Acting for

791.43 Act
Acting for America : movie
stars of the 1980s

$24.95
ocn429634768
06/07/2010

# STAR

AMERICAN CULTURE / AMERICAN CINEMA

# DECADES

Each volume in the series Star Decades: American Culture/American Cinema presents original essays analyzing the movie star against the background of contemporary American cultural history. As icon, as mediated personality, and as object of audience fascination and desire, the Hollywood star remains the model for celebrity in modern culture and represents a paradoxical combination of achievement, talent, ability, luck, authenticity, superficiality, and ordinariness. In all of the volumes, stardom is studied as an effect of, and influence on, the particular historical and industrial contexts that enabled a star to be "discovered," to be featured in films, to be promoted and publicized, and ultimately to become a recognizable and admired—even sometimes notorious—feature of the cultural landscape. Understanding when, how, and why a star "makes it," dazzling for a brief moment or enduring across decades, is especially relevant given the ongoing importance of mediated celebrity in an increasingly visualized world. We hope that our approach produces at least some of the surprises and delight for our readers that stars themselves do.

ADRIENNE L. McLEAN AND MURRAY POMERANCE
SERIES EDITORS

Jennifer Bean, ed., *Flickers of Desire: Movie Stars of the 1910s*

Patrice Petro, ed., *Idols of Modernity: Movie Stars of the 1920s*

Adrienne L. McLean, ed., *Glamour in a Golden Age: Movie Stars of the 1930s*

Sean Griffin, ed., *What Dreams Were Made Of: Movie Stars of the 1940s*

R. Barton Palmer, ed., *Larger Than Life: Movie Stars of the 1950s*

Pamela R. Wojcik, ed., *New Constellations: Movie Stars of the 1960s*

James Morrison, ed., *Hollywood Reborn: Movie Stars of the 1970s*

Robert Eberwein, ed., *Acting for America: Movie Stars of the 1980s*

Anna Everett, ed., *Pretty People: Movie Stars of the 1990s*

Murray Pomerance, ed., *Shining in Shadows: Movie Stars of the 2000s*

# Acting for America

## Movie Stars of the

# 1980s
★☆★★★★★★★★★★

EDITED BY

ROBERT EBERWEIN

RUTGERS UNIVERSITY PRESS

NEW BRUNSWICK, NEW JERSEY, AND LONDON

LIBRARY OF CONGRESS CATALOGING-IN-PUBLICATION DATA

Acting for America : movie stars of the 1980s / edited Robert Eberwein.
    p.  cm. — (Star decades — American culture/American cinema)
Includes bibliographical references and index.
ISBN  978-0-8135-4759-6  (hardcover : alk. paper)
ISBN  978-0-8135-4760-2  (pbk. : alk. paper)
    1. Motion picture actors and actresses—United States—Biography.  I. Eberwein,
Robert T., 1940–    .
PN1998.2.A245  2010
791.4302'80922—dc22
[B]
                                                              2009030961

A British Cataloging-in-Publication record for this book is available from the British
Library.

Visit our Web site: http://rutgerspress.rutgers.edu

Manufactured in the United States of America

For my students

# CONTENTS

★★★★★★★★★★★★

Acknowledgments         ix

Introduction: Stardom in the 1980s         1
ROBERT EBERWEIN

1   Robert De Niro: Star as Actor Auteur         19
AARON BAKER

2   Sylvester Stallone and Arnold Schwarzenegger:
Androgynous Macho Men         36
REBECCA BELL-METEREAU

3   Jessica Lange and Sissy Spacek: Country Girls         57
WILLIAM BROWN

4   Mel Gibson and Tom Cruise: Rebellion and Conformity         77
MICHAEL DeANGELIS

5   Michael J. Fox and the Brat Pack: Contrasting Identities         99
ROBERT EBERWEIN

6   Eddie Murphy: The Rise and Fall of the Golden Child         120
KRIN GABBARD

7   Sigourney Weaver: Woman Warrior, Working Girl         139
CHRIS HOLMLUND

8   Harrison Ford: A Well-Tempered Machismo         160
ADAM KNEE

9   Sally Field and Goldie Hawn: Feminism, Post-feminism,
and Cactus Flower Politics         180
CHRISTINA LANE

10   Meryl Streep: Feminism and Femininity in the Era of Backlash         201
LINDA MIZEJEWSKI

11   Clint Eastwood and Bruce Willis: Enforcers Left and Right         223
JAMES MORRISON

12   Steve Martin and John Candy: Penny Wise and Pound Foolish         243
JERRY MOSHER

**In the Wings**                                    263
ROBERT EBERWEIN

**Works Cited**                                     271
**Contributors**                                    279
**Index**                                           281

# ACKNOWLEDGMENTS
☆☆★★★★★★★★

I want to thank all the contributors for their illuminating essays, rapid responses to questions, and cheerful cooperation. The series editors Adrienne McLean and Murray Pomerance have offered timely and helpful guidance on all matters. It has been a privilege to have another book overseen with characteristic wisdom by Leslie Mitchner, associate director and editor in chief of Rutgers University Press. Marilyn Campbell, director of preproduction, as always, provided calming guidance. Alison Hack, production coordinator, helped once again. And it is a pleasure to have been helped by someone new to me at the Press, Katie Keeran. Eric Schramm's copyediting was very helpful. I am grateful for the assistance of Barbara Hall and other helpful individuals at the Margaret Herrick Library, Academy of Motion Picture Arts and Sciences. I appreciate the cooperation of Derek Davidson and Ronald Mandelbaum at Photofest, Inc. Thanks also to Peter Lehman and William Luhr. At Oakland University, Virinder Moudgil, senior vice president and provost, provided support for research. Susan Hawkins, chair of the Department of English, was, typically, kind and helpful, as were Cynthia Ferrara and Becky Fernandez. Yet again, colleagues in the Kresge Library assisted me in gathering information. And Jane was, as usual, Jane.

# Acting for America

# Introduction
## Stardom in the 1980s

ROBERT EBERWEIN

Rarely do we perceive the significance of everything that's happening as we live through a given historical moment. While I was aware of major historical events and trends that are mentioned in these pages, it would be misleading to say that I entirely "got" the decade of the 1980s as I experienced it. I didn't understand all its complex issues or ramifications any more than any of us comprehend fully the period we're living in right now. More complete knowledge and fuller understanding are, inevitably, retrospective. But watching the films now that were made at a time we lived through uncomprehendingly can be a prime source of information in this regard.

Some of the actors and actresses to be discussed here were already visibly established stars before the 1980s; for example, Clint Eastwood and Harrison Ford had achieved success and prominence in the 1970s. Some had already won or been nominated for Oscars: Robert De Niro, Sally Field, Goldie Hawn, Sylvester Stallone, and Meryl Streep. Others had begun to make impressions or be noticed: John Candy, Mel Gibson, Jessica Lange, Steve Martin, Arnold Schwarzenegger, Sissy Spacek, and Sigourney Weaver. The rest were all new to the screen, and rose to varying levels of prominence after their first appearances in the 1980s: Tom Cruise, Michael J. Fox, members of the Brat Pack, Eddie Murphy, and Bruce Willis. While these major stars are important for obvious reasons such as their talent (signaled by the number of nominations and awards) and power at the box office (measured by theatrical grosses and salaries), it's important to understand that their star images were realized in the unique context of this particular decade.

### ★★★★★ Historical Background

While a number of important political events occurred in the 1980s, we must be cautious about suggesting that any one of them "explains" what's distinctive about the decade. One obvious claimant for major importance is the shift in political power in the United States from the presidency of liberal Democrat Jimmy Carter, who lost the 1980 election, to that of the conservative Republican Ronald Reagan (1981–1989). Reagan won the election primarily for two reasons: Carter's disgrace for his failed attempt in 1980 to rescue American hostages held by Iranian terrorists, and a general shift in political sentiment in the country toward more conservative positions. A former Democrat and movie star of the 1940s and 1950s, and a host of popular television series in the 1950s and 1960s, Reagan came to office leading an attack against big government spending and taxing; posing an aggressive stance against America's enemies, especially the Soviet Union; and issuing a call for a return to more conservative moral values.

The first of these agendas led to the development of "Reaganomics," an economic policy characterized by supply-side principles that promoted reducing taxes for the wealthy. The assumption was that their increased spending would "trickle down," having a salutary effect on the economy as a whole. Although the policy didn't work, and a significant recession occurred in 1982, for a time economic news was generally positive; but in October 1987 the stock market experienced a significant collapse, falling over 30 percent over a few days. More concerns were prompted by financial scandals, especially the downfall of junk-bond king Michael Milken. Public opinion associated the Yuppie culture, one ruled by Young Urban Professionals, with the world of banking and high finance. For many, Gordon Gekko, a central character in Oliver Stone's 1987 film *Wall Street*, served as the definitive emblem of the financial excesses, in particular because of his claim that "greed is good." Tom Wolfe's novel *The Bonfire of the Vanities* (1987) also skewered the world of business and high finance and introduced the disparaging expression "masters of the universe" to describe the sense of importance characterizing the most self-absorbed of the corporate rich.

Reagan's second agenda involved trying to create an elaborate missile defense system for use against incoming nuclear warheads. Full development of this program, nicknamed "Star Wars," did not occur, although billions of dollars were committed to it. Relations between Reagan and Soviet leaders gradually improved, leading to a 1985 summit meeting with General Secretary Mikhail Gorbachev. By the end of the decade, the USSR had lost significant power, a result of massive economic problems caused in part by its unsuccessful war in Afghanistan. A general revolt against Soviet communism ensued, evidenced in the tearing down of the Berlin Wall in 1989. But the tensions between the United States and communist countries did not end completely. In China the communists were still very much in power, as demonstrated in the massacre of Chinese students protesting in Tiananmen Square in 1989. Both the tearing down of the Berlin Wall and the Chinese protests were captured on television, resonating throughout the world.

The third agenda appeared in criticism of the social behavior and initiatives of the 1960s and 1970s that had extended into the 1980s: the Women's Liberation movement and call for the passage of the Equal Rights Amendment; gay and premarital sex; and the growing drug culture. The ERA failed to pass. The coming of AIDS (acquired immune deficiency syndrome) provoked widespread fear of homosexual activities, in some cases linked to drugs. Controversies intensified about sex education. Reagan's answer to dealing with what he and the conservatives perceived as dangerous sexual and drug activity was embodied in First Lady Nancy Reagan's "Just Say No" campaign. This was very much in accord with conservative religious and social principles espoused by such evangelical leaders as James Dobson, founder of Focus on the Family (1977) and the Family Research Council (1981). Dobson served on the Commission on Pornography chaired by Attorney General Edwin Meese. While (not surprisingly) the report released in 1986 was highly critical of pornography, its findings and recommendations failed to generate much support or any legal actions to curb the perceived threat.

International and political tensions of the period included assassination attempts on Reagan and Pope John Paul II, and the murders of Egyptian and Indian leaders Anwar Sadat and Indira Gandhi. The United States went to war briefly in Grenada in 1983. Many terrorist attacks occurred around the world, arguably the most egregious being the bombings of the American embassy and marine barracks in Beirut in April and October 1983, which killed hundreds; hijackings of airplanes and ships in 1985; and the Libyan bombing of Pan Am flight 103 over Lockerbie, Scotland, in 1988, killing 259 passengers. Attempts to ease tensions with Iran led to a complicated scheme that involved selling them arms and using the monies illegally to finance a covert war against the Sandinistas in Nicaragua. While the political fallout from the congressional investigation of the Iran-Contra affair was considerable, Reagan emerged virtually unscathed and left office with his popularity still intact.

## ★★★★★ Technology

Major developments in computers, communications, and media occurred in the decade. The date of Super Bowl XVIII, 24 January

1984, is important, for on that day Ridley Scott's award-winning commercial introducing Apple's Macintosh computer aired for the first time. In a setting that evokes the world of George Orwell's novel *1984*, dronelike males march into a vast hall and then watch a Big Brother figure ranting on a large screen. A young woman in shorts and a halter top runs into the hall carrying a sledge hammer that she throws against the screen, causing it to explode. This is followed by a voiceover and print message: "On January 24 Apple will introduce Macintosh. And you'll see why 1984 won't be like '1984.'" The Mac, which enjoyed phenomenal sales, revolutionized the industry, providing the first advanced graphics system to give so much command over the display and manipulation of information. The next year Microsoft introduced its Windows operating system. By 1989, significant advances had been made that would lead to the creation of the World Wide Web. Other notable developments occurred with the introduction of Motorola's mobile cell phone and the CD-ROM.

Even before these appeared, the VCR and videotape had begun to attract buyers, including those who were not deterred by the format war between Sony's Beta and JVC's VHS systems. The latter ultimately won (an earlier version of the recent war between High Definition DVD and Blu-Ray). It was becoming increasingly easier and cheaper to watch films and stars in one's home. In a key judicial decision, the Supreme Court prevented film companies from claiming copyright infringement for films recorded on tape. Now filmed entertainment was readily and increasingly available cheaply in the home. Small video rental operations that began in the first part of the decade were soon put out of business by larger operations like Blockbuster, which grew into the largest tape rental operation in the country by 1989 (http://www.fundinguniverse.com/company-histories/Blockbuster-Inc-Company-History.html). Videotape gave a second distribution life to films (not to mention creating a wildly successful market for pornography that could now be viewed in private without attending public theaters). Laserdiscs, introduced in 1981, offered another way to watch films, but the format never became as popular as VHS.

Meanwhile, the cable television industry was experiencing massive growth. There were seventy-nine networks in 1990, up from twenty-eight in 1980, with fifty-four channels available to sixty million homes. Ted Turner introduced two of the major new ones: CNN (Cable News Network) in 1980 and TNT (Turner Network Television) in 1988. While TimeWarner's HBO and Viacom's Showtime focused primarily on presenting films, their respective subsidiaries, Cinemax and The Movie Channel, showed films exclusively, as did American Movie Classics. Initially, audiences watching films on all these pay channels could see them without censorship or commercials, but eventually AMC had to change this practice once it became part of tiered cable offerings rather than strictly a pay channel. Looking at these developments from today's perspective, it is apparent that the 1980s provided the foundation for today's viewers who can watch films downloaded from the Internet on a computer, a cell phone, or on a high-definition television linked to a DVD player or computer.

☆☆☆★★ **Social Issues**

Of all the cable channels that appeared in the 1980s, MTV can claim the greatest importance within the entertainment industry. Beginning in 1981, the channel became the touchstone for all forms of popular music among youths, expanding from rock 'n' roll into punk, heavy metal, hip-hop, rap, and grunge. Among its significant aspects, it offered a point of entry to filmmakers like David Fincher, who began his career by making music videos. His award-winning "Express Yourself" (1989) appropriates elements of Fritz Lang's *Metropolis* (1927) and stars Madonna as a woman who subjects men to her desires. It manifests a radical image of female empowerment and plays off Madonna's reputation for sexual allure and personal rebellion against social norms. She was already a worldwide phenomenon, having made indelible impressions with her earlier videos, such as "Like a Virgin" (1985) and "Papa Don't Preach" (1987). Her influence as an icon of female power and a model of fashion for teenage girls, supported in part by her role in the financially successful *Desperately Seeking Susan* (1985), extended into the next decade, underscored by the immense popularity of "Vogue," another Fincher video in early 1990.

Madonna represents the most radical female entertainer in the decade rebelling against conservative cultural and behavioral norms. From a different direction, leaders of the National Organization of Women (founded in 1966) such as Eleanor Smeal and Judy Goldsmith worked actively in the 1980s for women's rights. Molly Yard organized two marches on Washington to protest the efforts of Reagan's successor, President George H. W. Bush, to overturn the Supreme Court's earlier *Roe v. Wade* decision. Two notable events occurred when Sandra Day O'Connor was appointed as the first female justice on the Supreme Court in 1981, and Geraldine Ferraro was selected as Walter Mondale's vice presidential candidate in 1984.

The 1980s also saw the increased development of feminist and gender studies, many specifically addressing the way our responses to female stars are affected by industrial and technical practices. Some work complemented the earlier work of Laura Mulvey (see "Visual Pleasure") demonstrating the importance of psychoanalysis in helping us understand how star images are constructed and processed (see De Lauretis; Silverman). As some essays in this volume make clear, films can be seen to reflect the various stages through which feminism was passing in the 1980s. Sympathetic support for the advances in gay liberation that had begun in the 1960s and 1970s was informed by the attention being paid to the roles of gays in history and the arts (see D'Emilio; Russo).

A counterpart to Madonna as a sexual rebel in a different medium was Robert Mapplethorpe, a gay photographer whose explicit homoerotic works prompted the arrest of a museum director in Ohio where his works were shown, and a protest against the Corcoran Gallery in Washington for refusing to display them. Mapplethorpe's death from AIDS in 1989 was one of many in the 1980s caused by HIV, the human immunodeficiency virus. By that point, worldwide attention was focused on the disease, which began striking gay men in the early 1980s, and then spread to drug users, recipients of blood transfusions from HIV-positive donors, and straight sexual partners. First called the "gay cancer," AIDS quickly reached epidemic proportions, largely because of the initial inability of doctors and scientists to isolate the virus and find a way to counteract its ravaging effects. One of the most significant deaths that drew attention to AIDS was that of actor Rock Hudson in 1985, an event that stunned the entertainment industry and the world, given his status as one of the most popular leading men in film. Susan Sontag's famous short story "The Way We Live Now" was the first fictional work of note to address the disease (*New Yorker*, 24 November 1986). Randy Shilts's bestselling book *And the Band Played On* (1987) gave a history of the origins of the disease and the early misfires in developing effective treatment and prevention.

African Americans experienced many positive kinds of recognition, including a number of "firsts": Arthur Ashe playing on the Davis Cup tennis team; Gwendolyn Brooks winning a Pulitzer Prize for poetry; and Chappie James being appointed a four-star general in the air force. Certainly the most famous African American entertainer was Michael Jackson, who made what remains the most successful album in history, 1982's *Thriller*. The music video of that number, directed by John Landis the next year, is generally regarded as one of the greatest ever made. And "The Cosby Show" (1984–1992), which concerned a happy upper-middle-class black family headed by a doctor, played by the popular entertainer Bill Cosby, was a phenomenally successful television show, claiming first place for several years in the television ratings.

## ☆☆★★★ Culture

Other popular television series were also family-centered. Michael J. Fox starred in "Family Ties" (1982–1987) as the ultraconservative son of parents who had been hippies. This followed "The Cosby Show" on NBC's Thursday night schedule, both dominating the ratings and offering a decided contrast to "Dynasty" (1981–1989), a night-time high-fashion soap-opera that depicted the lives of a very unhappy super-rich family in Colorado, and "Dallas" (1978–1991), about an equally dysfunctional dynasty in Texas. "thirtysomething" (1987–1991), developed by Edward Zwick, concentrated on two advertising partners and their wives. "Golden Girls" (1985–1992) looked exclusively at a group of older, unmarried women living in Florida, while "Roseanne" (1988–1997) concerned a middle-class family unit in Illinois. Different kinds of families were constituted by characters who were not at all related to one another, such as the group dispatching cabs in "Taxi" (1978–1982), including Danny De Vito, and the crowd that hung out at the "Cheers" bar (1982–1993), Kelsey Grammer among them.

Various network dramatic series were extremely popular. Crime shows focused on males included "Hill Street Blues" (1981–1987) and "Miami Vice" (1984–1989). "Magnum P.I." (1980–1988) starred Tom Selleck as a private investigator in Hawaii. Women were the cops in "Cagney and Lacey" (1982–1988). "21 Jump Street" (1987–1990) concentrated on a group of very young police officers (including Johnny Depp). "Moonlighting" (1985–1989) featured Bruce Willis as part of a private investigating team. "L.A. Law" (1986–1994) looked at crime from the perspective of lawyers. The hospital drama "St. Elsewhere" (1982–1988), which featured Denzel Washington, anticipated the growth of such series in the next decade.

Live coverage afforded by television gave audiences the chance to witness other important events in addition to the fall of the Berlin Wall and the protests in Tiananmen Square. Much of the world watched the wedding of Lady Diana and Prince Charles in London on 29 July 1981. A very different experience occurred for the horrified viewers in the United States who watched the disastrous explosion of the Challenger spacecraft on 28 January 1986. As would occur with the shots of the plane striking the World Trade Center on 9/11, news stations presented a seemingly endless loop of the actual moment of the astronauts' deaths as the spacecraft burst into its eerie smoke-swirled free-fall.

## ★★★★★★ Film in the 1980s

Ronald Reagan figures in at least one of the assumptions about developments in the film industry during this period. Stephen Prince has called into question what he calls "myths" about the film business at this time, such as the following: "Blockbusters took over the industry, leading to a general lowering and coarsening of the quality of filmmaking; the films of George Lucas and Steven Spielberg epitomized this blockbuster style and proved detrimentally influential on a generation of American filmmaking; and Hollywood mirrored the politics of the Reagan period, shifting to the political right and helping to popularize the Cold War politics of the Era" (Prince, *American* 1; also see Palmer). While he points out ways in which some of these assertions can be supported, Prince's argument is that since the 1980s were much more complex, we cannot accept unquestioningly many of the standard generalizations. He explains how other developments in the industry need to be factored into any analysis, most notably the technological shifts and advances represented by videotape and video games, and the massive changes in the way films were financed once the various studios became parts of conglomerates (Prince *New Pot*).

It is certainly true that "high concept" works were produced by Don Simpson and Jerry Bruckheimer with "simple" storylines, "aggressive editing and a skillful blend of visual imagery and popular music" (*New Pot* 210; also see Wyatt). And, as will be clear, some of the stars discussed in this volume appeared in high concept and blockbuster action films, for example Tom Cruise in *Top Gun* (1986). But many other kinds of popular genres do not lend themselves to the standard generalizations. For example, two major kinds of films were developed and marketed to teenagers: comedies and slasher films. In the first category were those set mostly in high schools dealing with teenage anxieties and loves. Many, like John Hughes's *Pretty in Pink* and *Ferris Bueller's Day Off* (both 1986), were rated PG-13. Part teen comedy, part time-travel suspense film, Robert Zemeckis's *Back to the Future* (1985) was the highest grossing film of the year ($198 million). Some films were R-rated and dealt more candidly with sex, such as the first *Porky's* (1981) and *Fast Times at Ridgemont High* (1982) (see Doherty; Shary). Other teen-oriented films had a serious focus, even while containing comic aspects, such as *Lucas* (1986). A few were serious and presented sometimes painful examinations of youth culture and issues of growing up, such as Francis Ford Coppola's *The Outsiders* and *Rumble Fish* (both 1983). Two 1986 films focused on youths coming to terms with death: *Stand by Me* and *River's Edge*. One of the most popular films of the decade was Steven Spielberg's poignant and haunting *E.T.* (1982), about the friendship that develops between a young boy and an alien creature inadvertently left behind by his companions.

The major horror films focused primarily on evil beings attacking promiscuous teenagers. John Carpenter's classic *Halloween* (1978) occasioned three sequels in the 1980s about the relentless Michael Myers. Wes Craven's *A Nightmare on Elm Street* (1984), about Freddy, a ghost who attacks teenagers, initiated an R-rated franchise that yielded three sequels in the decade. The third major horror series aimed at teenagers was Sean Cunningham's *Friday the 13th* (1980), which resulted in six sequels in the 1980s (see Clover). As has been argued, the two genres complement one another in that the search for sexual gratification played for laughs in the comedies is punished in the slasher films with death.

Musical films were more popular than they had been in the 1970s. The decade began with Alan Parker's *Fame* (1980), which shows how teenagers train and develop at a performing arts school in New York City. The highly successful *Flashdance* (1983), about a young woman who is a factory worker but who wants to be a dancer, initiated a fashion trend (http://www.reelviews.net/php_review_template.php?identifier=1612). In *Footloose* (1984) Kevin Bacon plays a talented teen who introduces dancing to a repressed group of teenagers in a small town. And in *Dirty Dancing* (1987) Patrick Swayze plays an instructor whose dance lessons enhance the previously ordinary life of the heroine. Other comedies not specifically connected to teens included *Police Academy* (1984), the *Ghostbusters* films (1984, 1989), *Stripes* (1981), *Back to School* (1986), *Raising Arizona* (1987), *Beetle Juice* (1988), and *Three Men and a Baby*, the highest grossing film of 1987 ($168 million).

While films in the *Star Wars* and *Indiana Jones* series were huge successes for George Lucas and Steven Spielberg, a number of serious dramas triumphed at the Oscars (and many did well financially) including Best Picture winners *Ordinary People* (1980), *Chariots of Fire* (1981), *Gandhi* (1982), *Terms of Endearment* (1983), *Amadeus* (1984), *Out of Africa* (1985), *Platoon* (1986), *The Last Emperor* (1987), *Rain Man* (1988), and *Driving Miss Daisy* (1989).

*Platoon's* win was particularly significant, since it treated American involvement in the Vietnam War negatively and was made by Oliver Stone, a veteran, who won Best Director for it and for another Vietnam film, based

Jihmi Kennedy, Denzel Washington, and Morgan Freeman in *Glory*. Courtesy Photofest. Copyright TriStar Pictures, 1989.

on the true story of veteran Ron Kovic, *Born on the Fourth of July* (1989). Stanley Kubrick's *Full Metal Jacket* (1987) was another highly respected film that was critical of the war. Other Vietnam films of note included *Hamburger Hill* (1987), John Irvin's fact-based film about a platoon's ten-day efforts to capture a hill in Vietnam; and Brian De Palma's *Casualties of War* (1989), also based on a true story, about a soldier who risks his life by exposing members of a platoon who rape and kill a young Vietnamese woman.

An opposite view of America's involvement in the war emerged in the immensely popular Sylvester Stallone films *First Blood* (1982) and *Rambo: First Blood Part II* (1985), about the experiences of a Vietnam veteran. His support of the war and his desire to "win this time" by rescuing Americans still held hostage have been connected to Reagan. According to Susan Jeffords: "While those on the left caricatured Reagan's militarism by referring to him in political cartoons as 'Ronbo,' Reagan himself quipped at a press conference after the release of hostages in Lebanon, 'Boy, I saw *Rambo* last night. Now I know what to do the next time this happens'" (*Hard Bodies* 28). Other war films of note included Clint Eastwood's *Heartbreak Ridge* (1986) about the U.S. invasion of Grenada in 1983, and Edward Zwick's *Glory* (1989), featuring Morgan Freeman and Denzel Washington in a work based on the true story of an African American regiment fighting for the North in the Civil War; Washington won the Best Supporting Actor Oscar.

*Glory* joined a number of other films in the 1980s offering positive roles to African Americans, who had not been represented to such an extent in positive starring roles in films of earlier decades, particularly in 1970s blaxploitation films. In contrast to these, Whoopi Goldberg and Oprah Winfrey appeared in Steven Spielberg's *The Color Purple* (1985), an adaptation of Alice Walker's novel. Eddie Murphy scored in a number of highly successful comedies, such as *Beverly Hills Cop* (1984) and its sequel (1987). Danny Glover was a cop partner of Mel Gibson in *Lethal Weapon* (1987) and *Lethal Weapon 2* (1989). Morgan Freeman received an Oscar nomination for *Driving Miss Daisy* (1989), and Spike Lee made an indelible impression as a major American black filmmaker. His *Do the Right Thing* (1989), which was shown at the Cannes Film Festival, offers an edgy examination of negative aspects of race relations in the 1980s, referring directly to the troubling Howard Beach and Tawana Brawley incidents that had polarized segments of the New York City community.

Several important films focused on women and their lives. The comedy *Nine to Five* (1980) shows three female office workers putting their oafish and sexist male boss in his place. *Working Girl* (1988) approached life and politics in the office from a secretary's perspective. The biographical films *Coal Miner's Daughter* (1980) and *Frances* (1982) offered sympathetic accounts of a singer and a film star. The relationship of mothers and daughters is at the center of *Terms of Endearment* (1983) and *Steel Magnolias* (1989). *Aliens* (1986) confirmed that a woman could be the principal star of an action film.

Although only a few films, all independent productions like *Parting Glances* (1986), dealt with gays and their experience of AIDS, some gay- and lesbian-themed dramas that weren't about the disease were financed by the major studios, among them *Cruising* (1980), *Making Love* (1982), *Personal Best* (1982), and *Desert Hearts* (1985). The first, about a homicidal maniac, occasioned angry protests from those who thought it demonized gays by presenting such negative images of them. Blake Edwards's gender-bending comedy *Victor/Victoria* (1982) offered a positive view of gays, as did two English films: *My Beautiful Laundrette* (1985) and *Maurice* (1987). The three plays that constituted Harvey Fierstein's *Torch Song Trilogy* were made into one feature-length film in 1988. Independent filmmaker Lizzie Borden made two important films about lesbians: *Born in Flames* (1983) and *Working Girls* (1986).

## ★★★★★ Notable Established Stars of the 1980s

Films of the decade featured many stars who were already well established and introduced a number who would enjoy stardom for

Jane Fonda, Dolly Parton, and Lily Tomlin in *Nine to Five*, as strong women who put their male boss in his place. Courtesy Photofest. Copyright IPC Films Twentieth Century-Fox, 1980.

the first time. Sean Connery, forever identified as the first star of the James Bond franchise, gave up that persona after *Never Say Never Again* (1983) and won acclaim as a monk in *The Name of the Rose* (1986) and an Oscar for Best Supporting Actor as a G-man in *The Untouchables* (1987). He ended the decade as a new member of the enormously successful franchise started earlier by Steven Spielberg when he played Harrison Ford's father in *Indiana Jones and the Last Crusade* (1989).

After a promising start to his film career in the 1970s, Michael Douglas became a significant star presence in this decade. He made three financially successful comedies with Kathleen Turner: *Romancing the Stone* (1984), *The Jewel of the Nile* (1985), and *The War of the Roses* (1989). He won an Oscar for Best Actor as the greedy and immoral Gordon Gekko in *Wall Street* and praise as a cheating and remorseful husband in the worldwide success *Fatal Attraction*, the second highest grossing film of 1987 (over $156 million).

After two Oscar-nominated performances in *Bonnie and Clyde* (1967) and *Chinatown* (1974) and a win for Best Actress for *Network* (1976), Faye Dunaway appeared less often in 1980s films, but gave two indelible and courageous performances, one as the troubled superstar Joan Crawford in *Mommie Dearest* (1981) and another as a drunk in *Barfly* (1987). She was much more actively present in television specials and series such as "Christopher Columbus" (1985).

Jane Fonda was less active in films during the 1980s, concentrating on her phenomenally successful workout videos. Nonetheless, having won two Oscars in the 1970s for *Klute* (1971) and *Coming Home* (1978), Fonda remained a star presence. She was one of the aggrieved office workers in the successful *Nine to Five*, and received two more Oscar nominations in the 1980s, one for *On Golden Pond* (1981), in which she played the daughter of her real father, Henry Fonda, and the other for *The Morning After* (1986), in which she appeared as a drunk.

Jodie Foster, who at age fourteen was one of the youngest Oscar nominees in history for *Taxi Driver* (1976), continued her artistic development in *The Hotel New Hampshire* (1984) and in a number of lesser known films such as *Siesta* and *Five Corners* (both 1987). She won her first Best Actress Oscar in 1988 playing a rape victim in *The Accused*. Women's rights are at the center of this important film that focuses on the way a woman from a lower class can be disadvantaged and abused by the legal system.

Dustin Hoffman, who had been a star since the 1960s, triumphed playing a cross-dressing out-of-work actor in the 1982 comedy *Tootsie*, the year's second highest earner after *The Return of the Jedi*. He appeared with Warren Beatty in the disastrous critical and financial failure *Ishtar* (1987), but ended the decade on a high note, winning the Oscar for Best Actor playing Tom Cruise's autistic brother in *Rain Man* (1988), and then joining Sean Connery in *Family Business* (1989), a modest comic success.

Bette Midler became famous as an entertainer in the 1970s for her performances at the gay Continental Baths in New York City. Her first major film performance in *The Rose* (1979) as a singer-drug addict (modeled on Janis Joplin) earned her an Oscar nomination. Her film work in the 1980s confirmed her status not just as a gay icon but as a hugely talented comedic star who appeared in such hits as *Down and Out in Beverly Hills* (1986), *Ruthless People* (1986), and *Outrageous Fortune* (1987). *Beaches* (1988), one of her most successful films, was a tearjerker about female friendship, demonstrating again that her skills included serious drama as well as comedy.

Paul Newman, who had become a major star in the 1950s, climaxed a three-decades-long career with his first Oscar win for Best Actor (at age sixty-two) in *The Color of Money* (1987). He was playing an older version of the pool-playing character he had introduced twenty-five years earlier in *The Hustler* (1962), for which he had also been nominated. Two of his seven other Oscar nominations came for films in the 1980s, as an editor in *Absence of Malice* (1981) and an alcoholic lawyer in *The Verdict* (1982). Jack Nicholson's career in films also began in the 1950s, although in a minor way. He had earlier been an Oscar nominee for *Chinatown* and then a winner for *One Flew Over the Cuckoo's Nest* (1975) before adding another Oscar in the 1980s as Shirley MacLaine's boyfriend in *Terms of Endearment* (1983). For his famed role as The Joker in *Batman* (1989), he became the highest paid male actor in film history, since his contract gave subsidiary percentage rights, which ultimately exceeded $50 million.

Al Pacino had become famous playing Michael Corleone in *The Godfather* (1972), and received one of his four Oscar nominations as Best Actor in *The Godfather: Part II* (1974). He began the 1980s by taking on the challenging and widely criticized role of a cop investigating murders of gay men in the controversial *Cruising*. His other films in the decade confirmed his star status, as a playwright in the comedy *Author! Author!* (1980), and as a cop in love with a woman who may be a killer in *Sea of Love* (1989). Even more than his persona as Michael Corleone, though, it was playing Tony Montana in Brian De Palma's *Scarface* (1983) that gave Pacino his best known role as the ultimate gangster.

Robert Redford continued to be a major presence, with starring roles as a warden in *Brubaker* (1980), a baseball player in *The Natural* (1984), and as Meryl Streep's lover in the Best Picture Oscar–winner *Out of Africa*. Notable for winning an Oscar in 1980 for his first directorial effort, *Ordinary People*, Redford has been the single most important individual in developing and supporting the growth of independent film in the United States, beginning with his founding of the Sundance Institute in 1981.

## ★★★★★★ New Faces for the Decade

Many talented actors and actresses who were appearing in films for the first time in the 1980s achieved stardom. Matthew Broderick started his star-making career with *War Games* (1983), a comedy about the possibility of nuclear war that connected in a timely manner with the Cold War tensions of the period. John Hughes's *Ferris Bueller's Day Off* was a massive hit that capitalized on the current popularity of teen movies. After appearing in two adaptations of well-known plays in 1988, *Biloxi Blues* and *Torch Song Trilogy*, he starred in the award-winning *Glory*, and with Sean Connery and Dustin Hoffman in *Family Business*.

Already a famous singer/comic performer as the partner and wife of Sonny Bono, and a popular entertainer in the 1970s, Cher became a presence in films in the 1980s, first by recreating the role she had had in the play *Come Back to the Five and Dime, Jimmy Dean, Jimmy Dean* (1982), and then as Meryl Streep's lesbian friend in *Silkwood* (Oscar nomination, 1983), a caring mother of a disfigured boy in *Mask* (1985), one of the women connected to the demonic Jack Nicholson in *The Witches of Eastwick* (1987), and the conflicted fiancée and girlfriend of brothers in *Moonstruck* (1987), for which she won an Oscar.

Glenn Close's entrance into film was very impressive and earned her five Oscar nominations in the 1980s. The first came for a supporting role in her debut film, *The World According to Garp* (1982). All the rest were for Best Actress: playing the wife who hosts the reunion of mourners in *The Big Chill* (1983), clearly a vitally important film for many of the names mentioned here; Robert Redford's love interest in *The Natural*; and a devious French aristocrat in the costume drama *Dangerous Liaisons* (1988). As a mentally unstable home wrecker in *Fatal Attraction*, she created a character whose behavior and fate as a successful independent woman obsessed with a man (Michael Douglas) elicited an enormous amount of contentious debate in venues ranging from popular reviews to scholarly articles. Some saw the film as an overt attack on feminism and women's advances in the business world.

Kevin Costner's early career in films was unremarkable, including his nonspeaking and faceless credit as a corpse in *The Big Chill*, but became notable in the later part of the decade. He played G-man Eliot Ness in *The Untouchables* and a Russian counterspy the same year in *No Way Out* (1987), and cemented his stardom in two films about baseball: as a player, Susan Sarandon's love interest in *Bull Durham* (1988), and as a visionary farmer who builds a baseball diamond in the highly successful *Field of Dreams*

Glenn Close and Michael Douglas as the adulterous couple in the controversial hit *Fatal Attraction*. Courtesy Photofest. Copyright Paramount Pictures, 1987.

(1989), which gave a memorable phrase to film history: "If you build it, he will come."

William Hurt's career in the 1980s spanned many genres, beginning with science fiction in *Altered States* (1980), followed by a famous film noir, *Body Heat* (1981), which made stars of him and Kathleen Turner and introduced conventions of the erotic thriller into American film. He was one of many important stars who formed the ensemble cast of *The Big Chill*. His next major role in *Kiss of the Spider Woman* (1985), as a gay transvestite (at the height of the AIDS hysteria), won him an Oscar. *Broadcast News* (1987) and (again with Turner) *The Accidental Tourist* (1988) cemented his star status.

Michael Keaton became a star in the 1980s playing very different kinds of parts. He had a huge hit that spoke to the advances of women's liberation when he played a house husband whose wife is the breadwinner in the comedy *Mr. Mom* (1983); a creepy-funny ghost in Tim Burton's *Beetle Juice* (1988); an addict trying to get *Clean and Sober* (1988); and Bruce Wayne in *Batman*, the number one film of 1989 that earned over $250 million.

Like Keaton a success in both comic and serious roles, Kevin Kline, another star of *The Big Chill*, triumphed as both a comic talent in *A Fish Called Wanda* (1988), for which he won the Oscar as Best Supporting Actor, and as a serious performer in *Sophie's Choice* (1982), the western *Silverado* (1985), and *Cry Freedom* (1987), based on the true story of a crusading journalist investigating the death of African leader Steve Biko, played by Denzel Washington.

Already a superstar of country and western music, Dolly Parton became a film star in 1980 when she joined Jane Fonda and Lily Tomlin in *Nine to Five*, which grossed $103 million. *The Best Little Whorehouse in Texas* (1982), with Burt Reynolds, confirmed her star appeal. *Rhinestone* (1984), her next film, in which she plays the part of someone trying to remake Sylvester Stallone's character, was a critical and financial failure, but she ended the decade in the very successful ensemble drama *Steel Magnolias* as one of the supportive women in a beauty shop.

Michelle Pfeiffer was also in *Dangerous Liaisons*, receiving her first Oscar nomination for Supporting Actress playing an innocent young girl. In 1989 she was nominated as Best Actress for *The Fabulous Baker Boys* in which as a nightclub singer she performs a justly famous rendition of "Making Whoopee." She joined Cher and Susan Sarandon as one of *The Witches of Eastwick*, and acted with another of the stars discussed in this volume, Mel Gibson, in *Tequila Sunrise* (1988). But it is her role as Elvira, the girlfriend of Tony Montana (Al Pacino), in *Scarface* that is probably most familiar to today's viewers. Her performance as a bored, coke-snorting beauty demonstrated enormous talent and star presence.

Kathleen Turner's stardom came from both comic and serious roles. The three comedies mentioned above that she made with Michael Douglas were very successful. And she received an Oscar nomination for *Peggy Sue Got Married* (1986), a comedy drama in which the forty-ish heroine revisits her earlier physical teenaged self. But she is remembered most vividly as the sensuous and amoral sexpots she plays in *Body Heat*, in which she tricks her lover into murdering her husband and then leaves him to suffer the consequences, and the highly censored *Crimes of Passion* (1984). Her performance in the first brought the world of film noir into the 1980s with an uncompromising sexual frankness. In the second she leads a dual existence as a businesswoman by day and a prostitute by night. This film's sex scenes led to cuts in order to avoid an X rating.

Robin Williams was an enormously popular entertainer known for the television series "Mork and Mindy" (1978–1982), in which he played a space alien, and his wild and zany appearances on talk shows. His film work cemented his status as an important star, beginning with *Popeye* (1980), followed by *The World According to Garp, Moscow on the Hudson* (1984), and a biographical film based on the experiences of Adrian Cronauer, a disk jockey in Saigon, in *Good Morning Vietnam* (1987), for which he received an Oscar nomination. The film had the fourth highest gross in 1987. Williams showed his serious side again as an actor as a popular English teacher in *Dead Poets' Society* (1989), a dimension he would capitalize on in the next decade in *Awakenings* (1990) and his Oscar-winning performance in *Good Will Hunting* (1997).

## ★★★★★ A Word about the Title

*Acting for America* was chosen as the title for this volume because so many of the stars' films are inflected directly or indirectly by issues of concern to the country in the 1980s. These include the aftermath of the Vietnam War; the advances of African Americans; grass-roots social activism; increased attention to youth; the empowerment of women; conflicts between conservative and liberal outlooks; and aspects of masculinity. Some stars can be considered in relation to more than one of these. As the following essays demonstrate, certainly part of their appeal follows from the way their star images draw attention to and stimulate consideration of these concerns.

# ★★★★★★★★★★★
# Robert De Niro
## Star as Actor Auteur

AARON BAKER

By the time he received the Best Actor Academy Award for his performance in *Raging Bull* (1980), Robert De Niro's critical reputation was firmly in place. He had already been nominated twice, in 1976 for *Taxi Driver* and in 1978 for *The Deer Hunter,* and had won as Best Supporting Actor for *The Godfather: Part II* in 1974. De Niro's second Academy Award for playing prizefighter Jake LaMotta also solidified his association with Martin Scorsese, who had directed three of his films: *Mean Streets* (1973), *Taxi Driver,* and *New York, New York* (1977). While both men enjoyed substantial critical success as a result of their collaboration, during the 1980s Scorsese's influence on De Niro would also manifest itself in the actor's ability to establish an auteurist formal and thematic pattern in his film performances. De Niro's creative vision appears in his choice of roles, his

research into a character's background, his willingness to change his physical appearance to portray a character, the improvisatory contributions he
often made to dialogue, and the thematic continuity of consistently playing
characters who commented on the social construction of masculinity.

Paul McDonald has explained that while the film industry needs to sell
very expensive movie products to audiences "who have very little idea
what they will get," "stars names are one of the mechanism's used . . . to
predetermine audience expectations" ("Stars" 155). By 1980 the name
Robert De Niro conveyed a star image with clearly defined traits: anger,
alienation, and violence—what one critic called his "often fearsome screen
presence . . . full of choked rage" (Schruers 43). De Niro's most celebrated
parts from the 1970s had established those characteristics, and some of his
twelve movie roles in the 1980s continued to reinforce them. Yet the anger
and violence of De Niro's highest profile roles from the 1980s, particularly
in *Raging Bull, The King of Comedy* (1982), *Once Upon a Time in America*
(1984), *The Mission* (1986), and *The Untouchables* (1987), increasingly gave
his star image a dimension of social critique directed at what Robin Wood
has called Hollywood's version of "the Ideal Male: the virile adventurer,
potent . . . man of action" (*Hitchcock* 291). Writing in 1985, Robert Ray
named this male character who is central to so many Hollywood movies the
"outlaw hero," who disregards the laws of the larger society in favor of his
own "private notions of right and wrong" (59). Several of De Niro's 1980s
roles built on the delusional vigilantism of his Travis Bickle character in *Taxi
Driver* to show the potential danger of such self-righteous violence. As a
counterweight to these antisocial characters, De Niro also sought to diver-
sify his roles somewhat, playing more patient, cooperative men in *True Confessions* (1981), *Falling in Love* (1984), and *Jacknife* (1989) as an alternative
to the destructiveness of the outlaw hero's narcissistic and violent self-
assertion.

Besides his acting and collaboration with Scorsese, by the 1980s De
Niro had also become known for a stubborn refusal to share information
about his personal life; Jay Carr in 1988 called him "Hollywood's most
unreachable actor" (*Chicago Tribune*, 24 July 1988, 13:6). Such insistence on
privacy compromised De Niro's ability to fit the model of Hollywood stars
that Richard Dyer has defined as a pairing of movie roles and contextualizing
media discourse (*Heavenly Bodies* 2–3). De Niro's resistance to self-revelation,
combined with his tendency to play parts critical of the individualized masculinity typical for A-list actors, limited his stardom by denying audiences
the voyeuristic access to a behind-the-scenes view of the glamorous personal life expected from stars, as well as by keeping him from roles that

transferred such a charismatic, empowered identity into heroic lead characters. In 1987, De Niro hired Creative Artists Agency (CAA), run by the hottest agent in Hollywood, Michael Ovitz, to represent him. His plan was to modify his image as a serious actor who always played "dark" dramatic roles with an action comedy, *Midnight Run*, a CAA package set up by screenwriter George Gallo and director Martin Brest (Baxter 268–69). De Niro went so far as to grant a rare interview to *Rolling Stone* in 1988 to promote *Midnight Run*, yet even as he worked to enhance the film's commercial potential, his two main comments about its artistic merits offset his outsider image in favor of social connection and collaboration: the emotional scene in which his character sees his estranged daughter gave the story, in De Niro's view, "some weight," and he thought it important that he had been able to work successfully with co-star Charles Grodin (Schruers 45). Yet in the 1990s De Niro held onto the violent outsider persona, as films such as *Goodfellas* (1990), *Cape Fear* (1991), and *Heat* (1995) showed, and while he went on to do more comedy with *Analyze This* (1999), *Meet the Parents* (2000), *Meet the Fockers* (2004), and *Stardust* (2007), all these parts have continued to illustrate the destructive effects of, or actively reject, a self-absorbed, violent masculinity.

## ★★★★★  De Niro's Acting

In his 1980s roles De Niro exemplified Barry King's idea that skilled acting requires the ability to "disappear into the part" and impersonate a character, as opposed to the "personification" typical of star vehicles. Star turns, in King's words, place "emphasis on what is unique to the actor, displacing emphasis from what an actor can do *qua* actor onto what actor *qua* person or biographical entity is" (168, 178). The Method style of acting that asks for expression of the actor's own experience and emotions King describes as an adaptation of film performance to the need for stars, allowing bankable performers to present their personalities rather than having to become the character (179). Richard Maltby agrees that the profit motive of Hollywood stars limits narrative complexity by how "the commercial imperatives of the star system require that stars are always visible through their characters" (384).

Stella Adler, De Niro's teacher at the New School in New York in the early 1960s, made a point of rejecting the use of emotional memory central to Lee Strasberg's Actor's Studio version of the Method, stating instead that "acting is not neurosis. It's about character" (Baxter 43). De Niro's emphasis in his 1980s roles on the careful creation of character through advance research, transformation of his physical appearance, and improvisation all fit Adler's approach, following her statement that one of the most important ideas she learned from her study with Stanislavski was that "the use of your own life is more limited than your imagination" (Baxter 198). In a 1984 interview after working together on *Falling in Love*, Meryl Streep described De Niro's ability to contribute to improvisation: "He's incapable of a false move. . . . So when there's something wrong with the writing, he just can't do it. Then everyone realizes the scene's wrong and we fix it" (*Newsweek*, 3 December 1984, 78). Scorsese has also emphasized the importance of improvisation in describing his work with De Niro as a means of getting to "the truth of the situation" (Hodenfield 134). "We improvise . . . rewrite the scene, and then we shoot it," Scorsese explained, adding that several of De Niro's most famous moments as an actor—such as Travis Bickle's "You talking to me?" monologue and the argument in the back room of the bar with Harvey Keitel in *Mean Streets*—were improvisations (Brunette 13, 43; DeCurtis 184).

As has been typical throughout his acting career, De Niro spent extensive time and effort preparing for the *Raging Bull* role. He trained hard for the boxing sequences, losing fifteen pounds getting into shape to play the fighter in his prime, taking boxing lessons from LaMotta himself, and sparring for weeks under the tutelage of professional trainer Al Silvani. LaMotta claimed that De Niro was so successful in his physical preparation that he would have ranked among the top twenty middleweights in the world (Baxter 197–98). De Niro, cinematographer Michael Chapman, and director Martin Scorsese also carefully mapped out the choreography of the fight scenes in *Raging Bull*, which were shot largely from inside the ring to give viewers a close-up view. Between takes of the boxing sequences, De Niro would often punch a bag to keep himself in character (Baxter 200).

Once the fight scenes were shot, production of *Raging Bull* went on hiatus while De Niro continued his preparation for the role by gaining weight to play LaMotta after he retired from the ring. The actor went to Paris and Rome for a four-month eating tour, increasing his weight from 145 to 215 pounds. The additional weight made the last two weeks of shooting strenuous for De Niro, as he found himself short of breath and suffering from high blood pressure (Baxter 201).

On De Niro's obsessive preparation, Barry King comments that, in the case of *Raging Bull*, his pursuit of realism by transforming his body was also a response to the creative limitations involved in a collaborative production process (177). Chapman's cinematography, Scorsese's direction, and Thelma Schoonmaker's editing all contributed to the stylized, expressionist quality

De Niro as Jake LaMotta in *Raging Bull*. Copyright United Artists, 1980.

of the Jake LaMotta character—what Joseph McBride described in *Variety*: "Scorsese and editor Thelma Schoonmaker . . . make highly effective use of slow motion in the fights and elsewhere to take the film out of objective reality into the subjectivity of LaMotta's mind" (12 November 1980). However, the physical verisimilitude of the character came primarily from what King called De Niro's extreme steps to change his weight in pursuit of "an authenticating sense of character outside the process of filming" (175).

De Niro's intense commitment to transforming his body to play LaMotta also asserted his creative input in defining the character's arc. The boxer's decline from a trim young man full of what Richard Corliss calls "animal energy" to the obesity of his post-prizefighting life parallels LaMotta's loss of control over his career to Mafia manipulation, and the growing dysfunction of his marriages and relationship with his brother Joey (Joe Pesci) (*Time*, 24 November 1980, 100). As LaMotta becomes increasingly aware of his inability to avoid mob control of his career, as well as to manage his appetites for sex and food, he begins to feel an intense frustration that feeds his paranoid jealousy about the infidelity of his wife, Vicky (Kathy Moriarty), his distrust of Joey, and his weight gain.

An early scene establishes how the nexus of food, sex, and domestic violence will define LaMotta's frustration and how De Niro will employ his signature naturalistic acting style to represent his character's obsession with control. Angry about a recent defeat in Cleveland, Jake accuses his first wife, Emma (Lori Anne Flax), of unjustified jealousy over other women while he was away for the bout, and then yells at her to bring his steak: "Don't overcook it . . . it defeats its own purpose . . . It's like a piece of charcoal! Bring it over here!" Emma reacts angrily and, grabbing her by the hair, Jake pushes his wife into the bedroom. During the couple's fight, Joey arrives and the two men have the following exchange:

> JOEY: You can't . . . put up with this fuckin braciole here . . . What's wrong?
>
> JAKE (after a long silence): My hands, I got these small hands . . . I ain't never gonna fight Joe Louis . . . the best there is. . . . And you asking me what's wrong.
>
> JOEY: You're crazy . . . He's a heavyweight and you're a middleweight . . . Why go crazy thinking about it?
>
> JAKE: Hit me in the face.

Joey begins punching his brother in the face, growing ever angrier as Jake questions his manhood to spur him on. To increase Pesci's indignation, De Niro would insult him between takes. Before a shot in the later scene in which Jake interrogates Joey about infidelity with Vicky, De Niro surprised his co-star by asking him, "Did you fuck your mother?" (Baxter 201).

Along with his emphasis on preparation, physical transformation, and improvisation, De Niro's acting style in *Raging Bull* and his other 1980s films employed performance techniques demonstrated in the scene with Joey and Emma: a colloquial, urban style of speech and physical self-assertion, as well as deliberate discontinuity created by elliptical or overlapping dialogue or acts of seemingly random, spontaneous violence—what might be called "moments of expressive incoherence" that suggest cracks in the character's outer façade, allowing for the expression of inner repression or deep motivations (Naremore 278). The escalation in the scene seems motivated less by the actions or comments of the other characters than by how they express Jake's frustration. The sudden outburst of anger about the steak demonstrates Jake's volatile temper, and Joey's subsequent comment— "You can't . . . put up with this fuckin' braciole"—refers to Emma using a term for stuffed meat from Italian American cuisine that implies the sexual subtext of the boxer's frustration. Jake's unexpected redirection of the conversation and insistence that his brother hit him exemplifies the deliberate discontinuity of De Niro's performance style, as well as its function to express latent subjectivity.

More because of the spectacle of his weight gain than these acting techniques, De Niro's performance in *Raging Bull* set a new standard. Kevin Hayes commented that "since *Raging Bull*, the willingness to gain weight for a part has become a mark of an actor's dedication to the role" (7). Hayes gave the example of Charlize Theron putting on "considerable" weight to portray serial killer Aileen Wuornos in *Monster* (2003), and quotes a reviewer who said of her Oscar-winning performance that "not since *Raging Bull* 'has there been a transformation this powerful and effective'" (7). Chazz Palminteri summed up the influence of De Niro's physical change for *Raging Bull*, comparing it to Brando's Method-inspired 1947 performance in the theater production of *A Streetcar Named Desire*: "Marlon Brando changed acting when he walked across the stage in *A Streetcar Named Desire*. De Niro changed it with *Raging Bull*. At that time, no actors transformed themselves the way he did. They do it now. But they do it because of him" (Betty Cortina, "Robert De Niro," *Entertainment Weekly*, Winter 1999, 85).

De Niro's concentrated dedication of his creative energies to build complex characters in his 1980s performances adhered to King's idea of impersonation as defining the standard in film acting, and the actor's own view that "to transform yourself into something entirely new—that was genius" (Baxter 29). The outlaw hero is generally acted with a representational verisimilitude to convey that its version of morality and agency is plausible and "real." In contrast, De Niro's research and physical transformation for roles, his ability to create a colloquial verisimilitude through improvisation—the expressive incoherence of a character like Rupert Pupkin in *The King of Comedy*, mixing manic ambition with comic cool, or indigenous people signifying a cultural reality opposite his highly stylized acting as Rodrigo Mendozo in *The Mission*—all these aspects of his performances foregrounded the artificiality of his roles and indicted the dishonesty of star turns that deny their own construction.

Moreover, the very process of star construction was central to De Niro's role in Scorsese's *The King of Comedy*. Rupert Pupkin is obsessed with achieving stardom by any means necessary, including kidnapping and threatening talk show host Jerry Langford (Jerry Lewis). The relevance of this commentary on American infatuation with celebrity was underscored by John Hinckley's attempt to assassinate President Reagan while the film was in the last stages of preproduction. The shooting was motivated by Hinckley's fascination with a star, Jodie Foster, whose attention he hoped to gain just as De Niro's Travis Bickle became obsessed with Foster's character in *Taxi Driver*, and just as Rupert wants the attention of Langford in the later Scorsese film.

De Niro's 1980s performances critique the outlaw hero star role by distorting it, creating characters who abuse its ideals of self-reliance and willingness to fight for justice by using violence selfishly to protect themselves from their own fears and insecurities. As he rehearses his nightclub act in the last scene of *Raging Bull*, Jake LaMotta bungles the Terry Malloy "I coulda been a contender" lines from *On the Waterfront* (1954) that he invokes to blame his brother Joey for his failure and rage. Likewise, De Niro's gangster characters in Sergio Leone's *Once Upon a Time in America* and Brian De Palma's *The Untouchables* fail in their attempt to use language to explain away selfish, violent behavior. De Niro's roles as David "Noodles" Aaronson and as Al Capone in these films therefore exemplify Sarah Kozloff's observation that movie gangsters are frequently as profligate with words as they are with violence, using both to intimidate and control others (207).

To get the role of Noodles, De Niro had to convince Leone of his ability to play the character both in his thirties and as a man in his sixties. Yet even after the actor's usual painstaking research about the Lower East Side Jewish gangsters and his careful preparation of the right kind of makeup to simulate aging, Leone, who had been working on the project for fifteen years and often spoke of actors as marionettes he controlled, was still reluctant to concede creative control. The Italian director's strong commitment to his stylized vision for the gangster film was made clear by his decision to shoot it primarily on elaborate sets at Cinecittà in Rome, and his conception of Noodles didn't allow for the degree of realism and improvisational freedom De Niro expected. As Elizabeth McGovern, who played Noodles's childhood sweetheart Deborah, put it, "De Niro was so fixed on realistic detail and Sergio couldn't care less about realistic detail" (Frayling 446). Leone himself recalled working with De Niro as a situation in which "Bob lives the script: he repeats it to himself 100,000 times at home, and when he comes on the set he gives off a sense of improvisation and spontaneity" (439). To some degree Leone did allow De Niro his realist aesthetic, shooting his scenes as the younger Noodles before those as a man in his sixties, a scheduling turn that cost the production a million and a half dollars (449).

Yet it was perhaps the director's biggest allowance for what he called "more reality within the dream" that impacted De Niro's performance the most (Frayling 441). Noodles's violent pathology manifests itself in two rapes that he commits, the first during a robbery and the second of Deborah after she tells him of her plans to leave for a career in Hollywood. Richard Godden explains the rapes as a blunt statement by the director about Hollywood's dishonest omission of sexual violence, stating that "Leone's recording of the rape articulates the dysfunction between bodies in images and bodies themselves" (384). McGovern supported this view when she stated that the rape of her character "didn't glamorize violent sex. . . . He [Leone] is making a gangster film, and . . . you can't make that kind of film unless you profile . . . an extremely brutish and limited kind of person" (Frayling 448). Nonetheless, De Niro experienced the unpleasant results of having his character positioned in such a critique after *Once Upon a Time in America* was shown at Cannes in May 1984, when he had to face the angry reaction of several women in the audience to the two rape scenes. One of the women confronted De Niro directly in a press conference after the screening, describing the assaults as "blatant, gratuitous violence" (Baxter 240).

## ★★★★★ A Kinder, Gentler Masculinity

As if reacting to the limitations on his creative control in *Once Upon a Time in America*, De Niro took a more active role in the conception of his next film, *Falling in Love*, and commented that he saw the part as "something different to anything I had done before and for that reason alone it seemed like a good idea" (Baxter 237). Yet even as the romantic lead in *Falling in Love* modified the social misfit persona that had come to define his star image, De Niro continued to focus his energy on extensive preparation, physical transformation, and improvisational dialogue to construct a character that commented on masculinity.

Once he became interested in Michael Cristofer's script, De Niro sent it to Meryl Streep, hoping that together they could replicate the success from their collaboration in *The Deer Hunter* six years earlier. Paramount was interested in the project for exactly that reason, and to convince studio head Michael Eisner, De Niro and Streep met in December 1983 to improvise new dialogue to add to the script. Eisner liked the changes and authorized the film's $13 million budget (Pfaff and Emerson 100).

*Falling in Love* parallels the discontent of its two lead characters, Frank, an architectural engineer, and Molly, a commercial artist, both of whom work in Manhattan and live comfortably in Westchester County. Both are dissatisfied with their jobs, marriages, and family lives, and after a chance meeting while Christmas shopping at Rizzoli's on Fifth Avenue and again later on a commuter train, they begin a relationship. The story carefully traces not only the growth of their intense infatuation with each other but the simultaneous indecision and guilt both feel about breaking up their marriages.

De Niro created a character in *Falling in Love* that critiqued a careerist, consumerist idea of masculinity. Sociologist Michael Kimmel describes Frank's dissatisfaction as the "loneliness [and] emptiness" of "breadwinner . . . men feeling like cogs in the corporate machine," who find "conspicuous consumption . . . hardly a compensation" (176). Kimmel attributes the large amount of "men's liberation" literature published in the 1970s to the

Colorful clothing in *Falling in Love*. Copyright Paramount Pictures, 1984.

presence in American society of "many men . . . living lives of quiet desperation—working in boring and unfulfilling jobs, trapped in unhappy marriages with little or no relationship with their children" (185). Frank clearly
feels such dissatisfaction with his marriage, family life, and job, despite the
latter's monetary rewards. He twice rebuffs his boss's attempts to convince
him that a transfer to Houston would move him "five steps up the ladder,"
he reminds his wife that it was her idea to have kids, and after a morning
spent Christmas shopping he meets his friend Ed (Harvey Keitel) and sarcastically describes how economic security doesn't compensate for his emotional distance from his family: "I just spent a fortune buying all the wrong
gifts for everybody, so I feel great."

In addition to the cooperative improvisation that improved the script,
De Niro also relied on Streep to help him create the Frank character physically. She suggested losing the extra weight he still carried from *Raging Bull*,
which he did, giving him a trim appearance that helped the forty-one-year-
old De Niro more effectively portray a man still young enough to be dissatisfied with sacrificing sexual desire in favor of a settled life. De Niro and
Streep also used costumes effectively to communicate their choice of life
change. In the film's early scenes the unhappy lives of both characters are
represented by the muted tans, grays, and khaki of their clothing. Frank
appears several times in crewneck sweaters and a nondescript tan wind-
breaker, and Molly in a trench coat and skirts and tops cut so wide that they
conceal the shape of her body. As the romance between the characters

develops, however, both externalize their emotions through their clothing, and in the film's last scene Frank wears a rich green sport coat with a purple tie and Molly a brightly colored sweater underneath a blue wool coat with a fur collar.

Two other 1980s roles that gave De Niro the opportunity to portray a patient, cooperative image of masculinity were his roles as Rodrigo Mendoza in the period film *The Mission* and as Vietnam veteran Joseph Megessey in *Jacknife*. But unlike *Falling in Love*, in which his character from the start marked a break from the anger and violence of his star image, De Niro's performances in *The Mission* and *Jacknife* show the process of rejecting the violent isolation of the outlaw hero for a kinder, gentler masculinity.

In *The Mission* De Niro presented a character redefined as he gives up arrogance and slave trading for Christian gospel and community. Accustomed to improvising his dialogue, De Niro wasn't comfortable with the formal language of Robert Bolt's screenplay, but the script worked to establish the initial pretension and self-absorption of Mendoza, a mercenary and slave trader in eighteenth-century Paraguay. Jesuit priest and activist Daniel Berrigan, who had a small part and worked as an advisor for the film, described De Niro's Mendoza, riding into the marketplace with a group of Guarani slaves, dressed in knee-high leather boots, his hair pulled tightly back and armed with a long sword, as "arrogant Satan on parade" ("The Mission Diary," *American Film*, November 1986, 24). We also hear Mendoza's self-absorption articulated in the film's early scenes. He dismisses the attempts of Jesuit missionaries to help the Indians he enslaves, tells his brother Felipe (Aidan Quinn) to find a woman ("About women I am always right, you know that"), and responds with anger ("So me you do not love? . . . So I have no need?") when the woman Rodrigo wants, Carlotta (Cherie Lunghi), tells him she loves his sibling instead.

Enraged by Carlotta's decision, Mendoza kills his brother, and to assuage his guilt he joins a Jesuit priest, Father Gabriel (Jeremy Irons), to help save the Guarani he had formerly enslaved from Portuguese landowners who force them to work on banana plantations. Mendoza's arrogant language disappears in the nine-minute scene of De Niro climbing up steep waterfalls, barefoot and pulling a heavy mesh bag filled with armor and weapons, to reach the isolated area where the Indians live. Upon finally reaching the top, he breaks into tears. Even as Mendoza returns to violence in a futile attempt to help the Guarani resist Portuguese soldiers, the ideas of community and nonviolence endorsed by the film—what Berrigan called its "contrary vision"—win out; Mendoza is finally told: "If might is right, love has no place in the world" (Berrigan, *American Film*, November 1986, 26).

Echoing his famous roles in *Taxi Driver* and *The Deer Hunter*, De Niro in *Jacknife* again played a Vietnam veteran scarred by his experience of the war. Joseph Megessey initially displays maladjusted behavior, showing up unexpectedly very early in the morning at the home of his war buddy Davy (Ed Harris) to go fishing, and later telling Davy's sister Martha that she is "built like a brick shithouse." Moreover, in two early scenes he appears inclined toward violence as an expression of his alienation: in one, he drives Davy's truck recklessly while howling like a dog and yelling "Just a crazy fuckin' bastard, that's me, right," and in another, when Martha rejects his advances, he puts his fist through a window in frustration.

De Niro used his skill with physical transformation to represent how, unlike those earlier Vietnam veteran characters, Megessey controls the destructive force of the anger and alienation resulting from the war experience. As an outward sign of his adjustment, when Martha invites him to the prom at the high school where she teaches, Megessey cuts off the beard that recalled De Niro's Mike Vronsky character from *The Deer Hunter*, and discards the cowboy boots alluding to Travis Bickle's obsession with frontier justice. Even when Davy drunkenly confronts Megessey during the prom about taking his sister out, De Niro reacts with patience and generosity that demonstrate an understanding of his friend's feelings of self-hatred caused by the fear he felt in battle. The desire for social connection that De Niro expresses through the physical transformation of the Megessey character is articulated in a scene with another friend from Vietnam, Jake (Charles Dutton), who tells him: "Makes me feel good to know I'm not alone. . . . People alone they just waste away slow. That's true for all people . . . not just vets." In describing his preparation talking with men who had fought in Vietnam, De Niro reported finding a greater openness and strength by the late 1980s when he made *Jacknife* than when he appeared in *The Deer Hunter*, implying that it impacted the Megessey role: "I met a lot of guys when I was doing *Deer Hunter*. . . . The war was more immediate. . . . You never really talked with them about the pain. . . . But when I met the vets for this film they were more able to deal with things like that" (Dougan 203).

## ★★★★★ A Peaceful Man

Al Capone in *The Untouchables* was De Niro's highest-profile performance of the 1980s. Earlier oversimplified film representations of the mobster challenged De Niro to portray Capone more accurately. Asked by Jack Kroll in *Newsweek* what attracted him to the role, he responded: "I've never seen [him] done the way it should be done. Capone wasn't just pure evil. He had to be a politician, an administrator, he had to have something going for him other than just fear." The extensive material available about the life of the famous gangster also gave De Niro ample opportunity for the kind of research and preparation he relished. He looked at old photos, saw movies in which Capone had been represented, and read the gangster's newspaper coverage, including one account of a psychiatrist who treated Capone and was killed when he got too personal—a likely source of the Mafia boss in analysis that De Niro would later portray in *Analyze This*. For the Capone role De Niro undertook the most radical alteration of his physical appearance since *Raging Bull*. He again gained a significant amount of weight—twenty-five pounds over five weeks—by consuming large amounts of pasta, potatoes, desserts, and beer. De Niro acknowledged the psychological challenge of putting on so much weight again, calling it "very depressing," yet he also stated that he wished he could have added even more, and indeed he wore a latex body suit to augment his bulk as well as plugs to broaden his nose (Kroll, "De Niro as Capone: The Magnificent Obsessive," *Newsweek*, 22 July 1987, 64). He also spent hours getting his hair cut to simulate Capone's baldness and trying on the Armani wardrobe developed for the role.

Besides the historical richness of the part, De Niro was attracted to *The Untouchables* by the opportunity to work again with Brian De Palma. The two had started their movie careers together twenty years earlier with three small independent films, *Greetings* (1968), *The Wedding Party* (1969), and *Hi, Mom!* (1970). Thus when producer Art Linson expressed doubt about how the laconic, now-svelte De Niro would realistically portray the portly, verbose Capone, De Palma could reassure him about the actor's dedication to preparation and his acting skills (Kroll, "Magnificent Obsessive," *Newsweek*, 22 July 1987, 64).

De Niro was also enthusiastic about David Mamet's screenplay. He had seen the playwright's *American Buffalo* and praised his writing as a "kind of vernacular poetry" appropriate for the elliptical, aggressive dialogue that De Niro had used so effectively in the past. The affinity between De Niro's approach to acting and Mamet's writing showed itself in a scene in which Capone speaks with reporters before attending an opera: "I have done nothing to hurt these people but they're angered at me so what do they do? Doctor up some income tax for which they got no case, to annoy me. To speak to me like men? No, to harass a peaceful man." The gangster's awkward syntax, slamming one phrase against the next, typifies the discontinuity and colloquial speech patterns of De Niro's realist acting style and subverts Capone's denial of criminal violence. The aggressive urban vernacular De

De Niro as Al Capone. "I'm a businessman." *The Untouchables*. Copyright Paramount Pictures, 1987.

Niro was famous for also comes out in full force in a later scene in which Capone learns that Eliot Ness (Kevin Costner) and his G-men have intercepted a large shipment of his bootleg liquor: "I want that son of a bitch dead! . . . I want you to get this fuck where he breathes. I want his family dead! I want his house burnt to the ground and I want to go in the middle of the night and piss on his ashes!"

Mamet commented in a 1989 interview that in his screenplay he "gave some good speeches to Mr. Capone," including the gangster's first appearance in the film (Case 102). De Palma opened that scene with a shot looking down on Capone in a barber's chair with titles explaining that 1930 in Chicago is "The time of Al Capone," in which "rival gangs battle for control of the lucrative bootlegging market." We then hear the reporters ask Capone about accusations of criminality and violence, to which he responds: "On the boat, it's bootlegging, on Lake Shore Drive, it's hospitality." The reporters laugh and he continues, "We laugh because it's funny and we laugh because it's true," concluding, "I'm a businessman. . . . There is violence in Chicago, of course, but not by me or by anybody I employ. . . . It's not good business."

During the scene following Capone's initial performance for the reporters, De Palma takes a position critical of the just-a-businessman claim when we see the mobster's assassins bomb a speakeasy whose owner won't buy his beer, and kill a young girl. Yet, even as De Palma vilifies Capone's violence, both here and in a scene in which he kills an inept subordinate with a baseball bat, we also see how the legal system, as represented by Ness and a Chicago cop, Malone (Sean Connery), also operated outside the law and according to a discriminatory logic that stigmatized Italian Americans. The legal system in *The Untouchables* imposes social control using the double standard Capone complained about in his opening remarks, calling into question whether the violence employed by the lawmen in the name of justice is in fact morally superior.

Allusion also adds to the moral complexity of the crime story centered on Capone and helps to move the film beyond the limits of genre. Mamet (who has described himself as "a devotee to Sergei Eisenstein and his theory of montage") and De Palma allude to the Soviet filmmaker's Odessa steps sequence from *Battleship Potemkin* (1925) in the scene in which Ness and his deputy, George Stone (Andy Garcia), apprehend the bookkeeper who will be the central witness in the tax evasion trial that would put Capone in prison (Kane 146). Mamet and De Palma thus cast the gangster story within a materialist context whereby Capone is not just the embodiment of the "pure evil" that De Niro criticized, but rather representative of a problematic criminal response to larger patterns of discrimination and social control. Certainly the scenes showing a bomb in a speakeasy or a brutal killing with a baseball bat undercut any chance that we might see the gangster's violence as justified. Instead, the parallels between De Niro's Capone and Connery's Malone—their similarly brutal violence and equally aggressive language—undermine the moral standing of both the mobster and the cop.

De Niro's elliptical style of delivering dialogue and his proven skill with vernacular language helped establish this critical parallel. Confronted by Ness, who threatens to shoot him in the lobby of the Lexington Hotel, Capone moves toward the government agent angrily and taunts him: "Fuck you. . . . If you were a man you would have done it . . . you punk." For his part, Connery plays Malone as if trying to match De Niro's coarse language and delivery. In one scene Malone insults the Irish police chief (Richard Bradford) with the remark, "You run with the fuckin' dagos" before they come to blows. When confronted by Capone's assassins, Malone again utters an ethnic slur, stating contemptuously: "Isn't it like a wop, brings a knife to a gunfight." Malone's biased language and taste for violence invoke the historical context of discrimination directed at Italians in Chicago in the period prior to Capone's rise, and undercut the moral and legal legitimacy claimed by Connery's character.

## ★★★★★ With a Hero like Travis . . .

While De Niro's role as Al Capone returned him to the violent outsider that he had begun to move away from, its parallel with Connery's bigoted, vigilante cop exposed the contradictions of Hollywood's endorsement of outlaw hero masculinity. The Capone role therefore fits into a thematic whole in De Niro's performances, going back to Bickle's psychotic delusion that the blood bath he initiates would restore law and order, a critique that Scorsese underscores visually with the Hitchcockian bird's-eye view of the results of Bickle's violence and that De Palma invokes when we look down upon Capone in the first scene in which he appears.

The seven roles from De Niro's 1980s films discussed here develop this critique of the outlaw hero established in *Taxi Driver* in various contexts. *Raging Bull* shows how selfishness and violence destroy a family. *The King of Comedy* returns to the idea from *Taxi Driver* that American society, in its obsession with celebrity, often ignores the cost sometimes required to achieve such individual distinction. (Jerry Lewis commented that he felt the ending was too easy on Rupert, who should have been shown as more violent, like Travis Bickle [Naremore 269].) In *Once Upon a Time in America*, the sexual violence of De Niro's character that Sergio Leone chose to emphasize made him more an example of violent entitlement than a critical response to it. His Al Capone in *The Untouchables* more successfully uses parallels of violence and hostile language between the mobster and the lawmen to call into question the story's celebration of Ness and the Untouchables as outlaw heroes, pointing instead to the need to see the conflict between the gangster and the G-men within a larger context of ethnicity and class politics. Finally, *The Mission* offers probably the most overt critique of the outlaw hero among De Niro's 1980s roles. It rejects the typical reconciliation of individualism and the interests of community in Hollywood films by showing how Mendoza dies to resist the greed of the Portugese landowners.

However, De Niro in the 1980s must surely have been aware of the potential obscurity for many viewers of these critiques of Hollywood's individualized masculinity, the possibility that audiences would see them as endorsements of violent self-assertion. After all, *The Untouchables*, fueled by the attention his performance received and the star power of Costner and Connery, was by far his biggest box-office hit of the decade, placing sixth on the list of top-earning American films in 1987. As a counterbalance, De Niro also took on the smaller, quieter roles in *The Mission, Falling in Love*, and *Jacknife* in which he could actively endorse an alternative, gentler, compromising kind of male character.

Richard Dyer has stated that the central interest of film stars comes from their articulation of "what it is to be a human being in contemporary society . . . the promise and the difficulty that the notion of individuality presents" (*Heavenly Bodies* 8). De Niro's performances in these 1980s films embodied this conflictual individuality, and his particular ability to use his considerable acting skills—both physical and linguistic—to create characters who pathologize or reject self-interest, as well as affirm a more positive, social image of masculinity, offered a particularly difficult and promising version of such star appeal.

# 2 ★★★★★★★★★★★
# Sylvester Stallone and Arnold Schwarzenegger
## Androgynous Macho Men

REBECCA BELL-METEREAU

The 1980s witnessed a profound shift in the nature of idealized masculinity and stardom, exemplified by the rise of Sylvester Stallone and Arnold Schwarzenegger as superstars. The bodies and films of these actors represent the super-sizing of muscles and publicity, and the two engaged in a constant dance of competition with each other for the position

_Rambo: First Blood Part II._ Courtesy Jerry Ohlinger. Copyright Anabasis, N.V., 1985.

_Conan the Barbarian._ Courtesy Jerry Ohlinger. Copyright Dino De Laurentiis Company/ Universal Pictures, 1982.

of top money-making star. A close look at how and why these two figures dominated the decade's box office is key to analyzing the complex relationship between marketing and gender in creating stardom. Although these two figures are most often associated with hyper-masculinity, their appeal for viewers does not lie exclusively in their identity as the stereotypical lone "macho man." Rather, both stars incorporate a complex and fascinating mixture of stereotypically masculine and feminine signals as inherent to their star personas. These contradictory gender cues are essential to both actors' commercial success, in part because they helped broaden the actors' appeal for female and gay audiences. Even as heterosexual manly men watch these stars with unalloyed pleasure, the erotic display of smooth, hairless bodies and bulging pectorals that look like large breasts conveys an androgynous identity hidden in plain sight for other viewers. During the 1980s, this counter-text brought in a whole new set of fans who enjoyed reading these stars' sexual identities in multiple ways—either consciously or unconsciously. At the same time, these two actors followed the path to international stardom through a web of primarily male economic and political networks, while their multilayered sexual identities spoke to deep ambivalence and anxiety over shifting social, political, and sexual roles.

As preeminent muscle men of the decade, Stallone and Schwarzenegger were inextricably bound to each other in a battle for fans and box office supremacy. They were well aware that they were competing for a similar viewing audience, and they spoke of each other publicly with the kind of openly boastful hostility one normally associates with the Worldwide Wrestling Federation. At one point, Schwarzenegger wished his temperamental girlfriend Brigitte Nielsen on Stallone: "She was obsessed with him [Schwarzenegger], she wanted to marry him, and he didn't know what to do. Arnold and Sylvester shared the same attorney and so he had the attorney introduce Brigitte Nielsen to Stallone, and Stallone ended up marrying her" (Leamer 216). In Stallone's 1986 *Rolling Stone* version of the story, Nielsen had been obsessed with Stallone since she was eleven and she essentially stalked him until she won him over (19 December 1986, 127). Similar competing narratives of the two actors abound during the 1980s, adding to their fascination for fans and viewers.

Rival ethnic identities also contributed to the dueling personas of these actors, whose speech and accents tied them to particular social and economic milieus. The almost monotone flatness of their voices hearkened back to John Wayne. Their semi-naked physiques evoked traditions of the 1950s bathing beauty contests, teenage beach movies, and a subsequent broader notion of self-conscious parody. Both actors modified their star personas by incorporating into their work the kind of irony that involves self-deprecating humor and exaggeration, typical of the growing camp sensibility noted by such critics as Richard Dyer. Their competitive transformations followed the rapidly shifting parameters of masculinity, femininity, and androgyny, as they raced to keep up with one another and with the moviegoing public's constantly changing social and sexual tastes.

## ★★★★★ Sylvester Stallone: Refashioning the Italian Stallion

Stallone's acting career, which began in 1970 with a pornographic film, moved through smaller parts to his triumphant appearance in the Academy Award–winning *Rocky* (1976). Throughout the 1980s his image and identity evolved in such films as *Victory* (1981), *Nighthawks* (1981), *First Blood* (1982), *Rocky III* (1982), *Rhinestone* (1984), *Rambo: First Blood Part II* (1985), *Rocky IV* (1985), *Rambo III* (1988), and *Tango & Cash* (1989). The media of the 1980s presented Stallone in contradictory terms, ranging from the "dumbest piece of meat in Hollywood" to the man who can talk "cogently on subjects ranging from geopolitics to poetry and bemoan the lost art of conversation" (*Ladies' Home Journal*, July 1988, 96). As the highest paid superstar of 1988, Stallone owned collections of weapons and art worth several hundred million dollars, and his physical activities ranged from "low culture" boxing to polo, the sport of aristocrats. Viewers tended to conflate his movie roles with his private life, and the rags-to-riches nature of his own biography supports this connection. He grew up in New York's Hell's Kitchen, and *Ladies' Home Journal* described him as "down to his last $100 when he sold the script of *Rocky*" (July 1988, 98). Stallone also mentioned that he had been approached to run for governor of California, but that he didn't feel he had the patience or aptitude for politics.

Publicity for Sylvester Stallone highlights the complexity and ambivalence of his troubled relationship to power and wealth. In a 1982 *Rolling Stone* article, Lawrence Grossberger discusses Stallone's cycles of success, excess, and failure, noting that "we love to wallow in the misfortune of others. Especially stars." The conspicuous consumption of the 1980s was writ large in its superstars, and Stallone's case exposes both the impulse toward indulgence and the resulting consequences, including guilt and regret. For example, immediately after purchasing an $80,000 Clénet, he found himself wondering, "What self-aggrandizing asshole would drive a car like that?" (Grossberger, *Rolling Stone*, 8 July 1982, 12). He immediately sold the car, along with a number of other status-symbol vehicles, paring his transportation down to a Toyota wagon. Stallone's path from failure to success and from poverty to extravagance appears in the trajectory of his film narratives during the 1980s, as he became a model for American manhood.

While viewers and critics tend to focus on how Stallone's star appeal resides in his power and stereotypically masculine attributes, other elements deserve attention as well. Many of the gestures, clothing choices, hairstyles, and psychological attributes of Stallone's heroes actually subvert conventions of the male-dominated action genre. In *Victory*, he wears a fitted blue soccer uniform, which makes him appear slight and almost boyish, hardly the image of the macho man. In *Nighthawks*, he sports flamboyantly stylish suits, and in the *Rocky* series, the silky textures of boxing shorts and dressing gowns emphasize his ambiguously androgynous appeal. Even in the early Rambo films, his long hair and headbands give him an almost girlish appearance, an apparent counterweight to the physical abuse heaped on his dirty sweating body. In most of his films of the 1980s, shots of his smooth, glistening, muscled chest send contradictory visual signals, just as his layered hairdo, complete with headbands and hoods, simultaneously suggests masculine and feminine styles. Moreover, the behavior of a number of his characters bespeaks a thinly veiled emotional vulnerability and neediness not usually associated with the lone male hero.

In *Victory*, Stallone establishes both his androgynous appeal and his international credentials as cocky outcast Captain Robert Hatch, goalie for the Allied Prisoners of War, a multinational soccer team set to play against an all-star Nazi team in Paris. The Germans hope to humiliate the Allies in this very public match, but the POW team plans to escape at halftime instead. Against logic, however, the POW group opts to finish the game, and even Stallone's loner character catches the sense of camaraderie. In the climactic scene, lyrical shots of Stallone playing in balletic slow motion crosscut to close-ups of a Nazi commander (Max Von Sydow) gazing at him approvingly. These looks of grudging admiration for Stallone's physicality can be read on several narrative levels: as nonpartisan appreciation of the sport, as old age looking wistfully at the strength and agility of youth, as repressed homoerotic voyeurism, and as foreshadowing of the Third Reich's defeat.

*Victory* is not a title that people immediately associate with Stallone's blockbuster career, but its emphasis on international teamwork, both within the narrative and in the real-world production itself, established the foundation for his worldwide stardom. The film is significant in the development of Stallone's stardom because of two important factors. First, it allowed him to establish a credible reputation by working with Old Hollywood's iconic action director, John Huston. Second, it brought him into partnership with a cast from around the world, including Michael Caine, Von Sydow, and such internationally popular soccer players as Pélé. He plays an American enlisted in the Canadian army who also has a French girlfriend, thus giving a nod to Canadian and French audiences as well.

That same year, Stallone appeared in a film that would become another franchise, playing a role that also emphasized his outcast underdog status and the apparent vulnerability, even softness, of his character. At the opening of *First Blood*, Stallone's John Rambo could be mistaken for a college student, with fluffy hair and a casual demeanor, strolling through the sunny countryside. Once he learns of the death of his black friend, Rambo's only surviving Vietnam War comrade, the psychological and meteorological weather changes. Rambo wanders through the rain, a pitiful, homeless figure almost stereotypically girlish in his quiet demeanor, and totally abject in his poverty and filth. Rambo remains sullen yet passively resistant as a sheriff harasses him and takes him to jail, where the officers compare him to an animal, a motif that is reiterated near the close of the film.

Torture and male nudity ensue—two popular staples of Stallone films of the 1980s—first placing Rambo in the shower as the object of the gaze of other males, and then causing the traumatized veteran to experience a Vietnam flashback to another situation where he was semi-naked and tortured. This agonizing scene in turn triggers one of Rambo's famous rampages in which he wreaks havoc on his surroundings and flees into the woods. In this pastoral setting, Stallone refashions his persona from the urban pugilist of the *Rocky* films to mountain man and guerilla fighter. At the same time that he appears to become more masculine in his aggressiveness and toughness, he also assumes conventionally feminine functions and clothing attributes. In his first designer challenge, he manages to create a rather dashing tunic from an old tarp and rope belt. Later, he tries his hand as seamstress on his own body, first extracting a tiny sewing kit from his knife hilt and then darning a broad gash in his arm with skill and delicacy.

At some point Rambo dons stylish headgear, which morphs from a leafy camouflage to a hippie-style sports headband that he wears throughout the remainder of the film. He finds food for himself (and in a parallel scene, his former colonel comments on Rambo's self-sufficiency, noting his ability to cook and his willingness to eat anything). Rambo's domestic life in the wilderness demonstrates that he is comfortable removed from society and surviving in the wild. Susan Jeffords argues that Rambo's externalization of conflict in this film and subsequent sequels represents a "pattern of internal amnesia" that is "typical of male action film sequences of the 1980s"

(*Hard Bodies* 246). Indeed, the "popularity and financial success of these films suggests that sequentiality itself was one of the mechanisms for Hollywood responses to crises in the representations and marketing of [U.S.] masculinities in this period" (247).

In *First Blood*, Rambo's return to the wild also works through the national nightmare of humiliating defeat in Vietnam by visually creating a descent into the hell of all things dark, abject, and feminine. Rats bite at him as he crawls through a slimy tunnel passage, a kind of psychological close encounter with Freud's *vagina dentata*—the toothed vagina. Throughout this ordeal, Stallone's demeanor often resembles that of a sleepwalker. Some critics would argue that his lack of affect during these scenes simply reveals his inability to act, but his behavior is also a credible imitation of someone suffering from post-traumatic stress disorder. His stoical manner also follows the popular Hollywood model of American masculinity that suffers in silence.

Despite his manly ability to withstand pain, Rambo's character endures humiliations that subtly undermine his traditional masculinity. For example, at one point a police officer who has been a father figure to Rambo hints at a homoerotic attachment between Rambo and his former colonel (Richard Crenna), asking if the colonel wants to give him a big sloppy kiss. By the end of the film, Rambo's character is not only placed in stereotypical female poses but is also emasculated and infantilized. Rambo rages at his own economic impotence and finally collapses, huddling against the older man like a child, his long locks and lower body position making him appear vulnerable and conventionally feminized. All of this drama is delivered with the utmost seriousness, presenting a figure that viewers are intended to see as a sacrificial rather than a triumphant hero.

The spectacle of the exposed and humiliated physique, what Rita Kempley calls the "sadomasochistic thing," is an integral part of Stallone's star image (*Washington Post*, 22 December 1989, 13). He offers the erotic display of the suffering male body, perhaps as an antidote to abuse or perhaps—for some viewers—as a booster to the visual thrill of witnessing such torture. In this welter of mixed signals, Stallone's progression throughout the 1980s mirrors cultural attitudes toward masculinity, as Jeffords and other critics have noted. Gaylyn Studlar and David Desser observe: "Rambo declares that 'the mind is the best weapon,' but Stallone's glistening hypermasculinity, emphasized in the kind of languid camera movements and fetishizing close-up usually reserved for female 'flashdancers,' visually insists otherwise" (9).

Even in the failed comedy *Rhinestone*, the androgynous elements of Stallone's persona surface in his choice of wardrobe, which ranges from colorful exhibitionist shirts, open to the waist, to flatly absurd rhinestone-covered cowboy suits, as the title suggests. The private interaction behind the scenes reveals that this famously bad movie was not simply a case of Stallone's inability to do comedy; it seems to be an example of his devotion to courtly love overcoming his own survival instincts. Finding Dolly Parton at a particularly low point in her life, Stallone set out to rehabilitate both the actress and her career as a country-and-western singer by writing a role that presented him as a buffoon and her as a sexy country diva. Parton claims that he virtually saved her life by encouraging her through one of the darkest emotional periods of her life: "It was an awful time for me. . . . Every day I thought, 'I wish I had the nerve to kill myself'" ("Dolly Parton Saved by Sylvester Stallone," starpulse.com). This personal side of Stallone's career reveals his own attempts to transform his star image and perhaps himself from macho icon to sensitive new-age hero, still trying to capitalize on his earlier successful star qualities.

On the heels of Stallone's failed comedy and his success with the tortured Rambo and Rocky characters, the sequels, *Rambo: First Blood Part II* and *Rocky IV*, came in at over $150 and $125 million, second and third in box office grosses for 1985 after *Back to the Future*. *Rambo: First Blood Part II* broke a record for distribution as the first picture ever released to over 2,000 screens at once (*Rambo: First Blood Part II*, imdb.com). It also boasted a sustained advertising campaign, opening in May and still receiving a full-page advertisement in the *New York Times* (opposite one for *Back to the Future*) in early July. The second Rambo film, often touted as the film in which the United States gets to win the Vietnam War, is controversial for its rewriting of history, as noted in Ian T. Haufrect's documentary *We Get to Win This Time* (2002). Originally written by James Cameron and featuring Rambo's character fresh from a mental institution, *Rambo: First Blood Part II* underwent drastic alteration under Stallone's pen. He changed the story so that Rambo was coming out of prison as an angry character destined to get revenge and leave bodies in his wake. The new Rambo fulfills multiple fantasies for American viewers bruised by defeat in Vietnam and insecure about the place of American manhood. The 1985 Rambo is much more violent, but his relationship to technology and femininity is still somewhat troubled, reflecting anxieties of a culture in the throes of technological and social change. Rambo uses a bow and arrow to pick off a sniper who couldn't hit him with a rifle, and in the climax, he shoots up a computer that stands for a corrupt political bureaucracy. In Stallone's version of the Vietnam story, the American is beloved by the Vietnamese, in the person of Julia Nickson-Soul as Co-Bao, who stands in for the entire Vietnamese people.

Also, Stallone takes time out to kiss this woman, who then conveniently dies in a sentimental farewell scene. Her presence, albeit transitory, gives a nod to the influence of multiracial and female viewers.

In *Rocky IV*, Stallone's hero sets himself up as natural man, comfortably training for his boxing match in a pastoral setting and using only ordinary physical means of strengthening himself. His opponent, the Russian Ivan Drago (Dolph Lundgren), trains scientifically, using technology and a cold, methodical approach. Despite his obvious mechanical advantage, with his hulking frame towering over Rocky, Drago nevertheless loses. This improbable narrative points to elements outside the confines of the story. Rocky's winning over Drago is not simply the defeat of a character; it can also be seen to represent Stallone's defeat of Schwarzenegger's clone; and beyond that, it is working-class America's defeat of the entire Soviet Union in a Cold War triumph.

*Rocky IV* opens with self-reflexive references to previous Rocky films, the experience of aging, and the filmmaking process itself. Rocky appears as the family man and sensitive new-age guy, with a child, wife, and grouchy uncle, all of whom he showers with affection and extravagant technology, as if to demonstrate how the star is entering a new, modern phase of his stardom. Technology and sensitivity appear in the domestic setting of Rocky's comfortable suburban abode. When Rocky arrives home, his son videotapes him as he gets out of the car, and this blurry black-and-white footage subtly calls attention to the real-life star's fame and constant exposure to the camera. Rocky gives a robot to his uncle for a birthday present, referencing the popularity of *E.T.* (1982) and other such films and demonstrating another beneficial use of technology. These positive depictions of technology are wedded to other images of Rocky in his new role as sensitive family man. Rocky describes himself as "nervous" about the gifts he gives, a narrative that echoes the star's attempts in interviews to portray himself as more complex, intelligent, and sensitive than his earlier star persona had suggested.

The film also abounds with direct references to technology and indirect references to Stallone's competitor for top star status, Arnold Schwarzenegger, associated with the mechanical cyborg/robot through his role the previous year as the Terminator. As the story progresses, technology receives less flattering treatment in its association with the unemotional, mechanical Drago. His expressionless voice and demeanor (not to mention the foreign accent that most Americans could scarcely distinguish as either Russian or Austrian) make humorless fun of the Schwarzenegger/Terminator figure. Furthermore, Drago's wife is played by Brigitte Nielsen (by now Stallone's

Sylvester Stallone, in *Rocky IV*, his face battered black and blue and his naked torso draped in the American flag, came to represent a certain segment of the American public who saw the United States as aggrieved, embittered, and misunderstood. Copyright Chartoff-Winkler Productions/Metro-Goldwyn Mayer, 1985.

wife), speaking for him and wearing a gray pants suit and short haircut. When Rocky's wife, Adrian (Talia Shire), attempts to control their relationship, the champ refuses to give in to her, thus establishing his manliness and independence.

Rocky goes to Russia to fight Drago, who has killed his longtime friend and fellow fighter Apollo Creed in a boxing match in the United States. Following Creed's death, a montage sequence alternating love scenes between Rocky and Adrian and scenes of Rocky and Apollo embracing has the effect of suggesting a homoerotic underpinning in the men's relationship. Rocky's preparation for the fight once in Russia contrasts sharply with that of Drago. Rocky trains in the snow, chops wood, runs, and pulls a dog sled, while Drago's training involves scientists, steroids, and machines. At the end of this sequence, Rocky scales a snow-covered rock mountain, an echo of mounting the Philadelphia Art Museum steps in the first Rocky film.

Political ideology infiltrated Stallone's Rocky and Rambo roles throughout the decade. Politically and religiously conservative admirers who perceived themselves to be besieged by godless communism made Stallone an iconic cultural figure. In *Rocky IV*, Rocky prays while a Gorbachev look-alike enters the auditorium; when the two fighters enter, Rocky faces universal boos while Drago receives cheers reminiscent of a Hitler rally. When Rocky finally lands a punch that cuts Drago, the gigantic fighter responds with surprise and confusion. The persistent Rocky eventually wins over the affection of the crowd as he deliberately takes punch after punch while the crowd begins to scream his name. Finally, Rocky begins his assault, the giant falls to the mat, and the crowd lifts Rocky to their shoulders as he is wrapped in the American flag. In his typically slurred speech, Stallone expresses an ideology that resonates both politically and socially: "What I'm trying to say is if I can change, then you can change. Everybody can change." When "Gorbachev" stands and applauds his words and comes into the ring, embracing his sweaty, flag-swathed body, Stallone/Rocky has overcome two important enemies. At a personal level, the actor has beaten the mechanical foreigner who represents his star nemesis, Schwarzenegger/ Terminator. In more political terms, Stallone overcomes the Soviet enemy and wins over the hearts and minds of the Russian people and their leader, all in a single encounter. This action aligns Stallone with President Reagan, who, in the eyes of his admirers, later managed the miraculous feat of bringing down Soviet communism and winning the admiration of the real Mikhail Gorbachev.

Instead of continuing along these conciliatory lines, Stallone's anticommunist *Rambo III*, set in Afghanistan, missed the target in message and timing, as relations between the United States and the Soviet Union had thawed by the date of its release. The film made almost $54 million domestically, but its budget came in at $65 million. At the same time, its worldwide gross was a respectable $189 million, a testament to the importance of the international appeal of Stallone's new ultra-violent persona. *Rambo III* made the 1990 *Guinness World Records* for the most violent film made until that date, with 108 onscreen kills and over 70 explosions (*Rambo III*, imdb.com). (The only film named simply *Rambo* [2008] would exceed those figures.)

By the end of the decade, Stallone had once again refashioned his image into a kind of banker cop, complete with glasses (to look intellectual), salon haircut, and Armani suits (to look rich), as well as a self-reflexive claim that "Rambo is a pussy" (to look sophisticated and witty). But just what does this statement mean, given the overtly homoerotic word and visual play featured in *Tango & Cash*? The constant references to homosexuality and gay marriage constitute a combined homophobic and homoerotic motif in the film. Stallone recognizes the need to alter his image in keeping with a swiftly changing public perception of gender roles. Throughout the decade, Stallone follows the path of Madonna in that he constantly reinvents himself, both as a star and as an iconic figure, in films identified with the essence of masculinity. He is not always successful, but he is always trying to locate the pulse of the American public. His desire to try out new images may well have contributed to the decline in popularity of his films with audiences attached to a particular star incarnation of Stallone.

A look at the marketing and critical reception for his films reveals a pattern of growing feminization and "homoeroticization" throughout the 1980s, finally culminating in *Tango & Cash*, which Kempley describes as follows: "Kurt Russell in drag, a slickery shower scene, come-hither repartee— all the suppressed homosexuality of the buddy movie genre surfaces in Sylvester Stallone's latest sadomasochistic man thing. 'Tango & Cash' is more like 'My Beautiful Laundrette' in the closet than it is a bad ripoff of 'Lethal Weapon'" (*Washington Post*, 22 December 1989, 13). Another critic writes with obvious relish: "An entire generation of American men were left extremely confused about their sexuality as a result of *Tango & Cash*" (Johnny Lieberman, ruthlessreviews.com).

When even a *Washington Post* critic recognizes the homoerotic subtext of a film, it is no longer a subtext. It is a text that indicates a self-conscious campy humor on the part of the filmmakers and cast. The star and the budgets for Stallone's films of the 1980s were over the top, capitalizing on a new camp sensibility and using capital in a new way, establishing a marketing pattern that continues to this day in blockbuster films. Tino Balio notes of the development of the ultra-high budget films and saturation booking: "The format was popularized by Carolco Pictures, an independent production company headed by Mario F. Kassar and Peter Hoffman that got its start with the *Rambo* movies starring Sylvester Stallone in the 1980s. Carving a niche for itself in the fast-growing foreign market, Carolco specialized in action-filled blockbusters and paid top stars like Sylvester Stallone and Arnold Schwarzenegger enormous fees to carry them" (Balio 24). But beyond these successful marketing strategies, the films of Sylvester Stallone serve as a cultural gender barometer, tracking the weather for the extremes of hyper-masculinity, ultra-femininity, and the liminal states between.

Just as multiple booking and the twin stardom of Stallone and Schwarzenegger boosted audience interest and financial competition, Stallone learned that he could increase his grosses and the psychological punch of the narratives by adding another popular actor to his films. Chris Holmlund argues that in *Lock Up* and *Tango & Cash*, which close the decade, a kind of doubling occurs: "Crucially, in both these films Stallone is no longer a loner, no longer a little Rocky or a big Rambo fighting unbeatable odds and winning impossible battles all by himself. Now he is joined by another man, a figure so like Stallone I call him the Stallone clone" ("Masculinity" 214). I would contend that this partnering actually begins early in his career with

*Victory*, where an older mentor leads the unwilling younger man into the teamwork and acceptance of the all-male social group. A similar male partnership occurs in *First Blood*, as a lone Rambo confronts and surrenders to the man who used to command him in Vietnam. Rambo takes on this Oedipal struggle against institutionalized authority, but he fails, left shackled and defeated in an ending that paves the way for triumphs in later sequels.

It is significant that neither of these films shows Stallone's character in a heterosexual relationship with a woman. One way to account for this omission of the feminine is that Stallone's character is the stereotypical "woman"—the object of our gaze, the recipient of our pity, and at the same time the rescuer of his own pitiful and abject self. Self-contained, Stallone plays both child and father, victim and rescuer, man and woman. Stallone has to act all the parts and, more significantly, he has to appeal to as many contradictory demographics as he can manage, a feat he seems to have mastered intuitively in his most successful vehicles.

Throughout these various incarnations, the exposure of Stallone's body is problematic, for, as Paul Fussell notes, "Truth to tell, every king is a bit of a queen" (52). And, as Richard Dyer observes, "Nakedness may also reveal the inadequacies of the body by comparison with social ideals. It may betray the relative similarity of male and female, white and non-white bodies, undo the remorseless insistences on difference and concomitant power carried by clothes and grooming. The exposed white male body is liable to pose the legitimacy of white male power: why should people who look like that—so unimpressive, so like others—have so much power?" (*White* 146).

In listening to the dialogue in the shower scene of *Tango & Cash*, one would think that director Andrei Konchalevsky had read Dyer's article. For example, when Cash (Kurt Russell) bends down to pick up the soap, Tango (Stallone) shies away, saying that he doesn't know him that well. At a surface level, this demonstrates Tango's rejection of physical intimacy, but the phrasing is peculiar. For a male heterosexual audience, it reassures the viewer that there is nothing "gay" about this scene. At the same time, other viewers may infer that if Tango knew him better he would be more comfortable with another naked man in such close physical proximity in the shower. Cash tells him not to flatter himself; he has seen Tango naked. Here, again, the overt denial of Tango's attractiveness reassures traditional male viewers that there is no possibility of attraction between the two. Meanwhile, it hints at two racy and subversive possibilities for gay or female viewers to snicker at. First, if Tango were more attractive, Cash would be interested. Second—an even more threatening possibility—Tango is not well endowed, a recurring inadequacy motif explored exhaustively in numerous films of the 1980s and noted by Peter Lehman and other gender critics. Lehman remarks on the "awkward visual structures that deny the view of the genitals" (125) even as characters discuss penis size, noting that the gender of the speakers determines the psychological function of either denying vulnerability or disavowing homoerotic desire (138).

## ★★★★★ Arnold Schwarzenegger: From Locks, Frocks, and Pecs to Intellect

Like Sylvester Stallone, Arnold Schwarzenegger began his career with an emphasis on the brutalized body as a site of both erotic attraction and masculine power. In the early 1980s, Schwarzenegger's *Conan* films established him as a figure who spoke little but whose actions were magically effective. His roles during the 1980s covered the gamut in terms of playing out viewer anxieties, embodying fantasies in distinctive character types, and expanding the popularity and commercial success of action genres. He began as muscle man in the *Conan* films, became a robot villain in *The Terminator* (1984), then reluctantly took on a contract-driven supporting role in *Red Sonja* (1985). Throughout his career in this decade, he took risks in creating his star identity.

Schwarzenegger's characters often enjoy a special relationship to machines and role playing, demonstrating cleverness or effortless manipulation—traditionally considered to be female survival tactics—to attain success. The old-fashioned masculine hero maintains a stolid and consistent identity and appearance, whereas Schwarzenegger's new male is prepared to shape-shift in a way more often associated with "feminine" adaptive behavior than with stereotypical "masculine" strength. Combined with cleverness, the sheer bulk and size of Schwarzenegger's body gives his characters a winning combination of wiles and weight.

From the outset of his film career, Schwarzenegger seemed to be highly aware of the importance of gender issues and women viewers to his success, as he placed himself opposite bold, aggressive female figures. In 1980, he played Mickey Hargitay in the television movie *The Jayne Mansfield Story*, and in *Red Sonja*, a spin-off of the Conan series that focused on the titular figure (Brigitte Nielsen), he played another male second fiddle. The red-headed Amazon Sonja tells the Conan-like Kalidor that she needs no man to help her, although, of course, he ends up helping her. At the close of the story, Kalidor instructs a child-king that he should never marry a woman unless she can defeat him in battle. At that point, Sonja and Kalidor engage in a few half-hearted sword parries and then close the film with a kiss.

Schwarzenegger was banking on the film's appeal to women and children, who play significant roles in the film, although he was not particularly pleased at "starring" in a film where he actually had only a supporting role. He himself "eschews this movie as one of his worst, yet he (laughingly) claims that it's an excellent disciplinary tool for his children: 'I tell them, if they get on my bad side, they'll be forced to watch *Red Sonja* ten times in a row. Consequently, none of my kids has ever given me much trouble'" (*Red Sonja*, imdb.com).

We see the seeds of Schwarzenegger's brutish and malleable trickster persona even in his first big hit, *Conan the Barbarian* (1982), in which he plays a young man determined to avenge his parents' death, which he witnessed as a boy. When the film flashes forward to the grown Conan, director John Milius takes full advantage of the cheesecake appeal of Schwarzenegger's body. Lingering low-angle close-ups focus on the handsome face, the bared chest, the long hair flowing in the wind. Through the course of the film, Conan moves from naïve boyhood to the role of young adventurer who is ready to experiment sexually and use deceptive charm to further his progress. The aggressiveness of other characters in pursuing Conan's body places him in the conventionally feminine role as the object of desire. On his way to kill the snake king, Thulsa Doom (James Earl Jones), Conan encounters two women who teach him to be wary and aggressive. The first one he has sex with turns into a demon, and he barely escapes with his life. Later, Conan meets a woman who asks him repeatedly if he wants to live forever, just before she jumps into danger and expects him to follow. These dangerous women would typify Schwarzenegger's future female counterparts throughout the 1980s.

Manipulation, ambiguous sexuality, and malleability also stand as signature characteristics of the star's roles, as exemplified when the character of Conan finally arrives at the camp of Thulsa Doom. He flirts with one of the male initiates, who tells him he shouldn't be afraid to expose his body. At this point, the man opens Conan's shirt to expose Schwarzenegger's bulging pectorals, and Conan suggests that they go off into the bush where people won't be able to see them. Once there, Conan delivers an elbow jab, steals his opponent's robe, and makes his way into the camp, where he eventually kills the rival king. This $20 million sword-and-sandal epic, produced by Dino De Laurentiis, fared well at the box office, grossing over $68 million worldwide, bringing international and bi-gender attention to Schwarzenegger and his semi-clothed body. As with Stallone, this global popularity was crucial to Schwarzenegger's rise as an international—therefore blockbuster—star.

This was the first in a long line of successes for the actor, who had parlayed thirteen world champion bodybuilding titles into starring roles almost from the start of his film-acting career. In order to understand how Schwarzenegger calculated and calibrated his star persona, it is worth first exploring how technology, marketing, and gender intersect in films of the 1980s, particularly in box office successes. Schwarzenegger made the choice during the mid-1980s to shift from fantasy to techno-fantasy, a key element in his popularity. Several top-grossing films of the 1980s and early 1990s feature males whose bodies are destroyed and rebuilt in the invulnerable shell of a robot, or feature cyborgs who become humanized by their contacts with people. *The Terminator* and *Terminator 2* (1991), as examples, both look to technology as a way of restoring the body of authority. Far right and left ideologies meet in these films in their suspicion of government. Their filmic assertion of violent action as a solution provides their common ground.

One of the mass cultural pleasures of the 1980s was a set of narratives and imagery that offered "two ways to a feeling of 'mastery': at the level of plot in which the hard-body hero masters his surroundings, most often by defeating enemies through violent physical action; and at the level of national plot, in which the same hero defeats national enemies, again through physical action" (Jeffords, *Hard Bodies* 28). Jeffords's argument brilliantly identifies the patterns of star heroes, their physical and emotional characteristics, and the ideologies represented by many of the top-grossing films of the period. What her analysis neglects, however, is full explanation of eroticization of the body, the contradictory fissures and sutures that indicate multiple interpretations and pleasures, particularly for heterosexual females or for other disempowered groups, such as gay and lesbian audiences, adolescents, and children.

This complexity of identification, voyeurism, and fetishism holds true even in Schwarzenegger's films, ordinarily considered purely "masculine" action fare. In *Acting Male*, Dennis Bingham claims that "the gaze at the male star often (though by no means always) deemphasizes the body and focuses on the face, upper body, and voice, as sites of individuality as well as avatars of 'sincerity' and 'coherence'" (18). However, Schwarzenegger's case serves as a strong counterexample to Bingham's latter assertion. Throughout the 1980s, his films featured various parts of his anatomy. He took pride in fashioning his own stardom, from the initial choice of scripts and concepts to such fine points as costuming and audience reception: "The only reason I show off my body in the movies is for believability. . . . Then we sell more tickets. It's designed for that purpose only" (*Mademoiselle*, October 1986, 88). His insistence on "believability" as his sole purpose for

Arnold Schwarzenegger often plays characters paired with macha females whose physical prowess sometimes challenges his own, here Maria Conchito Alonso in *The Running Man*. Copyright Braveworld Productions, 1987.

exhibitionism and the economic rationale behind this choice suggests discomfort with his role as object of desire.

It is somewhat ironic that Schwarzenegger's focus on functional muscularity appears in a *Mademoiselle* interview that actually reinforces his image as pure beefcake. Interviewer Diana Maychick asks about "scenes of his unadorned chest rippling like mad" and describes how "his boyish candor is finally subsumed by his bod," when "his chest peeks out in all its formidable glory" (October 1986, 88). Indeed, Schwarzenegger's protestations appear somewhat disingenuous when one considers how he himself discusses his voyeuristic appeal to women in a *Sports Illustrated* article. He describes how, after *The Running Man* (1987) came out, executive producer Keith Barish told him that women commented on his "cute ass," to which he responded, "Now I know which direction to take with my next movie" ("Hot Stuff," 7 December 1987, 90). As the accompanying still from *The Running Man* shows, he's comfortable sharing a scene in his underwear with tough co-star Maria Conchito Alonso. He made good on this promise in *Red Heat* (1988), with its extended opening scene featuring loving shots of Arnold's nude buttocks.

In *The Terminator*, Schwarzenegger was able to address different viewers' fantasies by including a range of characteristics, even within the role of an apparently one-dimensional, single-minded killing machine. The framing device opens with a quick introduction to the 2029 world of machines in a state of nonstop warfare against all remaining humans. The film then flashes back to the present (of the 1980s), but even these scenes of contemporary life have the same dystopic quality as the future world does—a kind of greasy, gray slickness. Into this world two time travelers land. The first is the Terminator, T-101, whose splendidly naked body stuns the viewer with its uncanny development and its offhanded and spectacularly violent actions. When he approaches three partying teenagers and asks for clothes, they foolishly make fun of his naked state. He grabs one of them, tears out his heart, and then smashes another young man against the wall. The remaining survivor quickly disrobes. Schwarzenegger then begins his mission, wearing a rather effeminate-looking beaded jacket, a size too small, thus emphasizing his largeness in a humorous way. The second visitor from the future arrives in a similar naked state, but his body is presented as vulnerable and damaged from the journey. He steals a bum's pants and runs off, with the police in hot pursuit. The narrative immediately sets up contradictory and shifting points of identification.

Although a viewer might naturally sympathize with innocent victims, Schwarzenegger's demeanor is peculiarly winning and humorous in his blunt ferocity and determination. When we meet Sarah (Linda Hamilton), and learn that someone seems to be systematically killing women named Sarah Connor, our reasons for liking her reside in her ineptitude and vulnerability. Throughout the film, she and the Terminator stand in counterpoint to each other, and at any given moment one might just as readily identify with Schwarzenegger's ruthless robot. When the cyborg recreates the female voice of Sarah's mother, viewers must admire the guile and cleverness of this human machine in pretending to be a middle-aged woman. The voice of Sarah's mother is heard, thus turning the robot into a woman, temporarily, in the minds of the listeners who are fooled until Schwarzenegger's face appears onscreen. Particularly appealing are his spare, clever one-liners. When he says his famous "I'll be back," with his distinctive Austrian accent, the average audience takes particular delight as he returns in a giant vehicle that smashes its way into a building.

Such tag lines have become a trademark of Schwarzenegger's star persona, but equally important is his handling of physical detail. As a bodybuilder, he is keenly aware that an essential part of his star quality rests in his own physical appearance in tandem with the visual cues surrounding him. It is no accident that his roles often emphasize the color red and that two of his film have "red" in the titles: *Red Sonja* and *Red Heat*. With an MBA from the University of Wisconsin-Superior, Schwarzenegger was well aware of market studies showing that the color red creates excitement in consumers. Of course, any actor who specializes in action roles relies on the power of red blood in the filmic landscape to arouse viewers, but not all stars employ colors in the same ways. When Stallone uses red—as he often does both in wounds and in clothing—it is usually in conjunction with white and blue, to reinforce the patriotism of his message.

In contrast, the remaining color palette for Schwarzenegger's blood-drenched films seems to be black and various shades of metallic gray, associated with technology, in works that generally depict machines as ultimately triumphant. In *Predator* (1987), when the camera picks up the viewpoint of the eponymous technological shapeshifting alien, the predator's vision appears as heat-seeking, with red signaling life forms to be destroyed. Schwarzenegger covers his entire body and face with gray mud, to foil the creature's heat-sensitive vision, and only the rims of his eyes and lips provide slashes of red color. These scenes visually imitate the mud-covered warriors in *Apocalypse Now* (1979) and Stallone's *Rambo: First Blood Part II*. When James Cameron uses a red filter in *The Terminator* to turn the entire screen red in Schwarzenegger's film, it signals to the audience that we are now viewing the world from T-101's mechanical perspective, and we are encouraged to sympathize with that exciting point of view in spite of ourselves.

Cameron engineers this unwilling identification in one of the most shocking and memorable scenes after T-101's arm and head are injured. Although this sequence emphasizes the purely mechanical structure of T-101's body, it also humanizes the character by allowing the audience to witness his self-repair. In a gesture that seems to pay conscious homage to Stallone's self-surgery in *First Blood*, Schwarzenegger sews up his injured arm. Then he tops the scene by removing his damaged eyeball, staring through the red glowing lens into the mirror, where he sees a face in severe need of a makeover. Unable to repair his damaged face, T-101 opts for the stylish Oakley sunglasses to conceal his missing parts. This creates his famous Terminator look, which subsequently created a market boom for the brand out in the "real" world after the film's success. The look and the personality of both the terminator and Conan roles established Schwarzenegger's star brand. Less idealistic, more international, and at once more sadistic and comical, he looked to a mythical past and then to a dystopic future as his source of financial and social power. Schwarzenegger's screen persona addresses viewers' anxieties about the human body's vulnerability and weakness, dependency, domination by machines, and changing gender roles.

In *Red Heat*, Schwarzenegger goes over the top in displaying his muscles and playing on his star identity. The opening begins with a scene set in

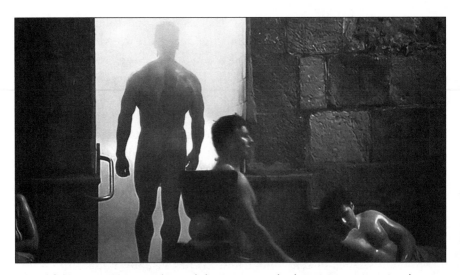

Arnold Schwarzenegger soon learned that women and other viewers appreciated scenes in which he exposed his physical attributes as much as the censors would allow, as in this shot from *Red Heat*. Copyright Carolco Pictures, 1988.

Russia that looks at first like a gay bathhouse. Muscle-bound semi-nude men parade through the steamy underground world, capturing the admiring gaze of men and women alike. Schwarzenegger's nude figure appears prominently, and to introduce him the camera begins at his feet and tilts up to reveal his body, clad in nothing but a tiny towel. This exposure of the body employs camera movements usually reserved for female pin-ups, but in the context of the bathhouse the scene contains elements of gay subculture as well. The shots of a naked Schwarzenegger from behind also pay homage to *The Terminator* and reinforce his image as an unbeatable killing machine. Having called up these connotations, the film then allays any ensuing anxieties as it shifts to the traditional events of the action genre and a brawl ensues. In a clever twist on the usual fight scene, Schwarzenegger and his muscle-bound opponent burst through a window onto a snow-covered roof and continue to battle semi-nude in the snow. When Schwarzenegger goes to the United States and teams up with the character played by Jim Belushi, the two actors have a charming chemistry that maximizes the humorousness of Schwarzenegger's stiff, mechanical persona. In the end, Schwarzenegger's deadpan character wins over his partner and the entire American police force.

Schwarzenegger's final film of the decade, *Twins* (1988), acknowledges the existence of Stallone's muscular star presence when the naïve character Julius comes to the United States from a desert island and, gazing in wonder at everything, sees a movie poster for *Rambo III*. Looking at Stallone's bicep, Julius compares it to his own and then gestures to indicate that Stallone's muscles are inferior. While *Twins* highlights this rivalry and Schwarzenegger's hard musculature, it portrays Julius as a stereotypically "soft" character in subtle ways, particularly in his relative passivity and his adulation for what he calls "feminine" traits. At one point, he describes to his brother (Danny De Vito) how much he admires women's characteristics of sensitivity and compassion, and the brother says knowingly, "You're a virgin." Julius replies demurely, "That's private." When he finally does lose his virginity, it is the woman who takes the lead. The film's blend of comedy, romance, and mild action placed Schwarzenegger's body front and center in a lucrative production that received generally positive reviews. The star would go on in the next decade to play a role even more overtly feminine, in which he becomes pregnant and gives birth (*Junior* [1994]).

★★★★★ **Schwarzenegger versus Stallone: The Anxiety of Imitation**

Despite Stallone and Schwarzenegger's parallel rise in popularity in action films, several crucial elements distinguish Schwarzenegger's successful star formula from that of Stallone. If Stallone's films focus on his position as underdog and suffering victim, Schwarzenegger's roles typically emphasize his invulnerability, showing him killing without emotion or coolly taunting his enemies before calmly destroying them. During the early and middle 1980s, Stallone is the old-fashioned masochist, bound to traditions of the old world, while Schwarzenegger begins in a fantastic past and soon becomes the sadistic fighting machine of the future. Both stars would completely shift gears by the end of the decade, in remarkably similar ways. After the success of *Rocky IV* in 1985, with the U.S. champ defeating the Russian Ivan Drago, Schwarzenegger in *Red Heat* plays a Soviet cop named Ivan Danko, who is (rather improbably) working in the United States trying to capture a Russian bad guy. Both Schwarzenegger and Stallone then close the decade in 1989 with a comedy in which they play supposedly intellectual types, a total reversal of their personas at the beginning of the 1980s. Stallone's attempts at humor have generally failed, in contrast to Schwarzenegger's comedies, at least according to critics and audiences. The latter's success may be attributed in part to his ability to read what audiences really want. Many viewers had passed through their fascination with the romantic and classical phases of hard-bodied heroes, and by the end of the 1980s they had moved on to a taste for revisionist fantasy and self-reflexive parody.

Schwarzenegger maintained an ironic stance in the various roles he played throughout the 1980s, and was on his way to becoming the archetypal modern, technological man, a representative of what Fred Glass calls the "New Bad Future" (NBF), a dystopic world often governed by machines (2–13). Roger Ebert noted in a review of *Red Heat* that "Schwarzenegger's whole career is based on his ability to see the humor in apparently hard-boiled situations" (*Chicago Sun-Times*, 17 June 1988). Stallone, on the other hand, cut a figure more comfortable with the romantic and sentimental views of the individual's relationship to government. Both actors portray characters justifiably suspicious of authority, but Stallone's hero is more likely to be seriously outraged or hurt. Schwarzenegger's protagonist, on the other hand, simply gets even and tosses off a quip to his unfortunate victims before destroying them, usually with apparent ease.

Throughout the 1980s, both Schwarzenegger and Stallone rose in tandem with each other and with the ascending influence of women, minorities, and technology. They played roles that increasingly emphasized androgynous elements beneath a hyper-masculine veneer, and they capitalized on their screen personas, their private lives, and their political identities as stand-ins for the conflicted psyche of a nation. Stallone took on "clone partners" and an almost masochistic persona often associated with stereotypically feminine sacrifice, while the manipulative and sometimes mercurial Schwarzenegger often teamed with powerful "macha" female figures. Both actors displayed their bodies in seductive ways previously reserved for women's roles, offering themselves as objects of the desirous gaze of characters in the film and spectators in the viewing audience. Their willingness to exploit the full spectrum of human sexuality, as well as their adaptability, international appeal, and business savvy were all integral to their unprecedented success as iconic musclemen, social forces, and blockbuster stars of the 1980s.

# 3 ★★★★★★★★★★★

# Jessica Lange and Sissy Spacek
## Country Girls

WILLIAM BROWN

Scholarship on 1980s cinema regularly considers Jessica Lange and Sissy Spacek in the same breath (Prince, *Pot of Gold* 177; Palmer 273). Molly Haskell consistently puts the two side by side, characterizing them (with Sally Field) as "country women who wear spunk the way Sylvester Stallone sports muscles . . . [and as female] candidates for canonization, superior to everyone else on the screen and remote from the rest of us" (*From Reverence* 372–73). Haskell notes that if Jane Fonda, Barbra

---

*Coal Miner's Daughter.* Copyright Universal Pictures, 1980.
*Frances.* Copyright Brooksfilms/EMI Films, 1982.

Streisand, and Goldie Hawn were the decade's most bankable female stars, "at a slightly lower rung of bankability, Jessica Lange and Sissy Spacek have been able to initiate and develop smaller projects" (376), before noting that they provided an alternative to the "kiddie movies and special effects super-spectacles" typical of the 1980s, superspectacles that may even have enabled their stardom by making enough profit to help fund smaller projects (398).

Reasons for the pairing of these two actresses are several. First, both had significant roles as popular female country singers in two of the decade's most noted music biopics, Spacek as Loretta Lynn in *Coal Miner's Daughter* (1980) and Lange as Patsy Cline in *Sweet Dreams* (1985). Second, both figured prominently in a cycle of films sometimes referred to as the "Dust Bowl Trilogy" (Emerson and Pfaff 136), three films released in 1984 that dealt with the plight of small farm owners: two set in contemporary times, *Country* (Lange) and *The River* (Spacek), and a third set during the Depression, *Places in the Heart* (which starred Sally Field). A fourth film, *The Dollmaker*, starring Jane Fonda, which was made for television that same year, is sometimes included in this cycle (Palmer 252–53), not least because Fonda spoke before Congress in 1985, along with Lange and Spacek, in order to raise awareness of the 1980s "farm crisis," which saw the Federal Housing Administration (FHA) foreclose on numerous small farms around the country, an event that in turn spurred the formation of Farm Aid, musical concerts staged as bene-fits for family farms (Bonnen 193–94; Dyer, "Rural" 54–57; Palmer 246–54; Prince, *Pot of Gold* 314; Whillock 27–31). Lange and Spacek's joint appear-ance before Congress was followed by their first joint appearance in a film, *Crimes of the Heart* (1986), in which they play two of three sisters reunited in their hometown after one of them, Babe (Spacek), is arrested for shooting her husband (the third sister is played by Diane Keaton).

In addition to their roles as country singers, farmwomen, and screen sis-ters, Spacek and Lange also have further similarities. Besides earning high wages, both have a stated antipathy toward Hollywood in that neither has lived there except temporarily and for professional reasons, each preferring to forgo glitz and glamour for a quiet life in the country.[1] Both Lange and Spacek also have romantic relationships with men in the movie industry: the former has for a long time lived with playwright, actor, and director Sam Shepard, while the latter has long been married to art-director-turned-director Jack Fisk. An understanding of them and their roles is enhanced by the non-cinematic texts such as interviews and profiles that accompany their films. Even if they both maintain a distance between themselves and Hollywood, that they are in relatively high-profile relationships has made them the stuff of celebrity fanfare.

However, their (clichéd?) decision not to be a part of the Hollywood glitterati also means that both are associated with a form of stardom based more upon their commitment to developing acting abilities than upon a desire for celebrity. According to Christine Geraghty, this would make of Lange and Spacek "professionals" as opposed to "celebrities" (187). Barry King, meanwhile, might describe this form of stardom as "impersonation," in that Spacek and Lange can be said to "inhabit" their roles, rather than simply to play thinly veiled versions of themselves, this latter being a form of stardom that King terms "personification" (King 167–82). As we shall see, however, in the work of both actresses there are consistent trends that bear similarities to their offscreen personae, such that both tread an ambiguous path between impersonation and personification as King defines these terms.

Their status as stars famous for impersonation is mirrored in the perceived quality of their work, with both actresses continually present on the list of Oscar nominees during the 1980s, Spacek for Best Actress in 1981 (winning for *Coal Miner's Daughter*), 1983 (*Missing*), 1985 (*The River*), and 1987 (*Crimes of the Heart*)—as well as in 2002 for *In the Bedroom* (2001); Lange in 1983 for Best Actress (*Frances*) and for Best Supporting Actress (*Tootsie*), winning the latter award, as well as for Best Actress in 1985 (*Country*), 1986 (*Sweet Dreams*), 1990 (*Music Box*, 1989), and 1995 (*Blue Sky*, for which she won her second Oscar). In addition to their repeated presence at the Academy Awards, both actresses are in part recognized for their business acumen, since both moved into producing films in the mid-1980s, putting together *Country* and *Raggedy Man* (1981) through their production companies Prairie Films ("Jessica Lange," *American Film*, June 1987, 7) and Blackbird Productions (Libby Slate, "An Interview with Sissy Spacek," *American Premiere*, Winter 1986, 11).[2] This again serves to heighten the perception of Spacek and Lange as professionals committed to producing quality work that they believe in rather than to simply being famous. Finally, their decision repeatedly to play strong women in 1980s cinema is yet another reason, as Haskell points out, that Lange and Spacek are often considered together in histories of 1980s Hollywood cinema.

There are also differences between the actresses, not least in terms of how they are presented onscreen. This chapter is a study of their respective performances, particularly in light of the continued feminist discourse that surrounds actresses in general. While both often (and very capably) play strong women, the moments when each has had greatest success also rely in part upon the conservative, as opposed to progressive, nature of their roles—and so this chapter also offers their performances and personae up to ideological critique.

## ★★★★★ Women in the Masculine 1980s

Typical of many 1980s stars, Lange and Spacek were in part enabled in their success by the rise of the powerful agent, since both were at Creative Artists Agency under "star" agent Michael Ovitz (Prince, *Pot of Gold* 168). However, Lange and Spacek were atypical in that they are commonly associated with "progressive" films—with the strong female characters they feature—and not the "impoverished" cinema that was 1980s "Reaganite entertainment" (Britton "Blissing"; Wood *Hollywood . . . and Beyond*; Wood "80s"), that action-packed and masculine domain defined by what Susan Jeffords calls "hard bodies," and characterized by fantasy, science fiction, and comedy films (Jeffords *Hard Bodies*; Prince, *Pot of Gold* 3).

Of the two actresses, Lange more often worked in these mainstream genres. She had her first break as Dwan, the Fay Wray character in Dino De Laurentiis's remake of *King Kong* (1976), before making Bob Fosse's film version of his stage musical *All That Jazz* (1979) and the critical and commercial housewives-turned-crooks flop, *How to Beat the High Co$t of Living* (1980). She caused something of a stir for her raunchy portrayal of fiendish housewife Cora in *The Postman Always Rings Twice* (1981), but her commercial breakthrough was as ingénue actress Julie in *Tootsie*, a package film put together by Ovitz (Prince, *Pot of Gold* 168), and for which Lange won an Oscar. Yet the film arguably offers us an atypical Lange role, in that Julie is not so much a progressive female as another "dumb blonde" actress who is deprived of agency: it is implied that Julie maintains a television gig because of her relationship with the producer. A single mother, she might be perceived as strong, but there is also a sense that her independence masks her desire to have a stable family back home on her father's farm.

This we can compare to Lange's turn as troubled actress Frances Farmer in *Frances*, which came out the same year, and without which Lange has said she would not have won the award for *Tootsie* (*American Film*, August 1990, 14–19). While Julie can only free herself from the tyranny of male executives through the help of a man, Frances is a strong character who strives for her independence both professionally and in her personal life, refusing to accept the various terms and conditions that her studio contract holder, Paramount, lays down. Frances is committed to an insane asylum through a misunderstanding by her mother (Kim Stanley), and although the film does not present a happy ending per se—or perhaps even *because* the film does not present a happy ending—it becomes an embittered attack on the male-authored objectification of women that was studio-era Hollywood, and which continued in the 1980s through films like *Tootsie*.

With roles in *King Kong* (fantasy) and *How to Beat the High Co$t of Living* and *Tootsie* (comedies), Lange appeared more often than Spacek in commercial genre films of the era. However, as mentioned, these films were atypical for these actresses. Even when Lange starred in what we might term a "hard bodied" film, she did so in a unique manner. As Babs Rogers Grey in *Everybody's All-American* (1988), Lange plays a beauty queen, a housewife, a mother, and a successful businesswoman in the shadow of husband and American football star Gavin "The Grey Ghost" Grey (Dennis Quaid). In spite of its emphasis on sports and homosocial bonding (plenty of scenes featuring footballers being "men" together), *Everybody's All-American* is not quite a celebration of Reaganite masculinity. Although Lange has been outspoken in her dissatisfaction with the film (*American Film*, August 1990, 15; Linda Bird Francke, "American Independent," *Interview*, December 1989, 57), *Everybody's All-American* is rather a critique of Gavin's short-sighted and would-be glorious lifestyle in favor of the more mundane approach adopted by Babs. The film is not without its problems in terms of the representation of women (Babs is, after all, a beauty queen), but her progression from a submissive beauty who "just wants to be Mrs. Gavin Grey" to mother and then to assertive businesswoman, all while Gavin is floundering with his diminishing virility, suggests that the film is at least intended as a critique rather than a celebration of the "American dream."

Instead of taking part in the 1980s macho aesthetic, Lange and Spacek are identified predominantly with politically engaged films that often attempt to deal with the plight of individual women in various circumstances and situations. Neither is particularly associated with the masculinized women that we find in the late 1970s and 1980s films of actresses like Sigourney Weaver (*Alien* [1979]; *Aliens* [1986]; *Working Girl* [1988])—even if, as noted above, Haskell compares these women to that epitome of 1980s hard bodies, Sylvester Stallone. Rather, we see in Lange and Spacek that which Haskell also identifies as the "fragmented, schizophrenic, but oddly hopeful presence" of women in 1980s Hollywood (372). They do not play sensational power bitches who have forsaken individuality for self-assertion, nor, *Tootsie* aside, do they play second-fiddle sounding boards for their films' male heroes. Instead they represent—even if at times problematically—strong women who can work and have a family and (sometimes) have a successful relationship.

Given Haskell's concept of "superwomen," it is not surprising to find her including Marie Ragghianti in this category (372). Marie became famous for fighting corruption in the state government of Tennessee and was instrumental in contributing to the downfall and imprisonment of various officials, including the governor. We might wonder why she should be called a "superwoman" for working and having a family, and director Roger Donaldson (*Marie*, 1985) normalizes Marie in his adoption of what Sarah Harwood identifies as the predominant "realist" style of 1980s Hollywood cinema, offering no exceptional or overly rhetorical camerawork or editing to suggest Marie's extraordinariness (Harwood 32). The rather depressing implication of Haskell's conclusion is that what Marie manages to achieve is beyond the abilities of "ordinary" people, regardless of their sex.

Hollywood cinema certainly does not typically follow Cesare Zavattini's wish for cinema to be about "ordinary" folk to whom "nothing" happens (see Bazin 67). Indeed, it is bent upon depicting extraordinary individuals who, by merely being featured on the big screen—as characters or as actors—are perhaps deprived of their ordinariness in favor of some extraordinary individuality. But can we not take it in good faith that a film like *Marie* at least tries to depict its protagonist as an ordinary individual in exceptional circumstances, rather than as an extraordinary woman predestined for greatness—the idea of predestined greatness being, after all, the phallocentric myth peddled in boys' films from *Star Wars* to *The Matrix* to *Harry Potter*?

Looking at Marie Ragghianti as an incarnation of Spacek's stardom, rather than from the feminist point of view adopted by Haskell (women as "types" in films), can we not work through the contradiction between ordinariness and extraordinariness, between types and individuals, by saying, after Richard Dyer (*Stars* 49–50), that the star does indeed marry the ordinary to the extraordinary, the type to the individual (stars come across as being normal and familiar, even if they are [marketed as] exceptional individuals), rather than keeping them eternally at odds with each other? Haskell seems at times to want to have her cake and eat it: though neither a masculinized/threatening woman nor a passive object of the gaze, Marie is cast as "extraordinary" and thus as not a "real" but a "super" woman. Had the film featured her failure, however, whether as mother or as professional trying to uphold her integrity in the face of state corruption, one suspects that her inability to be both mother and worker would similarly have led to a critique of the would-be implicit and conservative message that women should not try to take on both motherhood and a job (even though the high cost of living practically demands it in Western societies, regardless of whether or not parenthood should be or is a full-time occupation).

## ★★★★★ Biopics

The strong but ordinary women often played by Lange and Spacek conform to certain genres that were popular in the 1980s, even if these genres are not the ones (action, fantasy, science fiction, comedy) that are typically believed to define the decade. *Coal Miner's Daughter*, *Frances*, *Sweet Dreams*, and *Marie* are all biopics, while *Missing* and *Music Box* are fictionalized versions of true stories, and *Crimes of the Heart* is arguably a woman's melodrama in the mold of other 1980s films such as *Terms of Endearment* (1983), *Beaches* (1988) and *Steel Magnolias* (1989). That in these seven films both Spacek's and Lange's characters come to assert a strong femininity (individuals who remain feminine, as opposed to being ersatz males) shows that these actresses functioned against the grain of the major trends of 1980s cinema, which saw women gradually disappearing from the screen (Prince, *Pot of Gold* 174; Krämer 201). Their continued success—and in roles that were atypical of the period—is indeed a testament to Lange's and Spacek's star power and charisma. Lange and Spacek both come to stand for a continued female (even feminist) presence in 1980s Hollywood, a period Robin Wood describes as "antifeminist" in character (*Hollywood . . . and Beyond* 183).

Jesse Schlotterbeck has identified the ways in which songs have played a narrative role in recent Hollywood musical biopics such as *Beyond the Sea* (2004) and *Ray* (2004); that is, the themes of the songs reflect, comment upon, or even advance the narrative content of the film, bringing the musical biopic closer to the musical in terms of genre. Schlotterbeck compares these recent films to *Coal Miner's Daughter* and *Sweet Dreams*, in which the music is portrayed not as emotional expression but as work: music is positioned "more as an artistic form and career choice than a forum for personal expression. The performer's knack for a particular musical style leads to a career choice that forces him to adjust to a demanding lifestyle" (84). That the films are about music as labor is reflected in the title of *Coal Miner's Daughter*: Loretta Lynn (née Webb) is the daughter of a man who was similarly defined by his work. While this is not true of the title of *Sweet Dreams*, the film does also sacrifice "the spontaneity of the classical musical . . . in favour of a more faithful depiction of touring and songwriting as labor" (85).

That both films associate Spacek and Lange with labor—as happens in many of their other films—heightens the sense in which they are considered professionals rather than celebrities, as well as offering us female characters capable of material success. That both films are about performers, however, does offer us conceptual problems. Although we see the work that goes into stardom, rather than seeing stardom mythologized as simply a mode of being, these women are also performers on stages, and thus are arguably objectified in the way that Laura Mulvey has so memorably described ("Visual Pleasure"). This is truer of *Sweet Dreams* than *Coal Miner's*

Jessica Lange mimes Patsy Cline in *Sweet Dreams*. Copyright HBO/Silver Screen Partners, 1985.

*Daughter*. In that film, we are never really sutured into the point of view of any obsessive or leering fans: when Lynn performs at the Grand Ole Opry for the first time, we are given her nervous backstage point of view rather than that of fans waiting for her to come onstage, and the only time we explicitly see the reactions of fans is when we see their confused response to Lynn's final onstage breakdown. *Sweet Dreams*, however, immediately sutures us into a male point of view as Charlie Dick (Ed Harris) enters into a bar at the film's beginning and is struck by a woman performing onstage, she of course being Patsy Cline. Cline is much more the conservative female to-be-looked-at than is Lynn in *Coal Miner's Daughter*, not least because Cline is already onstage when the film begins. Cline's fame is assumed, while Lynn must work for hers.

One could argue that the films actively critique the spectacular nature of performed femininity, positing instead an authentic femininity. David Brackett, for example, observes a progression in Lynn's appearance and musical style from simple and homely to slick and "artificial," especially through her use of makeup (270). Brackett continues:

> Loretta ultimately does suffer a decline, symbiotically linked to her embrace of artifice and country pop, which is overtly connected in the film to her health problems and "road weariness": she suffers from headaches and physical ailments that culminate in her having a breakdown on stage. The opposition between "hard country" and "country pop" thus reinforces other antinomies that drive the film's narrative: innocence/ambition, authenticity/ artificiality, natural healthiness/poor health, supportive relationships/ strained relationships. (270)

Similarly, in *Sweet Dreams*, "Patsy grows more distant from Charley [*sic*] . . . as she moves toward a slicker show, cosmopolitan appearance, and more pop-oriented material" (272). However, while Brackett might read the films as a critique of performed femininity (favoring instead "authentic" females), that the films seemingly have Lynn and Cline "punished" for their increasing "artificiality" is also problematic since it proposes that there is a "natural" feminine authenticity that is somehow not a construct.

Furthermore, for all of the female performers' success, there is a suggestion that masculine authority underwrites the films. *Coal Miner's Daughter* may emphasize the work that goes into Lynn's evolution as a singer-songwriter and the difficulties that such a life entails, but she is still arguably the product of male endeavor: the daughter of a coal miner, she is famous as Loretta Lynn, not Loretta Webb, and there is a sense—at least early in the film—that it is her husband, Doo (Tommy Lee Jones), who enables her career by giving Loretta her name, buying her a guitar, and taking her to recording studios. Doo may come to recognize that he can no longer help Loretta, who has become part of a music industry that is beyond his ken, but there still seems to be a masculine agenda at work in the film. Furthermore, that in both films Doo and Charlie turn to drink in the face of their wives' success suggests the implicitly conservative nature of the projects: the collapse of the family unit is both de facto negative and seemingly the inevitable outcome of women working—as performers no less—instead of staying at home and standing by their men.

In the same way that Cline is already onstage at the start of *Sweet Dreams*, suggesting that she is more objectified than Lynn (and that *Sweet Dreams* is a more conservative film), this is also reflected in the film's attitude toward work. If both films emphasize hard work, real life, and authenticity, in *Coal Miner's Daughter* this is rendered more convincingly because Spacek really did sing Lynn's songs (as well as release albums of her own; see Emerson and Pfaff 117), while Lange was miming along to Cline's music (see Brost). Spacek really does work; Lange pretends to work. If both are professionals more than celebrities, Lange is more of a celebrity than Spacek.[3]

That said, although both *Coal Miner's Daughter* and *Sweet Dreams* see Lange and Spacek emerge, to greater and lesser degrees, as hard-working actors, the music biopic does arguably and paradoxically heighten a performer's star status. Cynthia Rose writes of the difficulty that a film star must inevitably face in trying to play a music star, since to do so convincingly, the film star must sacrifice her own personality for that of the role (14–16). However, Rose also says that actors can reorder the biopic to their own concerns, meaning that the actors assert their own stardom over that of the music star they are portraying. The less a film star is identified with the role of the music star that she portrays, the more that film star's stardom is reaffirmed. By *not* singing Patsy Cline's songs, one might argue that Jessica Lange becomes more prominent as a star, if less regarded as an actress.[4]

## ★★★★★ Glamour

Both Lange and Spacek are associated with "real life" in *Sweet Dreams* and *Coal Miner's Daughter* because country music is perceived to be "of the people" (Brost). Furthermore, Lange and Spacek are more generally associated with real life because they often play real people: Lange in *Frances*, *Sweet Dreams*, and to a certain extent *Music Box*; Spacek in *Coal Miner's Daughter*, *Marie*, and to a certain extent *Missing*. These real people are also defined by their work, even when they are famous (*Sweet Dreams*, *Coal Miner's Daughter*, *Frances*), suggesting realistic films starring professionals, not stars. However, Lange is more often associated with glamorous females—and thus with stardom—than is Spacek: Patsy Cline, Frances Farmer, and Julie in *Tootsie* are all performers (as is Meg in *Crimes of the Heart*), even if their relationship with glamour is ambivalent, while Lynn must work harder than Cline for her fame and Marie Ragghianti is thrust into the media spotlight out of circumstance and not out of choice.

Both Ann Talbot (Lange), the lawyer who in *Music Box* defends her father (Armin Mueller-Stahl) against accusations of being a Nazi war criminal, and Beth Horman (Spacek), the wife of journalist Charles Horman (John Shea) who in *Missing* has been "disappeared" by the post-Allende military regime in Pinochet's Chile, are "real" people who must work in order to achieve their goals. However, even here Ann, like Patsy Cline, is already successful (as a lawyer) when *Music Box* begins, while Beth, like Marie Ragghianti and Loretta Lynn, must become good at what she does (trying to find her husband). Spacek must work (or work harder) to achieve her goals, something reaffirmed in *Coal Miner's Daughter*, where Lynn's bemused first meeting with Cline (here played by Beverly D'Angelo) also posits Cline as already—and thus somehow "naturally"—famous.

There is an irony that emerges when we consider Lange's miming of Patsy Cline's songs in *Sweet Dreams*, for Lange did a lot of work on her speaking voice to make it sound like Cline's (*Interview*, April 2006, 72). And, as Kent Jones says, Lange has a "physical use of voice, which makes any given line reading a musical event" (36). If Lange plays vocal characters who have a vocal range, Spacek, who, as noted, did sing in *Coal Miner's Daughter*, often plays taciturn or softly spoken characters who do not. When her characters are vocal and do speak, as in *Coal Miner's Daughter, Missing,* and *Marie,* we see them finding their voices, so to speak. There is a sense of progression in these films, in that Spacek's characters must find their voice, while Lange's are already vocal.

Lesley Chow explains how a voice, particularly a low voice of the kind that we associate with Jessica Lange, can be both attractive and seductive, while Spacek's is perhaps girlish. Spacek for a long time played young girls (Sally Hibbin, "Star Profile: Sissy Spacek," *Films and Filming,* April 1985, 4). Lange played desirable women, even if their attitude toward their desirability is ambivalent, as in *Frances, Sweet Dreams,* and *Everybody's All-American.* She is associated more often than Spacek with glamour, an effect reinforced in Lange's role as Carly Marshall in *Blue Sky,* where, from the opening credits depicting magazine images of glamorous stars such as Marilyn Monroe, Carly is associated with what Marjorie Rosen has called "Mammary Madness," an idealized form of femininity constructed for the pleasure of men. We first see Carly/Lange in that most hackneyed of advertising images: sunbathing semi-naked on a beach and "appreciated" from above by husband Hank (Tommy Lee Jones) and a helicopter pilot. Hank is out trying to measure radiation levels; it is Carly who radiates the most.

Lange's "glamorous" characters, particularly Frances Farmer, Carly Marshall, and Babs Rogers Grey, are defined in a way by their simultaneous resistance toward and embrace of their glamorous or would-be glamorous styles. This ambivalence means that they are understood as "crazy." Since these women cannot cope with trying to be autonomous individuals in a world where they are also the objects of male desire, this "othering" of female characters as crazy is problematic even if critical of the patriarchal system of desire, into which Lange's turn as "Crazy Cora" in *The Postman Always Rings Twice* also fits. They show us women who are what Sue Harper has called "mad, bad, and dangerous to know," hence the description "Lunatic Lange" (Julia Cameron, "Jessica Lange," *American Film,* January 1983, 35).[5]

Lange's glamorous nature is reflected in the makeup and framing that often accompany her characters. Although not always blond or dressed in ball gowns à la *Frances* and *Everybody's All-American,* Lange is often filmed through screens, windows, or behind a thin chimney of tobacco smoke (consider the first time we see her smoking through a bus window in *Crimes of the Heart*), and she more often than not wears sunglasses. To an extent, these devices hide Lange from us. But in the same way that the glamorizing effects of makeup could also be said to hide real faces, so, too, do these devices heighten Lange's glamour. They both mediate her (seen through a window, it is as if Lange's characters are icons on a screen within the various films' diegeses) and render her exotic. Her sunglasses suggest distance, mystique, and heat, while the more mundane spectacles that Lange wears offscreen but never onscreen suggest the ability to look back rather than to be looked at (Gene Siskel, "Lange Suffering," *Time Out*, 1 August 1990, 17).

This perception of Lange as a glamorous object of desire is nowhere more explicit than in the words of her biographer, J. T. Jeffries:

> Jessica Lange *is* a movie star, in the good old-fashioned sense of the word. . . . Without necessarily wanting to be, Jessica Lange has become consecrated as the blonde American goddess of her generation. . . . Here, at last, is an actress worth lusting after. . . . Sally Field, Sissy Spacek, Jane Fonda—let them doff the faded cotton dresses, lose the makeup, carry the politically correct roles. Alone among these women, Jessica Lange lives as pure image. She bears the mantle of an icon unique to American cinema: the blonde movie star. . . . Lange has a real woman's body, not some skinny, aerobic tautness, but good-sized thighs, a torso you could get lost in, and the best eyebrows in the business.    (2–5)

As much as Jeffries presents Lange as masturbatory fantasy, he recognizes that she does not necessarily want to be the blond goddess but assumes the role almost unwillingly. This furthers the contradictions inherent in Lange and perhaps absent in Spacek. Lange's glamour is matched by her acting ability.

## ☆☆★★★ Performance

James Naremore and Andrew Klevan have suggested that more studies need to be done on performance in cinema in order that scholars might more fully appreciate what work goes into creating memorable characters. The status of Lange and Spacek as "professional" actors who "impersonate" characters is very much linked to their performance style, which in turn reflects the "professional" nature of the characters they play.

I have argued that Lange is perhaps more a star than Spacek for *not* singing Patsy Cline's songs, her old-fashioned stardom also reaffirmed by her seeming glamour. However, in addition to her ability to transform her voice, Lange's ability to perform has also been of note to scholars. Kent Jones says that "Lange works from a basic vocabulary of moves that is retooled and modulated for every character: hand movements for emphasis that are sometimes sweeping, sometimes delicate, never less than exquisite; a penchant for quick change-ups in speed, lunges forward, and wounded withdrawals . . . a fully dimensional sense of her own body and a very unusual if not singular feeling for line and volume" (36).

Lange has also been associated with fearlessness when acting (Jones; Vineberg, "Acting" 26). She herself feels that actresses nowadays do not take enough risks (*Premiere*, November 2003, 68), suggesting both her ability to identify with her roles and her ability convincingly to create characters. In particular, responses to *Frances* could not but blur the distinctions between Lange and Farmer (Tony Crawley, "Why Jessica Lange Is Playing Frances Farmer," *Films Illustrated*, January 1982, 128–32; Crawley, "Jessica Lange as Frances Farmer in the Film that Hollywood Feared," *Photoplay*, April 1983, 10–12; Frank and Krohn; Hibbin, "Star Profile: Lange," *Films and Filming*, February 1985, 4–5). This suggests that she indeed "impersonates" her characters (after Barry King), something Gene Siskel affirms when he says that Lange, whom he considers more an actor than a star, "uses a range of acting methods, orthodox and unorthodox, in order to realise her characters" ("Lange Suffering," *Time Out*, 1 August 1990, 17). For *Music Box*, for example, Lange studied lawyers, wrote a Hungarian past for her character, and made the house where certain scenes were filmed her home (16–18).

Although her acting has been less discussed in critical circles, Spacek is similarly associated with impersonation, not least because she does not remember performing key scenes in her films, so into her characters does she become ("Is Sissy About to Make Another Clean Sweep with *Raggedy Man*?" *Photoplay*, March 1982, 13). She is also associated with method acting, having studied under Lee Strasberg at the Actors' Studio in New York (Hibbin, "Star Profile: Spacek," *Films and Filming*, 4). Both Lange and Spacek are therefore associated with creating convincing characters, even if, as Karen Hollinger has argued (after Richard Maltby), the Method is inherently patriarchal and misogynist because it associates "good acting with the expression of masculine emotion . . . and actresses in female-oriented genres like the 'woman's film' became increasingly connected with the emotionally excessive acting of the tearjerker" (15). I am not saying that either actress systematically or regularly uses the Method, for even Spacek felt limitations with it by the time she made *3 Women* (Emerson and Pfaff 59). But both are associated with an acting style of impersonation that lessens their star status in favor of recognition as actors, even if Lange's characters are more glamorous and thus more star-like than Spacek's. We may recall that Hollinger, citing Alan Lovell, says that the work of stars is as worthy of the same consideration and esteem as the work of actors (54).

Of course, Spacek's characters have an ambivalent relationship with glamour. Spacek, who in real life was a homecoming queen, cheerleader, and majorette (Emerson and Pfaff 14), played the title role in *Carrie* in 1976, the girl who is vindictively made a prom queen as part of an elaborate hoax, the implication being that Spacek/Carrie is actually not glamorous. If Lange's characters rebel against the objectification of women from within (they are the objects of the male gaze but do not necessarily like it), Spacek's seem to rebel against it from without (they are not the object of the male gaze, or if they are, they are so in a problematic way). Nita in *Raggedy Man*, Marie, Jessie Cates in *'night Mother* (1986), Gussie Sawyer in *Violets Are Blue . . .* (1986), and Babe Magrath in *Crimes of the Heart* are all single, divorced, or getting divorced. Even though Babe is significantly more "glamorous" than many other characters that Spacek has played, she is not necessarily as glamorous as her sister Meg, who is a (failed) singer/performer, and who is of course played by Jessica Lange.

If often single, and if not as glamorous as Lange's characters (Spacek is associated with an absence of makeup and is not so noticeably shot in an iconographic way), Spacek's characters still seem to have as strong an effect as Lange's on the other characters with whom they interact. For both actors, their characters become involved with a veritable litany of alcoholics, if they are not heavy drinkers themselves. Booze plays a central role in *How to Beat the High Co$t of Living, Coal Miner's Daughter, Frances, Missing, Country, The River, Crimes of the Heart, Far North* (1988), and *Everybody's All-American*. To hypothesize this apparent alcohol dependency, it seems as if the hard-drinking or drunk characters of these films use the escapist effects of alcohol to distance themselves from the reality that surrounds them. This suggests indirectly that the films aim to be realistic: a surfeit of reality causes the escapism of drinking. It perhaps also reaffirms an association between Spacek and Lange and reality: their performances are very realistic, so real that they and those around them need a drink just to put some distance between them and the unbearable facts of life. Even if not glamorous, Spacek, as much as the "glamorous" Lange, drives her men away, to drink, or to kill—or, also like Lange, she herself leaves her men, goes "mad" (Babe shoots her husband in *Crimes of the Heart*), and/or drinks a lot, too. Not that these are "good" traits (they suggest that women and men are mutually intolerable), but they do testify to the effect that Lange and Spacek have on those around them and vice versa, which in turn suggests a certain "realism" as far as the performances of their characters are concerned. This is also reflected in the fact that few of their films are lighthearted: *Crimes of the Heart* has comic elements but is not a comedy, while *'night Mother* veers from a fairly comic opening to downright tragedy. For this reason, the films do not conform to the escapist fantasies typical of 1980s Reaganite cinema, which itself, like alcohol, sought to put distance between audiences and the reality that they inhabited.

## ★★★★★ Country Girls

If Spacek and Lange play women who are not very easy to live with, and/or who have difficulty living with themselves (drunks, killers, etc.), their films do not easily fit into genres either, even if they both had notable success in biopics. Prince says that the "salient social and cultural issues of the 1980s surfaced in films *outside* the familiar frameworks afforded by genre. Cycles of film coalesced about diverse issues, including the Midwest farm crisis that triggered a rash of small-farm foreclosures" (*Pot of Gold* 314; my emphasis). If Spacek's and Lange's films are associated with reality/realism, then it makes sense that their work falls outside conventional genres—and I end this chapter by looking in greater detail at their non-generic films associated with rural America: *Country, The River*, and, to a lesser extent, *Far North*.

Robert Fish says that "American cinema has a long tradition of coding the rural affirmatively in relation to the values, moralities and landscapes of the city" (4). Meanwhile, Catherine Fowler and Gillian Helfield argue that "underlying all rural cinema is a contemporary consciousness that complicates yet also specializes its apparent attachment to the past, while at the same time drawing it nearer to the concerns of urban cinema" (11). At a time of rampant capitalism during the Reagan era (Prince, *Pot of Gold* 314–15), with its emphasis on development through urbanization, it seems logical that there would be films that stand in opposition to the urban "hyperreality" of American cities (see Eco), and which put forward a nostalgic view of the

Jessica Lange as Jewel Ivy in *Country*. Copyright Touchstone Pictures, 1984.

American countryside as somehow authentic and/or truly American (the countryside as tied to the nation—see Fowler and Helfield 11). In their analysis of Iowa as depicted in American cinema during World War II, Marty Knepper and John Lawrence see the "agrarian ethos as fundamental to democracy" (336), something that we also see implicitly affirmed in *Country, The River,* and *Far North.* Each deals with the struggles of farmers, and perhaps even with the death of traditional farming (and thus America's traditional democratic values), even if the films, particularly *Country* and *The River,* put forward hopeful messages in the end (people unite to stop the land from falling into the hands of major industries).

As noted earlier, Spacek and Lange are associated with the country in both their films and their private lives, which in turn lends to them a perceived authenticity, even if at the expense of their status as "impersonators" (that they are country girls in real life suggests that they are also "personifiers").

This authenticity takes on a political dimension when we consider how both the films and the actresses themselves took part in the campaign against the farm crisis in the build-up to the Farm Security Act in 1985 (Bonnen 193–94). And, being political, this authenticity can only be regarded as authentic if we redefine the word not according to its popular definition as "true" or "genuine" but as being consciously constructed (authenticity from the Greek "auto-hentes," which means "self-creation," as pointed out by Richard Kearney [54]).

To ask whether one can gain access to a "true" or "real" American identity, particularly in an era when national identity is considered an invention that belongs to "imagined communities" (see Anderson), is problematic, not least because it presupposes that such a thing exists (even if beyond reach). While Bonnen has critiqued 1980s U.S. rural policy (and Lange and Spacek's campaigning) as not really reflecting the true rural population (it was aimed more or less exclusively at the farming community and no one else), his argument does indeed seem to presuppose a "true" rural community that has an identity or essence that can be defined. However, by pointing out the ways in which the rural became conflated politically with farming in the 1980s, Bonnen is useful in establishing the constructed (and thus unnatural or inauthentic) nature of rural authenticity as posited by Lange and Spacek in their films and in their political work for farmers.

Jennifer Holt says that 1980s Hollywood involved "a synergy between industry and politics that would prove to be far more powerful than any other in Hollywood history" (28). If Reaganite entertainment is already political, the political films that are *Country* and *The River* (as well as *Far North*) are

Sissy Spacek as Mae Garvey in *The River*. Copyright Universal Pictures, 1984.

also Reaganite, and thus as much reaffirmations of the specific nature of Reagan's America as critiques of it. Of the earlier Iowa films, Knepper and Lawrence conclude that "a pastoral view of heartland America becomes increasingly difficult to accept as real on screen, but it seems to fill a psychic need in Americans" (336). As much can be said of the Lange and Spacek films, which come to act as a release valve for anxiety in an age when capitalism runs riot ("Greed is good" being the touchstone line of Oliver Stone's *Wall Street* [1987]). For all of their supposed realism, these films are as much if not more an artificial construct as the more mainstream films that Britton and Wood berate (and their conservative nature may be reflected in the acting methods employed, in that Lange and Spacek adopt a style that is close enough to the Method to be similarly misogynist in outlook).

That Lange could produce *Country* (and that Sam Shepard directed *Far North*) was enabled through the rise of the agent and the increased star power that this entailed. Lange always worked as a participant in and never really as an opponent to the economic system that contributed to the very rural crisis that she subsequently tried to prevent. It is apt that Prince defines the 1980s talent pool as an "oligopoly": rather than a cinema both free and accessible for all, these films are part of a cinema that was predicated upon the competition, exclusivity, and avarice that in the 1980s did not solve but furthered America's unrecognized class inequalities (160–85).

Appeals to some mythical American past and real way of life are backward-looking and conservative in nature: they demand the undoing of what damage Reaganomics wrought on the social infrastructure of the

United States. Sadly, such a demand is impossible to realize without adopting a substantially more radical (and inclusive) stance. Going backward (and in a way that features social exclusion: farmers, not peasants, are saved, as Bonnen explains) is not a way out of the irreversible trap that is the passing of human time, even if 1980s Hollywood, perhaps in acknowledgment of the damage being done, dreamed of a return to earlier times in time-travel narratives such as *Back to the Future* (1985) and *Peggy Sue Got Married* (1986).

In an interview Lange noted: "All those Midwestern traits—honesty, simplicity, lack of ambition—those virtues I used to see as dull, I now see as admirable" (Andy Webster, *Premiere*, April 1985, 160). Herein we perhaps detect a hint of condescension toward those of whom Lange speaks: rural inhabitants as simple and as lacking in ambition. Perhaps it is for this reason that Fred Schruers does not gawk longingly at Lange as her biographer does, but rather contends that she and her companion Sam Shepard, "for all their insistence on staying close to the heartland sod . . . seem more comfortable with the *concept* of Middle Americans than the reality. . . . Lange cried when she delivered her self-penned plea to Congress on behalf of America's hard-pressed farmers, and did so sincerely; but one wonders if she and Shepard resemble the guy in the old aphorism who loves mankind—'It's the people I can't stand'" ("Lange-Froid," *Premiere*, January 1990, 54).

Is it that in Lange's and Spacek's films, we do not see the progressive, anti-establishment, or perhaps even revolutionary ideology that at first seems apparent? While both actors do play strong women who can hold down careers and raise a family and keep a lover and change the world in a positive way by convincing others to help them, and while they are thus progressive as characters and also as actresses, it is the films themselves, films that they have helped to shape, that are conservative in their need to control and/or contain them. It is not that Lange and Spacek play or actually are superwomen who are impossible or even undesirable on account of their perfection (although this is a legitimate if problematic criticism to make), but that the films in which they appear subvert them and are conservative in nature. To take one example, *Frances* ends up reaffirming the star system by having Farmer end unhappily, leaving one with the impression that Lange, so closely aligned with Farmer, is also dependent on Hollywood and glamour, even if she insists she is resolutely against it. The utopian endings of *Country* and *The River* (although tempered in the latter film: Scott Glenn's evil Joe Wade will be back) also confirm the same. Happy, escapist, short-term solutions to problems function simply to reinforce what they supposedly critique.

Both Lange and Spacek, while thought of and promoting themselves as professional impersonators, are still stars, whose existence as such is dependent upon exclusivity, individuality, and celebrity. To argue that a celebrity's work often goes unrecognized is important (see Lovell). But definitively to separate "professionals" from "celebrities" runs the risk of suggesting that professionals can leave celebrity behind. There is no blame to be given to people who become celebrities. However, if professionalism is, in the cases of Lange and Spacek, used to cover over celebrity, it is incorporated into their celebrity: they are serious country girls famous for playing serious country girls, both onscreen and off. If Frances Farmer had chosen (or been depicted as choosing) not to be an actress and to be happy/happier as a result, then perhaps there might have been a progressive politics in *Frances*, suggesting work toward a common as opposed to an exclusive wealth.

Eighties cinema, including the oppositional cinema that the "Dust Bowl" films seem to constitute (together with, among others, *Frances, Missing, Marie, Everybody's All-American*), cannot but be a product of its time, as must those people who helped to make it. The films considered here and featuring Jessica Lange and Sissy Spacek are also products of their time. As such, they are inherently tied to the politics of the Reagan era, a part of it as much as they claim to stand against it, and perhaps ideologically more for it than even they realize or claim. It is an impossible situation from which there is perhaps no escape: how to find a way out of a destructive and unrestrained capitalism in the grip of which we always and perhaps unwittingly remain. Professionalism, to be recognized, becomes celebrity, the cult of the individual. One cannot speak out against celebrity, or the wider capitalist processes, typified by Hollywood, that enable it. To emphasize individuals in the collective struggle, in the struggle for collectivity, is a sure way to undermine that struggle.

Perhaps *'night Mother* points to a way out: suicide, not just as an act of desperation but, as Spacek's Jessie tries to argue with her mother (Anne Bancroft), as a progressive act of choice: to choose not to be a part (anymore) of this crazy, individualistic, exclusive, and damaging system that is life under capitalism. Jessie (too individualistically) removes herself from the screen, the suicide taking place behind a closed door. In so doing, Jessie/Spacek removes herself from life, this impossible contradiction in which the subject, as individual, is always at odds with (the idea of) the collective.

One more paradox: I have mourned the fact that Frances Farmer did not find happiness by embracing "real" life and rejecting the cinema, but perhaps the non-life that is being on the screen is also the escape from her individual self, the death that Frances misses, but to which she is denied a return. Existing as an individual is what separates us from the possibility of a collective existence, while cinema is, as Laura Mulvey has said, death twenty-four times a second, a freedom from life offered by the fixity and stillness of the image (even if the images—plural—give us the illusion of movement). Perhaps it is precisely in cinema that we can find freedom, but this must be a cinema for everyone, and not just for the happy few. Under Reagan, Lange and Spacek fought through cinema for a more equitable life; but they did not do so enough. They are not ordinary people but stars; and as such, they could never achieve what their films ostensibly promote. Instead, they retained and even increased their power and standing, albeit via slightly alternative means, within the exclusive power system that is Hollywood.

### NOTES

1. On Lange, see Linda Bird Francke, "American Independent," *Interview*, December 1989, 57–60, 128–29; Jeff Dawson, "Mrs. Blue Sky," *Empire*, June 1995, 82–83; George Hadley-Garcia, "No More Monkey Business for Jessica Lange," *Prevue*, April 1984, 61–64; Sally Hibbin, "Star Profile: Jessica Lange," *Films and Filming*, February 1985, 4–5; Andy Webster, "Jessica Lange," *Premiere*, April 1995, 160. On Spacek, see Emerson and Pfaff; Nancy Mills, "Big Sissy," *Stills*, 24 February 1986, 17; and Libby Slate, "An Interview with Sissy Spacek," *American Premiere*, Winter 1986, 8–11.

2. "The company started out as Flying Armadillo Productions, after the Texas state animal, but it seemed too specific. 'Spacek' is actually pronounced 'Spah-check,' which is Czech for 'blackbird,' so that's why it's Blackbird Productions." Slate, *American Premiere*, Winter 1986, 11.

3. It is ironic that the authenticity of Spacek is connected to her ability to work—her authenticity is more constructed or the result of labor than is Lange's, which seems less true but which is arguably more natural because less work is involved.

4. The reverse might also hold true: by singing Loretta Lynn's songs herself, Sissy Spacek shapes Lynn more greatly than does Lange, who mimes and lets the "real" Cline into her performance, thereby suggesting that Spacek is the greater star (or should we say "better actor"?). This perhaps depends on how much we feel that we are watching "Sissy Spacek as Loretta Lynn" or "Loretta Lynn as played by Sissy Spacek," if the reader will permit the distinction. That is, do we believe in the character or simply see an actor performing?

5. It is ironic that Lange won the Oscar for her spectacular turn in *Blue Sky*, since it is perhaps also a negative portrayal of a woman. It does, however, suggest the seeming sexism that underlies Hollywood's awarding body. A similar sexism is also revealed in writing on Lange, for example by J. T. Jeffries, as well as by Siskel ("Lange Suffering," *Time Out*, 1 August 1990, 17), who wonders why Lange does not do more *Tootsie*-style roles instead of "serious" films.

# 4 ★★★★★★★★★★★
# Mel Gibson and
# Tom Cruise
## Rebellion and Conformity

MICHAEL deANGELIS

Top Gun (1986) and the first installment of the popular *Lethal Weapon* series (1987) successfully secured and sustained the marquee value of Tom Cruise and Mel Gibson, emerging superstars whose celebrity has persisted across several decades to the present. Both films are classic representatives of the action film genre that the decade popularized, and both could be described as "buddy" films—yet the actors themselves and the reasons for the success they had enjoyed since the start of the decade are widely divergent. If a star persona develops through a series of films and extra-cinematic star texts progressively across the span of a career, each of these films signals a strategic point in the evolving cross-project personas of Cruise and Gibson (on star texts in fantasy and the melodramatic mode see Desjardins; Gledhill; and DeAngelis). As critics noted, with *Top Gun* Cruise's persona was branching out from an imposed image as a teen actor with ties to the Brat Pack. For Gibson, *Lethal Weapon* was just as crucial a transitional work, marketing the wildness of his "Mad Max" persona for a broader audience market.

One common element in both actors' careers is a connection to the role of the outsider/rebel, emerging at the forefront in American culture in the transition from the 1970s to the more politically conservative 1980s. The outsider image that helped to propel New York–born (1956), Australia-raised Mel Gibson to Hollywood stardom at the start of the decade is tied to a perception of "otherness" that curiously rendered him accessible to a wide range of audiences across national, sexual, and gender boundaries; as the decade progressed, however, the appeal of Gibson's persona would anchor him to the role of family-values advocate trying to retain his association with rebellion even as he began to alienate segments of the viewing audience whom he had initially engaged. In the span of the same decade, Tom Cruise, who was turning eighteen in 1980, initially secured a teen rebel image that was subsumed by the discourse of All-Americanism, thereafter sustaining his rebel status across projects that many perceived as much more conservatively conformist before becoming more reflective in his final films of the decade.

## ★★★★★ Mel Gibson: Marketable Ambiguities in the Early 1980s

Mel Gibson has never played a self-avowed homosexual character; indeed, his pronouncements against gays at the start of the 1990s secured his politics as homophobic. Yet his popularity in America in the early 1980s—along with his association with rebellion—correlates directly with versions of masculinity that were being influenced by gay culture. According to an article in *Macleans*, "Society was changing long before the emergence of the homosexual culture. The contraceptive pill, the increased role of the state in taking care of the infirm or the elderly and the technological advances that made it possible for women to leave the family and go to work, all started heterosexual culture moving in the direction of gay values" (Lawrence O'Toole, "Gay Style," 18 February 1980, 46). The first half of the decade also witnessed the increasing cultural prominence of the "New Man," the health- and class-conscious independent male who had apparently rectified the social conditions that had made it difficult for men to live on their own, including the neutralization of sexual stigmas about remaining unmarried (see Paul

Theroux, "The Male Myth," *New York Times Magazine*, 27 November 1983, 116; Neal Karlen and Nikki Finke Greenberg, "The New Man's Lament," *Newsweek*, 16 July 1984, 82; Barbara Ehrenreich, "A Feminist's View of the New Man," *New York Times Magazine*, 20 May 1984, 36–48).

By the time that Gibson had established himself as a star of the Australian New Wave, "gay style" had pervaded American consumer culture to the extent that the boundaries between "straight" and "gay" were often blurred. The success of disco had already made gay cultural phenomena accessible to and accepted by the mainstream. The ultra-macho hard bodies of the Village People epitomized gay culture's contemporary obsession with hypermasculinity even as the group encouraged its audiences to fantasize about being them and being *like* them. Gibson's initial popularity in America coincided with a cultural moment when the concept of "ambiguity" in the definition of star personas—including a version of masculinity described as strong yet inherently vulnerable—signaled a form of character depth. While neither his publicists nor Gibson himself ever actively promoted a perception of the star as gay, his image benefited from the press's ability to construct him as receptive to identifications and desires across the ever more permeable boundaries of gender and sexuality. In a 1983 *Newsweek* cover story, David Ansen traces the success of new "incredible hunks" such as Gibson to the gay-to-straight crossover phenomenon popularizing underwear ads, beefcake calendars, and fitness planners. "Homosexuality always celebrated beauty," Ansen argues, "and . . . the general acceptance of a gay subculture has encouraged an outspoken appreciation of masculine sexuality in the mainstream culture" ("The Incredible Hunks," 23 May 1983, 48). The fantasy of Gibson constructed by his early films and promotional materials is also one of accessibility. This fantasy tempers traditional macho imagery to produce a more universally acceptable male body that conflates strength and vulnerability. This body is hard and impermeable yet also natural, authentic, human, and within reach as an object of identification and desire.

Gibson's early star discourse softens beefcake hypermacho into a more accessible and human framework. The firm and agile body becomes a site of receptivity and invitation, and Gibson tempers excessive muscularity to avoid perceptions of narcissistic self-obsession. *Newsweek* comments that in *The Road Warrior* (1982), Gibson emanates "a quiet, unnarcissistic intensity" and "easy, unswaggering masculinity" (Charles Michener, "'Shane' in Black Leather," 31 May 1982, 67), and *People*'s 1983 story of this male "heartthrob" notes "the astonishing dichotomy between the image and the man" who never actively seeks the desire that his fans invest in him (Jim Callo, "Up from Down Under," 14 February 1983, 99). If Gibson's naturally rugged body conformed to a working-class male image that had been pro-moted to pre-Stonewall gays as an ideal, this image also established the actor's authenticity and a self-imposed distance from superstar status. Gib-son's roots are unmistakably working class, reiterated in his roles in his first two American-produced box office successes in the early 1980s. In *Gallipoli* (1981), Frank is a poor railroad worker from Perth, and *The Road Warrior*'s Mad Max is an ex-police officer.

Gibson's ability to avoid categorical definition establishes his rebel sta-tus: he is strong but not maniacally aggressive, a sexual object who never solicits his own objectification. Early press material also connects Gibson to rebellion through "locative ambiguities" that consistently dis-place his per-sona. His stateside popularity emerges from a hybridization of nationalities that references the Australian "New Wave" cinema's attempt to transcend specific national allegiances. In an article in *Cinefantastique*, Bob Villard explains that prior to the release of *Mad Max* in 1979, Australian cinema had historically proven to be too insular for "the highly lucrative American market," and producer Byron Kennedy and director George Miller "con-spired to overcome the 'ethnicity' of their homeland" with a film that strove to "obliterate the fact that the story's action was filmed in Australia" ("Road Warriors," May-June 1982, 6). The attempt to construct a "*cross-cultural*, mythical hero, one who could triumph over evil in all markets" was pros-perous in countries as culturally diverse as Japan, Germany, Great Britain, and eventually the United States.

His first two successful American releases, *Gallipoli* and *The Road War-rior*, foreground national identity even as they disguise it to secure an inter-national following. Biographical facts of Gibson's upbringing enhance locative ambiguities: Gibson's grandmother was Australian, but the star was born in Peekskill, New York, and spent his childhood there until age twelve, marking Gibson's emergence onto the American celebrity scene in the early 1980s as also a return to his own homeland ("Hollywood Can Wait," *Newsweek*, 31 May 1982, 67). Gibson is sometimes Australian, sometimes American, and other times neither; his heritage readily transcends national boundaries. The mainstream American press both preserves Gibson's cross-cultural marketing potential while correlating his national outsider status with his popularity in America. *Newsweek* remarks upon his "hint of Down Under humor [that] may be quintessentially Australian but is also the stuff of an international male star" (Michener, "'Shane' in Black Leather," *News-week*, 31 May 1982, 70).

In the early 1980s, such locative ambiguities polarize city and country to suggest that the road to stardom has made Gibson an outsider, a figure who belongs in neither of the two places he has chosen to call "home." While the actor's origins remain in the rural setting of upstate New York, his inherited home of Australia becomes the heartland whose roots he risks losing, even though the home where Gibson resided at the time that he made both *Gallipoli* and *The Road Warrior* was in metropolitan Sydney. *Newsweek* explains that Gibson "is in no hurry to get to Hollywood: 'It's not a question of Australian loyalty. I just want to do interesting work. I'm not going to go to Hollywood just because it's Hollywood.'" Later, the article explains that while Gibson "remains an American citizen . . . his outlook is totally Australian. 'I'm in tune with this place [Australia]. . . . But I can speak with an American accent—with a bit of effort'" ("Hollywood Can Wait," 31 May 1982, 67).

Gibson can appeal to his audiences as a working-class, heterosexual, Australian male who denies his status as a sexual object. Given the historically specific circumstances of the early 1980s, however, these attributes of identity can also be drastically reconfigured: his working-class roots also make him accessible as an embodiment of a masculinity that also addresses gay desire—indeed, a version of elemental masculinity that gay American culture was instrumental in promoting as an ideal to be emulated and desired. And star texts even manage to transform a male sexual objectification—also promoted by gay culture—as an aspect of feminine vulnerability that curiously reinforces his status as a strong, intense, and entirely masculine man. His biographers would later elaborate upon the star's skillful execution of this gender sleight-of-hand. David Ragan notes: "Close-ups of his unusual green [?] eyes show up over and over, and in *Mad Max* the camera repeatedly focuses on his black leather boots and then pans slowly, tantalizingly upward. . . . If that sounds like a treatment usually given only to female stars, it is. But the only thing remotely feminine about Gibson is the vulnerability he projects. . . . Audiences sense that there's a peculiar mix of elements in this particular psyche, and they're right" (31).

In a 1981 review of Peter Weir's *Gallipoli* in the gay-targeted journal *After Dark*, Dan Yakir explains: "To those who complain that the movie lacks a love affair, Gibson responds, 'But there was a love story—in a male sense. It was a very strong mateship. At that time, those fellows really depended on one another" ("Those Gallipoli Boys," November 1981, 46). An executive from the Robert Stigwood Organization (RSO), *Gallipoli*'s producer, states that the company "markets gayness, but the product it markets is a lot less gay than the Stigwood Organization is. We know the secret of broadening gayness so that it sells to straights. And that's really what you're after, isn't it? How gayness is penetrating the straight marketplace in ways

"But there was a love story—in a male sense": Archie Hamilton (Mark Lee) and Frank Dunne (Gibson) in *Gallipoli*. Courtesy Photofest. Copyright Paramount Pictures, 1981.

straights can't identify. . . . We've helped put gays out there as a market like women and blacks, but you can't say that yet" (John Lombardi, "Selling Gays to the Masses," *Village Voice*, 30 June 1975, 10).

The window of access to gay and straight readings of the film is the buddy genre that had been popularized in 1970s Hollywood cinema. The film itself concerns the parallel paths of two runners turned soldiers, the devoted nationalist Archie Hamilton (Mark Lee) and his loyal follower Frank Dunne (Gibson) in the Australian outback during the first years of World War I. In its harrowing climax at Gallipoli, Archie and his fellow soldiers leap over trenches to be slaughtered by the Turks as Frank screams in agony over his inability to prevent his friend's senseless death. Among the attributes that Robin Wood ascribes to the buddy film are the absence of any identifiable "home" where the male protagonists could be said to belong, a "male love story" that subverts the classical Hollywood cinema's narrative trajectory toward a union of the heterosexual couple and the integration of the nuclear family, and the death of at least one of the two protagonists, which precludes any possibility that the relationship will be "consummated" (Wood, *Vietnam* [1986] 222–44).

For different reasons, both male protagonists are eager to escape the confines of the home, and Frank's aimless wanderings are motivated by a sense of restlessness that mark him as an unanchored figure, his alienation from his domestic environment exacerbated by a more universal alienation from the outback that largely comprises the film's setting where most of the story transpires. He never belongs where he is at any given moment. Frank questions Archie's assertion that masculinity is a function of patriotism, and *Gallipoli* confronts themes and topics that inform American sexual politics of the early 1980s: the problems of conforming to a traditionally accepted masculinity, and the problems of love between men. Gay critic Simon Watney suggests, "In many ways . . . *Gallipoli* goes further [than other contemporary films that present self-identified gay male protagonists] in showing sexuality as a system of regulative constraints, with its careful depiction of conflicting values and expectations about masculinity and male behavior" (122). The *Advocate* describes the film as an "antiwar masterpiece [and] one of the most intensely moving (albeit non-physical) love stories between men ever to grace the screen" (31 January 1982, 47).

*The Road Warrior* reiterates *Gallipoli*'s strategy of securing Gibson's universal accessibility through ambiguities of character identity. The film's vast, barren landscape echoes the characterization of a hero largely stripped of identifiable human attributes. As the voiceover narrative suggests, he has become a "burnt-out shell of a man" defined primarily by the loss of his family. His black leather boots, pants, and jacket with torn-off right sleeve are the only remaining signs of his former identity as a police officer as Max races through the remote wilderness in his rusted-out, banged-up V-8 interceptor, unshaven and unwashed. Yet this extensive paring away of identifiable human attributes results in the characterization of a rebel whose self-imposed distance from human emotions signals both strength and vulnerability, and the film uses a similar strategy in the representation of Max's body as an object of identification and desire that could play into homosexual desire without soliciting it exclusively. Indeed, the physical display of much more muscular and traditionally "macho" male stars of the 1980s is more directly tied to such aggression, punishment, and inflicted torture, as is the case with Sylvester Stallone in the Rambo films *First Blood* (1982) and *Rambo: First Blood Part II* (1985), and with Arnold Schwarzenegger in *Conan the Barbarian* (1982) and *Commando* (1985). Yet the representation of Max's body interweaves these seemingly opposed possibilities. While Max's objectification is clearly linked to punishment and aggression endured at the hands of other males, the mediating "look" at the displayed body is often ambiguous, emanating sometimes from his brutal punishers, and elsewhere only from his audience's perspective.

In *Gallipoli* and *The Road Warrior* as well as early press articles, structured ambiguities of character and narrative accommodate categorically elusive readings of the star persona—as Australian and American, masculinized and feminized, strong and vulnerable, gay and straight—while withholding identifiable character attributes. What is consistent during this period, however, is a composite star image as pan-accessible. With respect to such multiple subject positions of access to Gibson, the star discourse would never again be quite as accommodating as it had been in the early 1980s, since transformations of his persona cumulatively delimit these positions of access in ways that "resolve" it within the progressive "narrative" that constitutes his career from the mid-1980s to the present. With ideological shifts in his stardom, changes in mainstream perceptions of homosexuality, and shifts in gay politics, Gibson becomes progressively less accessible to "alternative" fantasy constructions.

## ★★★★★ Conservative Politics: Gibson as Family Man

The conservative political climate of the Reagan/Bush years, as well as its emphasis upon the reintegration of the stable nuclear family, deeply affected mainstream cinema's strategies in continuing to accommodate alternative readings of star personas such as Gibson's. Hollywood's early

1980s "gay new wave" featuring films such as Arthur Hiller's *Making Love* (1982), James Burrows's undercover cop/gay buddy film *Partners* (1982), and Blake Edwards's gender and sexual "performance" study *Victor/Victoria* (1982) failed to sustain itself, largely due to the increasing social visibility of the new "gay cancer" that would come to be known as AIDS. By the middle of the decade, conservative political factions were taking more reactionary measures against gay culture, as reflected in William F. Buckley's recommendation that AIDS carriers be tattooed, and Pat Buchanan's suggestion that AIDS was just punishment for offenders against the moral order. The conservative cultural climate might not have altered Mel Gibson's "universal" accessibility to American audiences across sexual lines, especially since the publicity strategies of targeting gay audiences never involved self-acknowledged gay characterizations. Still, the later part of the decade progressively constructs a more conservative version of Gibson that stands for the same family values that ultra-conservative factions were promoting as a counteractive to a moral indecency that the gay "lifestyle" epitomized.

Peter Weir's 1982 film *The Year of Living Dangerously* is pivotal in this transformation of the star's accessibility. In this film, ABS newsman Guy Hamilton (Gibson) embodies some of the same characteristics of Max Rockatansky. Guy is a loner and an outsider to the culture in which he has been thrust—here, the politically unstable setting of Sukarno's Indonesia in 1965. In the first half of the film, Guy also develops into a figure whose heroism is defined by his empathy and sensitivity to the dire social and economic conditions that the Indonesians face, and by his ability to gain the trust of news photographer Billy Kwan (Linda Hunt), who opens up professional opportunities for this cultural newcomer. "We're not quite at home with the world," comments Billy, referring to the fact that each of them is of two worlds, with Guy's heritage being both Australian and American. Extending the affiliation with Max, Guy's exposed, sweat-glistening upper body is often filmed from overhead and high angle shots that highlight both his vulnerability and universal accessibility, since these shots are not motivated by any suggestion of the protagonist's punishment. Unlike the previous films, however, the trajectory of this hero's path does center upon the promise of a successful heterosexual union, here with the British government attaché Jill Bryant (Sigourney Weaver). Guy aggressively pursues Jill from the moment he meets her, and after violating her trust in an opportunity to further his career, he becomes yet more resolute in his determination to reconnect with her, which he does in the film's final shot.

As a result of this highly successful film, the popular press became much more motivated to investigate aspects of the star's offscreen persona, and Gibson's subsequent transformation from Australian actor to international superstar was stressful and uneasy. Before appearing in his first American-made film in 1984 (Mark Rydell's *The River*), details of Gibson's personal life were rarely revealed, but his popularity was rising so quickly that he was solicited to make a series of four films in less than two years: *The Bounty* (1984), *The River, Mrs. Soffel* (1984), and *Mad Max: Beyond Thunderdome* (1985). In a 1985 article that deemed Gibson "The Sexiest Man Alive," *People* magazine reports that Gibson's star status had begun to affect the actor: he was arrested for drunk driving while filming *Mrs. Soffel* in Toronto, and he would attack the press for misrepresenting and misquoting him in interviews (Michele Green, "The Dish from Down Under," 4 February 1985, 70–76). Biographer Roland Perry reports that he was frequently drunk and incommunicative on the *Thunderdome* set (136). After completing *Thunderdome*, Gibson took a long-term hiatus from filmmaking and returned to his new ranch in Australia to spend time with his family. Gibson's disenchantment with the trappings of his newfound stardom stems from his perceived lack of control over his own image, exacerbated by the media's misperceptions of his "real" identity and the blurring of the boundaries between his public and private life that he struggled in vain to keep separate. Curiously, the texts reveal more details of his personal life (including his hatred of the press), even as they support Gibson's right to keep his private life "private," by positing Gibson's stable family life as a therapeutic counteractive to the deceitful media industries.

The locative ambiguities that promoted a universal accessibility are now also used to signal a conflict between incongruous versions of his image that the press promotes: a 1987 *Mademoiselle* article describes a "dichotomy of roots" that leads to Gibson's observation that "I'm not really at home in either place" (Diana Maychick, "Mel Gibson Unbuttoned," March 1987, 232). And in *People*'s "Sexiest Man Alive" piece, the ambiguities are depicted as an internal conflict: he has become on "outsider" because he is worn out by his work, unhappy with his current film project (*Thunderdome*), and angry with the press for drawing attention to this very unhappiness.

Beginning in the mid-1980s, the rebel star who feels out of place in Australia and America—and, indeed, in his own body—finds the only place that he can call "home" to be wherever his family is. The family man is the "real" Mel Gibson, and everything else is a disingenuous fabrication imposed by the film industry and the press. Green reports that "if there is anywhere that Gibson seems at ease, it is in the embrace of his family," which was rapidly expanding throughout the 1980s (*People*, 4 February 1985). This emphasis upon family life is sufficiently flexible to permit a continuity with many aspects of his early, pre-Hollywood screen image. The father who is only "himself" in the undisturbed privacy of his own home (be it one of two new ranches in Australia and Montana) becomes the ultimate sign of authenticity. Gibson is a good father because he was always meant to be a father.

The new "family" advocate version of the star requires no radical adjustment to the strategies used to construct Gibson's early image. A masculinity that was initially largely unselfconscious appears even more so as a natural by-product of fatherhood. According to a 1985 article in *McCall's*, Gibson's "wife, Robyn, jokes that he maintains his muscles by lifting infants" (Elizabeth Darcy, "Mel Gibson: Superstar . . . Super Dad!," January 1985, 79), and *Ladies' Home Journal* reports that this "quiet, down-to-earth family man with clear priorities," who is "hooked on fatherhood," "doesn't work on maintaining his good looks and rarely even exercises" ("Mel Gibson: From Macho Man to Family Man," August 1987, 72–73). While the emphasis upon fatherhood and family values continues to render the star authentic, it also resolves ambiguities that had previously been kept open in the interests of promoting a universal accessibility that crossed lines of sexual orientation. As a result of his tendency to be "brutally honest" in his interviews, Gibson was closing off alternative readings of his star persona. He tells Diana Maychick in *Mademoiselle* that "they [the press] always concentrate on the dark, silent facade of 'Mad Max' . . . or this 'sexiest man alive' trash. Those are cartoon images. . . . Nobody like that can laugh with his kids. So they leave that part out. Well, that's the part that counts" ("Gibson Unbuttoned," March 1987, 234).

By 1987, Gibson was using his celebrity status to support ultraconservative candidate Robert Taylor in the Australian federal elections. Biographer James Oram notes that Gibson, described as being "so conservative [that] he made Ronald Reagan seem like a pointy-headed Liberal," applauded as Taylor exclaimed during a rally that "our nation today is suffering a massive increase in child abuse, drug abuse, suicide, pornography and the AIDS thing" (120). Around the same time, as Oram reports, Gibson began his "personal dispute" with a Catholic Church that had abandoned the traditions of the Tridentine Mass. He became openly hostile in a television interview when Barbara Walters questioned his and Robyn's decision not to practice birth control (12). The man whom director Mark Rydell described as "very respectful of women" (Darcy, "Mel Gibson: Superstar," *McCall's*, January 1985, 114) was later quoted as saying, "I think that word, feminist, is bull. Feminism is a term invented by some woman who just got jilted" (Oram 12).

Gibson's new, late 1980s image of ultraconservative advocate for family values finds a convenient narrative mouthpiece in his role as Martin Riggs, the cop/hero of the four highly successful *Lethal Weapon* films (1987–1998, the first two grossing $65 million and $147 million, respectively, in their years of release). Gibson's portrayal of Riggs in the first installment of the series combines earlier characters and films that initially established his popularity in America. As biographer Neil Sinyard notes, character continuity can be found in "a dimension of madness in his onscreen persona: from *Mad Max* to *Hamlet* via *Lethal Weapon* is a very logical route. . . . There is even a common cause for this craziness and inner violence. These heroes have been unhinged by the violent destruction of their family lives and by the death of their wives and/or other loved ones" (10). While Martin Riggs certainly owes much to Mad Max, *Lethal Weapon* as a buddy film owes just as much to *Gallipoli*: both films portray an intimate bond between male lead protagonists. And the *Lethal Weapon* series displays the objectified male body even more. Despite these similarities, however, the series aligns itself with the publicity texts of the late 1980s to resolve the ambiguities of the earlier persona and signal the birth of a specifically more conservative and less rebellious image of Gibson.

The star's move from pan-accessible object of desire to conservative and heterosexual family man correlates with a transformation in the buddy film genre occurring in the late 1980s. As Robin Wood suggests, if the earlier films in the genre configured the home as consistently absent, the later films are more concerned with the "restoration of the home [which becomes] synonymous with the restoration of the symbolic Father" (*Vietnam* [1986] 241). Riggs eventually does recapture the foundations of a home in the heterosexual union with the Rene Russo character in the series' third installment, and in the first two films, he finds a most adequate "substitute" in the family of Roger Murtaugh (Danny Glover), to whose home he returns with his dog for Christmas dinner in the final scene of the first film. As the classic Reagan-era hero, he rescues Murtaugh's daughter from the hands of a drug lord, yet Riggs also upholds patriarchy on the national front.

*Lethal Weapon* clearly distinguishes between heroes and villains on the basis of domestic and national allegiances to a "law" that *The Road Warrior* leaves more ambiguous (and that *Gallipoli*'s narrative yet more radically questions the point of upholding), and it also resolves any ambiguities regarding what it considers to be the acceptable version of masculinity. Riggs is a "lethal weapon" who is rendered vulnerable to reminders of his own emotional loss: he jabs a revolver into his mouth early in the first film, ready to pull the trigger and breaking down in tears as he holds his dead wife's picture. This vulnerability is initially tied to the objectified male body: the camera first reveals an entirely naked Martin (with only his back side visible) getting out of bed with a cigarette as he moves to the refrigerator to grab a beer. Yet two subsequent and laboriously protracted "exposures" of the stripped male body are clearly motivated by another male villain's aggression. In the first, Martin is naked from waist up, suspended from a hook and tortured by being doused with water while prodded with an electrical current. In a later scene, he strips off his shirt in a fight with the final villain (Gary Busey) as Murtaugh and other fellow police officers cheer Riggs on. Each instance is configured as a test of masculinity that, according to Steve Neale's paradigm, justifies the male body display by associating it with punishment and violence, thereby securing the heterosexuality of viewing subject and object viewed (see Neale "Masculinity"). And in each case, Martin passes the test. He never gives in.

## ★★★★★ Tom Cruise, All-American

Tom Cruise's persona features different start and end points than Gibson's, tailored to the specific ideological conditions and eccentricities of the era and evidencing Hollywood's ability simultaneously to secure and promote discrete versions of star-level masculinity. Both versions of Cruise often employ and elicit similar aspects of human character and disposition to produce results that do not appear to have very much in common. The most obvious difference concerns age—a factor that would figure more prominently in 1980 than in 1989. With Cruise in the 1980s we see the very strategic shaping of an all-American hero and an "entrepreneurial rebel," even if what it means ideologically to be either heroic or rebellious shifts significantly through the decade. Cruise evolves from a teenager who plays with the toys real soldiers play with in *Taps* (1981) to a much more mature role in which playing at being an all-American results in psychological trauma and the loss of the use of his lower body in *Born on the Fourth of July* (1989).

Cruise was only nineteen and a half years old when *Taps*, his first major film, was released in December 1981. He portrays hot-headed Captain David Shawn, the cadet who remains so resolved to defend his Bunker Hill Academy from being razed for a new condominium development that he opens fire with a machine gun on the police officers to whom the rest of the cadets have surrendered at the end of the film, maniacally screaming, "It's beautiful, man! It's beautiful!" This film marks the initial stage of Cruise's development of a unique brat-trait that stayed with him throughout the decade: the playful yet strategically confident juggling of a long and powerful appendage, from the machine gun of *Taps* to the fighter planes of *Top Gun* to the pool cues of Martin Scorsese's *The Color of Money* (1986) to the bartender's liquor bottles of *Cocktail* (1988) to his own body, gymnastically flipping on the hoods of abandoned cars (*The Outsiders*, 1983) or on his parents' sofa (*Risky Business*, 1983).

Once it started to matter what Tom Cruise experienced as a child and how he behaved with his older and more experienced directors and co-stars—that is, as soon as his own stardom was secured as something more sustainable than that of just another teenage actor—the press began to construct Cruise as a "mature" character with extended staying power in Hollywood. By the latter part of the decade, Cruise would be molded into something of an anti-brat, an exceptionally respectful young man who conformed to what might be expected of a hero. "Nearly everyone has mentioned his politeness," explains Aljean Harmetz in a 1987 article in the *New York Times*. "But from a movie star, it is, nevertheless, a shock" ("Crossing the Line to Stardom," 7 June 1987, 1). David Ansen argues that, in marked contrast to "rebel" movie stars of the past, Cruise harbors a "deferential formality" and "essential decency": "Tom Cruise's favorite four-letter word is 'ma'am.' As for three letters, 'sir' is high on the list" ("Cruise Guns for the Top," *Newsweek*, 9 June 1986, 72).

A polite and respectful attitude toward others does not in itself generate sufficient character depth to resonate with audiences across the span of a career. Accordingly, what Paul Chutkow describes as a "permanent freeze into a Reebok caricature of the All-American Boy" ("The Private Life of Tom Cruise," *New York Times*, 17 December 1989, 1) eventually comes to secure another type of outsider status that distinguishes Cruise from other young actors of the time. While they inherited and enjoyed the benefits of having financially successful star parents, Cruise came from humble roots and had to carve his own path to success. He explains: "Our family didn't have enough money to feed me" (*San Diego Union Tribune*, 7 July 1990, E1). Cruise was dyslexic. His parents divorced when he was still a child. "After a divorce, you feel so vulnerable," he confesses in an interview with *Rolling Stone*. "I went through a period . . . of really wanting to be accepted, wanting love and attention from people. But I never really seemed to fit in anywhere." In the same piece, *Risky Business* co-star Rebecca DeMornay (whom Cruise dated after the film's release) confirms that "there's definitely something different about kids who come from broken homes. They have this sort of *searching* quality, because you're searching for love and affection, if you've been robbed of a substantial amount of time with your parents. I think that's true of Tom" (Christopher Connelly, *Rolling Stone*, 19 June 1986, 92, emphasis in the original).

Unlike Gibson, Cruise is constructed as "his own man" from the start of his career, well aware of the ways in which Hollywood might attempt to redirect his persona along its own paths and determined not to let this happen. *Rolling Stone* columnist Lynn Hirschberg's 1988 piece on Cruise begins by noting how the actor has successfully controlled the interview by insisting that it take place on the "neutral ground" of the interviewer's hotel room ("A Conversation with Tom Cruise," 11 August 1988, 44). She continues with a keen description of the roots of Cruise's success: "A combination of shrewdness and all-American boyishness is one of the reasons that Cruise has been so successful in his career. Yet there is an edge: Cruise is serious about his goals. He's like a boy scout—thoughtful and brave and loyal and all the rest—but his honest-to-gosh good-guyness is mixed with steely determination. And that's what audiences find so compelling" (46). Problems and obstacles never become the setting for crisis or trauma: as David Ansen explains, Cruise has "no guilty Freudian secrets in his closet, no paralyzing self-doubts" ("The Big Hustle," *Newsweek*, 13 October 1986, 68). Instead, Tom Cruise constructs such problems as mere challenges that can and will be overcome.

Cruise's own self-descriptions are instrumental in perpetuating his image as a hero who triumphs over adversity. Referring to circumstances of his childhood—that because his family moved often he was constantly forced to attend new schools and connect with new classmates—he says, "In every different place, I became a different person. You've got to create your own world when you move like that. That was just my way of dealing with things. When you have to cope with a lot of problems, you are either going to sink or you are going to swim. You're either going to take the challenge and rise to the occasion or it's just going to devour you. Am I going to survive? Or am I going to get eaten alive? And I was trying to survive the best I could" (Hirschberg, *Rolling Stone*, 11 August 1988, 88). Yet as his interviewers and commentators clarify, Cruise's "steely determination" never hardens his persona into a fixture of inaccessibility, because it is inextricably woven with character attributes that endear him to his audiences: cleanliness, cute boyishness, and politeness.

What this winning combination also begins to shape is an image of masculinity designed as a national restorative, a return to the union of the strong body and sound decision-making capabilities. As Susan Jeffords explains, the Reagan era witnessed a move to reclaim the health of a nation

weakened by the "soft body" international policies of the Carter administration through a reassertion of masculine strength, confidence, and deci-
siveness (*Hard Bodies* 11). Cruise successfully markets these attributes
within a corporeal "package" that keeps getting harder as the roles progress
toward hyper-erect *Top Gun*. Yet the strength of the body (always undeniable, but by the time of *Top Gun*, almost imposing) consistently remains
linked to the strength of Cruise's sound entrepreneurial spirit.

Responding in 1983 to observations that he has been perceived as a
"sex object," Cruise comments: "It doesn't matter to me. . . . I just focus on
what I want and what I want to do, and everything outside of that is just
there, and it happens" (Tom Shales, "Cruising Speed," *Washington Post*, 30
August 1983, B1). The solipsistic nature of such "focus" dovetails elegantly
with the resolve and determination of Joel Goodsen, the appropriately
named heroic figure of Cruise's 1983 breakthrough film *Risky Business*. The
plot concerns the teenage son and only child of higher-than-upper-middle-
class parents away on vacation from their home in the affluent Chicago
suburb of Glencoe, leaving Joel, with the help of some friends, to navigate
the unfamiliar territories of awakening sexuality. After a "first time" sexual
encounter with call girl Lana (DeMornay) takes an unexpected turn when
Joel discovers his mother's expensive crystal egg missing from his living
room the following morning, Joel weaves through a series of adventures
that induce him to display his expertise in business management: property
acquisitions, bargaining, risk management, decision making, and, most
notoriously, the launching of a successful enterprise, as Joel and Lana transform the Glencoe estate into a brothel to earn money to repair his father's
Porsche, which Joel has let sink into Lake Michigan. The film relentlessly
demonstrates the inevitability of his success at whatever he decides upon
pursuing—even a spot in an Ivy League school, secured when a Princeton
interviewer who appears unexpectedly at the brothel bash becomes another
very satisfied customer.

As Cruise's first fully developed character, Joel becomes the successful
vehicle for connecting good heterosexual sex with good business sense. The
film also establishes a paradoxical aspect of Cruise's persona upon which his
subsequent films would build—the hero who is both a rebellious outsider
and blatant conformist. In one way, Joel is portrayed as just another clean-
cut white American kid whose desire to have his first sexual encounter
underpins an unlikely yet ultimately fulfilling fantasy of sexual and capitalist excess. Sporting dark sunglasses in the opening and closing scenes of
the film, coolly revving the motor of his father's Porsche in front of a group
of girls, taking the risky move of having sex with Lana on a midnight train

The teen rebel entrepreneur: Joel Goodsen (Cruise) in *Risky Business*. Courtesy Photofest. Copyright Warner Bros. Pictures, 1983.

through the city, or holding his own in negotiations with pimps who want the prostitutes he has borrowed returned to their rightful "owners," Joel embodies the spirit of the cool dude, someone who dares to set himself apart from the pack. To the extent that the film succeeds in retaining its sense of irony and cynicism about the terms under which it has established the sex/business connection, it manages to sustain Cruise's rebel image.

Yet ultimately the film celebrates the capitalist practices toward which the film at first appears to direct cynicism. First, on the basis of class privilege, Joel already has everything he needs, and accordingly all of the film's bargaining and negotiating of valuable inanimate objects and female bodies is relegated to the realm of play, an exercise in trade-based capitalism that has no consequences behind the celebration of its own excessive display. Unlike Joel himself, the pimps and prostitutes that briefly move in and out of his life exist in a social realm that the film codes as abnormal, yet the narrative is structured to secure the audience's identification not with struggling outsiders but with the agents of affluent privilege, encouraging its viewers to gasp in horror as Joel fails to prevent the Porsche from being submerged, and conveying upper-class anxiety of loss in its slow-motion pan of the delicate and costly crystal egg that the pimp has returned to Joel in a football toss. As much as the film tries to be risky, it is much more concerned with celebrating the successful business practices of the rich and privileged, the ultimate stakes for its hero being set not very high at all (if Joel doesn't get into Princeton, he'll just settle for the University of Illinois). Accordingly, and despite its attempt to code Joel as a rebel, the hero of *Risky Business* remains much more enmeshed in the logic of social and economic conformity. Indeed, given the Reagan era's promotion of the "healthy body" that promises to restore the strength of the nation, Joel becomes a willing advocate of the prevailing conservative ideology of the mid-1980s.

By far Cruise's most financially successful film of the decade (and, at $177 million, the highest grossing film of 1986), *Top Gun* presents the star/ hero with an even more paradoxical combination of rebellion and conformity. The film concerns overly confident Lt. Pete "Maverick" Mitchell, in training to become a fighter pilot at the navy's distinctive Fighter Weapons School, and his efforts to prove himself as the leader of his class while successfully wooing Charlotte "Charlie" Blackwood (Kelly McGillis), who turns out to be one of his instructors. The film does much to establish Maverick as a classic rebel. He drives a motorcycle and likes to work alone. He is also a rule breaker, gleefully engaging in unauthorized fly-by's that bring his fighter jet into danger. During one mission, acting against the advice of his colleagues, he decides to pursue one final "enemy" plane even though he has very little remaining fuel in his own jet. Maverick's rebellion is configured in terms of cockiness that some label a fearlessness the navy desperately needs, but which many of his fellow trainees perceive as impulsive recklessness. The only signs of Maverick's vulnerability involve a thinly conceived backstory regarding his conflicted relationship with his father, whose death has left him with no remaining family except for his close friend and partner, Lt. Nick "Goose" Bradshaw (Anthony Edwards).

The paradox inherent in *Top Gun*'s emphasis upon Maverick's restlessness relates to this rebel's choice of career paths. As Rob Edelman aptly explains in his review, the fact that Maverick "fits the classic rebel mold" makes it all the more perplexing that, "by choice, he has become a navy pilot, rather than a Wild One or a Rebel Without a Cause. . . . If he's such a 'maverick' . . . why is he in the navy, where the rule is conformity?" (41). Edelman proposes that Maverick is aligned with Hollywood's contemporary preference for "one-dimensionally macho" heroes, figures whose invulnerability evidences a tendency to associate effective leadership skills with the ability to conform. I would assert that the admixture of rebellion and conformity through Maverick comprises a strategy to eroticize military operations in an attempt to render ideologically conservative political positions more palatable to mass audiences. In 1986 America, Tom Cruise is a most appropriate vehicle to effect such a strategy. In Paramount's "Handbook of Production Information" for the film, co-producer Don Simpson explains that Cruise "was the first person we considered for this film, so we didn't get involved in going after anyone else. We went out and got Tom Cruise" (9).

Among a number of possible reasons for this choice was the excellent fit between the role of Maverick and Cruise's already established star persona, marked by the same spirit of the entrepreneurial rebel that Joel emblematizes in *Risky Business*. With their drive, their determination, and their alignment with all-American values, the two characters share much common ground. They also share a philosophy of life as "play"—an eagerness to engage in a series of adventures with seemingly unexpectable consequences—even if in Maverick's case the stakes of such games end up being considerably more deadly (playmate Goose ends up dead in a flight maneuver gone bad). Maverick perfectly embodies the entrepreneurial rebel image, and he makes it even sexier than Joel ever could—not only in its depiction of his steamy relationship with Charlie, but also through the testosterone-heavy emphasis upon the hard male bodies of Maverick and his fellow trainees. Goose tells Maverick, "You live your life between your legs, man." Harder yet and equally eroticized are the glistening, more impermeable bodies of the jets themselves, filmed in romantic silhouette throughout the film, and subjected to the occasional stolen caress of a trainee. At an introductory training session in which details of this magnificent hardware and technology are described, one of the trainees exclaims, "This gives me a hard on!" "Don't tease me," his friend warns. With such breathtaking excitement, it is not surprising that the U.S. Navy endorsed the film (Edelman 42), and that it served as such an effective recruiting tool.

After *Top Gun* and toward the end of the decade, as Mel Gibson was shaping the family-man version of the rebel image, Cruise's roles were gradually becoming more reflective—with his performance as pool hustler Vincent Lauria in *The Color of Money* (the big stick is still something of an object of fascination for him) and with more demonstrable self-questioning in *Rain Man* (1988), which revives much of the star discourse on locative ambiguities in its depiction of an unanchored man who is aching for meaningful family connections, and which traces the evolution of his character Charlie Babbitt from insensitive, greedy, and jealous brother to a guardian and friend with a conscience. Yet it is with the film featuring a most suitable end-of-the-decade narrative, characterization, and performance that

Pool hustler with a big stick: Vincent Lauria (Cruise) in *The Color of Money*. Courtesy Photofest and Buena Vista Pictures. Copyright Buena Vista Pictures, 1986.

the transformation of Cruise from cocky teen rebel to more mature and reflective adult actor is most pronounced—*Born on the Fourth of July* (1989). The film traces the story of marines paraplegic Ron Kovic, from the period prior to his enlistment in the early 1960s, through his traumatizing experiences in Vietnam where he was injured, and then to his return to the United States, first as an embittered defender of the government's military involvement in Southeast Asia and later as an even more vehement war protester and social advocate.

The film serves as a turning point for Cruise, even while it simultaneously permits him to sustain attributes that made him appealing to audiences from the start of the decade. If he was a perfect choice for *Top Gun* on the basis of an already established all-American and entrepreneurial rebel status, the casting of Cruise as Kovic is even more suitable (and ingenious) because it enables transformations of the star persona and the character he plays to progress along parallel paths and echo each other. Even if Oliver Stone "uses his star's All-American persona for ironic generalizations," as *Newsweek* observes, the strategy is still effective because it reveals a depth of character (of both Kovic and the star) that broadens Cruise's range for future projects ("Bringing It All Back Home," 25 December 1989, 74). Cruise/Kovic's experience of and participation in the tragedies of war disrupts the "play" philosophy Joel Goodsen and Maverick had upheld, with a reminder that actions executed in the interest of preserving traditional American values can also have actual, longstanding consequences. His previous characters' associations with macho hypersexuality are also turned inside out as the hero comes to lament the loss of the use of his sexual organ, making his plea of "I want to be a man again!" yet more resonant, and previewing other, more socially committed demonstrations of his manhood in the latter part of the film.

There might appear to be some element of risk in the star's decision to portray a character that comes to question the all-Americanism so instrumental to audiences' perception of his persona. Through his transformation in the role, however, Cruise emerges as a version of the American hero who is no longer trapped by prevailing definitions of patriotism. And he even manages to sustain the entrepreneurial aspect of his persona as a man who does whatever he can to beat the odds—first to stay alive, then to regain the use of his legs, and ultimately to influence the nation's perspective on an unjust war.

Ultimately, the extratexual and cinematic star discourse of Mel Gibson and Tom Cruise in the 1980s relies extensively on versions of the depth model of persona development. In Gibson's case, a persona that from the beginning was "deep," strategically navigating though ambiguities of home, nationality, and sexuality, eventually came to ground and anchor itself in a version of the star that was much more "situated" in the heterosexual nuclear family, even as this persona retained prior associations with rebellion that made Gibson famous as Mad Max. For Cruise, the trajectory is largely reversed, as an actor initially defined by his connection with teen films, and later by his embodiment of an all-American entrepreneurial rebel consonant with the prevailing conservative ideology of the time, eventually coming to take on a role that appears to question and recontextualize the attributes that had made him famous. Both celebrated actors ended the 1980s by leaving their audiences with a clear sense that there was something else, and something more, to be discovered about them.

# 5 ★★★★★★★★★★★
# Michael J. Fox
# and the Brat Pack
## Contrasting Identities

ROBERT EBERWEIN

Michael J. Fox. Courtesy Photofest.

*The Breakfast Club*: Judd Nelson, Emilio Estevez, Ally Sheedy, Molly Ringwald, Anthony Michael Hall. Courtesy Photofest. Copyright Universal Pictures, 1985.

*St. Elmo's Fire*. Standing: Emilio Estevez, Demi Moore, Rob Lowe. Seated: Ally Sheedy, Judd Nelson, Mare Winningham, Andrew McCarthy. Courtesy Photofest. Copyright Columbia Pictures, 1985.

Construction of these actors' identities occurred in a somewhat different manner than that seen with the others discussed in this volume. Having had varying levels of success earlier in the decade, the actors to be examined here all achieved major stardom in the summer of 1985. Michael J. Fox, already well known for his role as Alex P. Keaton, the archconservative, Ronald Reagan–worshipping son of liberal parents on sitcom television, had a box office triumph as Marty McFly in Robert Zemeckis's *Back to the Future*, the number-one film for the year (nearly $198 million). By the end of the summer Fox had solidified his position as a bankable star with *Teen Wolf* ($33 million) and become an iconic figure of adulation and even affection for fans and the media. The engaging youthful teenagers he portrayed in both films became the starting point for the parallel developments of his offscreen identity as a boy growing into manhood, an actor maturing into more adult roles, and a model of unthreatening and gentle masculinity.

In contrast to Fox were the eight actors who found themselves saddled with the media-imposed collective identity of the "Brat Pack." Five were already familiar to audiences from their appearance in John Hughes's successful *The Breakfast Club* (1985, $45 million; sixteenth in earnings): Emilio Estevez, Anthony Michael Hall, Judd Nelson, Molly Ringwald, and Ally Sheedy. Estevez, Nelson, and Sheedy joined Rob Lowe, Andrew McCarthy, and Demi Moore the same year in another solid hit, Joel Schumacher's *St. Elmo's Fire* ($37 million, twenty-third in earnings). These actors came to be known as members of the Brat Pack after David Blum coined the term with specific reference to Estevez, Lowe, and Nelson, as well as actors who had appeared in *Taps* (1981): Tom Cruise, Timothy Hutton, and Sean Penn ("Hollywood's Brat Pack," *New York*, 10 June 1985, 43).

By the end of the decade, while Fox was still a major star, the media had moved from treating him as a kid to presenting him as a grown-up man, happily married to Tracy Pollan, and a new father, as well as a talented, versatile actor. One theme in his coverage that had first appeared in 1985 still prevailed as the decade ended: Fox was not like anyone in the Brat Pack. Only two of the eight actors considered members of that media-constructed group were continuing to have successful films: Estevez in *Young Guns* (1988) and McCarthy in *Weekend at Bernie's* (1989). Beginning in 1985, one of the constant themes dominating media coverage of the Brat Pack was their mutual denial of the collective identity that had been imposed on them.

## ★★★★★ Fox: From Boy to Man

The Canadian-born Fox, one of five children of a career army man, quit high school and came to the United States in 1980 to be an actor. His first career break occurred in 1982 when he got the part of Alex Keaton on "Family Ties," the NBC comedy that ran from 1982 to 1989 and began the process of making him a star. Among his awards for this series were three consecutive Emmys from 1986 to 1988 as "Outstanding Lead Actor in a Comedy Series," and the Golden Globe in 1989 for "Best Performance by an Actor in a TV Series." Obviously the conservative teenager who supported Ronald Reagan appealed to the president, who said "Family Ties" was his favorite television show in 1985.

Taking the part of Marty McFly in *Back to the Future* was an even more important moment in Fox's professional life. Although executive producer Steven Spielberg initially wanted him, his work on "Family Ties" precluded taking the part, which was given to Eric Stoltz. When the latter's work was deemed inappropriate for the part after filming began, Fox replaced him, even though this meant enduring a grueling schedule that had him working on the television show during the day, filming *Back to the Future* at night—usually into the early morning hours—and then returning to NBC the next morning at 9:30. *Back to the Future* opened on 3 July to generally favorable reviews and strong box office (fourth-highest weekend opening in 1985). Its huge gross handily beat the distant second, *Rambo: First Blood Part II* ($150 million).

Clearly Fox was one of the most important appeals of *Back to the Future*. In *Lucky Man*, his autobiography, he speaks about the affinity between himself and "the character of Marty McFly—a skateboarding, girl-chasing, high school rock and roll musician—[who] seemed like the kind of guy I could play in my sleep" (Fox 89). In the press release, Fox underscored this image and said his "favorite scene . . . takes place in 1955 when he performs Chuck Berry's classic 'Johnny B. Goode' . . . 'I was able to live out two fantasies . . . I've always wanted to do a big budget feature . . . and . . . to be a rich rock star. In [*Back to the Future*] I get to do both" (Universal News Press Department, 5 June 1985, 2–3). This dynamo of energy who dashes rather than walks in the film is much closer to the car-racing character he had played in the otherwise forgettable made-for-TV film *High School U.S.A.* (1983) than to the Alex of "Family Ties." His show was number two in the ratings, as the lead-in to the top-rated series that followed it, "The Cosby Show," a combination that dominated the 1984–85 season.

Fox as a rock star in his favorite scene in *Back to the Future*. Courtesy Photofest. Copyright Universal Pictures, 1985.

While not all reviewers responded positively to Fox's performance in *Back to the Future*, those who did were effusive. Richard Corliss referred to "the ingratiating Fox" (*Time*, 1 July 1985, 62). Jack Kroll found him "perfect" (*Newsweek*, 8 July 1985, 76). J. Hoberman predicted correctly that if the film "didn't knock some of the box-office wind out of *Rambo*'s sails this weekend, nothing will" (*Village Voice*, 2 July 1985, 48). And Joseph Gelmes sounded a note that got at Fox's uniqueness: "an ingratiating, plucky little guy who reminds me of a young Mickey Rooney of the 1980s—an easygoing, gulp, gosh, unadventurous young guy who rises to the challenges of fantastic events" (*Newsday*, 3 July 1985, 2:41). Gelmes's comment is one of several from critics who compare Fox and Rooney. The likeable, nonthreatening, short bundle of talented energy who could do anything was quickly elevated by the media, which filled in the blanks with references to his facial and other physical injuries sustained by playing hockey in Canada; his continuing interest in rock 'n' roll; and his romantic history with his female co-stars.

Writing in *People* a month after the opening of the film, Richard Sanders indicated that Fox had received the full publicity treatment in Hollywood: "His face looms on two Sunset Boulevard billboards—one for the low-budget comedy *Teen Wolf* and another for [*Back to the Future*]." The author made the first of what would be constant references in the media to Fox's private life, specifically his automobile, a "$20,000 Nissan 300ZX Turbo," and his girlfriend, Nancy McKeon, the co-star in both *High School U.S.A* and *Poison Ivy* (1985), another made-for-TV movie ("Michael J. Fox Leaps into Stardom after Zooming Back to the Future," *People*, 12 August 1985, 82).

Fox's rise as a superstar from 1985 on invites examination of how aspects of the character Marty served as a basis for appreciating the actor Fox's reception. As we will see, a similar kind of melding of parts in films and actual personalities occurs with the Brat Pack. The DeLorean in *Back to the Future* can be seen as one element involved in constructing the star image of Fox. To blast off into the past/future, the car has to reach a speed of 88 miles per hour. One aspect of Fox's life mentioned constantly in the media was his love of fast cars. In fact, one can chart his rise in Hollywood's financial stratosphere by the kinds of cars he drives, from the Turbo, purchased in the early 1980s after he had been working for a while on "Family Ties," to his Ferrari, one of several cars in his garage by the year 1987. Alan Richman mentions in an interview that Fox didn't even have a car when he started the series, and includes a description of his ride with Fox in his Ferrari: "Ordinarily a man of simple tastes and complex feelings, he is for the moment a man of extravagant tastes and one simple feeling: He wants to go fast. He Andrettis his way down Gower Avenue, screams in consternation when he misshifts, vows to make up for it . . . hits the Hollywood Freeway at 85 mph, weaves around a Datsun, dials his car phone, lights a second cigarette, slams in a rock tape, gets happier all the time." But this speed-limit violating image is immediately qualified by the author: "Usually, he does not require the services of a $70,000 sports car to find happiness. Almost any childlike pleasure will do. He loves acting like a kid, and when asked if he has a favorite role, he mentions a home movie of himself at 5, riding his bike while holding a snake by the tail" ("Little Big Man," *People*, 20 April 1987, 96).

The image of a man who is still a kid at heart figures pervasively in the articles and interviews, and is factored into commentary on his choice of films from 1985 to 1989. The sense of the child about to develop clearly helps explain his appeal to everyone—as a brother, the boy next door, and every mother's dream for her daughter—and foregrounds his decisions to make films that allowed him to grow as an actor and literally start acting/ behaving like an adult onscreen. Before this transition, one writer said Fox "looks like a chain-smoking choirboy" (Patrick Goldstein, "Fox's Rockin' Roll," *L.A. Calendar*, 3 August 1986, 19). The image recurred a few months later, as Bruce Buschel told Fox: "There's your famous face on the newsstand with a story that paints you as a choirboy Cagney" ("Little Big Man," *GQ*, December 1986, 227). Mark Morrison described him as looking like "an all-American Innocent on spring break" ("The New Short Kid Hits It Big," *US*, 29 July 1985, 25). Six months later, he called him "the hottest kid in Hollywood" (*US*, 27 January 1986, 20).

The range and variety of magazines following Fox is staggering. In January 1987, he was one of the young actors pictured on the cover of *Tiger Beat*, the teen celebrity magazine. Shortly afterward, one reporter in a fashion magazine said he "has the white-teeth smile and wholesome good looks of a teenage magazine pin up" (Susan Alai, "The Year of the Fox," *W*, 9–16 March 1987, 22). He was on the 12 March cover of *Rolling Stone*. The next month a writer for a traditional woman's magazine commented on his cross-generational appeal: "A recent public opinion poll ranked him as the most popular male celebrity in America after Bill Cosby" (Susan Granger, "Michael J. Fox: TV's Favorite Son Is Short of Stature but Long in Talent," *Ladies' Home Journal*, April 1987, 112). In an interview in *Playboy*, he explained how he learned the facts of life but refused to go into details about his first sexual experience in order not to embarrass the woman (David Rensen, "20 Questions," June 1987, 130). In September, he was on the cover of *Playgirl*, the issue reporting on their "9th annual ten sexiest

men in America [contest]." Fox remarked on this kind of widespread coverage at the time. A newsstand in his neighborhood had a number of magazines showing him on the cover: "Every now and then, during the
post-*Back to the Future* eighties, I'd stop by and . . . discreetly scan the racks
. . . surveying the versions of myself on display—*People, US, GQ, TV Guide,
MAD, Cracked, AdWeek, Variety, McCall's, Family Circle, The National Enquirer,
The Star, The Globe, Seventeen, 16, Tiger Beat, Bop.* . . ." He reflected on them
as a measure of his star status: "On the cover of *People* I was the boy next
door, *GQ* a well-groomed yuppie, *Playgirl* a sex symbol. . . . I found myself
in the labyrinthine fun house of American mega-celebrity" (Fox 94).

In 1987 Fox starred in two films that took him beyond teenaged roles.
He was now the "Little Big Guy" for *McCall's* ("Family Ties: Little Big Guy
Michael J. Fox," August 1987, 70) and the "Little Big Man" for *People* (20
April 1987, 86). The first of these more adult roles was as Joe Rasnick, a factory worker/rock musician, in *Light of Day* (1987). He plays a decent young
man who tries to serve as a peace-keeping bridge between his sister (Joan
Jett), a fellow musician, and their mother (Gena Rowlands). For the first
time in his films, Fox does not scamper down halls or ride a skateboard as
he moves frantically from one crisis to another. Instead he drives a beat-up
van from town to town as the rock group seeks gigs. The film had a
respectable opening in third place, with a $3.5 million weekend gross, but
it would eventually make only $10 million, nothing like the success of his
previous film. At least one critic thought Fox's own age suited the role: "Fox
is the most popular 25-year-old teenager in America today . . . [and] brings
to the grim and depressing world of [the film] that quality of enduring sincerity that helps keep the rating of TV's 'Family Ties' so high. . . . Playing a
character close to his actual age, Fox gives a heartbreaker of a performance"
(Joseph Gelmes, *Newsday*, 6 February 1987, 3:3). But Michael Wilmington,
even though sympathetic, saw a problem in the age: Fox "stretches himself,
subverting his usual cute-kid person, and even playing his own guitar riffs.
. . . But he can't disguise the fact that, though Fox's presence obviously got
the movie made, he seems wrong for the part. The fact that he seems so
unformed—which enables him to play teenagers believably—works against
him here" (*L.A. Times Calendar*, 6 February 1987, 1).

Fox's next film, *The Secret of My Succe$s* (1987), a sophisticated comedy
with strong elements of farce, returned him to his winning box-office days,
with over twice the opening weekend revenue of *Light of Day* ($7.7 million)
and a domestic gross of $67 million. In it he plays Brantley Foster, a recent
business school graduate who leaves his native Kansas for New York. There
he works in the mail room for his uncle Howard (Richard Jordan), who

runs a huge corporation, is seduced by his aunt Vera (Margaret Whitton), pretends to be an executive in the company, and meets and falls in love with Christy Wills (Helen Slater), who is having an affair with his uncle. The film's two-staged climax exposes and resolves the romantic complexities, and Brantley and his aunt end up in control of the company.

The public liked it more than some of the critics. In a harsh review, David Denby clearly stressed Fox's own immaturity as a problem and found him "miscast as a movie star. Tiny, hairless, and smooth, with an unnervingly placid face—the face of a wizened child—Fox looks likes he's been dipped in polyurethane. If you spilled something on him, he would wipe clean" (*New York*, 27 April 1987, 126). The snide remark echoes Patricia Schroeder's constantly repeated characterization of Ronald Reagan in 1983 as the "teflon president" (Pat Schroeder, thinkexist.com). Denby added more physical insults about "the whirling little man . . . a superconfident twerp, running down endless halls" (128). In fact, Fox had switched from running down halls in high schools to those in modernist office buildings in New York, a transition that clearly didn't work for these critics. The "boy next door" had morphed unpleasantly into a suit.

Fox's most pronounced move away from teenaged roles came in 1988 when he starred in *Bright Lights, Big City*, playing a fact checker for a *New Yorker*–like magazine, hanging out with a fast-living crowd, and snorting cocaine. "Michael J. Fox Grows Up," said the cover of *US* (18 April 1988). Interestingly, the character played by Tracy Pollan, his future wife, is definitely not part of that scene, which his character will ultimately abandon. But even though Fox had chosen a more challenging and adult role, residual references to the boy-child image persisted. One writer described him as "the luminary, movie-star, comedian, dramatic actor, Pepsi pitchman, teen idol, Hollywood mogul, impulsive boy wonder, savvy and thoughtful adult. . . . Fox, now 26, wears all those labels like a charmed coat of many colors." Still, the writer observed, "Fox is ready to leave Alex behind, ready to become an adult, an actor." Fox told him: "I have to challenge that perception of me. That squeaky-clean thing is not something I've consciously planned." In fact, Jay McInerny, who adapted the film from his novel, said in an interview that Fox was particularly appropriate for the part: "The very fact that Fox is so endearing is something everybody felt was needed" (Steve Weinstein, "Michael J. Fox: Boy Next Door Ready for Some New Risks," *L.A. Times Calendar*, 31 March 1988, 1, 13). When the film opened, a full-page advertisement in the *New York Times* carried a blurb saying, "Alex Keaton grows up . . . and then some . . . A truly powerful picture that reveals dynamic new dimensions in the acting style of Michael J. Fox" (1 April 1988, C11).

Fox and Tracy Pollan (his future wife) in *Bright Lights, Big City*. Courtesy Photofest. Copyright CST Telecommunications/Mirage, 1988.

Fox's most demanding role thus far came the next year in Brian De Palma's *Casualties of War*, based on a true story written by David Rabe. Fox plays PFC Eriksson, who was part of a platoon that kidnapped, raped, and murdered a young Vietnamese woman. Eriksson protested, did not participate, and even risked his life to report the perpetrators, who were all court-martialed and imprisoned. Two 1989 articles display the media's recognition of his growth: "An Actor Who Insists on Being Serious" (Aljean Harmetz, *New York Times*, 10 August 1989, C13); "Michael J. Fox: Life as a Man" (Rick Tolander, *Premiere*, October 1989, 84–90). But even now he was not immune from those who wouldn't let him escape the childish persona. One writer described him as appearing "startlingly like a Michael J. Fox doll. . . . He seems smaller, even, than he does onscreen, more squeaky-clean." Fox commented on his public image and relevance for this film: "'OK,' he says, 'if people look at me as someone who's very accessible . . . the boy-next-door type of thing . . . why not say, 'OK, if you're comfortable with me, let me take you to hell and see how that works.'" He says the film is important for him in moving beyond comedy: "'I wasn't looking forward to doing something so emotionally draining . . . ' Fox says, boyish face clouding over" (Kathy Huffhines, interview in *Hartford Courant*, 3 September 1989, 67).

*Casualties of War's* domestic gross of $18 million did not come close to its $22 million production cost. Still, in each of his unsuccessful films Fox had been pushing himself as an artist, taking on increasingly challenging roles. What's interesting about *Casualties*, as opposed to the other films that failed, is that it drew on what audiences had accepted as the essence of Fox the person: his basic decency, goodness, and likeability—character traits that were constantly being reinforced by the media. Steve Pond quotes De Palma: "I thought Michael would embody the sort of innocent young American boy that the audience had sort of grown to like and identify with from his television series . . . and I wanted to put that boy through this" ("Facing the Future," *GQ*, November 1989, 271). De Palma made a similar comment on Fox in the "Biography" section of the Columbia Pictures press book: "Michael brings a strength and conviction and emotional depth to the character of Eriksson. It was a terribly difficult role because the character is under extreme psychological and emotional pressures throughout the movie, and Michael had a tremendous sense of integrity in everything he did" (Columbia Press Book 1989, 1–2).

The period 1985 to 1989 saw him rise from popular television personality to megastar, starting with *Back to the Future*. Having worked strenuously to emerge from teenage roles by taking those that specifically underscored his maturity as an adult, Fox concluded the decade by literally going back to *Back to the Future*. In November, the first sequel to that film opened on the Thanksgiving holiday with a highly impressive weekend gross of $28 million and an eventual take of $119 million. But even though Fox was again playing Marty, this time he came at the role from a different direction, as a seasoned adult film actor who was still youthful enough to make Marty believable, rather than as someone who was not that far from actual teenage years. Instead of playing a role that extended his image as a sharp teenager, an actor with an impressive range and incredible energy was again playing a teenager, but this time by choice rather than necessity.

## ★★★★★ Distinguishing (the) Fox from the Pack

In the period 1985–1989, the constant theme in media coverage of Michael J. Fox was his likeability. In contrast, the inception of the Brat Pack began in an article that presented them as strikingly *un*likeable.

The process of contrasting Fox and the Brat Packers started in the summer of 1985 when they all achieved stardom. The originating media sin that simultaneously created and stigmatized the Brat Pack occurred in David Blum's article in the 10 June 1985 issue of *New York* magazine describing his interview with Estevez, Lowe, and Nelson at the Hard Rock Café in Los Angeles. On the cover, a still cropped from the film *St. Elmo's Fire*, opening

28 June, showed Estevez, Lowe, and Nelson in the bar of the film's title. Blum described the extensive beer drinking, noting that by the end of his interview the men were on "their fifth or sixth round of Coronas" (47), and offered numerous less-than-positive examples of their behavior and attitudes: connecting with women at the bar, speaking dismissively of an actor who hasn't had recent success at the box office, and trying to get into a movie theater using clout rather than tickets. He said Estevez "is already accustomed to privilege and appears to revel in the attention heaped upon him almost everywhere he goes. He has a reputation in Hollywood as a superstud" (44). He assigned titles to these men and to others included in membership: Estevez as "unofficial president," Lowe, "The Most Beautiful Face," Nelson, "The Overrated One" (42). Blum acknowledged disputes over the actual membership in a disparaging way: "Everyone in Hollywood differs over who belongs. . . . That is because they are basing their decision on such trivial matters as whose movie is the biggest hit, whose star is rising and falling, and whose face is on the cover of *Rolling Stone* and whose isn't. And occasionally, some poor, misguided fool bases his judgment on whose talent is the greatest" (42). Blum's sarcastic remark about talent was matched by his refusal to suggest that any of these three were talented and his implicit criticism of their lack of acting training: "What distinguishes these young actors from generations past is that most of them have skipped the one step toward success that was required of the generation of Marlon Brando, and even that of Robert De Niro and Al Pacino: years of acting study" (43).[1]

Within two months, an article in *People* included a cautionary statement: "Don't mistake Michael J. Fox for another member of the Brat Pack. While Judd Nelson and Emilio Estevez and Rob Lowe are busy posturing in *St. Elmo's Fire*, Fox is becoming the hottest kid on the Hollywood block" ("Michael J. Fox Leaps into Stardom," 12 August 1985, 82). Implicit in the differentiation is the criticism of the other men as lacking Fox's personal charm. "Of course, it's too early to tell whether success will spoil this buoyant boy wonder. 'Family Ties' creator Gary Goldberg, who lauds Michael's down-to-earth values, predicts that it won't. 'I don't think Michael even knows what the Brat Pack is,' he says" (83).

A *GQ* reporter described him the next year as "the antidote to the Brat Pack and the answer to the country's future" (Bruce Buschel, "Little Big Man," *GQ*, December 1986, 227–28). Interestingly, Fox had read for John Hughes, who wanted to cast him as Ducky in *Pretty in Pink* (1986) but was unable to because of the "Family Ties" schedule. Hughes told Mark Morrison that Fox "was my favorite actor who I've never worked with" and contrasted him with members of the Brat Pack: "The Brat Packers all play things pretty serious; it's a brooding, more internal style. He's a very free guy—he just wings it. That excitement translates onscreen" ("Hottest Kid in Hollywood," *US*, 27 January 1986, 24). A writer in *Good Housekeeping* in 1987 contrasted his roots with those of the Brat Pack: Fox had "become a household name at an early age. Yet, unlike many of the today's 'brat pack' stars, he didn't have special advantages growing up" (Mimi Kashah, "Michael J. Fox by Michael J. Fox," August 1987, 54). The title of Desson Howe's review of *Bright Lights, Big City* alludes to the pack: "Bright Lights, Brat City." But he does not suggest Fox is like them. In fact, for Howe, "He does not seem the ideal casting choice at first" (washingtonpost.com, 1 April 1988).

## ☆☆☆★★  The Name Shame

Almost two years later, Blum still retained his terminology. In "The Brat Pack Strikes Back: Why One Writer Is Weary of His Words," Blum reflected on his 1985 commentary, noting that he would be rich if he had a nickel for every time the phrase had been used. But he stuck to the concept, saying the phrase was an "excellent way to describe the actors I'd gotten to know ever so slightly. . . . They had acted like—well, I might as well say it, brats" (*L.A. Times Magazine*, 21 June 1987, 8–9).

It is uncertain who exactly first used the phrase "Rat Pack," the obvious model for Blum's choice of names, but we do know that it came from someone within the group of stars from the 1950s and 1960s that included Lauren Bacall, Joey Bishop, Humphrey Bogart, Sammy Davis Jr., Judy Garland, Peter Lawford, Shirley MacLaine, and Dean Martin. It is important to realize that stories of the "Brat Pack" were being conveyed to teen audiences that would not have been aware of (and undoubtedly would not have cared about) these linguistic-historical roots. An unsigned article in *Teen* identified the members and suggested comparisons to contemporary readers: "Some of your parents' favorite actors—Frank Sinatra, Dean Martin, Sammy Davis Jr.—were known as the Rat Pack of the '60s. The Brat Packers of the '80s have a lot in common with these stars. Their career friendships carry over into their personal lives. Their movies make big bucks at the box office. And they can get away with almost anything, except an unsuccessful film" ("A New Look at the Brat Pack," *Teen*, June 1987, 56).

But unlike all the friends in the close-knit Rat Pack, whose members were already famous or well known by the time the term was applied to them, the young actors lumped into Blum's category and added immediately afterward were certainly not as well known or tightly connected.

While some had had some starring or supporting roles and others were friends, they were different in kind from their predecessors in that not every one knew the others. Even more to the point, as noted below, most of them inveighed against Blum and the title he had given them. That is, this was a membership designation imposed upon them from without.

The Hard Rock Café that served as the location of Blum's interview with three of them complemented the filmic primal sites that played into their identities as members: the school library in *The Breakfast Club* and the Georgetown hangout in *St. Elmo's Fire*. In the first, which appeared prior to Blum's article, Estevez, Hall, Nelson, Ringwald, and Sheedy spend a Saturday in detention for violating various school policies or committing infractions. One could argue, in fact (several months before the appearance of Blum's article), that they had acted like brats. The most serious punishable acts include Estevez's character bullying a classmate in the locker room, Hall's bringing a weapon to school, and Nelson's behaving generally like a thug.

In the second film, Estevez, Lowe, McCarthy, Moore, Nelson, and Sheedy play recent Georgetown University graduates trying to sort out their lives, without a lot of success. Again, their behavior is less than admirable: Estevez, the St. Elmo's bartender who immaturely pursues an older medical school student; Lowe, a philandering husband who neglects his family and young child; Moore, a coke addict out of a job (the actress's known drug problems were an inevitable subtext in this regard); Sheedy, a designer living with Nelson, an unprincipled operator who constantly cheats on her and switches political affiliations for advancement; and McCarthy, Nelson's journalist friend, secretly in love with Sheedy, who finally opts to choose neither at this time. (The only one of the friends who shows signs of maturity is played by Mare Winningham, who was not considered part of the Brat Pack and did not appear again with any of them.) The advertising for the film emphasized sensuality. When it opened, the full-page spread in the 28 June *New York Times* showed a photograph of the principal actors with the tag line: "The heat this summer is at St. Elmo's Fire" (C9). A subsequent ad two weeks later used a blurb from ABC TV's Joel Siegel: "This cast is the class of the summer of '85. They set St. Elmo's on fire" (12 July, C12). The reference to "summer of '85" alludes to *Summer of '42* (1971), a film about sexual initiation. The same heat motif theme appears in ads for *Blue City* (1986), a film with Nelson and Sheedy: "It's the coolest heat you'll ever feel" (*New York Times*, 2 May 1986, C15).

Although none of the advertisements for their films ever mentioned the Brat Pack, critics quickly acknowledged and appropriated the term. David Denby began his review by referring to his colleague's earlier article in *New*

*York Magazine*: "I'm gratified to have read in these pages that the young actors in *St. Elmo's Fire* dig one another . . . because nobody above the age of fifteen is going to like what they have done in their movie. On the other hand, the picture is a bash for pre-teens. . . . [The film] isn't drama, it's gossip, and peculiarly early-adolescent gossip. . . . The turbidly self-important treatment of these vacuous college graduates . . . is like a TV sitcom without jokes" (15 July 1985, 66). Rex Reed lacerated the film while raising a major question about the issue of the actors' status as stars: "Having established a new generation of stars nobody ever heard of, Hollywood is now risking a hernia trying to find suitable vehicles for them to star in. . . . The film serves only one purpose—to showcase the talents of seven new stars labeled 'Hollywood's Brat Pack'" (*New York Post*, 28 June 1985, 43). Of course, Blum hadn't mentioned any of the women as members in his list, but they were nonetheless included by Reed, as well as by Jack Kroll, who found the film "a cinematic Whitman's Sampler, a handy way to check out a generation of the new young stars who've become known as Hollywood's whiz kids, or brat pack" (*Newsweek*, 1 July 1985, 55).

The stigma of the Brat Pack figured in reviews of subsequent films. Nelson and Sheedy next appeared together in *Blue City*, a work with elements of film noir in which Nelson played a disaffected young man, assisted by Sheedy, trying to find out who murdered his father. The film performed weakly at the box office compared to *St. Elmo's Fire* ($6.9 million as opposed to $37.8 million), and was blasted by one critic who was put off by its blend of "youth-market" appeal with film noir (*Newsday*, 2 May 1986, 3:3). But the film offered Rex Reed evidence that "the Hollywood Brat Pack is not going to go away" (*New York Post*, 2 May 1986, 2).

The term continued to be used as a critical hammer in a review of *About Last Night* (1986), which follows the love affair of Lowe and Moore from a one-night stand through to love, separation, and finally the possibility of reunion. Even when praising Rob Lowe, two critics did so with backhanded slaps at the Brat Pack. One called it "one of the best American films of the year. . . . Rob Lowe, heretofore callow Brat Packer, is affecting" (Kroll, *Newsweek*, 14 July 1986, 69). Another said, "Rob Lowe at least proves himself to be more than just a pretty Brat Packer face" (Anne Bilson, *Monthly Film Bulletin*, 10 October 1986, 301).

Some reviewers noted the actors' extension of Brat Pack characteristics into different genres. One saw the cast of the teen-age vampire film *Lost Boys* (1987), in particular Kiefer Sutherland, as constituting "a second-generation brat pack" (Mike McGrady, *Newsday*, 31 July 1987, 5). Kim Newman commented skeptically on the youth-oriented stars of Christopher Cain's *Young*

*Guns* (1988), which concerns the early days of Billy the Kid, played by Estevez: *"Young Guns,* in this era of 'high concept,' announces itself through its teen magazine-oriented casting and use of an MTV rock soundtrack as the Brat Pack Western" (*Monthly Film Bulletin,* January 1989, 6).

Some reviewers were sympathetic to the way members of the group were used in films. Hughes, who wrote *Pretty in Pink,* in which Ringwald's character longs for a date to the prom with Andrew McCarthy's, was the object of a negative review: "As in *Sixteen Candles,* Ringwald walks through *Pretty in Pink* looking dazed. 'Why am I wearing such tacky sub-*Annie Hall* outfits?' her pained expression seems to ask. 'Because Hughes wants to make you the brat-pack Diane Keaton,' my empathic instincts answered" (Barry Walters, *Village Voice,* 4 March 1986, 60). In a review of *From the Hip* (1987), which starred Nelson, and *Mannequin* (1987), with McCarthy, Vince Aletta suggested a degree of sympathy for the Brat Packers, even as he criticized them, Hughes, and the industry: "As the brat pack grows up, gets its diplomas from John Hughes High, and sets forth into the wider world, you'd expect these spoiled, egocentric characters to have some trouble adjusting. But judging from two mess-for-success comedies of upward mobility . . . it's not the actors who can't handle adult life—it's Hollywood" (*Village Voice,* 3 March 1987, 59).

## ★★★★★ Denials

While Fox was if anything slightly bemused at finding himself in the "labyrinthine fun house of American mega-celebrity" as a result of the treatment he received by a variety of magazines, quite the opposite was true for the alleged members of the Brat Pack. Examination of interviews and articles reveals a curious disconnect. They criticized the imposition of the title and denied its appropriateness, but sometimes the description of their activities seemed to confirm the kind of clubby intimacy the title implied.

For example, writing on Sheedy—like Nelson, a child of wealth and privilege—Jeffrey Lantz reported: "Much has been made of the camaraderie of the so-called Brat Pack, but Ally doesn't socialize with the gang from *St. Elmo's Fire.* 'There's just not that much to say when we're not working. Most of my friends are not movie actors.' (Schumacher insists that the Brat Packers 'are all very separate individuals.') Between pictures, Ally writes in her journals, strolls the beach, reads philosophy" ("The Meteoric Rise of Hollywood's Busiest Young Actress," *American Film,* November 1985, 28). Somewhat contradicting this assertion, six months later John Skow said of

Sheedy, "Good sense rules her life although she's been known to wander off go-cart driving with Brat Packers Emilio Estevez and Judd Nelson" ("Greetings to the Class of 1986," *Time*, 26 May 1986, 72). A month later, according to Esther Fine, "She really hates reading that the current crop of young actors and actresses—herself as well as others such as Judd Nelson, Rob Lowe, Molly Ringwald and Emilio Estevez—has been labeled the 'brat pack'" ("Ally Sheedy's Film Career Tracks the Image of Youth in the 1980s," *New York Times*, 22 June 1986, 2:2).

Interviews reveal the actors' pronounced anger about Blum's article. In one, prior to the release of *Young Guns*, Estevez lamented the previous treatment of *Wisdom* (1986): "'Ultimately,' says Estevez, after noting that the film has received many compliments since it was released on cable, 'fuck the critics, 'cause they tried to really break me down, and the only thing it did is make me stronger—'cause everybody in Hollywood knew what they were doing, and the public knew what they were doing.' Why does he feel he was a target? 'I'm sure it was coming off the whole B.P. thing.' B.P.? Ahhh—Brat Pack. 'We're still fighting the term three years later'" (Fred Schruers, "Young Guns," *Premiere*, August 1988, 49). The next year Paul Freeman reported that Estevez "bristles at the Brat Pack label he picked up. . . . 'There was a stigma attached to that term. . . . We were portrayed as rude, money-grabbers who had unsavory lifestyles. It wasn't true'" (interview with Estevez, *TV Entertainment Monthly*, July 1989, 9).

Nelson became equally angry when discussing Blum's article a month after its appearance: "'I'm telling you . . . There are going to be a whole lot of stories coming out about all of us, this so-called gang of young Hollywood actors. But it won't be happening here, because we won't do them. Not after we got sandbagged by *New York Magazine*.' Nelson began breathing faster, scraping his hands along the brick. He was visibly agitated. 'If you'd asked me about the "Brat Pack" stuff first thing, it would have been a very short interview. . . . I'm so sick of every single person I talk to bringing up the "Brat Pack"'" (Rick Lyman, "Breakfast Club Street Punk Is St. Elmo's Yuppie," *Long Beach Press Telegram*, 10 July 1985, PT Extra, 5).

He was still smoldering two year later (and admittedly suffering from a hangover) during an interview with Jennifer Warren in which he expressed concern about the public's perception of him: "Nelson thinks it has everything to do with the 'Brat Pack' image, an outdated media label that refuses to die and has always made his blood curdle anyway. It's almost as if the public has confused his image with that of John Bender, the harsh unlikable character he played in *The Breakfast Club*" ("He Intimidates People Who Don't Like Him Because of That," *TV Guide*, 7 November 1987, 9). To counter such an image the writer quotes his friend Sheedy: "I *adore* him. . . . He's got a really warm heart" (10).

Anthony Michael Hall's publicity was tinged by his alleged membership. Even without referring to the Pack, at least one reviewer of John Hughes's *Weird Science* (1985), Hall's next film after *The Breakfast Club*, used language that evoked it: he had had "an honest sweetness" in *Sixteen Candles* in which he plays a geeky teenager who succeeds in losing his virginity, but "he is outgrowing the role. . . . He should be let out of the play pen to grown up on screen; he doesn't need to hold the patent on the bratty bright kid" (Sheila Benson, *L.A. Times Calendar*, 25 August 1985, 1). Even though he hadn't been mentioned in Blum's article, he made one of the earliest disavowals of any connection to the Brat Pack. He told *Los Angeles Times* reporter Kristine McKenna in August 1985: "The so-called Brat Pack was the invention of some journalist, and I don't consider those people my peer group. . . . I don't like being lumped in with a herd of people. . . . I have my own thing to say." In yet another example of how the media provide information designed to humanize stars, he's described as "not above the enthusiasm of a normal teen-ager. Arrive to interview him and music is blasting, his hats are sprawled around the floor, and he's eating Rice Krispies out of the box." More: "He's reading Dostoevsky and Malcolm X for enjoyment" ("Manchild in Filmland," 2 August 1985, 1, 13). Two years later, Laura Fissinger covered the young star in an article titled "Anthony Michael Hall: He's Sweet, He's Talented—and He Knows . . . The Ten Commandments of Surviving Teen Stardom." Among these is "Thou shalt have the right look." The writer uses this rule to contrast him with members of the Brat Pack: "No, not *that* look. Not the Rob Lowe pretty-boy look or the Judd Nelson angry-boy look or the Emilio Estevez smolder-boy look in any of the hottrotting brands of humma-humma in what is currently called 'Hollywood's Brat Pack'" (*US*, 26 August 1986, 46).

But by 1988, various examples of Hall's immaturity and personal lack of self-control had considerably lowered his reputation. McKenna was already treating her previous interviewee as someone making a comeback, in "On the Rebound with Anthony Michael Hall": "Hollywood hugged Hall when he was barely beyond childhood, sudden stardom nearly proved his undoing. Catapulted into the public eye at a point when he was going through his obligatory stint of teen-age rebellion." By this point Hall was already being perceived as a kind of failure. Although he had been the youngest member on "Saturday Night Live" in 1986, "'I was rude to a lot of people,' he confesses. 'I was drinking on the set . . . and had a problem with alcohol that I've taken steps to take care of'" (McKenna, "On the

Rebound," *Los Angeles Times*, 3 April 1988, 22, 344). He was dumped by Stanley Kubrick, who had chosen him to play Private Joker in *Full Metal Jacket* (1987).

The irony of McKenna's description of Hall as a normal teenager is underscored by an earlier article in *People* about Hall and Ringwald when they were making *Sixteen Candles* in 1984, prior to the coining of Blum's phrase. Accompanying the article are pictures of them with their on-set tutors; Hall is playing basketball with his. The writer cautions: "Do not think these are average kids. 'I'm not a typical teenager,' Molly announces . . . 'I'm not normal but that's good because if I were normal I'd be bored to death, really'" ("Sixteen Candles: Sweet Teens Graduate to Stardom by Acting their Age," 4 June 1984, 57–58). In fact, during the period 1984–1989, Ringwald's personal behavior emerged as among the most normal and least conflicted of all the alleged members of the group. The daughter of a stable marriage with a partially blind father, she appeared on the cover of *Time* with the caption "Ain't She Sweet" and was given a long and warmly written profile by Richard Corliss titled, "Well, Hello Molly!" (26 May 1986, 65–71). He didn't mention the dreaded Brat Pack name at all. Rather, he described talking with her and following her as she drove around Los Angeles shopping—an interesting contrast to Blum's description of hanging out with Estevez, Lowe, and Nelson as they went bar-hopping. Corliss cited Pauline Kael's assessment of Ringwald's "charismatic normality."

Andrew McCarthy, also a child of privilege and, like Nelson, a prep school graduate, was Ringwald's co-star and love interest in *Pretty in Pink* and *Fresh Horses* (1988), but they had no off-set relationship. McCarthy specifically denied any connection with the group, other than his presence in movies with them. An interviewer commented: "Mention the term 'Brat Pack' and McCarthy's eyes widen as he asks, 'What does it mean? That's just some writer being terribly clever. I don't live in L.A. I don't hang out at the Hard Rock Café. I don't know what it means when you're talking about Andrew McCarthy'" (Diana Maychick, "A Chat with a Brat," *Mademoiselle*, February 1986, 58). In an article that retrospectively surveyed them a decade later, McCarthy indicated that he "wants to set the record straight. He was never a Brat. 'The media made up this sort of tribe. . . . I don't think I've seen any of these people since we finished *St. Elmo's Fire*. And . . . I've never met Anthony Michael Hall'" (Samantha Miller and Dan Jewel, "The Brat Pack Actors, Once Everywhere, Went Mostly Nowhere," *People*, 19 April 1999, 116). His comment confirms the sense that both he and Ringwald had the most peripheral connection to the group and also, it should be noted, possibly the least controversial lives.

As to Demi Moore, Vanda Krefft lauded her in *Elle*: "Among Brat Pack peers, who often seem like roadshow versions of real stars, Moore distinguishes herself with genuine talent" ("Wising Up," August 1986, 26). The article included information about her personal life (the child of poor parents, a failed marriage, background working on *General Hospital*), commentary on her affection for her fiancée Estevez, with whom she was starring in *Wisdom*, his first film as director, information about her current reading (Dostoyevsky, Kundera), and details about the price of Moore's outfit for the photo shoot (a total of $1,160). In July 1986, Jack Curry suggested: "If Hollywood's Brat Pack had a women's auxiliary, Demi Moore would be the member of the sisterhood missing the most meetings" because of all her obligations and attention to personal development: "I feel like I'm on a constant search. It's an ongoing process of working out my character defects" ("Demi Moore: Brat Pack Distaffer," *Cosmopolitan*, July 1986, 116). Two years later, after she had married Bruce Willis, she appeared on the cover of *US* and was interviewed by Cyndie Stivers, who referred to her as "the Brat Pack Madonna" ("The *US* Interview," 16 May 1988, 15). Asked if she felt like part of the group, Moore said: "I never really tied it to me. I did *one* film with these people. I was, like, the outsider. But it wasn't like it was written. Emilio is one of the most gracious people I know, and it was strange to see him portrayed as this arrogant, ungrateful person. It was the guys going out—but I loved that they had this kind of friendship." She admits that she and Sheedy didn't have the same kind of "camaraderie [as the men]. I just didn't think we found what they did fun. We had our own [ways] 'Let's sit down, let's talk and steam vegetables.' For Ally and I, let me tell you, that would be about our speed" (18).

Even though Ringwald and Hall dated in 1984 while making *Sixteen Candles*, the only serious romantic relationship to occur in the group was between Estevez and Moore. This was featured prominently in coverage of them as he was making *Wisdom*, in which he and Moore become Bonnie and Clyde–style bank robbers in order to protect the financial rights of the poor. In a supportive article in 1986, Michael Danahy described the couple's behavior when Moore visited the studio: "They are planning a fall wedding. Both their careers are ablaze, and there is little time to waste. They smooch a bit, settle some details, exchange I-love-you's. . . . As soon as she is out of earshot, Estevez launches a salvo of not entirely bias-free praise. 'She's incredible in *About Last Night* . . . So in touch with herself and her emotions, and so relaxed'" ("Emilio Estevez's Running with a New Crowd These Days," *Globe and Mail*, 31 October 1986, D3). Moore had had several sex scenes with Rob Lowe in that film, an issue that was raised when he was

Demi Moore and Rob Lowe in *About Last Night*. Courtesy Photofest. Copyright Delphi V
Productions/TriStar Pictures, 1986.

interviewed in *Playgirl*. He talked about the awkwardness: "It's very difficult
going out with anyone in this business, and this is the first step to paying
the price. It hasn't affected any of our relationships. It's great, because now
Demi and I have a common ground, as well as Emilio and I" (Roberta
Smoodin, "Beautiful Dreamer: Thinking Out Loud with the Leader of the
Brat Pack," *Playgirl*, January 1987).

A related issue surfaced in relation to Nelson and Sheedy, who were
good friends. He responded to an interviewer's question about the awkwardness involved in doing a sex scene with Sheedy in *Blue City*: "Yes it was
very awkward. Probably the most awkward I've ever felt acting in my life.
. . . She is more like a sister. So we had to do this scene. I just didn't feel
right. I wanted to say, 'Wait a minute. An older brother should not do this
to a sister'" (Margy Rochelin, *Interview*, December 1986, 144).

A very different aspect of on-camera sexual behavior occurred in regard
to Rob Lowe, the son of wealthy parents and brother of Chad, another actor
and a pal of the Estevez-Sheen brothers. After hanging out with his friends
Nelson and Sheedy at the Democratic National Convention in Atlanta in
July 1988, he taped himself and another man having sex with two females
(one of them underage) in a hotel room. One of the females took the tape
and circulated it. It also included the record of an earlier sexual encounter,

this time with Lowe, a woman, and a man. Coverage of the ensuing notoriety, trial, and punishment (community service) often referred to his membership in the Brat Pack in addition to using captions for articles that played off on an uncanny connection to the winner of the Palme d'Or in Cannes in May 1989, Steven Soderbergh's *sex, lies, and videotape*. The most extreme example appeared in Mike Sager's article in *Rolling Stone*: "Rob Lowe's Girl Trouble: Sex, Litigation, and Videotape, How a Trip to the 1988 Democratic Convention Led to a Party He'll Never Forget" (24 August 1989). The article, which begins with a grainy photo of Lowe, seen from behind on the bed, describes how other magazines dealt with the scandal: "Shortly after the revelation of the sex tape, Lowe was pulled from the cover of *Teen* magazine's back-to-school issue. . . . In early June, a woman's clothing line bestowed upon Lowe the No Excuses Award. Lowe was pictured in a full page ad in *Women's Wear Daily*: How Lowe Can You Go?" (133). One article on the scandal included a reference to another disastrous career move. Citing him as "a prominent member of a group of young actors known collectively as the Brat Pack," the writer observed: "Most recently he was seen on the Academy Awards telecast dancing with Snow White and singing 'Proud Mary'" (Jacqueline Trescott, "Rob Lowe Sued over Pornographic Video," *Washington Post*, 20 May 1989, C9). That production number is commonly considered to be probably the worst in the entire history of the Academy Awards.

Michael J. Fox's personal development as an adult literally growing up in public view had proceeded in tandem with his growth as an actor taking more mature roles and asserting his identity and independence in a way that gave him the confidence and the authority to go back to *Back to the Future*. The second installment (1989) earned $119 million, the third (1990) $88 million. In contrast, the denial by the actors of their affiliation with the Brat Pack was a rather desperate and even pathetic attempt to assert their personal identities and refuse a construction foisted on them in "The Summer of 1985." Hall, Moore, Nelson, Sheedy, and Ringwald ended the decade with progressively underperforming films and diminished grosses. Only Estevez, with *Young Guns* in 1988 ($45 million), and McCarthy, with Ted Kotcheff's *Weekend at Bernie's* in 1989 ($30 million), had films that came close to or exceeded the earnings of either of the two films associated with the Brat Pack.

NOTES

1. He includes others, such as Tom Cruise, "The Hottest of Them All"; Timothy Hutton, "The Only One with an Oscar"; Matt Dillon, "The One Least Likely to Replace Marlon Brando"; Nicolas Cage, "The Ethnic Chair"; and Sean Penn, "The Most Gifted of Them All" (43). The fullest categorization of the Brat Pack appears in Pulver and Davies.

# 6 ★★★★★★★★★★★

# Eddie Murphy
## The Rise and Fall
## of the Golden Child

KRIN GABBARD

The first twenty-four minutes of *48 Hrs.* are entirely consistent with the other films that Walter Hill had directed. It opens with the villain, Albert Ganz (James Remar), staging a bloody escape from a prison road gang, complete with the over-Foleyed sounds of gunshots. Cut to Jack Cates (Nick Nolte), a blond-haired, barrel-chested detective with issues. After an argument with his girlfriend, Cates finds himself in a shoot-out at the hotel where Ganz and the man who helped him escape have settled in

*Beverly Hills Cop.* Courtesy Jerry Ohlinger. Copyright Eddie Murphy Productions/Paramount Pictures, 1984.

with a pair of prostitutes. While cops are bloodied and hysterical women are knocked about, Cates is forced to stand by and watch as Ganz kills a fellow detective with Cates's own large pistol. In a line that accurately describes most of the men in Hill's film, the prostitute who had been with Ganz before the fireworks says, "I think he likes shootin' cops better than he likes gettin' laid."

Searching for someone who can help him track down Ganz, Cates travels to a prison to speak with a former member of Ganz's gang, Reggie Hammond. Once inside the prison, Cates hears a falsetto voice punching out the lyrics to "Roxanne," a song made famous by the British rocker Sting. Even though the audience is not supposed to know that the voice belongs to Reggie Hammond until after Cates has spent almost an entire minute walking through the halls of the prison hearing the voice, the film has changed. It no longer belongs to Walter Hill. When we finally discover the source of the singing, we see Eddie Murphy as Reggie Hammond reclining in his jail cell, his eyes closed, his ears encased in headphones, singing his ass off. This young black man with the powerful falsetto bears no resemblance whatsoever to the unmusical, taciturn, hypermasculine heroes in most of Hill's work. Indeed, throughout the making of *48 Hrs.*, Murphy resisted Hill's direction, insisting on several changes to the script and to his character, a part that was originally written for Richard Pryor. Murphy even insisted that the name of his character be changed from "Willie Biggs" to "Reggie Hammond." At age twenty-one and in his first film, Eddie Murphy was already something of an auteur. Although witnesses say that there was friction on the set between Hill and Murphy, the director has said that he bears Eddie no ill will and that he is happy to continue cashing the large residual checks that *48 Hrs.* still brings him. In its first year of release, the film took in over $75 million in domestic rentals and was among the year's top moneymakers.

A book on stars of the 1980s is tailor-made for Eddie Murphy. No other star experienced so dramatic a rise and fall in a single decade. Between 1980 and 1989, Murphy moved from obscurity to popularity, then to spectacular popularity, and finally to a major decline. A great deal of his success was surely due to his ability to find the tiny needle's eye that African American entertainers had to pass through in the 1980s if they hoped to find a large audience. For most of the decade he managed to be *of* black America but not *in* black America. He was inevitably surrounded by white actors, and his characters' best efforts were almost always directed toward white people. After his many hits, however, audiences and reviewers were extremely disappointed by *Harlem Nights* (1989), the one and only film that

Eddie Murphy and Nick Nolte in *48 Hrs.* Courtesy Jerry Ohlinger. Copyright Paramount Pictures, 1982.

lists Murphy as both writer and director. It was also the first film in which he was joined by a large group of black performers in a milieu that, although it took place in a fantasy Harlem of fifty years earlier, was still Harlem. For this reason and a handful of others, Murphy definitively reached the bottom of a career arc in 1989.

## ★★★★★ A Precocious Impressionist

If you saw Eddie Murphy in his first seasons on "Saturday Night Live," you understand how he could so completely remake a film like *48 Hrs.*, not to mention *Trading Places* (1983) and *Beverly Hills Cop* (1984), the hugely successful vehicles that followed. With spot-on impersonations of everyone from Buckwheat to Richard Simmons and with a consummate sense of what works on camera, Murphy dominated every "Saturday Night Live" scene in which he appeared, even after he had just joined the cast in the 1980–81 season. Now, in the first post–Lorne Michaels season of the show, Murphy was surrounded by several mediocre comedians who, with the single exception of Joe Piscopo, did not last. In the next two seasons, Murphy was clearly the star and almost single-handedly brought back some of the glory of the original show.

By the early 1980s, writers for "Saturday Night Live" and many other shows were moving away from the type of ridicule regularly inflicted on black performers such as Garrett Morris, who consistently played stereotypes. But even if writers strayed in that direction, Murphy stopped it. He would not be cast in the Morris mold as a token African American. Virtually all the writers were white, middle-class graduates of elite universities. They had little sense of where Murphy should fit, and since he rejected much of what they wrote, he usually ended up on the set all by himself if he was on the set at all. In fact, in the first season he was not listed as a star but as a "featured performer." Even after Murphy had become the biggest star on the show, he was still alone on the stage on most occasions. But by this time, he was alone in sketches he himself had written, often with the few writers who understood his talent. "All you had to do with Eddie at that time was be a real good stenographer," said one writer (Shales and Miller 247).

Murphy's stunning success in his first Hollywood films must be considered alongside the fate of various other graduates from "SNL." Although we recall the first seasons of the show—with performers such as John Belushi, Dan Aykroyd, Chevy Chase, Gilda Radner, and Bill Murray—as a breakthrough in American humor and the history of television, with few exceptions, such as National Lampoon's *Animal House* (1978) with John Belushi and *The Blues Brothers* (1980) with Belushi and Dan Aykroyd, films that starred the original cast members were seldom successful. Murray, arguably the most distinguished actor among the first generation of "SNL" regulars, did not begin a period of critical acclaim until his breakthrough performance in *Groundhog Day* (1993). Eddie Murphy might have failed as he made his way through the cinematic wilderness after his early triumph on the show. He did indeed have his failures, but only after a run of such monumental success that it would have turned an ordinary mortal into a basket case. At least at first, Murphy managed to keep his head.

## ☆☆★★★ A Star Is Born

When he first caught the public imagination, the media constructed the young Eddie Murphy as a curious amalgam of streetwise ghetto boy and dutiful son from a middle-class Long Island suburb. The press was fond of pointing out his early escape from a bombed-out neighborhood in Brooklyn to the tree-lined streets of Roosevelt, Long Island. Murphy's biographers have reported that his father was killed by an angry girlfriend when Eddie was six, but in his interviews Murphy said that he barely remembered his natural father, who left his mother several years before his death. Murphy also neglected to mention that his mother became ill after the separation, and that Eddie and his brother spent time in foster care with an abusive woman Murphy would later call "a black Nazi." But after Murphy's natural mother recovered, she found a new husband. Murphy's stepfather was sufficiently affluent to transport the family to more comfortable surroundings in the year that Eddie turned eleven. Even though he was not a bad provider, the stepfather could be unpredictable and irascible. He also taught his sons how to box. Murphy regularly told interviewers about the night his stepfather came home drunk on a payday. He put a roll of bills on a table and told his sons that it was theirs if they could defeat him in a boxing match. According to Murphy, "We beat the shit out of the motherfucker" (Sanello 6). In the slightly romanticized, slightly racist imaginations of white Americans, Murphy had his share of street cred.

He also had a reputation as a stalwart young man devoted to his family and uninterested in drugs, alcohol, and even cigarettes. When CBS's "60 Minutes" devoted a segment to him in a 1983 broadcast, Murphy was filmed sitting on the floor next to shelves filled with books in an otherwise empty house. He had recently bought the house because of its proximity to his parents' home. The previous occupant had chosen to leave behind the books, thus providing the TV cameras with an opportunity to show Murphy settling into a household with at least the beginnings of classic domesticity. In this as well as in several other televised interviews, Murphy was consistently good-humored and agreeable, exhibiting none of the egomania for which he would soon become notorious. In the print media, however, his ego was on display, even at the same time that he was filming the CBS interview. He told *Ebony* magazine, for example, "When I die, I don't want to be stuck back there in a little box among the other obituaries. I want the front page" (Walter Leavey, "Eddie Murphy," *Ebony*, April 1983, 94).

Although Murphy seemed to have it all together from the first moment he stepped in front of the cameras on "Saturday Night Live," he probably proved his mettle most definitively when he was suddenly asked to do a part of his stand-up comedy routine at the end of the sixth show of his first season. Somehow the episode had wound down with four minutes to spare. Now, emerged from a childhood when he had devoted boundless energies to imitating everything from cartoon characters to Elvis Presley; profoundly influenced by the great African American comedians Bill Cosby and Richard Pryor no less than by Bob Hope; having long since perfected a large group of impressions; and following Richard Pryor's lead in making abundant use of profanity and African American slang, he was fully capable of making a smooth transition to G-rated entertainment when he was called upon at the last minute to do his stand-up act for NBC's cameras at the end of the im-perfectly scripted episode.

Murphy's early success on television was surely related to his ability to provide this kind of unthreatening crossover humor. Many of his routines on "Saturday Night Live" took an ironic approach to the popular entertain-ment that his middle-class childhood had made available to him but still emphasized his persona as a streetwise black man. Perhaps the best example of this unique blend of comic traditions was "Mr. Robinson's Neighbor-hood," a takeoff of the long-lived and popular PBS hit, "Mister Rogers' Neighborhood" (1968–2001). An ordained Presbyterian minister, Fred Rogers began each program by singing warmly about how much he wanted the young audience to be his friends, as he changed out of his sports jacket and into a cardigan sweater and settled into what was presented as his own house. Mr. Rogers was the perfect model for Murphy's Mr. Robinson, a black man in a shabby ghetto apartment. Like Rogers, Mr. Robinson had a benev-olent grin and a child-friendly mode of speaking. It soon became apparent, however, that a great deal of anger lay just below the surface of this pleas-ing demeanor. In one episode of "Mr. Robinson's Neighborhood," Murphy established that he, like the real Mr. Rogers, lived alone, but Murphy's char-acter made reference to a recently departed wife. "I'm so glad the bitch is gone," he exclaimed without abandoning his smiling delivery.

Murphy also delighted audiences with his impression of Buckwheat, another character extremely familiar to young adults who had grown up watching the old *Our Gang* comedies on television. With a fright wig and an extravagantly inaccurate system of pronunciation, Murphy's Buckwheat brought back vivid recollections of a character from another era of African American representation. Rather than embracing a racist stereotype, however, Murphy was bringing an ironic sensibility to his impression along with an infectious delight in the character's impenetrably happy demeanor. Much the same can be said of a completely different character, Raheem Abdul Muhammad, an angry militant who reviewed recent movies, always with the simple criterion of whether or not the films featured black people. When Ron Howard appeared on Raheem's program to promote his first major directorial effort, *Night Shift* (1982), Raheem was stunned to learn that the film was about pimps at the same time that it contained no black people. "I don't know whether to say thank you or punch you in your mouth, man," he exclaimed. Like Buckwheat, however, Murphy's Raheem always had a twinkle in his eye. It was obvious that Murphy took neither his character's politics nor his anger seriously and that he enjoyed sharing a laugh with the audience about the absurdity of it all. Writing in 1983 about Murphy's use of foul language, the critic Gene Lyons observed, "With Murphy you don't squirm, you giggle: he's not bad, just naughty—between the blue words he makes a point of letting audiences know he's the cleanest-cut comic around" ("Laughing with Eddie," *Newsweek*, 3 January 1983, 46). Much the same can be said of his television and movie personae.

Especially in the African American press, Eddie's abstemiousness was held up as a defense against his detractors, including several black ones. Fellow comedian Franklin Ajaye was especially critical of Murphy's imitations of Buckwheat, Raheem Abdul Muhammad, and another one of his "SNL" characters, a pimp named Velvet Jones. "Does he have any social consciousness?" asked Ajaye. Murphy responded by insisting that his humor in no way slowed the progress of African Americans. "It's stuff like 'The Jeffersons' that's a step back for blacks" (Leavey, "Eddie Murphy," *Ebony*, April 1983, 92).

But most African Americans were ecstatic about the success of Eddie Murphy on "Saturday Night Live." In the early 1980s, there were very few dynamic young black men on television who were not essentially castrated (think Jimmy Walker on "Good Times" or Emmanuel Lewis on "Webster"). A young, confident, attractive black man with an important role on a television program was virtually unknown. Not until 1984 did Bill Cosby take over the top spot in the TV ratings, but he did it playing the aging, thoroughly assimilated, unprovocative Cliff Huxtable.

Black audiences took special delight in one of Murphy's most famous sketches, "White Like Me." Supposedly relying on the services of the most talented African American makeup artists, Murphy enters the everyday world of New York City in the convincing guise of a white businessman. On a bus he encounters a group of typically jaded, willfully anonymous New Yorkers. When the only recognizably black person on the bus leaves, the group suddenly becomes a party. The bus driver turns on a recording of "Cabaret," and a female passenger rips off her coat and becomes a scantily clad cocktail waitress serving free drinks. Later, when the white-faced Eddie goes to a bank to ask for a loan, he is initially turned down by a black clerk. But an older white man in the bank tells the black man to take his break and smilingly hands a pile of cash to Murphy. "Just take what you want, Mr. White. Pay it back any time . . . or don't. We don't care." The sketch ends with Murphy and his staff of black makeup experts staring at the audience and warning them that they can never know if they are in fact dealing with "real" white people. In the "White Like Me" sketch, Murphy was speaking more directly than usual to his black audience. Later, he would put his career at peril by speaking to them even more directly. In general, Eddie Murphy has been most successful when he is, in the words of Manthia Diawara, "deterritorialised" from black culture (71).

## ★★★★★ They Called Him "Money"

Although in *48 Hrs.* Murphy was co-starring with the veteran leading man Nick Nolte, the success of the film has been accurately credited to Eddie Murphy and only to him. It would be difficult to imagine a twenty-one-year-old actor who had never even worked as an extra in motion pictures projecting so much self-confidence and professionalism in his first film. For one thing, as Reggie, Murphy does not let Nolte intimidate him. He never backs down or even blinks when Cates/Nolte gets up in his face. At the same time, he brightens many scenes with a light comic touch that was nonexistent in earlier films directed by Walter Hill. A good example is a scene shortly after Reggie's release into Cates's custody when the two go after Luther (David Patrick Kelly), another former member of the gang who may be able to lead them to Ganz. After Luther takes a shot at Cates, the detective chases Luther out of his apartment. Reggie opens a car door at the exact right moment so that Luther bangs into it and takes a pratfall. As Luther lies on the street in pain, Reggie, smiling, asks pleasantly, "What's happenin,' Luther? I'm sorry about the door, man. Did that hurt? It looked real painful when you slammed into it." This line was clearly written by Eddie. Early in the filming process, he refused to use terms such as "jive turkey" and "sucka" that were in the first draft of the script and were more typical of Hollywood Blackspeak.

The most famous scene in *48 Hrs.* comes halfway through the film when Reggie walks into Torchy's, a bar for wannabe cowboys, one of whom actually yells "Yee Hah" as he watches a bare-breasted dancer in chaps and a cowboy hat. Reggie quickly takes complete command of the situation, letting no one in the large collection of entirely hostile whites get the better of him. He expertly punches out the first man who challenges him and threatens to destroy the bar if he does not get the information he seeks. It is at Torchy's that he utters his famous line to a crowd of beer-drinking rednecks: "I'm your worst fuckin' nightmare. A nigger with a badge, and that means I got permission to kick your fuckin' ass whenever I feel like it."

At its conclusion, *48 Hrs.* continues to function simultaneously as a hard-boiled Walter Hill thriller and as an Eddie Murphy comedy. Having finally cornered the sociopathic Ganz, Cates has a showdown with the villain in a back alley. Ganz, however, has grabbed Reggie and holds him up as a shield while pointing a gun to his head. Reggie yells at Cates, urging him to shoot Ganz as quickly as possible. Like a gunfighter in the Old West, a grimly determined Cates gets off a fast shot to Ganz's chest before any harm comes to Reggie. With Ganz expiring hysterically ("I can't believe it. You shot me!"), Reggie is even more hysterical. Appalled that the dour, purposeful Cates actually took the shot, he shouts, "Are you crazy? I was bluffin'!" Right up until the end, the two stars are perfect foils.

Indeed, the relationship that develops between Cates and Reggie may be what gave the film so much traction with audiences. It should come as no surprise that serious bonding between black and white heroes is completely consistent with Hollywood ideology. When a white man and a black man co-star, we are likely to see racial tension develop early, as when Cates refers to Reggie as "Watermelon." By the end, however, as the two begin to collaborate and grow to respect each other, they even develop some mutual affection. This was the case in *The Defiant Ones* (1958), *In the Heat of the Night* (1967), *Silver Streak* (1976), *Lethal Weapon* (1987), *Die Hard* (1988), *Robin Hood: Prince of Thieves* (1991), and many other Hollywood films. Even before the birth of the cinema, we can find the same situation in *Huckleberry Finn*, *Moby Dick*, and *The Last of the Mohicans*, American novels in which white men have life-changing encounters with a male, colored Other. As many critics in literary and cinema studies have argued (Fiedler; Gabbard; Penley; Pfeil; Wiegman; Willis), fantasies of a white man and a black man finding their common humanity essentially let white Americans off the hook. If, like the heroes of these books and films, a white man can win the love and devotion of a single powerful, dark-skinned man, a great deal of history can be forgotten and overcome. All those years of repression, disenfranchisement, and racial hatred can be erased, at least for the white man who can point to his dark friend and claim to be innocent of it all. White people who become emotionally involved in these representations of white/black bonding have an even easier time of it.

If only white racism were so easily overcome and the past so easily forgiven. But there is more to this fantasy than simple reconciliation. For one thing, it inevitably requires that the black man remain subservient on some level, on occasion even sacrificing himself for the white protagonist. For another, the black man is typically denied the real freedoms available to his white mate. Consider the conclusion of *48 Hrs.* Cates gives Reggie permission to spend some time with Candy (Olivia Brown), an attractive woman he has met in a bar. With Ganz and his gang safely dispatched, the white cop waits patiently for Reggie to finish so that he can escort him back to prison. We see Reggie saying good-bye to this especially agreeable young black woman. It is clear that the two have made love and that Candy has feelings for Reggie. In matter-of-fact fashion, however, Reggie assures her that he will be back in six months and that he will take her out for dinner. Out on the street, he shows much more emotion when he reconciles with Cates, even lighting his cigarette. Cates immediately realizes that Reggie has stolen his lighter, but they now speak as equals, and for the first time in the film, Cates smiles.

Gender analysis is especially important for Murphy's early work because he has presented himself as an attractive black man with strong sexual desires, even if he is often asexual in his films. The scenes with Olivia Brown in *48 Hrs.* are practically anomalous in his films of the 1980s. Murphy would surely not have been quite so successful if his blackness and his sexuality were not so thoroughly contained during this decade.

Even in the Torchy's sequence in *48 Hrs.*, where Reggie successfully intimidates a house full of hostile patrons, he finds ways to make himself less threatening to the white members of his audience. After he tells the crowd at Torchy's that "there's a new sheriff in town, and his name is Reggie Hammond," he bulges his eyes in what is clearly a reference to minstrel traditions. Shortly after he has acquired some useful information and walked calmly out of the bar without a scratch, he says to Cates, "I'll be good from now on, Mr. Cates," imitating Eddie "Rochester" Anderson, the loyal retainer of Jack Benny and another figure with roots in plantation stereotypes. Don't forget that when Reggie sings "Roxanne" at the beginning of a film, he has taken up a song associated with a white Brit rather than with a black American. Not to put too fine a point on it, but the African American singing group performing in the one black bar Reggie visits, and the source of the film's theme song, "(The Boys Are) Back in Town," has adopted a highly unthreatening title, the Busboys.

Herman Beavers has also noticed the powerfully erotic component to Murphy's performance during the Torchy's scene. When Reggie walks into the bar, the camera dwells on a bare-breasted dancer entertaining the patrons. She is clearly the center of attention for much of the opening section of this sequence. But the stripper completely disappears when Reggie declares his presence. He has thoroughly replaced the erotic dancer as the object of the gaze (Beavers 269). Although the film casts Reggie as the hypermasculine center of the action, there is no denying the degree to which his violence and male display are eroticized, especially in a space that was completely sexualized just moments earlier by the female stripper.

In *Beverly Hills Cop*, Murphy is cast in an extremely similar situation when he leads the two white cops assigned to be his chaperones into a "titty bar." Once again, a major action sequence immediately follows the prominent exhibition of female flesh. In fact, the film incrementally allows Murphy's masculine display to replace the sight of naked female dancers. As he approaches the man who is about to pull out a large gun and demand the attention of the crowd, Murphy is centered in the foreground with a topless dancer on either side in the background. When he disarms the man with the rifle, he has made himself the undeniable center of attention, taking over from the criminal and the topless dancers who, like the bare-breasted woman at Torchy's, have disappeared.

If Murphy is the spectacular center of these films, he is also radically removed from black culture in virtually all his highly successful films in the early and mid-1980s. As Beavers points out in an essay that may be the most thorough analysis of Murphy's success, Murphy is seldom if ever portrayed within black culture. White viewers remain in their comfort zones because Murphy never ignites their anxiety about black people in groups. And his characters also express very little concern about his own people, inevitably devoting their efforts to situations involving white people only.

In *Trading Places*, Billy Ray Valentine has a few connections to the black community in the early scenes when he buys drinks for a group of prostitutes and tough-looking black men he met in prison. The filmmakers can only conceive of black culture in terms of freeloaders and ex-convicts. But Billy Ray unequivocally separates himself from all black characters once he acquires the assets and power of white capital. He is never again in the presence of black people until the final seconds of the film (although in one scene he is joined by Louis Winthorpe [Dan Aykroyd], who appears in blackface). In *Beverly Hills Cop*, Murphy's Axel Foley is never part of black

Eddie Murphy and Dan Aykroyd in *Trading Places*. Courtesy Jerry Ohlinger. Copyright Cinema Group Ventures/Paramount Pictures, 1983.

culture. He leaves Detroit for California after his white friend Mikey (James Russo)—a ne'er do well, but one who says to Murphy's character, "I love you, man"—is killed by the film's villains. Throughout *Beverly Hills Cop*, no black character plays any meaningful role in Axel's world.

Murphy's character is especially asexual in *Beverly Hills Cop*. When he arrives in Beverly Hills, Axel has a reunion with an attractive and well-dressed white woman, Jenny Summers (Lisa Eilbacher), presented as an old friend. The film never explains how a working-class black man like Axel Foley and an upper-middle-class white woman like Jenny can have a history together. And a nonsexual one at that. The part of Axel Foley was originally intended for Sylvester Stallone, and although the script had undergone numerous rewrites after Murphy joined the cast, the screenwriters clearly wanted to maintain Axel's extreme separation from black culture. In *Trading Places*, Winthorpe/Aykroyd meets and falls in love with a gorgeous prostitute played by Jamie Lee Curtis. Much of the film is devoted to their developing relationship, and they are together on the tropical island at the film's absurdly happy ending. In these same final moments of the film, Billy Ray is suddenly in the company of a bikini-clad black woman. She appears as if by magic, smiles, and utters not a word. *Trading*

*Places* has no idea how to conceive of a sympathetic black female who might actually be a good match for a character played by Murphy.

Nevertheless, in spite of the carefully circumscribed sphere in which Murphy's characters operated, he was still unusually empowered for a young black man in the America of the early 1980s. At the beginning of the Age of Reagan and Bush, young black men were still a source of major anxiety for most white Americans, and very few young black performers were granted as much license as Murphy in the scrupulously monitored, highly homogenized world of network television. Even as late as 1988 George H. W. Bush could be elected president by terrifying white Americans with television commercials built around Willie Horton, the sinister-looking black convict who assaulted a white couple in their home while he was on furlough from a Massachusetts prison. The voters' terror of young black males may explain why Murphy so often played a cop. He could be free-spirited, but he was always thoroughly bound by The Law. In no way could he be mistaken for Willie Horton.

In fact, I am tempted to suggest that the razor-thin Murphy of the 1980s and 1990s, who knew how to appeal to white Americans, set the stage for another slim black man, Barack Obama. In a rare co-authored essay, two critics for the *New York Times*, Manohla Dargis and A. O. Scott, have argued that the election of Obama must be seen in the context of a long parade of extremely popular African American performers. They point out that James Earl Jones, Morgan Freeman, Chris Rock, and Dennis Haysbert actually played the American president in movies or in a TV show ("How the Movies Made a President," 18 January 2009, Arts and Leisure, 1, 9). The critics also suggest that Sidney Poitier, Bill Cosby, Samuel L. Jackson, Will Smith, and several other black performers helped prepare Americans for an Obama presidency in one way or another. But the two only devote a few sentences to Murphy, who was actually born in 1961, the same year as Obama. No other young, brash, black performer ever charmed white Americans—and put them at ease—as compellingly as did Eddie Murphy. Dargis and Scott do not seem to understand that Obama might not have been received so warmly by so many if Murphy had not already taught white Americans that they can trust a young, ambitious, and dynamic black man.

## ★★★★★ Delirious and Derailed

If he was thoroughly deracinated from African American culture in his early work, Eddie Murphy was even more isolated in his two stand-up comedy films, *Eddie Murphy Delirious* (1983), originally broadcast on HBO, and *Eddie Murphy Raw* (1987), which had a theatrical release. In fact, except for a brief prologue in the second film, he is the only person onscreen for the duration of both. Whites could laugh at his transgressive, scatological patter and congratulate themselves on their appreciation of black culture. The white men in Murphy's audiences may even have fantasized about having some of the comedian's spontaneity and bravado, not to mention the sexual prowess he claims to possess. It was not the first time that whites have envied the masculine equipment of blacks. As Eric Lott has argued, white Americans were simultaneously ridiculing blacks and celebrating their phallic power as early as the 1830s in that uniquely American institution, the minstrel show. We can still see whites appropriating African American gestures of masculinity every time the white athlete spikes the ball and high-fives his teammates, every time the white rocker gyrates his hips and injects the gravel of authenticity into his voice, and every time the white comedian makes generous use of the word "motherfucker."

As a white Leftist, however, I take very little pleasure in watching *Delirious* and *Raw*. I found the films distasteful on first viewing, and I find them even more so now. For me, the gynophobia, homophobia, and narcissism that Murphy unceasingly projects in the concert films cast a shadow backward onto the Hollywood films and even onto the early appearances on "Saturday Night Live." Murphy's vile statements about gays and women in his stand-up routines make the traces of misogyny, homophobia, and macho posturing in the early work much more obvious and disturbing.

As Murphy himself freely admits in *Delirious*, his stand-up style comes from Richard Pryor. But if Pryor made abundant use of sexual slang and regularly referred to women as "bitches," he also projected vulnerability and even impotence. Murphy came of age in a middle-class household on Long Island and says that he never encountered racism during his childhood. Pryor grew up in his grandmother's brothel in Peoria, Illinois, and had more than his share of encounters with white racists. If Murphy's imitation of, say, Richard Simmons was dead-on, Pryor could be completely convincing when he impersonated several different breeds of talking dogs. And Pryor seldom if ever used foul language simply for shock effect. Not so Murphy, who was not ashamed to dwell on bathroom humor at length. We can draw a family tree with Dick Gregory and Bill Cosby at the trunk and a large limb for Pryor leading to a sprout for Murphy. After Murphy we can imagine new sprouts for Chris Rock, Wanda Sykes, and Dave Chapelle, but we would also have to posit a direct link between Murphy and Andrew "Dice" Clay, who spent a large portion of his act simply reciting obscene nursery rhymes.

And like Clay in his stand-up routines, Murphy is profoundly homophobic. Murphy begins *Delirious* by declaring that he is "afraid of gay people." He says he keeps moving around so that they can't watch his ass. And yet, Murphy appears in a flashy outfit with a brightly colored jacket matching his tight trousers. As E. Patrick Johnson has argued, black men need the image of the gay man to establish their masculine *bona fides*. They are then protected against charges that they themselves might be gay, a charge that is not unreasonable for a man like Murphy who displays himself on stage in tight pants. And who stripped down to his underpants on more than one occasion on "SNL." And whose movie characters inevitably have more intense relationships with men than with women. And who in 1997 was pulled over by police after he invited a male transvestite prostitute to join him in his car.

Just a few months after the release of *Delirious*, Murphy seemed to be backtracking from his homophobia in several scenes in *Beverly Hills Cop*. When he shows up at Harrow, the expensive club where he intends to face down the film's villain, Axel Foley gains entrance to the members-only restaurant by asking to speak with the film's villain, Victor Maitland (Steven Berkoff). Murphy himself wrote the dialogue for the moment when he adopts a gently effeminate demeanor and tells the maître d' that he needs to speak with Victor, "the gray-haired gentleman, very dark skin, Capricorn. Victor." When he explains that he must tell Victor that he has just come back from the clinic where he learned that he has "herpes simplex ten," the maître d' is happy to admit him to the restaurant so that he can deliver the message in person. At least for me, this impression of a gay man is funnier than it is offensive. Similarly, Murphy's Axel has great tolerance for Serge (Bronson Pinchot), the quirkily effeminate assistant in Maitland's art gallery. Axel even seems to enjoy the back-and-forth with Serge as much as Serge enjoys bantering with Axel. And early in *Beverly Hills Cop*, when Axel passes two men on the street dressed in outfits very similar to the one that Murphy had worn earlier in *Delirious*, he laughs out loud. Although he seems to be having a laugh at the expense of overdressed gay men, we can assume that he is also sharing an in-joke with fans who recognize the outfit. Are we to assume that Murphy is laughing at the idea that gay men would attempt to dress like him?

Homosexuality was not a topic in the bizarre Murphy vehicle from 1986, *The Golden Child*. As with all of Murphy's big-money films, Eddie played a role created for another star, in this case Mel Gibson. Even more so than in his previous films, Murphy's Chandler Jarrell is outside black culture in *The Golden Child*; although, as always, he speaks in African

American argot and expresses bewilderment at the cultural norms of the white mainstream. When the audience first meets Chandler, he is a Good Samaritan looking for information about a missing white child. The plot laboriously assigns him the complex and ultimately supernatural task of protecting a small Asian boy, clearly a fantasized version of the Dalai Lama. Not entirely asexual this time, Chandler is on the verge of a relationship with an attractive woman who appears to be South Asian, Kee Nang (Charlotte Lewis), one of several characters devoted to protecting the Golden Child. Even though she initially resists Chandler's advances, he chooses to sleep on the couch when she finally decides to invite him into her bed. Once again audiences are denied a scene with a sexualized Murphy. *Daily Variety* gave a good summary of *The Golden Child*: "A strange hybrid of Far Eastern mysticism, treacly sentimentality, diluted reworkings of Eddie Murphy's patented confrontation scenes across racial and cultural boundaries, and dragged-in ILM special effects monsters, film makes no sense on any level" (1 January 1986). It was his biggest critical failure to date.

In *Coming to America* (1988), Murphy was finally placed firmly in black culture, at least at first. But it is an African culture that has never existed. Playing an African prince looking for an American bride, Murphy was cast in a fantasy even more grotesque than *The Golden Child*. The film begins in the fictional African country Zamunda, where the royal family resembles medieval Arthurian royalty far more than modern postcolonial subjects. Ultimately, the film has little to say about the lived conditions of Africans and African Americans. Murphy's most interesting work in the film is not as the naïve African prince but as the several characters he plays under heavy makeup. As an aged black barber, a Jewish kibitzer at the barber shop, and a Rick James imitator, Murphy does some of his most original acting and paves the way for his polymorphous performances in the *Nutty Professor* films and much of the work that followed.

But *Coming to America* is probably best known for the lawsuit brought by newspaper columnist Art Buchwald, who claimed that the story by Murphy on which the film is built was stolen from a treatment he had written a few years earlier. The trial dragged on for several years, and Murphy and many in his entourage—which numbered approximately fifty employees at this time—testified at length about his business affairs. What little privacy Murphy had left was further compromised as the press regularly reported on a succession of unhappy affairs with women. Buchwald eventually received a small settlement that hardly covered his legal fees, but the shortfall did not stop several aggrieved and not-really-aggrieved parties from filing new lawsuits against Murphy and his production company. An actress named Michael Michele notoriously sued him for sexual harassment.

During the several years in which Murphy was making strikingly mediocre films such as *The Golden Child, Beverly Hills Cop II* (1987), and *Coming to America*, he was also giving up on his short-lived career as a vocalist. Partially because of the negative reviews his first recordings received, he committed a major career faux pas in 1985 and declined Stevie Wonder's request to appear in "We Are the World," the music video in which a large contingent of rock stars worked for free to raise money for famine relief in Africa. Everyone involved in the project came off smelling like a rose. The press congratulated all the singers for leaving their egos at the door when they made a video for a good cause. Perhaps an even bigger career mistake came a few years earlier when Murphy decided not to take the role played by Bill Murray in the mega-hit *Ghost Busters* (1984).

Nevertheless, all of Murphy's films prior to 1989 made good money: *48 Hrs., Trading Places, Beverly Hills Cop, Beverly Hills Cop II,* and *Coming to America* were all among their year's top five box-office performers. Even *The Golden Child* was the eighth biggest moneymaker of 1986. Murphy finally flopped with *Harlem Nights*, the first film for which he is listed as director and the first film for which he received sole writing credit. In the same year as the release of *Harlem Nights*, the ambitious television program "Who's Alan Watching," which Murphy produced and occasionally appeared in, was canceled.

Although Murphy is the star of *Harlem Nights*, the film's central character is arguably Sugar Ray, the owner of a lavish casino played by Richard Pryor. In *Eddie Murphy Raw*, his second concert film, Pryor is an important if unseen presence. Early in the stand-up act, Murphy does a spot-on imitation of Bill Cosby, who apparently called Murphy on the telephone and urged him to clean up his act. By portraying Cosby as sanctimonious and even prissy, Murphy inoculates himself against Cosby's charge that he was doing harm to young people who so admired Murphy that they dutifully imitated his prolific use of profanity. In his act, Murphy says that he ended his conversation with Cosby by saying, "I'm offended that you called. Fuck you." He then called Pryor to report the details of his conversation with Cosby. Murphy says that Pryor took his side, even adding, "Next time the motherfucker calls up, tell him he can suck *my* dick."

Pryor gives a surprisingly understated performance in *Harlem Nights*. In fact, so does Murphy. Eddie seems more interested in playing the stud than the comedian. Sadly, his idea of a powerful male figure is expressed in some extremely gynophobic moments, most notably in an extended fistfight with

Eddie Murphy and Richard Pryor in *Harlem Nights*. Courtesy Jerry Ohlinger. Copyright Eddie Murphy Productions/Paramount Pictures, 1989.

a madam played by Della Reese. The slugfest ends when Murphy's character realizes that he cannot win a bare-knuckled contest with this sturdy and
angry black woman. So, he shoots her in the foot with a pistol. Later in the
film he shoots another woman, this time leaving her dead. As it stands, the
film's extreme misogyny suggests that Murphy's anger against women was
allowed to boil over when, as the uncontested auteur of the film, he could
take the lid off his id.

In making *Harlem Nights* his own personal project, Murphy was surely
inspired by the sudden rise of Spike Lee in the late 1980s. Lee's first films
owed a fair share of their success to the richly compelling music composed
by the director's father, Bill Lee. Murphy saw to it that *Harlem Nights*—his
own attempt to reach a hungry black audience—also had great black music.
He hired the distinguished jazz pianist and composer Herbie Hancock, who
had played brilliantly with the Miles Davis Quintet in the early 1960s before
beginning a long career as a bandleader, composer, accompanist, and auteur
of music videos, such as the memorable "Rockit." He also provided music
for the inspired but suppressed film by Ivan Dixon, *The Spook Who Sat by the
Door* (1973), as well as Michelangelo Antonioni's sexy puzzle film, *Blow-Up*
(1966). For *Harlem Nights*, Hancock engagingly reproduced several songs
and arrangements by Duke Ellington who, more than any other composer
in the New York of the 1920s and 1930s, transcended the music of the dance
hall. Hancock's selection of music from the Ellington canon accurately

reflected Harlem night life in the 1930s when the action of the film supposedly takes place.

If the music is right, however, very little else is. For a film set in the 1930s, *Harlem Nights* is full of anachronisms such as fully integrated nightclubs, highly empowered black businessmen, and an easily outmaneuvered white power structure. The narrative is a confusing arrangement of poorly linked incidents. For the first time ever, a Murphy film lost money. Early in Murphy's career, Gene Lyons and Peter McAlevey wrote in *Newsweek*, "Eddie can tiptoe along the narrow line between anger and laughter in a way that shows everybody how silly we are to imprison ourselves with racial stereotypes. He thinks he can walk that line in his career" (7 January 1985, 48). But as the critics darkly hinted, Eddie was not able to sustain this elaborate balancing act. By presenting himself as a murderous but sexy black man in *Harlem Nights*, he also lost his white audience.

After his flop with *Harlem Nights*, it took Murphy several years to realize that he had a much better shot at retrieving his popularity if he connected with children and the childlike tastes of the mass audience. His star rose again in 1996 with *The Nutty Professor*, but only after he put quotation marks around his portrayal of that priapic sex machine, Buddy Love, the alter ego of the inept Professor Klump in *The Nutty Professor*. The real Eddie, the film suggested, was not the stud but rather the fat and lovable Klump. Regardless of how we wish to characterize this transformation in the history of African American representation, Murphy regained his stardom by definitively renouncing the potent black man he had so unsuccessfully embodied in *Harlem Nights*.

# 7 ★★★★★★★★★★★★
# Sigourney Weaver
## Woman Warrior, Working Girl

CHRIS HOLMLUND

For Sigourney Weaver, the 1980s were golden. Heartthrobs like Mel Gibson, William Hurt, Michael Caine, and Harrison Ford partnered her onscreen. She worked with top Hollywood directors, among them Ridley Scott, Mike Nichols, and Ivan Reitman. She earned three Academy Award nominations: Best Actress for *Aliens* (1986), Best Supporting Actress for *Working Girl* (1988), and Best Actress for *Gorillas in the Mist* (1988). Her face appeared on magazine covers. She did photo shoots for *Vogue* and *Harper's Bazaar*, modeling outfits designed by Karl Lagerfeld, Giorgio Armani, and Valentino Garavani. Her supporting performance in *Ghost*

139

*Busters* (1984) helped make that movie the highest grossing comedy at the time (nearly $240 million), and *Ghostbusters II* (1989) earned over $112 million in the United States alone. *Working Girl* did excellent business, too, taking in nearly $64 million domestically. By summer's end of 1986, almost as many people knew—and loved—Weaver's *Aliens* character, Ripley, as had cheered Stallone's pumped up ex-Vietnam vet Rambo in 1985. *Aliens* raked in $85 million domestically, another $46 million abroad. In mocking homage to Stallone, Weaver named the bellicose babe she played "Rambolina."

But Weaver was never really interested in being a star. "I prefer not to have any image, or any one image," she insisted (William McDonald, "Sigourney Weaver Eludes the Image Police," *New York Times*, 7 December 1997, Arts 17). Only with *Gorillas in the Mist* did she relish doing television and print promotional interviews, in large part because she liked educating viewers about the importance of protecting the gorillas. Her reluctance to appear in public means that a mere handful of interviews and articles rehearse her life during the decade, and only one unauthorized biography has ever been published about her.

## ★★★★★ Assiduous Actress, Reluctant Royalty

For Christine Geraghty, Sigourney Weaver's performances as Ripley demonstrate a "consistent sense of self" that seems to make her a "professional" star (197). At four *Alien* films and counting, she remains the only woman with an action franchise. But Geraghty qualifies her initial appraisal, citing several 1980s films as proof that Weaver's stardom is more complex than that of a "professional" star. Popular reportage comes to similar conclusions; witness Vanessa Lawrence's comment that "diversity is perhaps Weaver's strongest professional trait" ("Pillar of Strength," *Scoop*, March 2007, 46).

This diversity is partially attributable to the range of genres in which Weaver performed in the 1980s. But these genres are nevertheless linked, evidence of what Andrew Britton terms the "historical interpenetration of the genres" ("Stars and Genre" 203). In tune with the need to please multiple constituencies in theaters and audiences watching at home on video, the bigger-budget films in which Weaver performs during the 1980s consciously tap narrative, visual, and sonic elements drawn from and shared by several genres. And all somehow respond to contemporaneous foreign and domestic concerns such as: Who are "our" enemies? Do we have a responsibility to protect the environment, to save endangered species? Should women engage in combat? Are women warriors sexually appealing or unattractive, unwomanly? Should women be mothers first and foremost, or is it okay for them to work outside the home, to have careers?

Consider the character types, trumpeting tag lines, and multifaceted plots of Weaver's highest grossing and most critically acclaimed vehicles in this decade:

1. *The Year of Living Dangerously* (1982). Beautiful British Embassy attaché/ possible secret agent Jill Bryant (Weaver) succumbs to the charms of ambitious Aussie reporter Guy Hamilton (Mel Gibson) in steamy, riot-torn Indonesia under the watchful eye of dwarf Billy Kwan (Linda Hunt). Theirs is "a love caught in the fire of revolution." Set in 1965, a political thriller full of romance and drama.

2. *Ghost Busters*. Hard-working cellist Dana Barrett (Weaver) finds a hideous ghost in her refrigerator. "Who ya gonna call? Ghost busters!" When dark spirits turn her into a sex-obsessed, growling ghoul, her date, parapsychologist Dr. Peter Venkman (Bill Murray), along with his team of goofy co-workers, rescue her and save the city of New York from destruction. A slapstick comedy with romance, science fiction, and action overtones.

3. *Aliens*. "This time it's war" and "this time there's more." Forty-seven years after her first horrific experiences in space, warrant officer Ellen

*Aliens'* lovely, lonely leader of the pack. With the help of Space Marines and her right-hand "man," Private Vasquez (Jenette Goldstein, to Weaver's right), Warrant Officer Ripley takes on the aliens again. Courtesy Jerry Ohlinger. Copyright Twentieth Century-Fox Film Corporation, 1986.

Ripley (Weaver) is back in action fighting blood-sucking, death-dealing aliens. This time she is accompanied by a crew of gun-toting Space Marines and a little orphaned girl. Her foes, a giant egg-laying mother and myriad insect spawn, are helped by a yuppie traitor. Terror, death, and destruction culminate in a battle of the super moms. A science fiction/action/war film mélange.

4. *Gorillas in the Mist.* "In a land of beauty, wonder and danger, she would follow a dream, fall in love and risk her life to save the mountain gorillas from extinction." "At the far ends of the earth she found a reason to live, and a cause to fight for." In 1966, self-taught primatologist Dian Fossey (Weaver) travels to the mountains of the Belgian Congo and Rwanda to save the gorillas. In 1985, she is mysteriously murdered. Her beloved gorillas live on. An adventurer biopic with more than one love story.

5. *Working Girl.* A Cinderella success story for secretaries, heralded as "For anyone who's ever won. For anyone who's ever lost. And for everyone who's still in there trying." Tess McGill (Melanie Griffith) takes Wall Street by storm, replacing her conniving witch of a boss, Katherine Parker (Weaver), and stealing her handsome stock-trader boyfriend (Harrison Ford) into the bargain. A romantic fairy tale comedy.

As a supporting grid, the historically "interpenetrated" genres evidenced by these films, and by Weaver's lesser films as well, "constitute a distinct sub-set . . . of conventional relations which always precede the star" and render Weaver's stardom possible (Britton, "Stars and Genre" 198). A soupçon of romance, an insistence on independence, the ability to take action, the willingness—nay eagerness—to work outside the home and explore new lands all hew to generic conventions and provide common traits among her characters. Add to these baseline attributes a hefty dose of motherhood as "nature" and "nurture" in *Aliens, Gorillas in the Mist,* and *Ghostbusters II.*

Why Weaver was cast, however, is also linked to her physical qualities. As Barry King points out, bodily traits are always "already coded . . . [as] having . . . socially recognized attributes" (175). That Weaver is tall (5 feet 11 inches), with a strong jaw, thin lips, perfect teeth, erect posture, broad shoulders, small straight nose, striking eyes, elevated cheekbones, high forehead, and curly chestnut hair, makes her "right" for casting as assertive, powerful, attractive women. Her cultured vocabulary, precise speech patterns, and lack of regional accent mark her as educated and intelligent. Not surprisingly, critics marvel at her elegance and poise, proffering descriptions that stamp her as upper class, even aristocratic. Julie Cameron's appraisal is typical. For her, Weaver "looks the way a movie star should look—larger than life, exquisite, regal. . . . Tall, willowy, radiant, with porcelain skin and exquisitely chiseled bones, she would attract stares even without her star status" (*Chicago Tribune*, 13 July 1986, 13:4).

From the 1980s on, discussions in a number of venues such as news weeklies, popular magazines, and newspapers mine the same handful of biographical tidbits, crafting a star image that "fits" Weaver's physical traits and complements her casting. Her childhood is depicted as privileged. Born Susan Alexandra Weaver, she grew up surrounded by New York's entertainment elites. Her father, Pat, was president of NBC; her mother, British actress Elizabeth Inglis, was in *The 39 Steps* (1935). Even though her father eventually suffered career setbacks and financial losses, Weaver's teenage memories were not of deprivation, but rather of being shy and awkward. She attended private schools. At age thirteen or fourteen she changed her name from "Susan" to "Sigourney" because she was tall "and Susan was such a short name. To my ear Sigourney was a stage name—long and curvy, with a musical ring" (Richard Corliss, "The Years of Living Splendidly," *Time*, 28 July 1986, 61).

The ugly duckling blossomed into a lovely but rebellious swan. As an undergraduate majoring in English literature at Stanford, Weaver and her boyfriend dressed as elves and lived in a tree house. Did they smell? queried Dale Hrabi. "I was a clean elf . . . when I could find a shower." Weaver "bristled" at the suggestion that committing to an alternative elf lifestyle is "super-gay," then teasingly replied, "I don't think you should make generalizations about elves. They come in all flavors and colors" (82). At one anti–Vietnam War rally she played the lead in a guerrilla theater skit called *Alice in ROTC Land*. She was supposed to wave a copy of Mao's *Little Red Book* as she urged everyone to march to the Reserve Office Training Corps center in protest. She had forgotten to bring her copy, so she improvised and held up her little red address book. Hundreds of her classmates marched to the ROTC center and burned it down (Richard M. Levine, "Is This Face Funny?" *American Film*, 9 October 1983, 35).

Graduate school at Yale was profoundly disempowering. Weaver made a few friends, notably playwrights-to-be Christopher Durang, Wendy Wasserstein, and Albert Innaurato. But the Drama School faculty told her she had no future as an actress. For them, Meryl Streep was the golden girl, Weaver "uncastable" because of her height except perhaps in comedy. She was taught "to double-think every single gesture. . . . With every prop you used, you had to write down how you were going to use it. . . . It was so intellectual and so not what I needed. . . . I'm more of a gut person" (Scott Proudfit, "Out from the Shadows," backstagewest.com, 13 January 2000). She was miserable. Her approach to acting is to "just surrender to it." For her, "real acting comes from here [palm on chest] not from here [points to head]" (Cliff Rothman, "Exploring New Worlds," *Los Angeles Times*, 10 January 2000, F8).

After graduating she acted in off-off- and off-Broadway plays, many written by her former Yale Drama School friends.[1] Nineteen seventy-seven saw her first screen performance, in Woody Allen's *Annie Hall*. (She is Woody's date, waiting outside the movie theater, toward the end of the film.) Her breakthrough came in 1979, when she dazzled audiences and critics alike in Ridley Scott's *Alien*. The studio worried that her portrayal was too "hard." Its secretaries confirmed they liked her toughness (Pally 19).

She chose her roles carefully but recognized that you are always somehow cast on the basis of your last performance (*Chicago Tribune*, 13 July 1986, 13:5). Statements like "most of the women's roles I'm offered are just satellites to men. They twinkle briefly, then fade" led to her being labeled a feminist. If she is a feminist, she is certainly not a humorless one. Asked what adjectives she would apply to herself, she responded with characteristic wit: "Tall, willowy, elegant. And I would definitely include goddess. No, truthfully, it is a great relief if one has grown up tall to come across as willowy and graceful rather than awkward and clumsy" ("The Goddess and the Gorillas," *TV Entertainment*, October 1989, 22). She considers herself first and foremost an actor—not an actress, thank you. "An *actress* is someone who wears boa feathers," she told *American Film*. Then she looked down. She *was* wearing a pink feather boa (Levine, "Is This Face Funny?" 9 October 1983, 33).

That Weaver's physical traits and life experiences in many ways dovetail with her characters' traits and attitudes means she fits Robert Allen and Douglas Gomery's axiom that "stars are actors with biographies" (172). Worth emphasis is the fact that coverage of Weaver during the 1980s by both tabloid journalism and the establishment press was not only scanty but also decidedly ungossipy. Her stardom was grounded in her performances, not in celebrity appearances. Also, Weaver's acting evolved over the course of the decade, even if she was not a Method-based "performer" who expresses emotions through "every gesture and grimace" or "inarticulate speech" (Geraghty 193). Logically the awards came at the end of the 1980s. The choice in genres helped.

# ★★★★★ A Yankee Version of Athena: Co-Starring in Thrillers

In 1981, Weaver partnered with the Method-trained, blond, all-American William Hurt in *Eyewitness*. In 1986 she worked with polished professional Michael Caine in *Half Moon Street*. Most important, in 1982 she sizzled opposite Mel Gibson in *The Year of Living Dangerously*. Set in New York, London, and Indonesia, respectively, all three films "document and dramatize the acts of assassins, conspirators, or criminal governments, as well as the oppositional acts of victim-societies, countercultures, or martyrs" (Derry 103). Suspense is important, wound tightly though not exclusively around Weaver's figures. But the thriller is a notoriously elastic genre, and these films all enlist elements from related genres (see Rubin). All three engage with contemporary imperial concerns, updating that subset of adventure films Brian Taves terms the empire film (*The Romance of Adventure*), and all three revitalize romance, chipping away at conventional heterosexual partnerships and/or questioning traditional gender roles. Weaver prepared extensively for each part, calibrating her performances to complement those of her partners. In each film, her character constitutes a variation of what would become her signature star stamp: all are independent, intelligent, active professionals. Costuming, hair, and makeup are key. Never does Weaver wear trademark 1980s female attire. No puffy sleeves; no padded shoulders; no "poodle perms" for her here! She sports trousers and models couture evening wear.

The first film after *Breaking Away* (1979) from director-writer team Peter Yates and Steve Tesich, *Eyewitness* was widely anticipated. The Twentieth Century–Fox studio press kit describes the plot as "a spellbinding mystery of oddly mismatched characters thrown together by perilous circumstances" (2). Critics were less kind to the film, which includes a murder mystery, a terrorist plot, and a stalker romance. The mix appealed to Weaver, who liked playing wealthy Jewish journalist Tony Sokolow because "you're never sure who she is . . . Tony comes from a refined, cultured family. She could have a career as a classical musician, but she gets a job in hard news, which goes against her parents' expectations" (press kit, 6).

To prepare, she took horseback riding lessons, learned to play a Mendelssohn piano concerto, and accompanied WNEW-TV news reporter Aida Alvarez on assignments. "I watched Aida weave her magic. She makes you feel you're the most fascinating person in the world" (Chris Chase, "At the Movies," *New York Times*, 27 February 1991, C6). She took issue with Tesich's idea that Tony had grown up wanting to be male ("Why couldn't

Tony grow up wanting to be a young *woman?*") and disagreed with his decision to write Tony as someone without women friends, but she did not have
enough clout to force changes (Danny Peary, "Interview with Sigourney
Weaver," *Films and Filming*, 23 October 1981, 27).

Playing opposite Hurt was a joy: both agreed some things had to be
spontaneous. The film's promotional material emphasized romance over
suspense. *Playgirl*, the *New York Times*, *Rolling Stone*, and *Seventeen* all published a still of Tony interviewing Daryll, Hurt's character. *Time* and *Evening
Outlook* chose a still of the two seated on the Central Park grass, Weaver
leaning contentedly back against Hurt. Only *Newsweek, Marquee*, and the
*L.A. Herald Examiner* published images reminiscent of Hitchcock, one showing the two actors looking fearfully upward as they run, another featuring
Weaver screaming, a third proffering Hurt being attacked by his Doberman.

Several critics noticed Weaver's performance, but *Rolling Stone* named
the film one of the year's twenty-four worst (Stuart Byron, December 1981,
44). While it did poorly at the box office ($6 million gross, having cost $7.5
million), it is nonetheless Weaver's first high-profile role of the decade. Also
released by Twentieth Century–Fox, *Half Moon Street* is even less important
and another financial failure (grossing $1 million, an eighth of what it cost)
although of note because it lets her character, Lauren, a brainy call girl *cum*
foreign policy expert, fight the sexual double standard that codes casual sex
as damaging for women but not for men; and it gives Lauren explicitly feminist comments. "A lot of women like uncomplicated sex" is her motto.
With Weaver nude or partially nude in a number of scenes, *Playboy*
remarked appreciatively, "We keep a copy of this handy for the shot of
Sigourney Weaver topless on an exercise bike" (August 2004).

*The Year of Living Dangerously* is, in fact, Weaver's only successful 1980s
thriller. Thanks in part to MGM's novel release strategy—prints were sent
to a limited number of theaters in each area—the film did well ($6 million
cost, $10 million gross). But it contains multiple clichés and the happy Hol-
lywood ending shortchanges the complex story: miraculously, Guy (Gibson) and Jill (Weaver) embrace in long shot, safe in the doorway of the
plane taking them away from riots and revolution.

Based on a densely plotted novel by Australian writer C. J. Koch, the
film revolves around three interlocking narratives: Hamilton and Bryant's
romance, rising unrest during the last year of Sukarno's presidency, and the
curious tale of Billy Kwan, the dwarf photographer who serves as Guy's
guardian angel and guide. As in many of Peter Weir's films, mood is all.
Billy tells the tale, contributing reflections on the tumultuous times, introducing Guy and Jill, and charting the progress of their love. Romance is

central, though Weaver does not appear until twenty minutes in, wearing a demure one-piece bathing suit beside a posh swimming pool. Coolly she appraises Guy. Her voice is low; there's a faint British accent. At a party a week later, she dances with abandon, shimmying until the spaghetti straps of her full-skirted sun dress slip from her shoulders. How could Guy fail to notice her? Pauline Kael certainly noticed: "Weir knows what's spectacular about Sigourney Weaver: her brainy female-hunk physicality—her wide-awake dark eyes, the protruding lower lip, the strong, rounded, out-thrust jaw, and her hands, so large that when she embraces Gibson her five fingers encompass his back. . . . She uses her face and her body, and pours on the passion and laughter; she has the kind of capacity for enjoyment that the young Sophia Loren had" (*New Yorker*, 21 February 1983, 120–21).

Some inches taller than Gibson, Weaver nonetheless knew "how to play small, act petite" (Merle Ginsberg, "Leave it to Weaver," *People*, February 2000, 236). She enjoyed working with him, noting fondly that because he was only twenty-six at the time, "he was always trying to stay out all night, so the next day he would look tired and haggard, and look older" (Alex Simon, "Sigourney Weaver: From *Alien* to Comedienne," *Venice*, April 2001, 50). Weir had the two watch Cary Grant and Ingrid Bergman in *Notorious* (1946) to prepare, "so our love scenes would have that same sort of old-fashioned quality. The censors back then dictated that you could only kiss for so long, so they were kissing, then talking, kissing, then talking. Peter was very adamant that he didn't want to see any tongue" (49). Andrew Sarris found Weaver and Gibson "wondrously volcanic as two lovers erupting together on the edge of the abyss" ("Journalistic Ethics in Java," *Village Voice*, 1 February 1983, 59). In general critics were more taken with Hunt's performance; she, not Weaver, received an Academy Award, the first woman to do so for a role impersonating a man.

Although Sukarno coined the slogan "the year of living dangerously" with reference to Indonesia's efforts to chart a middle course independent of the United States or the Soviet Union, and signs protesting U.S. and British imperialism pepper the film, little information about Indonesian politics comes across. Shot in the Philippines following a decade of martial law, the production was seen as anti-Islamic and sparked riots and death threats to the cast and crew. Weir ordered everyone out and finished the film in Australia. Weaver was relieved. Not until *Gorillas in the Mist* would she again brave danger in a foreign land. With the exception of that and *Aliens*, she turned to comedies, accepting smaller, supporting roles in *Ghost Busters*, *Ghostbusters II*, and *Working Girl*.[2] Throughout the 1980s, in fact, she was convinced she was better at comedy than at romance or drama.

## ★★★★★ Sultry? Definitely. Silly? She Hopes So: Supporting Roles in Comedy

Weaver took full advantage of the opportunities afforded by comedies, which are even more amorphous than thrillers. A mode rather than a genre, comedy can combine with or parody virtually every other genre (see Neale, *Genre* 65–66; Neale and Krutnik). Primarily screwball comedies, *Ghost Busters* and *Ghostbusters II* nonetheless also revolve around the romance between Weaver and Murray, prefigure buddy action films like *Lethal Weapon* (1987), and take aim at earlier horror films like *Rosemary's Baby* (1968), *The Exorcist* (1973), and *The Omen* (1976). Part of the 1980s romantic comedy revival, *Working Girl* concentrates on the romance between Melanie Griffith and Harrison Ford, yet Weaver's and Joan Cusack's supporting performances add screwball touches.[3]

Weaver embraced the role of girlfriend/demon Dana Barrett in *Ghost Busters*. "I loved being the demon; that was my favorite part. . . . I loved levitating, and I loved turning into a dog. I loved all those things because . . . that's the kind of thing you usually do on stage" (Maguffee 152–53). She knew that "the work would be loose, crazy, and spontaneous. I've worked on the stage, so I've done a lot of improvisation, but this was a different atmosphere. . . . Having come out of Second City, the guys were all very generous. There was no ego" (press kit, 2).

A classical cellist, Dana lives in a modest apartment. Her wardrobe is unpretentious. When possessed she turns fiercely sexy. David Edelstein is one of many critics who loved Weaver's alternative look. "Her eyes grow dark, her cheekbones heavy, and her skirt is slashed to the hip revealing a pair of tall, supernaturally sinewy legs. (She really should do more of these exorcist movies)" (*Village Voice*, 12 June 1984). This is the image of Weaver that accompanied most reviews, with lustful neighbor Louis (Rick Moranis) at her side.

Kael prefers Weaver's toned-down performance as Dana: "When she stands talking to Murray, she's eye to eye with him, and she looks indestructible. She throws herself into her role" (*New Yorker*, 25 June 1984, 99). Whether as demon or Dana, however, opposite Murray Weaver conveys genuine comic chemistry. Loose-limbed and spunky, she meets his goofy sleaziness with earnest pragmatism.

As imperiled female victim, Dana sets the narrative in motion, yet the film's publicity campaign rarely recognized Weaver. Instead, in high-concept 1980s film fashion (see Wyatt), *Ghost Busters'* marketing began before release, with enigmatic posters featuring the logo and a single line of copy,

Louis Tully (Rick Moranis) ogles the demon-possessed Dana Barrett (Sigourney Weaver) in *Ghost Busters*. Courtesy Movie Star News. Copyright Columbia Pictures, 1984.

"Coming to Save the World This Summer," without explaining what the logo symbolized, mentioning the film, or invoking its stars. Ads were placed in the business, fashion, and sports pages, not the arts sections. Columbia purchased fifteen-second TV spots between primetime programs that again showed only the logo and the one line. The Friday before the film's release a music video featuring Ray Parker Jr.'s title song premiered. Thanks to the hype, an unprecedented 80-plus percent of the audience was aware of the film before its release ("Ghostbusters Overcomes Short Prod. Sked to Smash Results," *Variety*, 7 June 1984, 34). Block-booked into 1,200 theaters, *Ghost Busters* became the summer's biggest hit and the second highest grossing film of the year after *Beverly Hills Cop*. The theme song became a chart-topper. Released on video, the film also broke records (Tom Bierbaum, *"Ghost Busters* Sets Cassette Record, Tops Initial Order Revenues, Units," *Variety*, 16 October 1995, A26). Scores of products rode *Ghost Busters'* coat tails, among them a cereal called Ghost Busters ("They're here to save the world from dull spiritless breakfasts! Crunch bustin' fruit flavor with marshmallow ghosts!"). Murray and co-star Dan Aykroyd were hailed as comedy action stars. And the brouhaha surrounding the film's exhibition and franchise products meant that Weaver, too, netted fame she had not enjoyed since *Alien*. Logically, then, even though it took five years for the sequel to be made, it was clear she had to play Dana again.[4]

*Ghostbusters II* was released in 1989, a year when sequels were every studio's cash cow (the *Star Trek* series climbed to five; *Karate Kid* to three; *Friday the 13th* to eight; *Nightmare on Elm Street* to five). *Los Angeles Magazine* found it "the most cynically contrived" because so much of its plot works by substitution. Instead of the giant Marshmallow Man, there is the Statue of Liberty; instead of a creepy old apartment house on Central Park West, there is a creepy old museum; instead of the demons kidnapping Dana, now they kidnap her baby (Merrill Schindler, "Films," August 1989, 290). Most reviewers agreed the film was repetitive and contrived. But audiences did not care. Unpaid extras lined the streets where the film was shot chanting and yelling, "'Ghostbusters! Ghostbusters! Who are you going to call?'" (Adam Eisenberg, "*Ghostbusters II* for Laughs & Liberty," *American Cinematographer*, August 1989, 60). Thanks to new songs, a modified logo (the ghost now flashes a victory sign through the red bar), and the ubiquitous presence of the Ghostbuster "boys" in publicity photos, posters, and TV spots, the opening box office take was record-breaking, the final gross more than satisfactory. Of course this time there were more ancillary product lines, among them ghostbuster mugs, posters, T-shirts, plush toys, and Halloween costumes.

For Weaver the film's success ensured she was watched and worshiped. Significantly, however, she has no alter ego to motivate screwball moments in her performance. As the divorced, working mother of an eight-month-old baby, this Dana represents the rising numbers of single moms at the end of the 1980s (see Evans). Dana fights like a banshee to defend her baby. Weaver drew on skills honed in the *Alien* films to make her performance energetic and realistic, even though many sequences were shot using effects (see Ron Magid, "Busting Ghosts—Job That Keeps Returning," *American Cinematographer*, December 1989, 82). As she explained, "You need to use everything you've ever learned to invest the scenes with interest—take a scene like 'Let's seal this air duct' and make that work" (Fred Schruers, "On a Roll: Sigourney Weaver," *Elle*, March 1986, 97). Opposite Murray she plays Dana as initially guarded, then fondly bemused, and finally sincerely attached. On the set the two enjoyed a warm, teasing relationship. Just before her last close-up, for example, Murray goaded her: "You're not such a big deal when you're working with actors as tall as you are. . . . That's right! You can't work with Mel Gibson forever!" She giggled helplessly but nailed the take (Patrick Goldstein, "Return of the Money-Making Slime," *Rolling Stone*, 1 June 1989, 54).

Weaver's supporting role as Katherine Parker in *Working Girl* won her greater critical attention. Many critics hailed the film for reviving romantic comedy traditions and the Horatio Alger myth. A hit in the United States, Britain, and elsewhere, more than any of Weaver's other 1980s films *Working Girl* sparked discussions about the status of feminism and the rise of post-feminism, while it served as a reference point for debates about the glass ceiling and women in traditionally male occupations. Updating the populist appeal of *Nine to Five* (1980), *Working Girl* makes the evil boss a woman. For Cynthia Fuchs, the film thereby "raises two issues central to the Reagan-Bush era of kinder insider trading and gentler sexual discrimination, then wraps them up in romance ribbons: class and gender become topical fodder for formula" (51).

Dozens of writers interviewed actual secretaries and offered business fashion tips.[5] Twentieth Century–Fox promoted the film to 20,000 secretaries in thirty cities, sending *Working Girl*–emblazoned Post-Its, coffee mugs, paper-clip holders, and buttons that read, *"Working Girl*: There's More to Life than Smiling, Filing, and Dialing" (Nikkie Finke, "What Do the Real Secretaries Think?" *Los Angeles Times*, 17 December 1988, 1:7). Women loved the film, maybe because it was the only movie released that year featuring women in leading roles, maybe because it underscored the value of sisterhood through "the contrasting pairs of Tess and best friend Cyn (Cusack) and Tess and her new boss, Katherine (Weaver)" (Brunsdon 87). Tess models herself on Katherine, learning to speak cultivated English by mimicking the recording on Katherine's answering machine.

Cast because of her history as a cult feminist heroine, Weaver welcomed the opportunity to play a villain (Brunsdon 90). She spent weeks in brokerage houses observing Wall Street at work. Her carriage ensures that Katherine is the center of attention from the moment she strides into the office in a tailored grey suit, demure white blouse, pearls, a houndstooth gray-and-white coat slung over her shoulders, an expensive brown leather briefcase at her side. Once in her office she coaches Tess: "We have a uniform—simple, elegant, impeccable. 'Dress shabbily, they notice the dress. Dress elegantly, they notice the woman.' Coco Chanel." Eyes averted, she adds, "Rethink the jewelry," then gently promises, "It's a two-way street on my team. . . . Oh, and call me Katherine." Her superiority is visually transmitted later when Tess kneels on the floor, looking devotedly upward, helping Katherine on with new red ski boots. Katherine confides she plans to receive a marriage proposal that weekend: "You don't get anywhere in this world by waiting for something to come to you. You make it happen. Watch me, Tess. Learn from me!"

Pride literally goes before a fall here: Katherine flies off the ski slopes and breaks her leg. Weaver's voicing and gestures now become broad. Laid up in the hospital, she exhibits a campy control, slapping one doctor, giggling seductively with others. Back home she plays the sexy predator from her bed, slipping one negligee strap off her shoulder with a wink when Jack (Harrison Ford) appears, then grabbing him: "Tick! Tock! My biological clock! . . . Let's merge, you and I!" When she learns that Tess and Jack are an item and about to seal a major deal, she loses her patrician poise. Hobbling into a board meeting on crutches, she points one at Tess as if it were a rifle, screaming, "This woman is my secretary!"

## ★★★★★ Joan of the Aliens and the Apes: Starring Roles in Action/Adventure

The ability to send up identities is core to Weaver's stardom, and nowhere more visible than in her two starring roles in 1980s action/adventure films *Aliens* and *Gorillas in the Mist*. Both cinch her star status. Weaver's casting in the two films flouts the typical gender constraints of action and adventure films but hews to the action/adventure preference that heroes be workers. Ripley has a blue-collar background: she works as a loader before becoming a military advisor. Dian Fossey describes herself as a physical therapist who works with handicapped children. The Ripley role was, of course, originally written for a man. That Weaver was cast was thanks to James Cameron's desire to connect with women in the audience. As he told Richard Schickel, "It has been proved demographically that 80% of the time, it's women who decide which film to see" ("Help! They're Back!," *Newsweek*, 28 July 1986, 56). This hotly anticipated sequel opened in 1,400 theaters, an unprecedented 11 percent of them screening 70 mm prints, a big investment for Twentieth Century–Fox ("Fox Adds Number of *Aliens* Prints," *Hollywood Reporter*, 14 July 1986). The film grossed $10.1 million in the opening week. *Time* touted it as "The Summer's Scariest Movie" and placed that heading and a photograph of Weaver on its cover (28 July 1986).

Weaver had not been eager to do a second *Alien* film. Seeing the script, however, she felt playing the character again would offer a "challenge, to show how Ripley had aged and matured." She was intrigued by the fact that Ripley now had a dead daughter whose whole life she had slept through. The back story was shot but excised from the theatrical release. "With certain scenes gone, the ones that remained had some odd leaps in them. To my eye, I often seemed suddenly very emotional out of nowhere,"

Weaver complained (*Chicago Tribune*, 13 July 1986, 13:4–5). For her, Ripley became a "flame-throwing commando" (Teresa Carpenter, "At Long Last Sigourney," *Premiere*, October 1986, 5). She called James Cameron's obsession with armaments "pornographic" (John Powers, "Don't Tell Mom the *Terminator*'s Dead," *L.A. Weekly*, 5 July 1991, 32).

With *Aliens*' marines sporting U.S. flags on their uniforms and everyone talking about "nuking" the aliens during the period in which President Reagan was stockpiling weapons for possible "nuking" of the Soviet Union, no wonder the film was broadly understood as promoting right-wing agendas. The sequel sidles away from the original's critique of imperialism and "The Company," focusing audience antipathy on the alien queen and the yuppie company representative, Burke (Paul Reiser). That Burke's first name is Carter may be seen as an indictment of 1970s liberalism (Holmlund, "New Cold War Sequels and Remakes" 91). Like other 1980s action films obsessed with "getting to win this time," moreover, *Aliens* brings us a Ripley who suffers from nightmares (post-traumatic stress, anyone?) but nevertheless returns, like Rambo, to hunt for survivors, if now in steamy tunnels reminiscent not only of Vietnamese jungles but also of wombs.[6] Fears of sexuality and reproduction, of contagion and going soft, of illegal immigrants and welfare mothers all coalesce. The solution to these fears? War! For Reagan, similarly, Gallardo and Smith argue, everything was a "war": on drugs, on poverty, on pornography (63).

The majority of critics focused on Ripley as a character, ignoring Weaver's contributions. Many talked about Ripley's vulnerability to the threat of rape, most obvious in those scenes where she appears in her underwear. Yet when she dons a loader suit to fight the alien queen, all weakness seems to disappear. Feminist critics repeatedly argued that armed with artificial "muscles" that dwarf those of 1980s action heroes Arnold Schwarzenegger and Sylvester Stallone, Weaver/Ripley thereby exposes masculinity as a masquerade, as "musculinity" (Tasker, *Spectacular* 149), and that all the characters, not just Ripley, are simultaneously phallocentric and at risk (see Greenberg, "Fembo" 168).

Sociological "takes" tied worries about Ripley as warrior to debates around women in the military. The Equal Rights Amendment had been defeated in 1982, in large part on the grounds that it would expose women to unacceptable physical stress and dangers on the battlefield and "unman" male soldiers. But the 1980s did bring some gains for military women: by 1990–1991 and the Gulf War, 11 percent of the armed forces were female, with many women within range of enemy fire (see Katzenstein). Ripley's toughness is modified by *Aliens*'s emphasis on motherhood.

She becomes the adoptive mother of a missing child, thereby tapping into national concerns about missing children broadcast on milk cartons from 1984 on. That Newt (Carrie Henn) is blond and blue-eyed heightens the captivity-narrative stakes. Does Ripley's ultimate ability to make it alone prove that single moms can be successful parents? Thanks to Reagan's cuts to welfare and health care, the majority of single moms had little power in real life (Nancy Webber, "How *Aliens* Mirrors Feminine Fears," *Los Angeles Times*, 24 August 1986, 40). And what to make of Ripley's fear of biological motherhood, so graphically illustrated in her nightmares, or of the hints at a heterosexual romance?

Weaver's assessments of the character evidenced a "feminist" stance. "Women are the strongest characters in the film. Even the alien is more intelligent because of her maternal aspect. And who's interested in fighting a dumb monster? Newt is really the strongest: she's survived the longest, she's thinking the most clearly. The maternal experience for Ripley isn't a throwback. It could happen to a man. Besides, when Ripley and Newt are in danger they're *colleagues*. They postpone the mommy stuff till they're safe. Like any love story, this relationship must be earned. Ripley makes Newt a promise and she goes back to her to earn it." For Weaver this film was "the story of Ripley—a civilian—becoming a warrior, not a woman becoming a man. . . . I like the throne room scene where R attempts to negotiate peacefully with the bug queen. I also think it's important to have a woman save the day—especially for kids, who usually see only male heroes. . . . When the question of women being drafted came up a few years ago, I thought that there are some people who are better at fighting than others. Some of them are men, some women" (Pally 21). That the most gung-ho of the marines, Vasquez (Jenette Goldstein), is a woman who is clearly coded as lesbian surely pleased Weaver as well.

There were fewer debates around *Gorillas in the Mist*, in part because *Gorillas* was not as high-profile a production, in part because the script concentrates on a real individual. Marketing was deemed difficult: the film was not high concept and Weaver was not a superstar. But Universal, which distributed the film in the United States, spent $3 to $4 million on TV ads. One, aired on daytime soaps, showed Fossey as a woman choosing between her career and a married man who gets a divorce in order to marry her. A second, aired on "Good Morning America" and "The Today Show," was action-oriented and emphasized the film's exotic elements. A third, also featuring action sequences, ran nationally on the opening night of the Olympic Games. Opening small (fifteen theaters in twelve cities), by the following week 535 more theaters had been added (Geraldine Fabrikant,

"Advertising Plan Helps Risky Film to Succeed," *New York Times*, 4 October 1988, D23). Print ads and reviews in *Time, New York Times, Los Angeles Times, Wall Street Journal, Village Voice*, and *Ms.* showcased Weaver as the surrogate mom of young gorillas. Only *Newsweek* showed her with the Rwandan actors and her human co-star, Bryan Brown. A two-page ad in *Variety* joined the image of a gorilla with a letter from African Wildlife Foundation vice president Diane E. McMeekin congratulating Weaver on her performance: "I felt as if I were actually watching Dian again. Sigourney Weaver does an unbelievably good job of BEING Dian" (8 September 1988).

Fossey had wanted a film to be made from her autobiography. According to Weaver, she wanted "Brooke Shields to play her as a young woman and Elizabeth Taylor as an older one" ("Queen Kong," *Life*, October 1988, 40). Weaver prayed for the part. "I knew it was going to be the biggest opportunity I ever had," she told *Film Monthly* (Ken Ferguson, "Sigourney & Melanie," May 1989, 13). To prepare for grueling climbs to 12,000-foot elevations in the Rwandan mountains, she ran in the hills of Hawaii. She watched videotapes of Fossey dozens of times, studying her voice and picking up habits like chain-smoking (Teresa Carpenter, "At Long Last Sigourney," *Premiere*, October 1988, 42). She threw herself into the role, bringing a physicality to this performance that is unmatched by her others in the 1980s. Always a supporter, Kael noticed the difference: "Weaver's physical strength alone is inspiring in this movie, and there's a new freedom in her acting. She's so vivid that you immediately feel Dian Fossey's will and drive" (*New Yorker*, 17 October 1988). Edelstein wrote that "a new fearlessness has entered [Weaver's] acting—she'll inhabit a part if it kills her. . . . She has held on to her sense of absurdity; she isn't afraid to look foolish. As Dian Fossey she is magnificent" ("Joan of Apes," weavergorillas.blogspot .com). Weaver beams in wide-eyed wonder when she first spies the gorillas. Determined or enraged, her mouth turns down fiercely. There are brief love scenes, but these always occur after a special moment with the gorillas, Digit in particular. When Digit and Dian hold hands at one point in extreme close-up, Weaver's look of joy is transcendent.

Again and again, Weaver transforms herself into an "ape," lowering her head in submission, slapping her chest, picking at lice, grunting, and screaming. Her lower teeth tighten over her upper ones, her brows furrow, her jaw juts out. Although she tries also to convey Fossey's descent at the end of her life into drunken despair and disease (she suffered from emphysema), the logic of this part of her performance was lost on the cutting room floor. We never learn the answer to the challenge posed in the opening sequence, "To know who I am, and what it was that made me that

Gorilla mother, savior, lover: Sigourney Weaver as dedicated primatologist Dian Fossey in *Gorillas in the Mist.* Courtesy Jerry Ohlinger. Copyright Universal Pictures, 1988.

way," because we never see what must have been the minutiae of Fossey's work and we never learn much about Rwandan politics either, though these were central to the gorillas' destruction. Despite the film's emphasis on women's independence, moreover, it repeats the racist clichés of earlier empire adventures and adventurer biopics. The chief villain is white. With the exception of Sembagare (John Omirah Miluwi), who, thanks to his association with Fossey, "rises in life from the ranks of . . . village tour guide to responsible adjutant," virtually all Rwandans and Ugandans are portrayed as silent, superstitious spear throwers (Henry Sheehan, "Dian Takes Over Where Tarzan Leapt Off," *Reader*, 23 September 1988). Weaver's Fossey becomes the white sahib who towers over everyone except the gorillas.

The strength of her performance earned Weaver multiple nominations and awards. Unlike her nomination for Best Actress for *Aliens*, which was eclipsed by its Oscars for visual and sound effects, her nomination for Best Actress in *Gorillas* was enhanced and reinforced by her winning the Golden Globe for Best Performance by an Actress in a Drama, an award she shared with Shirley MacLaine and Jodie Foster. That same year she also won a Golden Globe for Best Performance in a Supporting Role for *Working Girl*.

## ☆☆★★★★ Game for Anything: Living Female Stardom

Throughout the 1980s Weaver never pursued dramatic roles. To close friend Christopher Durang she joked that she only got the part of Fossey because Jessica Lange was pregnant ("Dream Weaver," *Interview*, July 1988, 42). Instead, as we have seen, she worked in thrillers, comedies, and action/adventure movies. Almost all her 1980s films include action elements. Consistently she also appeared onstage, where an actor's physical qualities are less constraining (see King). She starred in several of Durang's comedies, for example, because "I like very experimental stuff— and movies can't be that, most of the time" (Leslie Bennetts, "Sigourney Weaver Portraying Portia in 'Merchant of Venice,'" *New York Times*, 21 December 1986, H5). She received a Tony Award for her role in David Rabe's *Hurlyburly*, and performed in regional productions of Shakespeare, Georges Feydeau, Harold Pinter, and Tennessee Williams.

She parodied in print what it means to be a movie star. In one mock interview for *Esquire*, for example, Durang asked her, "Tell me, how did you get the leading role in *Alien*?" "I slept with the director." *Eyewitness*? "I slept with the director and the writer and the crew." *The Year of Living Dangerously*? "I slept with the Australian consulate." *Ghost Busters*? "I slept with Menudo." "Here is a list of some of the questions *Esquire* would like me to ask you: Do you sleep in the nude? Do you make love by candlelight? Where do babies come from? Do you masturbate? Do you freebase cocaine?" "In no particular order: yes, no, no, yes, yes, L. L. Bean, yes, maybe, no, no, yes" ("Naked Lunch," July 1984, 73, 76). Accompanying photographs show the two seated side by side in evening wear, eating blinis, then putting their faces in their food. A second mock interview photo series, "Out of Sorts in Africa," features the two in a send-up of Meryl Streep's hit, *Out of Africa* (1985). Accompanying a photo of Weaver carrying two guns and Durang hefting a butterfly net, one caption reads: "Sigourney forced us to go hunting for our dinner." Another features a tall black actor as a "native" servant in 'fro, bead necklaces, and loincloth soothing the now-seated Weaver, the perplexed Durang at her side, one foot on a lionskin rug. The caption explains: "Sigourney became distraught at the mere mention of Meryl Streep" (*Esquire*, November 1986, 130–35).

From contemporary perspectives, how playfully fey Weaver's non-Hollywood performances are is more easily seen, although many certainly got the idea in the 1980s as well. In hindsight, some of Weaver's 1980s movies also seem more queer. What about the love that "strange little guy" Billy feels for her in *The Year of Living Dangerously*? Thanks to Vasquez and Ripley *Aliens* ranks as a queer classic. And what to make of those love scenes with Digit, the gorilla???!!! True, Weaver is happily married, but . . . if we look into her past, moreover, we learn that at the Ethel Walker School she played trouser roles that included Rudolph Valentino in an Arabian sheik show (Durang, "Dream Weaver," *Interview*, July 1988, 42). And she always acted, she said, for women in the audience. "I'm more concerned w/how other women respond to what I'm doing than I am that a man should look up at the screen and fall in love with me. Maybe I take that for granted. . . . Or maybe I'm acting for the women in men—the feminine side of men" (Dan Yakir, "Sultry? Definitely. Silly? She Hopes So," *Chicago Tribune*, 4–6 July 1986, 6).

We need to recognize that our perspectives on Sigourney Weaver's 1980s stardom are filtered through our own times. As Paul McDonald cautions, "Contextualising the meaning of stars is always open to the charge of presenting a simple 'reflectionist' history of stardom. . . . A balance needs to be struck between the signs and discourses which are particular to film stardom at any moment and a sense of the context of social beliefs and conditions in which the star circulates" ("Reconceptualizing Stardom" 179). Weaver would not say no. Her advice for living female stardom? "Perseverance and laughter, I think, are the two keys. And I also believe it's always better to say yes to something than to say no" (Proudfit, "Out from the Shadows," backstagewest.com).

### NOTES

1. Weaver thought that her life would revolve around work—until she met fellow Yale alum and theater director Jim Simpson. She asked *him* out, and they were married in 1984 by two ministers, one male, one female.

2. Because *Deal of the Century* (1983) and *Une femme ou deux* (1985) bombed at the box office I do not discuss them. It is worth noting that Weaver is paired with popular "Saturday Night Live" star Chevy Chase in the first and French/transnational superstar Gérard Depardieu in the second.

3. For a discussion of the differences between the screwball and romantic comedy traditions see Gehring.

4. A promotional photo visually acknowledges Weaver's importance. She perches atop a kneeling Murray. His hands and knees are on Harold Ramis and Dan Aykroyd. Both are also on hands and knees, with Ernie Hudson on hands and knees between them. Weaver's feet are on Hudson's head, her arms casually behind her head as she smiles for the camera (Patrick Goldstein, "Return of the Money-Making Slime," *Rolling Stone*, 1 June 1989, 52).

5. Titles include "How Plot of *Working Girl* Can Apply to Real-Life Role" (Rose-Marie Turk, *Los Angeles Times*, 1 January 1989, V1) and "*Working Girl* Hits Home with Wall Streeters" (Jane Applegate, *Los Angeles Times*, 8 January 1989, I5).

6. For Krin and Glen Gabbard, the "ambiguity of Weaver's screen persona, her phallicism and her move in *Aliens* and *Ghostbusters II* towards motherhood, is also part of the 'is-she-or-isn't-she dynamics of *Working Girl*'" (432).

# 8 ★★★★★★★★★★★★

# Harrison Ford
## A Well-Tempered Machismo

ADAM KNEE

Harrison Ford today remains a top Hollywood star of exceptional longevity, yet the 1980s are arguably the decade with which his star
image is most strongly bound up, the era of some of his greatest industry
successes. While the actor's image early in the 1980s was in many ways that
of a relatively conventional masculine action hero—principally as a result
of his successes in *Star Wars* (1977), its sequel *The Empire Strikes Back* (1980),
and *Raiders of the Lost Ark* (1981)—it significantly began to modulate by
mid-decade in such a way that strongly distinguished it from those of such
ascendant hard-body, Reaganite male stars as Arnold Schwarzenegger and

---

*Indiana Jones and the Temple of Doom.* Courtesy Movie Star News. Copyright Paramount
Pictures/Lucasfilm, 1984.

Sylvester Stallone (see Jeffords *Hard Bodies*). Ford's moderation from such machismo extremes is quite possibly one source of his popularity and is certainly central to his distinctiveness; indeed, this work of carefully controlling and tempering excessively macho traits itself becomes one of the defining characteristics of his own masculinity over the course of the decade, both narratively (in the internal struggles of the characters he portrays) and extradiegetically (in his efforts to guide his career by varying the kinds of roles he accepts).

★★★★★ **Crafting Hollywood Success**

The Indiana Jones and *Star Wars* films in particular aligned Ford with a certain old-guard—indeed nostalgic—and also distinctively American masculinity, in their epics of exploration, acquisition, and conquest both abroad and in outer space; and the particular neo-imperialist ethos implied therein clearly aligned with Reagan-era conceptions of America as an ascendant economic power (see Tomasulo "Mr. Jones"; Ryan and Kellner 217–43; Jeffords, *Hard Bodies* 1–23). Nevertheless, Ford's particular brand of machismo by the early eighties already has the seeds of its own critique within it: for example, in his characters' sometimes self-deprecating, tongue-in-cheek humor, as noted by Dyer (*Heavenly Bodies* 11) and others; and their cockiness and tendency to dispute with and remain detached from (but not attempt to overthrow) the institutions they serve. In *Star Wars*, for instance, although he does work to support the moral order represented by the rebels and to fight the evil Empire, his first (and for much of the time foremost) motivation is mercenary, and this streak (and outsider status) is referenced again in the early portions of *The Empire Strikes Back*. And while Ford continues to play characters who in various ways serve institutions of law and order, his is not an unyielding, hard-bodied American authority. Rather, Ford endeavors to temper the macho dimensions of his star image as it evolves, linking up with connotations not only of law, but also of humanity and sensitivity; strength and resilience; intelligence, skill, nuance, and deftness (both in his character roles and in the management of his career); rugged, virile masculine sexual attractiveness; and husbandly and fatherly concern for his loved ones.

Evidence of the perception of Ford as a cocky figure both onscreen and off, even at the start of the decade, can be found, for example, in Timothy White's *Rolling Stone* cover feature on the stars of the *Star Wars* series published at the time of the release of *The Empire Strikes Back*. Indeed, the article opens with Ford's sardonic commentary on the lack of opportunity for an individual actor to distinguish himself in a big-budget sci-fi ensemble piece like *Empire*; and in its brief background sketch of Ford the feature cites incidents that suggest his antipathy to institutional guidelines, specifically, his flunking out of college just before graduation and early termination of a contract at Columbia. Ford says, "I did a year and a half and got kicked out on my ass for being too difficult" ("Slaves to the Empire: The *Star Wars* Kids Talk Back," 24 July 1980, 36). The feature goes on to report, "With a little coaxing, Ford admits that 'to a certain degree,' Solo's cocky cachet is his own," relaying an anecdote from Ford about a scene where he changed a key line of dialogue to make it more true to his conception of his brash—and complex—character (37). In this same time period, a number of other feature articles were concordantly noting Ford's pickiness in choosing his roles—in particular, his initiative in avoiding science-fiction typecasting after *Star Wars* by appearing in *Heroes* (1977) (see *US*, 22 July 1980; *Starlog*, August 1980).

Evidence of just how substantially Ford's stock would soon rise appears in Michael Sragow's *Rolling Stone* feature at the time of the release of *Raiders of the Lost Ark*. Ford now has the cover to himself, in a close-up shot with the trademark Indy hat and whip, staring earnestly at the camera. The feature's description of Ford in the role of Jones, at first look "almost a parody of the imperial white explorer making the world his oyster," is consonant with his established characterization as a genre actor with a sardonic wit and a distinct intelligence. The accompanying interview confirms that Ford's physicality is not of the obsessively cultivated, hard-body type: "I'm not an athlete—I'm a notorious powderpuff. I'm one of the founding members of that chaotic underground of antijoggers. I don't train, I just say *I'm gonna do it*" (*"Raiders of the Lost Ark*: The Ultimate Saturday Matinee," 22 June 1981, 24).

Perhaps most significant here is the explicit articulation of what is arguably a supervising metaphor for Ford's career/star image. As in the earlier article, it is noted that after his stint at Columbia did not work out, Ford supported his family as a freelance carpenter. Here (as in other subsequent sources) reference is made to the fact that the "rough-hewn" Ford taught himself the trade, and Ford also draws an explicit comparison (one which, again, is brought up elsewhere) between the work of carpentry and that of acting: "Acting is basically like carpentry—if you know your craft, you figure out the logic of a particular job and submit yourself to it. It all comes down to detail" (24) (see the profiles in *US*, 22 July 1980, 4 August 1981, 20 June 1983; and *Starlog*, August 1980). A number of significant themes appear here. First, as a self-taught (rather than schooled or apprenticed) craftsman, Ford again can be seen as someone who tends to shirk established institutions, and what he has to offer, then, can be perceived as something genuine and home-grown, not overly refined and honed to external standards; the link can indeed be seen to Han Solo's image as a capable and independent mechanic. Second, in characterizing his acting as a form of craft, Ford anticipates a movement described, for example, by Yvonne Tasker (*Spectacular Bodies* 74), from a characterization of him as "star" (one known for a certain "star quality") to a perception of him as an "actor" (one who demonstrates distinctive skill as a performer) as well. And third, the particular craft deployed in this metaphor is one conventionally aligned with masculinity and physicality, but also with control over detail and nuance—the kind of careful control, I have suggested, that comes to characterize Ford's star discourse, both in his ability to guide his career away from stereotypical generic extremes and to temper the image of masculinity he projects.

Important as well is the fact that this account (like others) notes that the craft is taken up as a means of supporting a wife and children. Dutifulness in protecting those dependent upon him (especially those in a wife- or son-like relationship to him) is in fact already a trait linked with the Ford image by way of the Han Solo role; Solo's final action in *Star Wars* is the surprise protection of Luke Skywalker (Mark Hamill) as he is pursued during his assault on the Death Star, and he starts off *Empire* with another heroic rescue of his young friend ("That's two you owe me, Junior," Han chides Luke), continuing to come to the aid of him and Princess Leia (Carrie Fisher) numerous times during the film. Nor should the paradox be overlooked that it is because of Ford's own antipathy to a safe and controlled existence (at Columbia) that the need to find means of supporting family arises to begin with—just as it is Indiana Jones's derring-do, his affinity for adventure, discovery, and conquest, in refreshing contrast to his institutionalized academic career, that often puts those he feels obliged to protect in peril.

Indiana Jones's protective nature appears at the opening of *Raiders*, when he saves his assistant from dangerous booby traps while in pursuit of treasure in South America. When reintroduced to the former flame who becomes his partner in adventure, Marion (Karen Allen), he soon rescues her from torture at the hands of a Nazi agent, and saves her again from injury or death on numerous occasions throughout the course of the film. When, as the film moves toward its third act, his cohort Sallah (John Rhys-Davies) asks Jones how he is going to wrest the Ark of the Covenant from the Nazis as they speed away with it on a truck, he responds, "I don't know, I'm making this up as I go." But by this point, we have little doubt that he will indeed be able to pull this off, and, true to expectations, he emerges on a white horse moments later, shades of a classic Hollywood westerner coming to the rescue, only he happens to be pursuing Nazis across an Egyptian desert.

Aside from demonstrating a preternatural skill at getting himself and his friends out of dangerous situations, arising, it would seem, from a combination of both felicitous instincts and academic training, Jones (and by extension Ford) is figured here as a strongly erotic object of female desire, evident from early on in the film in a scene that features his female college students mooning over him as he lectures. And while Jones is not indifferent to such interest, particularly from Marion, it is significant that he does not often actively reciprocate, either because he employs self-control out of an understanding that it may distract from their mission or, in one humorous scene, because he is simply too exhausted to stay awake long enough to make love. Indeed, in both amorous and other matters, Marion is presented as very much a fairly even match for Jones, one who can readily hold her own in drinking and fighting. The result is a unique and refreshing chemistry between the two characters, an image of an action hero in a love relationship where he takes the woman seriously as an equal—an image underscoring Ford roles as someone heroic and macho, but also vulnerable and sensitive. Following as this does Ford's pairing with Fisher's also strong-willed Princess Leia, it helps further establish a pattern of Ford interacting with assertive female characters, something arguably possible in part because Ford's characters never take their own bravado and machismo all that seriously.

Beyond cementing the image of Ford as an action hero with a difference, *Raiders of the Lost Ark* also functioned to broaden Ford's fan base, aimed as it was at a much wider demographic than the more youth-oriented *Star Wars* films; and it simultaneously established him, along the lines of his character, as a (somewhat unintentional) sex symbol. As the cover tag-line for a profile in the December 1983 issue of *Playgirl* would subsequently describe him, "Harrison Ford: The Reluctant Sex Symbol." If Ford's interest was indeed in continuing to expand his reach and to avoid being typecast in youth-oriented science fiction roles, his next choice of vehicle, Ridley Scott's sci-fi action film *Blade Runner* (1982), might not seem a logical one. But the film does indeed continue to expand Ford's repertoire and refine (and make less juvenile) his star image at the same time it continues the development of Ford's association with action heroes who are nevertheless potentially vulnerable in romantic relationships.

*Blade Runner* highlights a number of the paradoxical elements of Ford's star image. He plays a violent enforcer of the law, employed in this case by the Los Angeles police department, but under duress; and his pursuit and

Ford in *Star Wars* as the rakish Han Solo. Courtesy Movie Star News. Copyright Lucasfilm/ Twentieth Century-Fox Film Corporation, 1977.

killings not of human criminals but of outlawed replicants cause him continual regret. Like Solo working for the rebels or Indiana Jones working for the U.S. government, the Ford character works here for an institution of authority but remains detached from it. As Deckard, Ford gives a hardboiled voiceover, in keeping with the noir referentiality of the film's style, and addresses others in a gruff manner, but this belies the emotions that hinder his work and that he increasingly feels for the replicants. It is again in a romantic relationship with a woman (albeit a nonhuman one) that the character's emotional vulnerability most strongly comes to the surface. In the scene which includes the commencement of the romance between Deckard and the replicant Rachael (Sean Young), Ford appears both emotionally and physically vulnerable, as, shirtless, he washes his face after an attempt on his life by another replicant. When he then straightens up to converse with Rachael and his bare torso fills the screen, Ford once more offers an image of male desirability, but this is plainly not a conventionalized image of hard-bodied eroticism; we are presented with a torso that (for once, in the early 1980s), while reasonably fit, does not have a hyperdefined musculature. This is an image of male physical attractiveness arguably linked more with accessibility and vulnerability than with power and aggressiveness. In point of fact, Deckard does turn physically aggressive a few minutes later, as he forcefully intervenes when Rachael tries to flee his initially gentle advances; however, he soon modulates back to a milder demeanor, with the film (in a politically retrograde gesture) clearly implying that Rachael is hardly unhappy at having been so detained.

Ford's next two screen appearances, both in hugely successful follow-ups to earlier adventure films, backtrack to more familiar territory, albeit with some revisions, again fairly well cementing his screen image. Whereas in *The Empire Strikes Back* Ford's Han Solo arguably becomes the narrative focus through his skill and judgment and rambunctious heroism, as well as his developing romance with Princess Leia, in *Return of the Jedi* (1983) the focus shifts back more toward Luke and the further development of his skills as a Jedi and his attempt to resolve issues regarding his relationship to Darth Vader. And as Luke has now clearly more fully matured, and is often the one saving Han rather than vice versa, Han no longer shows quite the fatherly (or brotherly) demeanor toward him he did in earlier episodes and does not refer to him as "kid" or "junior." On the other hand, in *Indiana Jones and the Temple of Doom* (1984), Ford's title character is quite plainly the narrative center, his qualities of heroism and protectiveness even more strongly asserted than in the earlier Indiana Jones film, while his traits of humor, sex appeal, and romantic restraint (along with his acquisitive impulses) are all kept intact.

These qualities can come even further to the fore in part because Indiana Jones now interacts with characters who, though spirited and assertive as his cohorts usually are, are nevertheless also plainly in need of protection (though once more this is partly because of the situations Jones gets them into). The earlier film's rough-and-ready Marion is now replaced by showgirl Willie Scott (Kate Capshaw). While she abhors the challenges of the outdoors, she also finds herself much attracted to Jones, who typically proves able to resist her amorous advances when distracted by the demands of his adventurous quest. Much as Jones has to look after her as they attempt to retrieve a stolen holy stone from a palace in the Indian jungle, he needs to devote even more care to his young sidekick Short Round (Jonathan Ke Quan), an orphaned Chinese boy he in effect adopted when he found him picking his pocket. While his overt comportment toward the boy is generally one of a (humorously played) irritation and antagonism, with the two often bickering over card games and the boy always quick to comment upon the elder's missteps, there is no mistaking the strong filial bond that exists between the two (suggested in particular in a number of scenes where Short Round emulates Jones), much further developing the fatherly tendencies already hinted at in the Han Solo persona.

Jones's figuration as a caring, protective transracial father, whose main goal is to retrieve the talisman that will help local Indian villagers and free their children from enslavement, works (as is typical with the Ford persona) to mitigate the fact that he is simultaneously placed in the classic position of the American imperialist, traveling across Asia to fulfill his desire for exotic artifacts. Indeed, the film goes out of its way to show that Jones is anything but the "ugly American" by demonstrating his knowledge of and sensitivity to local language and customs (as when he insists Willie make a show of eating the food the poor villagers have offered her, her revulsion not withstanding). As Jones not only adopts an underprivileged Asian boy but saves scores of Asian children from the terrors of the palace and allows them to return to their families, we see, paradoxically, how *Temple of Doom*, in an era of neoliberal economic policies that raised anew questions about the repercussions of Western trade practices in less developed countries, provides an image of a benevolent white American male freeing Asian children from forced labor at the hands of *their fellow countrymen*—in the process paving the way for the exploitation of Asian screens by Hollywood product.

Just how iconic the image of a benevolent and strong Jones/Ford is at this point is evident from the jarring effect of a sequence in which, under the influence of an evil priest's potion, he becomes everything antithetical to Jones/Ford—malevolent, gleefully abusive, and distinctly eroticized. He is presented in this scene shirtless and more noticeably toned than in earlier films, and willingly obliges the villains by starting to lower Willie into a pit of lava, brutally slapping Short Round when he tries to intervene. When the potion wears off, however, Jones changes back to his former self, the returned machismo thrust safely away as he openly expresses his love for the boy (and to a lesser extent for Willie).

One sign of the rapidly growing momentum of Ford's stardom, aside from the tremendous monetary success of all his early 1980s films, is the appearance near the time of the release of *Temple of Doom* of a mass-market star biography, *The Harrison Ford Story* (McKenzie). Title notwithstanding, the book has trouble fleshing out much of any story about the star, filled as it is instead with scene-by-scene plot synopses and pages of production background that have little to do with Ford. This suggests the extent to which a Ford star image had not yet strongly solidified. Making heavy use of previously published magazine interviews, the book recounts the now-familiar background of Ford's unhappy initial entry into the studio system, his departure and subsequent development of carpentry skills, and his occasional forays back to film acting in the 1970s, leading to his career-changing success in *Star Wars*; mention is also made of the minor car accident early in his career that yielded the signature scar on his chin. The book cites *Blade Runner* as "perhaps Ford's most important film" despite its initial lack of commercial or critical success, for the reason that "it was his first opportunity to sustain an *acting* performance in a starring role," and it thus most clearly established his bona fides (66).

The book's dominant theme is that despite his rise to fame in the early 1980s, Harrison Ford remains a level-headed "regular guy," uninterested in the Hollywood party scene and in being a recognized celebrity, and insisting on doing his own action stunts where reasonable: "His attitudes to fame, wealth and success have remained surprisingly consistent. He is proof, if proof were ever needed, that becoming a big-time movie star needn't change one's life for the worse. He has displayed an admirable ability to keep the craziness of Hollywood and film-making in general firmly in perspective. He isn't over-awed with his own on-screen image and can always be counted on for a breath of common sense in an all-too-looney business" (98).

## ★★★★★ Adjusting the Image

After his appearances in *Empire* and *Temple of Doom*, Harrison Ford's next role, in Peter Weir's *Witness* (1985), could be described as the one that was most important for the "maturing" of his star image in the 1980s on several interrelated levels: it articulates the multiple developing dimensions of his star persona in a refined and fully realized performance and in a vehicle aimed for a more mature audience demographic (even more so than *Blade Runner*, with its science-fiction trappings). As Philadelphia police officer John Book, Ford once more plays a character committed to upholding the law (as his surname might imply), but who also finds himself having to go against the organized institutions of the law on principle (when he discovers the corruption of his superior). The plot premise again has Ford/Book chiefly concerned with a woman (eventually a love interest) and a child (the love interest's son) dependent upon him for their protection, to which he is resolutely committed despite the woman's passing suspicions that his professional interests (in solving a case) might trump his concern for them (much as those under Indiana Jones's care often feel). More specifically, Book finds himself needing to protect a young Amish boy, Samuel Lapp (Lukas Haas), who has been witness to a murder during a visit to Philadelphia. Upon discovering a conspiracy in connection with the murder that goes to the top of his department—and finding that he and Samuel are in mortal danger because of it—he retreats with the boy and his mother, Rachel (Kelly McGillis), to their farm in rural Pennsylvania and, once there, the city cop attempts to blend in by adopting the appearance of an Amish man. During his rural sojourn, Rachel, a widow, develops romantic feelings for Book.

*Witness* worked as the quintessential star vehicle for Ford in showing the character's (and actor's) ability to skillfully control, maneuver, and adjust himself to function well in a number of disparate contexts, and to reconcile being at once upholder of the system and renegade; to be man of violence and man of thought and emotion, object of female desire and possessor of fatherly (and husbandly) qualities. Rachel at first expresses concern over her son having to spend too much time in the presence of a man "who goes around whacking people," but it is just moments later that Book, in his sensitivity to and awareness of Samuel, notices what no one else in his raucous precinct headquarters does: the boy's sudden recognition of the murderer (in fact a decorated officer) in a precinct photograph. The figuration of Book as a thinking man of action continues in the portrayal of his ability to skillfully whisk mother and son away to safety, despite their hot pursuit by top people in the police department. And he then demonstrates the craft and restraint to lay low by blending in with the Amish.

This notion of a skill at professional craft is very literally embodied in *Witness* with engagement of the motif of carpentry so central to Ford's 1980s image. This occurs in the rightly celebrated barn-raising sequence, in which Book helps ensure his acceptance by his temporarily adopted community and also firms up Rachel's admiration (and attraction) for him. Ford/Book's skill at carpentry signifies not only his adroitness, thoughtfulness, and masculine strength, but also his support of community and family. Nor is it merely incidental that carpentry figures centrally in the lead-in to an earlier scene that demonstrates Rachel's growing attraction. After a courtship call from a suitor for whom she has shown only lukewarm interest, Rachel delivers a glass of lemonade to Book, whom she finds (to her evident delight) displaying his woodworking skills in repairing an elaborate bird house he has previously damaged. Her sensual fascination with this man making use of her father's tools is particularly evident in a shot of her staring as he gulps down her lemonade, head tilted back and torso thus open to her, in one swoop. Discussion of his carpentry is picked up in the scene immediately following, where Rachel assists Book as he works on repairing his damaged car (thus demonstrating another set of manual skills) and reports to him that he has been invited to join the barn raising. At this point his tinkering leads to the car radio's coming on, and a rendition of Sam

Ford (as John Book) hiding out in Amish country in *Witness* with Kelly McGillis (as Rachel Lapp). Courtesy Movie Star News. Copyright Paramount Pictures/Edward S. Feldman Productions, 1985.

Cooke's "Wonderful World" can soon be heard. Book, happy to hear a familiar, old song, leads Rachel in a few dance steps before the pair is startled by the stern voice of her father-in-law.

In her discussion of Ford's acting in this important scene, Christine Geraghty highlights the significance of a modulation in the actor's more usual "seamless" mode of performance: "The tenderness of the scene," she argues, "depends upon the revelation, through gesture, of feeling which is normally hidden behind the Ford mask" (191). I would emphasize, however, that this modulation of approach and of emotion is also part of the broader figuration of Book's and Ford's dexterity, that Book's sensitivity and strength of character are projected here in part through his demonstrated nuance and skill in controlling both body and emotion.

As though building upon the facility we have just witnessed in carpentry and auto repair, we now have added other kinds of skills/handiness, a deftness first in Book's impromptu dancing, which he manages to pull off without the slightest hint of awkwardness despite the untutored feet of his dance partner, and also an emotional deftness. Before he dances with Rachel, Book holds her gaze with a serious look (as he walks around the car toward her) that appears to reveal his own attraction to her, but he soon breaks the tension by smiling and guiding her to dance with him. Singing along to the tune, in two instances he glides to a pause in which he again holds her gaze seriously and intently, but then smoothly modulates back into dance mode; in the second of these instances Book even appears briefly as though he is moving closer to kiss Rachel (in keeping with romantic genre conventions) before he shifts away. These highly meaningful pauses communicate both his interest in her and awareness of her emotions regarding him, but also his ability and his choice to keep their relationship within socially legitimized boundaries, to respect the moral order of the community (even if she herself might desire him to transgress this order) and to be worthy of her trust. Ford thus once again portrays a figure supportive of the dominant social order while also attuned to human emotions at odds with this order.

In point of fact, Book does eventually break down and give in to desire for Rachel toward the close of the film, seemingly in adherence to generic expectations—but the fact that the ostensible consummation of their relationship takes place offscreen (there is an abrupt edit away from their passionate kissing) would appear to speak to the difficulty such imagery would pose for the film's conceptualization of Book, as well as for Ford's image in 1985.

*Witness* can also be said to extend the racialized dimensions of Ford's stardom on a number of levels. Like Indiana Jones, John Book is the purveyor of a benevolent white male order, free of any exploitative motives as he moves into the realm of the ethnic Other (even if here a white Other) in order to ensure protection for all, in effect adopting a fatherless ethnic family (if only temporarily) as he does so. But another more overtly racial structure here is that of the largely urban crime drama featuring a white cop with a black partner up against a corrupt black colleague (and a white institutional power structure that supports him). Although *Witness* predates the bulk (although not all) of the interracial buddy police films that appeared in the 1980s, it significantly shares some of the underlying racial dynamics of those films. Christopher Ames (citing the work of Leslie Fiedler) emphasizes in particular how these films tend to evince a reversal of a classic relationship found in American literature between white and dark-skinned protagonists, wherein the former, in flight from civilization, must rely upon the superior wilderness skills of the latter to survive; in contrast, in the modern interethnic buddy film Ames describes, the refined (and indeed emasculated) black protagonist must depend upon the savagery and skill of the white protagonist for his salvation, and, ultimately, the return of his virility, such processes typically yielding utopian images of interracial masculine bonding.

Such a duality is writ large, indeed redoubled, in *Witness* in that Book's superior wilderness skills and strength contrast the diminutive and vulnerable nature of his African American partner Elden Carter (Brent Jennings) and the citified (even dandyish) nature of his chief African American antagonist, Detective James McFee (Danny Glover). McFee's incongruity with and ineptitude in the non-urban setting of the farm appears in his irritation over his shiny shoes becoming besmirched in manure when he arrives there (in a three-piece suit). Book's partner's symbolic emasculation is clearly suggested not only in his physically small stature, pointed out even by Samuel and emphasized in high angle shots of the detective, but also in his consistently nervous and frightened reactions to the machinations of the larger (and mostly white) villains around him—and ultimately in his death at the hands of these villains. Although Book is unable to protect his partner from murder (having been both more focused on the safety of the boy and not fully aware of the danger he was in), news of the murder and a desire to redress it are in fact what cause him to spring into (potentially dangerous) action in the film's third act. Book is thus still able to fulfill his heroic functions (though in a narrative structure much more built around heterosexual romance than homosocial bonding), and his character still conforms to the Ford star discourse of benevolent white masculinity. What is troubling from a critical race perspective, however, is that both main black characters are revealed to have inadequate skills to ensure their own survival, the film's more overt ideology of interethnic tolerance notwithstanding, and the final symbolic sharing of Book's virility is not with his African American partner in a definitive act of bonding but with his Amish rival in love (to whom he in effect cedes Rachel).

## ★★★★★ Further Departures

Ford's positive experience of expanding his acting range (to strong critical acclaim) and broadening his (adult) audience appeal, as well as his personal affinity to working with Weir, led to his readily accepting another, much more challenging and unconventional role immediately following *Witness*. On the surface, the character of Allie Fox in Weir's *The Mosquito Coast* (1986) might in fact appear to have many continuities with other Ford characters: here as elsewhere Ford plays a highly skilled handyman and a strong father figure, the film largely being presented through the perspective of Fox's young son Charlie (River Phoenix, who would go on to play a boyhood version of Indiana Jones in *Indiana Jones and the Last Crusade* three years later). Also like many other Ford characters, Fox is a self-styled maverick uncomfortable with dominant power structures and possessing an adventurous streak—one which leads him, very much in the mold of Indiana Jones, to seek excitement and glory in less developed parts of the world.

Despite these larger structural similarities, however, on balance Allie Fox is substantially different than most Ford characters during the decade. An eccentric, angry, and outspoken inventor, he abhors Western civilization (especially America's version of it) so much that he precipitately decides to move from the United States (with family in tow) to start a new way of living in an unsettled area of Central America, where his personal shortcomings come sharply to the surface. Fox (again like Indiana Jones) does have it in mind to help those in the foreign land to which he ventures, in this case by making use of a self-invented technology to cool jungle homes and produce ice, but he also reveals an intense drive to gain glory and recognition for his work, as well as to wield control over those with whom he interacts. Although visionary, Fox in his single-mindedness proves by turns megalomaniacal, dictatorial, abusive to his family, and murderous—an increasingly unlikable character very much at odds with the Ford star image. This lack of cohesion, however, is at most probably only a partial reason for the critical and commercial failure of the film. As a number of writers have pointed out, the film also suffers (by design or not) from a lack of any clear perspective on this unpleasant main protagonist, a dearth of cues to facilitate "reading" him (see, for example, Hentzi 10–11).

One clear indication of the continuing increase in Ford's cultural capital at the time was the appearance in 1987 of two general-audience biographies of the actor, one a slender mass-market paperback (Vare and Toledo), the other a more in-depth study (initially released in hardcover) by a British journalist with a track record in star biographies (Clinch). The Vare and Toledo paperback positions the actor as something of a renegade, a "star who hates Hollywood," always at odds with the system he is nevertheless part of (1). The more in-depth (and more polished) Clinch biography, while in large measure adhering to the same narrative contours as the other book, gains authority by using original interviews and drawing out several significant nuances, in particular in its opening assessment of his star image. Perhaps most significant is Clinch's repeated positioning of Ford as being on an order with the most legendary of Hollywood stars, opening her portrait with the assertion that he has been set apart by "star quality, the genuine, gilt-edged article, the kind they weren't supposed to make anymore," and noting the comparisons critics have frequently been inspired to draw between Ford and such icons as Humphrey Bogart and John Wayne, especially in the wake of *Raiders of the Lost Ark* (1).

While the appearance of two highly laudatory biographies of the actor in the same year goes a long way toward suggesting the progress of his career, such volumes rarely have much influence in shaping the star discourse in turn—especially in comparison to film roles themselves. And in terms of such film roles, Ford's career was arguably experiencing a lull around 1987. The coolly received, off-beat, auteur-directed *Mosquito Coast* was to be followed in early 1988 by another auteur work—the Roman Polanski thriller *Frantic*. These two films in combination with *Witness* marked a clear effort to further expand the actor's range and thus modify his star image. As Steve Oney's profile in *Premiere* (timed to coincide with the release of *Frantic*) put it, Polanski's film "should complete the process that *Witness* and *The Mosquito Coast* started: the elevation of Ford's place in the Hollywood pantheon from pulp genre hero to legitimate leading man" ("A Very Ordinary Man," March 1988, 46). Yet while the *Premiere* profile is prepared to accept Ford as a top screen actor, and quotes further comparisons to Bogart and Clark Gable, the article leaves the dominant impression (derived in large measure from an interview conducted in a town near Ford's Wyoming ranch) of a man almost angrily preoccupied with preserving the privacy of his personal life. The earlier discourse of a meticulous craftsman thus begins to shade in this account into that of an obsessive. In contrast to Clinch's characterization of the actor's extremely cautious and reserved but also "modest . . . likeable, informal" nature, Oney reports that, "distant, recalcitrant, on occasion a little surly, Ford is, in the end, a man who goes to greater lengths than most to control not only what is known about him but what he will or won't do" (51). Indeed, this qualitative shift in Ford's star discourse is already anticipated somewhat in a Kenneth Turan cover profile of the actor in the November 1986 issue of *GQ*, under the title "Harrison Ford Wants to Be Alone" and with a cover tag-line of "Hollywood's Mr. Mum."

*Frantic*, an uneven but nevertheless interesting film, is also relevant to this discussion in developing certain later shifts in Ford's image—on some level arguably even serving as a reflexive commentary on the inevitable aging of that image. Ford here plays a character who appears to be much more a part of the status quo than his previous characters in the decade, comfortably settling into married life as a successful physician (with teen children) and also showing signs of aging—emphasized in his repeated reaching for his reading glasses in early scenes of the film. While the character of Dr. Richard Walker at first appears comfortable with this state of affairs, the self-consciously Hitchcockian thriller that develops, in which his wife is kidnapped while they are on a conference trip to Paris, throws this existence into chaos. The largely nocturnal narrative in numerous ways hints at its own oneiric qualities and readily invites reading not only as a waking nightmare but as a middle-aged man's fantasy—one that involves throwing off the restrictions of a thoroughly bourgeois existence and pursuing law-breaking activities in the company of a voluptuous young French woman (Emmanuelle Seigner), albeit with the conscious justification that his aim is to rescue his wife. While the narrative economy requires that the young woman ultimately be killed off (appropriately, just before sunrise) in the process of saving the wife, a major portion of the narrative concerns the excitement of Walker's adventure with her—prowling the nightclubs and alleyways and even rooftops of Paris, fending off agents of various international powers, and developing a measure of trust and intimacy with his young and alluring new companion.

On one level, then, the text offers us two versions of Ford (as Walker) in one body—the one an aging, upper-middle-class, well-respected physician and devoted husband and father on a professional conference trip; and the other an adventurous, law-breaking, night-clubbing, virile American on a Parisian holiday, whose bare body (with visibly more toned muscles than in earlier Ford films) is exposed repeatedly, in one instance covered only by a stuffed animal. While this jibes with the sense of duality or contradiction already evident in Ford's star discourse (playing rakish characters who nevertheless ultimately support the status quo), it also speaks to a transitional moment for the star, the shift from an association with younger roles (in vehicles aimed largely for young audiences) to older, if not middle-aged ones.

## ★★★★★ Return to Form

After the exploration of darker dimensions of the Ford persona in two off-beat (and not high-grossing) productions, Ford's next career move, to return to more likeable characters in more crowd-pleasing genre pictures, was entirely in keeping with his consistent strategy in the decade of tempering potential excesses in his image and potential typecasting. In the romantic comedy *Working Girl*, released at the close of 1988, Ford as Jack Trainer is now most literally a Reagan-era organization man, a Wall

Street investment banker. And yet (in concordance with earlier roles), various dimensions of the characterization and narrative choices keep Trainer far from being another Gordon Gekko (the ruthless stockbroker famously portrayed by Michael Douglas in *Wall Street* the previous year). For example, as the boyfriend of Katherine Parker (Sigourney Weaver), the boss of the working-class protagonist Tess McGill (Melanie Griffith), he has a distinctly Yuppie class identification even though he is also characterized as only a mid-level employee still finding his footing in the business world (he admits he has "been in a little bit of a slump" deal-wise) and thus in narrative opposition to other men (and also some women) who have already ascended in the power hierarchy (see Tasker, *Working Girls* 41–43). That Trainer already has it in mind to break off his relationship with Parker and is attracted to McGill naturally also recommends him as a positive character, and one not overly invested in the system. Nor, indeed, do the major conflicts in the film really revolve around him, Ford in this case uncharacteristically playing what is in some sense a supporting role (though an important and top-billed one). Also somewhat uncharacteristic (though in keeping with the greater exposure of skin already evidenced in *Frantic*) is an overt positioning of Jack Trainer—and of Harrison Ford—as a sex object here, a prize McGill and Parker in effect compete for, whose attractiveness to women is made particularly evident in a scene where his decision to change his shirt in his office cubicle draws considerable (appreciative) attention from his female co-workers, as well as in a scene where several young women ogle him at a wedding party.

Ford followed up *Working Girl* with *Indiana Jones and the Last Crusade* in 1989—a film marking a return to Ford's successful action formulas. Yet while the film does revisit familiar territory and is arguably the first Ford film with strong appeal for teen audiences since 1984's *Temple of Doom*, it also continues the significant tendency in Ford's career to move more toward an adult audience. Although the film certainly delivers the expected action sequences, the adventure narrative is this time driven more than in the past by Indiana Jones's personal needs and emotional vulnerabilities (rather than, say, a drive for acquisition and excitement)—and this in turn provides a pretext for a deeper exploration of the protagonist's psyche than in earlier films. More specifically, Jones agrees to take on an assignment to find the Holy Grail primarily after learning that his father (a cold and unsupportive figure, about whom he has deeply conflicted emotions, played by Sean Connery) has disappeared while himself pursuing the relic. Another shift here in keeping with shifts in Ford's star persona is that Jones seems to be acquiring more of a sexualized identity. Whereas in the earlier

Ford tries his hand at romantic comedy in *Working Girl* with Melanie Griffith and Sigourney Weaver. Courtesy Movie Star News. Copyright Twentieth Century-Fox Film Corporation, 1988.

two entries, the female leads tended to be more sexually and romantically interested in Jones than vice versa, Jones in this instance shows immediate romantic attraction to the female lead, Dr. Elsa Schneider (Alison Doody), flirting unabashedly until a colleague reminds him of the urgent business at hand. When it turns out that this new object of his ardent affections (and, shortly thereafter, lover) has also been romantically involved with his father, Indiana's quest to gain his father's affections develops oedipal complications as well.

*The Last Crusade* accommodates this heavy element of oedipal intrigue within the confines of what is simultaneously a family entertainment vehicle in large measure by adopting a consistently comic tone (more so even than the previous two films in the series), in particular through its exceptionally witty and clever dialogue. This comic mode suits the Ford persona just fine here, especially because of Ford's appearance in a romantic comedy immediately before this film. The film's moral framework is able to accommodate having a female lead who sleeps with both Indy and his father by having her revealed to be a Nazi. Indiana's weakness for her, moreover, is (as the film's moral economy would imply) somewhat mitigated by the fact that she turns out to be at times less than fully comfortable with the practices of the Third Reich. Another sleight-of-hand keeps Indy from being seen as responsible for Schneider's demise: just as former lover Parker is seen to be largely hoisted with her own petard at the close of *Working Girl* (by being caught in a lie in a business deal), at *The Last Crusade*'s conclusion, Schneider falls to her death (even as Jones tries to save her) in greedily trying to reach the relic though it is beyond her grasp.

This somewhat more humanized version of Indiana Jones, and even more so the "frantic" image of Ford as Walker in the Polanski film, pave the way for more vulnerable, flawed, and ambiguous versions of the Ford persona that arise at the start of the 1990s—for example an adulterous district attorney accused of the murder of his former lover in *Presumed Innocent* (1990) (a film that finds Ford in lovemaking scenes that are more explicit than earlier ones) and an amoral and repugnant corporate lawyer whose personality changes completely following a shooting incident in *Regarding Henry* (1991). The character Ford portrays at the opening of the latter film is quite jarringly removed from most any other he played in the preceding decade—perhaps bringing to mind more than anything else the abusive nightmarish version of Indiana Jones briefly glimpsed in *Temple of Doom*, or the also abusive Allie Fox of *Mosquito Coast*. The impressive modulation in *Regarding Henry* from cutthroat attorney to speechless invalid to sensitive father and husband provides the consummate demonstration of the kind of absolute control in performance Ford was working on achieving throughout the 1980s. But at the same time the new image of Ford that develops in the second half of the film has all the hallmarks of a "kinder, gentler" white American masculinity emerging at the close of the Reagan era—one Susan Jeffords (specifically citing *Regarding Henry*) identifies as emblematic of a larger shift in Hollywood representations of masculinity occasioned in part by a simultaneous shift in American political concerns from foreign policy issues to domestic ones. As she describes it, at the turn of the decade, "*Retroactively*, the men of the 1980s are being given feelings, feelings that were, presumably, hidden behind their confrontational violence" (*Hard Bodies* 144–45). Yet though this formulation does apply quite literally to Harrison Ford's character in *Regarding Henry*, it is not nearly as germane to his overall star image: as this chapter has worked to show, Ford's distinctiveness as a male star of the 1980s was that the feelings had *always* been present.

# 9 ★★★★★★★★★★★★
# Sally Field and
# Goldie Hawn
## Feminism, Post-feminism, and Cactus Flower Politics

CHRISTINA LANE

Sally Field made celebrity history during her 1985 speech at the Oscars ceremony. Accepting her second Best Actress Academy Award, for *Places in the Heart* (1984), she declared, "And I've wanted more than anything to have your respect. The first time I didn't feel it. But this time I feel it. And I can't deny the fact that you like me . . . right now . . . you like me. Thank you." (Her speech soon morphed into a catchphrase that empha-

---

*Norma Rae.* Courtesy Jerry Ohlinger. Copyright Twentieth Century-Fox Film Corporation, 1979.

*Private Benjamin.* Courtesy Jerry Ohlinger. Copyright Warner Bros. Pictures, 1980.

sized weakness over strength: "You like me, you really like me.") A woman who was not afraid to expose her "need to be liked" clearly had cultural resonance in the 1980s, as her statement immediately became part of the lexicon of American popular culture. Goldie Hawn often expressed a similar sentiment. In an interview, she told Celeste Fremont that she knew she could appear flighty, but "I don't think of it as scatterbrained. . . . Everyone likes to be liked, so you put your most charming aspect forward" ("Goldie Hawn," *Playgirl*, November 1980, 39).

Field and Hawn speak to the contradictions of 1980s feminism. When seen as "intertexts," from a perspective further reinforced by their continual claims that they were (and remain) "best friends," the two stars illuminate how their feminist-star identities became newly defined from previous decades. It is instructive to place Field and Hawn alongside one another, as related stars, and as separate from other stars. This follows Richard deCordova's claim that to highlight the "actor-as-star" is to create "a specific path of intertextuality that extends outside of the text as a formal system" (20).

The two stars crossed paths repeatedly. The two continually told stories—in their films, offscreen representations, and self-accounts—that articulated a sense of being "in the process of" achieving political identity. What is most interesting about the staging of their stardom is that they were always "in-between" one political space and another, always inhabiting both past and present. As stars at a turning point—as the 1970s turned into the 1980s—Field and Hawn helped usher the past into the present.

For this reason, the two are best viewed as pre-feminist, feminist, and post-feminist all at the same time. They provide compelling illustrations of the states of feminism outlined by Susan Faludi in *Backlash*. She posits that in the 1980s, even though the majority of women supported feminist causes and cited the second wave movement as having positively impacted their lives, they distanced themselves from the term "feminist" (2nd ed. 2–7). This makes sense, Faludi asserts, given that the mass media, in conjunction with politicians, educators, doctors, and major corporations, was implying that the women's movement was the cause of women's inequities. She marks the middle of the decade as the first time the backlash becomes truly noticeable in popular culture, suggesting that it then strengthens in President Ronald Reagan's second term. Faludi makes a strong case, however, that overwhelming series of images—more than usual—were broadcasting the same message over and over again: it is time for the exhausted "superwoman" to admit that she (and feminism) were her own worst enemy and she would be much happier (and more feminist) at home (2, 4).

Field and Hawn achieved enormous critical acclaim and celebrity power as the 1970s gave way to the 1980s, with Field winning an Academy Award for her performance in *Norma Rae* (1979) and Hawn earning a nomination for *Private Benjamin* (1980). Nineteen eighty-four proved to be a pivotal year for both stars, with Field winning her second Academy Award (for *Places in the Heart*) and Hawn battling to bring *Swing Shift* to the screen. It is no coincidence that both *Places in the Heart* and *Swing Shift* revisit 1930s and 1940s proto-feminist struggles. The former features a recently widowed female farmer in the Depression era; the latter offers up Hawn as a Rosie-the-Riveter figure during World War II. These films mediate the complexities of middle-1980s feminism through a glance backward at what is presented as a simpler representation of female bonding and political community. While post-feminist discourse is very visibly reflected in representations of both stars, after 1984 Hawn becomes much more associated than Field with the individualistic, consumerist "lifestyle feminism" that defines post-feminism.

All of Field's and Hawn's films certainly have nuances and contradictions, but still their work between 1979 and 1984 specifically addresses concerns of gender equality, almost always going the additional step to connect gender discrimination to ideas about class, racism, or national militarization. They also speak to women's ambivalence about heterosexual norms and marital institutions, ending without romantic (heterosexual) closure and raising questions about coupling. More specifically, Field's and Hawn's characters begin to reimagine the worlds in which they live, pushing the ideological boundaries that dictate their social roles (see Tasker and Negra *Interrogating Postfeminism*). In addition, as their characters take on leadership they manifest a movement from self-focus toward community involvement and shared moral responsibility.

Between 1984 and 1989, the stars' films—and their representations in general—are inflected with more post-feminist discourse, evidencing a greater contest over meanings regarding the actresses' power, politics, and agency. Themes of domestic recuperation prevail, especially for Hawn (often with her apparent participation). Their aging was most certainly a factor—as each woman hit her forties in the middle 1980s—and led to their closer alignment with motherhood and the domestic sphere and a renegotiation of their past and present relationships to second wave feminism. Clearly the mid-decade intensification of post-feminism, which emphasized consumerism, leisure, lifestyle, and the self (over community involvement), was influencing their media discourse (see Tasker and Negra). In films such as Field's *Punchline* (1988) and *Steel Magnolias* (1989) and Hawn's *Swing Shift*, *Overboard* (1987), and *Bird on a Wire* (1990), the female protagonists are more self-centered, finding transformation through individual career choices or romantic decisions rather than in political community. The same theme appears in popular press accounts that relay the stars' growing satisfaction with their marriages, children, and homes. In these post-feminist representations, heterosexual romance and marriage become part of the solution rather than part of the problem (of female empowerment). Sally Field and Goldie Hawn showed women a way to go or—more aptly put—a way to grow.

## ★★★★★ First Acts: Signs and Salutes

"That's one of my dark secrets, the fact that I am totally apolitical. . . . I used to pretend that I care about all that because I figured no one wants to know you're that selfish. But, frankly, I care only about me" (Celeste Fremont, "Interview: Sally Field," *Playgirl*, July 1979, 91). This disclosure by Field, during her publicity for *Norma Rae*, is provocative on two counts. First, her "dark secret"—to care about "me"—may have been selfish, but it expressed a public desire of many post–second wave feminists. Her very choice of words poses a cultural question of the historical moment: what is political? Second, Field's revelation serves as a reminder that, at the beginning of the 1980s, the star was often constructed as "pre-political," but in such a way that foresaw her encounters with labor activism and women's rights as well as her own consciousness-raising.

This period in Field's career is compelling not because the star is "apolitical," as she suggests, but because she is in the midst of a transformation—a political awakening catalogued by the media from 1979 to 1982. A major part of Field's appeal is that she is a "transformative star," in the sense that the press represents her psychological and political turning points as a continual series of revelations. Field painted a telling self-portrait in 1980, observing, in a phrase that gave an article in *Ladies' Home Journal* its title, "I've been very cloistered in my life. I don't know many people, partly because of circumstances and partly because I started work so early. I didn't go to college. I haven't traveled. . . . There's a part of me that is just coming to life now" (Jeff Rovin, July 1985, 115). By January 1981, a contrast appears in Field's interviews, explicitly attributed to her participation in *Norma Rae*. The film chronicles the protagonist's struggle to unionize the rural southern textile factory in which she works, while also becoming more fully aware of the world around her (especially its sexism, racism, and anti-Semitism). Authors of many articles asserted that she was transformed by playing Norma Rae, who is a composite of several factory workers, but heavily based on activist Crystal Lee Sutton. With this role, the actress was not the same "Sally Field" as before. Many reviewers acted as if she had come out of nowhere, even though she had earned an Emmy for the television miniseries "Sybil" (1976). That Field was newly reinvented was testimony not only to her many years of daily study at the Lee Strasberg school, but to her new identification with working-class laborers, especially women. She went from (Method) acting to (political) action.

Whether it was the process of "performing" the character Norma Rae, or the broader experience of the picture's production, promotion, and acclaim, there appeared to be a major shift in her identity and, by extension, her persona. She remarked: "Even though I looked younger then, during all those television days . . . I felt like a very old person. . . . One of the least attractive things about me is that I've always tried to live in a closet. That way you don't have to think about what's 'out there.' Are there injustices? . . . Now I do want to know. . . . [I] could never see people very well, as a group, as a society or even as individuals" (Fred Robbins, "Sally Field: Coming Up Clover," *Saturday Evening Post*, January/February 1981, 68).

As implied by this remark, Field's accounts often generated a tension between narratives of political conversion and personal awakening. This was reinforced by her tendency to attribute her own transformation to *Norma Rae*'s formerly blacklisted director, Martin Ritt. As a result, a central question structured many of her interviews: to what degree was Field shaped by the feminist movement, and to what degree was she influenced by individual men? She created controversy during her acceptance speech for her first Academy Award, for *Norma Rae*, when she neglected to thank Crystal Lee Sutton or any of the female factory workers whose experiences had greatly informed the film. Field expressed gratitude to Ritt, exclaiming, "Ritt *was* Norma Rae." Within a few days, she tried to cover for the error, stating, "I hope that by thanking Marty Ritt, I was actually thanking all the women who had the courage to do what Norma Rae did." This only elided the working women further, insinuating a "cult of Marty" that appeared to preempt feminism for Field.

Ritt's attention to labor values figured in her comments on choice, agency, and the high priority of the "self." In 1980, Field told the *New York Times*, "I'm kind of at a crossroads in my career . . . trying to understand who I want to be and how I want to represent myself in the acting world now that I have the opportunity to choose for myself. I've really never had any kind of role model before, anyone like Marty [Ritt] who faced this kind of moral dilemma, if you can call it that: the morality of who am I within the context of my work" (Kirk Honeycutt, "Sally Field Maps a Career on

Back Roads," 12 October 1980, D24). Her films from this time—and particularly scenes in *Norma Rae*, such as that in which she confronts her pastor, and in *Absence of Malice* (1981), such as the climactic meeting with the attorney general—foreground "moral dilemmas" within work environments as well. These roles help portray the star primarily as a working woman, delving into principles related to labor and the public sphere.

The theme of work and the question of Field's dependency on men for empowerment—for which work was often the "answer"—were also represented as crucial concerns for her romantic life in the early 1980s. She had had a very public relationship with Burt Reynolds, one of the most powerful superstars of the day, for four years—from late 1976 to March 1980. They had co-starred in four films and graced the covers of a dozen magazines, as a leading Hollywood couple. In spring 1980, Field admitted that it was time to leave Reynolds in order to start making career decisions on her own and to look for seriously engaging work, rather than box office–driven material. She told the *New York Times* she distanced herself from Reynolds because "he thinks differently than I do and [just after *Norma Rae*'s success and during the 1979 film *Beyond the Poseidon Adventure*] I didn't believe in myself" (Honeycutt, "Field Maps a Career," 12 October 1980, D20).

This watershed article positions *Norma Rae* (and Ritt) as opening a major door in Field's life—a way for her to walk away from an increasingly stifling, career-damaging relationship with Reynolds. Sydney Pollack's *Absence of Malice* (with Paul Newman) and Ritt's *Back Roads* (1981) enabled her to take more dramatic risks and work with esteemed directors. By 1981, Field looked a lot like her former character, runaway bride Carrie in *Smokey and the Bandit* (1977), hitchhiking in a wedding gown, ready to throw off her veil and see where the road might lead. Only this time, she was *shedding* her ties with Reynolds in her liberation quest. About her realization that her relationship with the mega-star was disempowering, Field told interviewer Lawrence Grobel, "I came to the surface is what I did. I got mad" (*Playboy*, March 1986, 57). In the meantime, it looked as if another powerful female star was taking on the industry and leaving her romantic relationship behind. As yet another runaway bride, Goldie Hawn, would discard her wedding dress for boot camp, in the title role of *Private Benjamin*.

## ★★★★★ Second Acts: Double Talk

"Can [Hawn] be a good actress, a good producer and a good mother all at once?" This question, posed by David Ansen in his feature-length coverage of Hawn's success, offers one of many examples that portrayed Hawn as conflicted by multiple demands ("The Great Goldie Rush," *Newsweek*, 12 January 1981, 52). When she decided to make *Private Benjamin*, she was six months' pregnant and with a toddler at home. By the time it was released, she would be headed toward a divorce and single motherhood. Hawn's quality of accessibility meant that many of her followers felt close to her, sharing in the ideological contradictions that apparently structured her life. As she hit major obstacles in her personal life, in keeping with the confessional and therapeutic discourses of celebrity journalism in the 1980s, she openly shared them with reporters. This happened when she actually broke the news of her separation from Bill Hudson many pages into a *Playgirl* interview after pretending that her marriage was fine. In the middle of a long answer about passion in marriage, she responded, "I mean, I love to be high on love. But the most important thing to me is not that. I have to tell you something. (long pause) My husband and I are separating" (Fremont, "Goldie Hawn," *Playgirl*, November 1980, 113).

As all of this was occurring, the risk she had taken with *Private Benjamin* was paying off: producing a $10 million film, scoring a long-term contract with Warner Bros., launching a well-staffed production company, and receiving an Oscar nomination. Meanwhile, she was gracing the covers of *Newsweek, US, People, TV Guide, Playgirl*, and *Ms.* Throughout, she expressed second wave feminist sentiments, evidencing a discontent with the existing social order and looking to initiate institutional change.

With *Private Benjamin's* success, Hawn became a Hollywood powerhouse and in the process thwarted earlier stereotypes that had defined her as a sweet ingénue or dingbat. The media now painted her as a "master juggler" who somehow managed to put in fourteen-hour days, handle studio executives with "charm," and make it home to bathe the children and put them to bed at night. She appeared to be triumphant in this new role as "superwoman," a 1980s term for women who "wanted it all." As the decade progressed, however, it would become apparent that this star negotiated a constant balance of the socially aware feminist and the careerist, self-oriented post-feminist. Hawn's early 1980s representations underscore the options open to newly liberated women who were caught between two choices, to be a radicalized feminist or a self-designed superwoman.

These are binary terms for considering women's representations, yet they were ultimately the framework that the popular press used to portray Hawn. She functioned as a representational screen onto which the media projected dual queries (Would the second wave survive past the short term? Were women buckling under new pressures?) as two sides of the same coin. *Private Benjamin* brought these questions to the fore. It opens with a declaration that all that Judy wants "is a big house, nice clothes, two closets, a live-in maid, and a professional man for a husband." Fade up on Judy's wedding in progress, and, after a few sequences, we arrive at her wedding night. While consummating the marriage, with Judy still in her bridal gown, the groom falls dead of a heart attack. Once the wake is over, Judy sneaks out of her parents' house and disappears without a word—having made a conscious decision to stake a claim to her own life for the first time, thus connecting her with the wacky heiress figure from classical screwball comedies such as *It Happened One Night* (1934) and *My Man Godfrey* (1936), whose female characters become reborn and much more self-aware (Cavell 1–44). No matter that a few sequences later she will be duped into joining the army. It will not take long before she will make again the same choice: she salutes good-bye to the world of safety and privilege she has known and walks into the rigorous, unfamiliar territory of the all-female barracks. There, for a time at least, she will become a feminist in the military, a rare breed in 1980s Hollywood representation.

The basic premise of *Private Benjamin* is that this spoiled, Jewish woman has strengths she does not realize. She discovers her own resources first in the army, struggling not only against her male superiors but also against a controlling female, Captain Doreen Lewis (Eileen Brennan). Judy and her female platoon—a multi-racial and multi-ethnic crew—empower themselves by building physical strength, strategic abilities, and a growing awareness of their collective potential. They are seen engaged in a struggle to create a feminist space. She then moves to Paris to work in a high-powered position for the government. Upon taking her promotion, Judy is immediately isolated from the structuring bonds of her feminist community and her focus shifts to a search for a former one-night stand, a wealthy, elite Frenchman with whom she promptly falls in love. The film explicitly documents Judy's descent into numb misery and near insanity, as she chooses her relationship over her job and plans a wedding that only leads her to feel increasingly useless. As an answer to the forward movement of the army section—which seems clearly connected to the second wave feminist movement—the second section represents a cultural, and self-imposed, backlash. It is an allegory for the post-feminist, careerist, consumerist woman, who pours everything into her personal life without understanding the social, political, and psychological costs at stake.

Fortunately for Judy (and for us), as the film is ending and she stands at the altar, she returns to her senses. The rabbi is reading the vows and it is as though she wakes up, realizing that his words are in French, a language she does not understand. Hence, a connection occurs between this foreign language and the ("foreign") patriarchal language that confines her. Here and now, she calls off the wedding, but not before punching the groom in the face. After she has left her family and guests seated inside the groom's chateau, she steps onto the pavement outside to the beat of a marching band. Judy is Private Benjamin again. She walks into frame with her long, white gown gliding in the breeze, and her long hair flowing down her shoulders. She turns one last time toward the chateau, and toward the camera. Against the backdrop of a long dirt road lined with barren trees, Judy lifts off her flowing veil and—in a mock salute—casts it upward into the wind. She then turns and trudges up the long path, until she nearly disappears from view. The final image casts her as an alternative character in a blend of fairy tales—a countershot to Cinderella with a gesture toward Little Red Riding Hood and Snow White. Its dry, de-saturated landscape combined with a misty haze and the romantically dressed bride produce an ethereal, new-worldly effect.

Where this open-ended dirt road leads is anybody's guess. Literally and symbolically, the film ends here. Only one thing is certain: a groomless bride on a dirt path is a precarious image. Her future is unpredictable. It is the instability of Judy's final walk that is a defining characteristic of both 1980s feminism and Hawn's star persona. Early in the decade, the star, like her character, was poised to walk through uncharted territory—to reinvent her romantic life and hit a stride as a Hollywood executive. Yet, as will become clear below, many parallels occurred between Hawn's offscreen existence and Private Benjamin's. The two halves of the film created a pattern that structured the remainder of her 1980s films. They were governed by a binary tension between vocal, overtly political feminists and professionalized, individualistic women who struggled in ways they did not even recognize. Within a few years, she would look a lot more like the latter than the former. It is also notable that her star persona did not seem to accommodate these contradictory tensions as easily as Field's did.

## ★★★★★ Third Acts: New Inventions

Field's performance in *Places in the Heart* solidified her status as a serious actress and powerful force in the industry. Not only did she win her second Oscar, but she was finally having success with her own production company after repeated fits and starts. She had launched her initial company with Twentieth Century–Fox in late 1981 but did little as a new producer. In 1983, she moved to Columbia Pictures and joined with leading executive Laura Ziskin to start Fogwood Films. It would be 1985 before the release of their first venture, *Murphy's Romance*, but the press was rolling out major stories about Fogwood's forthcoming "impressive roster" as early as May 1984, six months before *Places* arrived in theaters.

Field's feminist transformation became fully evident in 1984. One of the greatest indicators was that she had taken hold of her career (by becoming a producer) and had done so by reaching out to other feminist-identified actresses. She explained to Grobel that when she was having trouble forming her first production company ("I couldn't even figure out whom to get to help figure out what to do"), she called on Jane Fonda, who had reached out to Field years before to little avail. Finally, Field "broke down and called Jane" and asked to meet. Over lunch, she disclosed, "I need to know how you do what you do. I'm completely lost . . . I feel so lonely here" (*Playboy*, March 1986, 116). Using the advice of actress-producers like Fonda and drawing on Ziskin's knowledge, Field developed Fogwood with confidence. In a 1984 *Los Angeles Times* story that emphasized her recent commitment to women's networking, she said that, in the face of struggles witnessed by producers Hawn, Jessica Lange, and Barbra Streisand, she had contemplated "getting the girls together" for support (Michael London, "Field's Newest Role as Actress-Producer," 9 May 1984, 12). With this new emphasis on female bonding, Field sounded much different from the "apolitical," "me-centered," and male-focused emphasis of her 1979 interviews.

If her shift in power was not influential enough, her performance as *Places in the Heart*'s Edna Spalding showed that her star persona was now directly engaged with contemporary feminist politics. Not surprisingly, the feminism of the film was tied to themes of labor. Director Robert Benton explicitly related women's empowerment to the trials (and victories) of farm work, given that this was a biographical tale based on his great-grand-mother's life (Aljean Harmetz, "Sally Field Has Propelled Herself," *New York Times*, 16 September 1984, 19). *Places* tells the story of a Texas widow who struggles to save her farm during the Depression, a battle that leads her to fight for equality for African Americans and migrant farm workers. Her identity moves from that of a domesticated, dependent housewife and mother to a hard-working landowner who stands up for herself, her family, and the workers who aid in rescuing her farm. "Working the land" takes on symbolic importance, both thematically and visually (given the numerous shots that track the growth of her burgeoning cotton fields).

This film transplants many feminist concerns of the 1970s and 1980s onto the life of a 1930s woman. Edna's struggle mediates tensions of second wave and post–second wave feminists because the character continually confronts conflicts that would have felt quite topical to its audience. For

*Places in the Heart* reinforces Field's down-to-earth image as well as her connection to Scarlett O'Hara. Courtesy Photofest. Copyright Delphi2 Productions/TriStar Pictures, 1984.

example, she must learn to write a check (with the help of an adversarial bank manager). She ultimately takes on the bank manager in an all-out war to prove her competence in the public sphere. Most women of the second wave had not overcome the same literal barriers—many (though not all) had not had to learn check-writing skills as adult women. But they were facing similar symbolic barriers such as being told by professionals that women could not purchase a house by themselves, make their own medical decisions, buy their own automobiles, and so on. Similarly, Edna is in the process of determining how to be a single mother, a struggle familiar to many women in the audience. Her experiences may well have resonated with those who felt they were living out the role of "husband and father" in a single-parent family.

In fact, one way to read *Places in the Heart* is that it proposes a redesigned, alternative nuclear family, a new paradigm that acknowledges politically altered social and familial relations. Not only does Edna invite the African American Moze (Danny Glover) to live on the farm, she also rents a room to a blind, eccentric man, Mr. Will (John Malkovich). By the end, Edna, Moze, and Mr. Will have become three-way parents to her son and daughter, although at times Mr. Will acts more like a sibling to them. The image they project, of a hybrid, makeshift family—whose many differences make it stronger, not weaker—is visually signified when a cyclone hits, forcing them to gather as a group in the tornado shelter.

For Field, *Places in the Heart* strengthened her image as pragmatic, unpretentious, and down to earth. Many press accounts reference the earth, soil, and land motifs that dominate the film. In an aptly titled interview in *L.A. Weekly*, Michael Wilmington and Ursula Schreck claim that her performance "is so rich and uncontrived, so warm and multi-layered and intensely emotional, it seems to have sprung right up through the soil itself" ("How Gidget Died," 12 October 1984, 40). Field, who had always exuded a comfortable, freshly scrubbed, "All-American" look, now achieved idol status as an icon of "Americanness" as she conjured up impressions of the nation's terra firma. *Places in the Heart* cemented this image, one introduced by *Norma Rae*.

The star's very American persona was buttressed by references to that Depression-era beacon of white, southern (American) femininity, Scarlett O'Hara. In a 1980 discussion of her efforts to quell her insecurity, Field had "joked about 'the fight between Cinderella and Scarlett O'Hara in me.' . . . Doesn't everybody think somebody else is really, ultimately, going to take care of them? Yet whenever I listened to anyone other than my own little voice, things always turned out wrong'" (Honeycutt, "Field Maps a Career," *New York Times*, 12 October 1980, D11). She preferred to find inspiration in Scarlett's strengths, imagining herself as a woman with "her fists clenched raised to the sky saying, 'I don't need a man'" (Sheila Weller, "Sally Field Learning to Please Herself," *McCall's*, January 1982, 79). By 1984, she had a different outlook. "I think somebody won," she told Scott Haller of *People*. "I don't feel like Cinderella anymore, and I don't feel like Scarlett O'Hara anymore. . . . But I feel like they got married and had a child and it turned out to be me" (15 October 1984, 121). This "daughter" of Cinderella and Scarlett relayed both characters' vulnerability and working-class alignment while very clearly articulating O'Hara's 1930s rugged, earth-bound determination.

*Places in the Heart* is a particularly good example of a film that bridges proto-feminism to post-feminism. Furthermore, its Depression-era setting helped secure Field's identity as "political," in ways that Hawn's World War II–era *Swing Shift* did not, as we will see. Perhaps the New Deal era's emphasis on coalition building played into the fluidity with which Field articulated and asserted feminism, whereas the divisiveness associated with the turbulent change in gender norms during the early 1940s made Hawn's film more loaded. It may also be that Hawn's previous "dingbat" image haunted her when it came to *Swing Shift*, illuminating the ways that Hawn and Field are simply different. Regardless, Hawn's "Rosie the Riveter" film suffered from a cultural backlash.

## ★★★★★ Fourth Acts: Turning Points

Thematic tensions always exist in the form of contradictions, but in the case of Goldie Hawn's films, it is remarkable how truly polar (as opposed to multiple and complex) these tensions were. The course of her films from 1980 to 1988 reveals the shift from feminism to post-feminism mentioned earlier in that they increasingly domesticate the star. While Hawn was indeed positioned for great success in 1980, the construction of her persona, films, and career was occurring within this broader context. Generally, it was a "re-masculinization" period for Hollywood and U.S. politics, as President Ronald Reagan rose to power and remained in office (Jeffords, *Hard Bodies* 12–13). The Reagan era followed a long struggle not just for women's rights but civil rights and gay rights. This presidency mobilized classical and contemporary film images that promoted a "sick" nation in need of rehabilitation. As Michael Rogin has eloquently argued, that administration won rollbacks on social programs by demonizing those political movements as social threats and invoking 1980s Ramboesque metaphors to mythologize American imperialism (32–38). During Reagan's first term, in which his political base was still building, the lingering effects of 1960s social movements still resonated heavily in the media. They were often posed as a question, such as, "Can women have it all?" By Reagan's second term, however, this question was answered with a firm "No."

The year 1984 marked the most profound break toward more conservative representation. With this in mind, *Private Benjamin*'s dichotomous structure most definitely serves as a model for situating Hawn's own shift from feminism to post-feminism. But the most marked shift in Hawn's persona—and in her entire career—came with the much-anticipated *Swing Shift*. Its critical and financial failure marked a downturn from which she could not recover, according to newspapers, magazines, voices from the industry, and the star herself. Conceived as a big-release epic that would join contemporary women's politics to the figure of Rosie the Riveter, it tells the story of World War II women sent to work in the factories while the men in their lives shipped off to military service. Hawn plays the housewife Kay Walsh, who starts to work in an airplane manufacturing plant when her husband enlists. She eventually falls in love with a trumpet-playing coworker, Lucky Lockhart (Kurt Russell), and is forced to make difficult choices about her marriage. (Hawn and Russell's offscreen relationship began on this picture.)

Warner Bros. signed the then up-and-coming Jonathan Demme to direct *Swing Shift*, but the film was plagued by creative differences between star and director and became a hotly contested site of meaning in Hawn's star biography. If, for several years, an unsteady balancing act had been performed by and through her stardom—between feminist politics and containment—then this film tipped the balance against Hollywood's view of her as a vocal, socially conscious woman. The story as told repeatedly by Hawn is that the turning point came at a screening of the rough cut. According to her, the protagonist had no arc and, more important, no conscience (Hawn 311). She felt that "the focus went off her at . . . very crucial moments, and so [did] . . . the studio." Even if *Swing Shift* was conceived as an ensemble piece, the central conflict for all the women would have no meaning if the protagonist did not establish the struggle. But her producing partner, Anthea Sylbert, claimed Hawn looked like "the blonde extra who'd been overpaid." Although she had ceded her producer's credit, Hawn retained approval rights, which gave her enough control to interrupt postproduction. Nevertheless, without any real power she became a go-between, mediating a relationship between the studio, various script doctors, and Demme, lacking the ability to enforce changes: "We'd have meetings, and the studio would say this and that. And nobody fought; [Demme] just turned around and didn't do it" (Ben Brantley, "Goldie's Second Takeoff," *Vanity Fair*, September 1989, 282).

The studio release was a "lowest common denominator" film, acceptable to Warners, disappointing but passable to Hawn, and completely out of Demme's hands. It failed at the box office and displeased critics. Popular press accounts berated Hawn as an egomaniac, a portrait that Warners did not dispute (publicly standing behind their director). The fact that Hawn suffered a major loss with *Swing Shift* but scored a major achievement in her love life with Russell merely reinforced the notion that she was relinquishing public power—or just downright losing it—and looking to a happy home life as a replacement.

*Swing Shift*'s role in Hawn's career—and in representations of Hollywood feminism in general—is made all the more compelling by the fact that there is a second rendering of the film—a Demme director's cut, which circulated as a bootleg in the late 1980s. Steve Vineberg in *Sight and Sound* compares the major differences of each version, describing Demme's cut as being most distinct in its rhythm and detail. It apparently has an "unslick and authentic-feeling" style, paying careful attention to all the female characters in the ensemble cast and showing how they increasingly grow into a new awareness as a group (*"Swing Shift"* 9). He finds Hawn's performance grittier and her character more conflicted. Demme shows us "everything that's inside Kay—how scared she is of going against the grain of old values the war and her new job are quickly making obsolete, how much it costs her every time she does, and how much she gains by the risks she takes" (10). Demme's cut—his portrait of Hawn—would certainly be an interesting sight to see, or, better yet, to have been viewed in mainstream markets. Filtered more daringly through this offbeat director's sensibilities, and fed more directly by a strain of independent women's cinema (such as the 1980 documentary *Rosie the Riveter*), who knows how her persona might have resonated with feminist criticism and filmmaking of the mid-eighties.

Vineberg criticizes Hawn for wanting to maintain a nice, "idealized" image and sustain clichés about proto-feminism and the war. Referring to Hawn as a real person, he also proposes that she saw parts of herself exposed on the screen in Demme's rough cut and insisted on taking control. Vineberg declares, "The irony is that Hawn didn't just slash Demme's canvas, but her own as well. Her performance in the unreleased version of *Swing Shift* is easily the finest work of her career" (*"Swing Shift"* 11). He, obviously, ascribes too much agency to Hawn and, regardless, the concern here has little to do with whether or not she was subconsciously insecure. The point is that "the making of *Swing Shift*" became narrativized as a symbolic loss of power for the star.

The film's centralization of feminist themes—its own precarious negotiation of political empowerment and recuperation—set it up to complicate Hawn's career. Its romantic appropriation of a 1940s version of feminism, and in particular a fantasy of World War II proto-feminism that longingly looked directly past the 1960s and 1970s second wave, put her star construction into further crisis. Mimi White provides an astute analysis of *Swing Shift*, showing how the character of Kay "projects the rise of feminism in the 1960s, but instead expresses [a political] 'out' in the narrative form of her immediate nostalgia" (325). In the representation of *Swing Shift*, proto-feminism is celebrated; more radical feminisms are elided, occluded, or expelled.

If Hawn was retreating into the domestic sphere, she was making an increasingly distinct impression in terms of her attitudes against marriage. This position was not a public stance, per se, but rather a way of modeling for other women "how not to get married." As she established her relationship with Russell, she made it known that neither of them had plans to legalize their co-habitation (which has lasted more than two decades as of this writing). For example, in 1988, when asked by a reporter if she had a term for describing their relationship, she answered, "live-ins, partners, lovers, companions, what? . . . There has to be a new word created in the English language for what we are. . . . But I certainly won't get married to give us a name" (Peter Hanning, "Goldie Hawn . . . Starting Over Again," *McCall's*, March 1988, 41). As a Hollywood star, she led the way in vocally legitimizing self-governed marriage or "opposite-sex domestic partnerships."

Hawn's persona—which by the late eighties had become defined through her status as part of an unmarried star couple—had balanced conservative and progressive definitions of coupling throughout the decade. It was a similar negotiation to the precarious balance of feminist politics. She once remarked, "I think eventually there's going to be a whole new system because marriage, evidently, is not working. But on the other hand, I feel commitment to a family unit is extremely important. Even if that is not the nuclear family. . . . Still, if I felt locked into the nice wife and mother image, I'd die" (Fremont, "Goldie Hawn," *Playgirl*, November 1980, 113). From 1980 on, her persona—by way of Hawn's comments and her example—invited other middle-class women to rethink the institution of marriage. Yet these challenges to marriage were fairly circumscribed: monogamy was valued and heterosexuality was never critiqued. In 1982, a friend stated, "Goldie's really a one-man woman" (Al Coombes and Mal Karman, "Goldie's Heartbreak Choice: Marriage or Career," *Ladies' Home Journal*, January 1982, 26). Hawn once declared, "I feel free, I feel I can do anything. I'm finally learning you don't have to be married to one thing—one medium, one idea—just to one man" (Brett Thayer, "Goldie," *Orange Coast*, April 1980, 12). It is in these representations of Hawn's relationship with a man that her status as a postfeminist crystallizes. Marriage is portrayed in both political and personal terms, with pragmatic and fiscal concerns dominating. By the mid-1980s,

Hawn's capitalist savvy was driving her marital decision making. And, the long tradition of lesbian and radical separatist critique of marriage within feminism was waning, as heterocentricity prevailed.

The star's second 1984 film, *Protocol*, sustained these trends. Produced by Hawn, it is a story about Sunny Davis, a cocktail waitress who inadvertently saves the president of the United States from assassination and is rewarded with a job as a high-powered diplomat. Her wide-eyed innocence and common sense make her a national media hero; they also help her halt a U.S. arms deal with an Arabian country. On the surface, *Protocol* appears to challenge the aforementioned Reagan-era remasculinization discourse with an alternative paradigm of female empowerment. It also provides a platform for Hawn to express her long-held anti-nuclear and pro-disarmament views. This film is additionally the most self-reflexive and intertextual of all her ventures, especially during a long montage that mixes magazine covers of the new celebrity Sunny with actual ones from Hawn's career. Spectators are encouraged to view *Protocol* transparently and make close comparisons between character and star. These blurred boundaries are reinforced by the fact that Hawn returned to her real-life roots, choosing this Washington storyline (she came from a Maryland suburb, just over the D.C. line) and shooting many of its scenes on location.

Given the close comparisons drawn between Sunny and Goldie, it is all the more significant that the film works against its own articulated interests. Its ostensibly political subject matter becomes deactivated because it concludes (in much the same way its inspiration, *Mr. Smith Goes to Washington* [1939], does) by implying that the nation's problems *and solutions* rest with individuals. Rather than critiquing the country's social and political systems, it ends by celebrating them. In addition, its message turns highly problematic when Sunny (as an American woman) rescues a group of Muslim women from their own patriarchal regime. Perhaps most obviously, its feminist message suffers a backlash effect: Sunny starts off as an independent and outspoken woman, yet ultimately she finds happiness in marriage, family, and local politics. Given the degree to which *Protocol* diffuses its own politicization of women's issues, Sunny may as well have become a corporate executive.

By the release of the Garry Marshall film *Overboard* (1987), the domestication of almost anything radical about Hawn appeared complete, except for the film's occasional pressure points that pushed their way to the surface. Hawn (who co-produced the film) plays an obnoxious, wealthy, bored wife (Joanna Stayton). She hires a working-class handyman (played by Russell) to make repairs on her yacht. After badgering him repeatedly, she

In *Overboard* Kurt Russell takes Goldie Hawn home to his cabin. Offscreen he was build-ing her a large cabin near their Colorado ranch. Courtesy Jerry Ohlinger. Copyright Hawn/ Sylbert Movie Company/Metro-Goldwyn-Mayer, 1987.

falls overboard (hence the film's title) and loses her memory. Russell's char-acter, Dean, decides to teach her a lesson in humility by convincing her that she is his wife and the mother of his four out-of-control children. By the end of the film, Joanna has come to prefer her new identity as wife and mother and fallen in love with Russell's character. In other words, follow-ing the general pattern of Hawn's star persona, this character's containment is complete—and, ironically, presented as self-determined.

*Overboard*'s logic of recuperation was reinforced by the film's publicity, which likened Russell to his character. Rugged and down to earth, he was the main reason that they had bought a seventy-acre ranch in Colorado. Their blended family of three children was growing up with cows, sheep, horses, and plenty of land. Judith Michaelson explains that they temporar-ily live in a four-bedroom house while they wait for Russell to build them a 5,000-square-foot cabin across the road ("Goldie Hawn—Just a Homebody After All?," *Los Angeles Times*, 24 December 1987, 1). Somehow, the presence of the hammer-holding, blue-jean-wearing Russell obscures the fact that this cabin will indeed be 5,000 square feet on an estate that actually makes up their third palatial residence. He appears to be simply a builder—just look-ing to provide for his wife and kids—mirroring his *Overboard* character and sealing off other possibilities of representation. Meanwhile, Hawn is "the picture of contentment as she lies on a chaise lounge in her living room . . . knitting clothes for the new baby of her close friend Meryl Streep" (Jeff Rovin, "Goldie Hawn's New Home," *Ladies' Home Journal*, September 1986, 75).

## ★★★★★ Fifth Act: Conclusions

Compared to Hawn, who even when domesticated fit the part of a junior mogul, Field came out the other side of the 1980s looking like a socially responsible, suburban soccer mom. Field's films from mid- to late decade continued to present her in roles where she gained a strengthened feminist perspective on life. Yet they also appeared to mirror her personal life, foregrounding the importance of romance and marriage. For example, in *Murphy's Romance* (her first producing effort), she plays Emma, a recent divorcée and single mother who moves to a small Arizona town and meets a much older Korean War veteran-turned-lefty (James Garner). Garner's character Murphy falls in love with Emma and helps her to launch a horse farm. Like so many of the female star's films, this one highlights hard work and labor. These values, and a love of the land, unite Emma and Murphy and ultimately indicate that their relationship will survive, whereas the one she had with her former husband (who returns) will not. *Murphy's Romance*, notably titled for the male role, ends with their clear decision to start a relationship, thus celebrating coupling and deemphasizing the woman's point of view, unlike her earlier, more female-centered, and open-ended films.

The 1988 picture *Punchline* also steers the protagonist's conflict toward a narrative conclusion that includes husband and family. Field's Lilah Krytsick is a lower-middle-class housewife and mother who decides to enter the world of professional stand-up comedy, against the wishes of her husband, John (John Goodman). *Punchline* traces the patterns of many of her films— Lilah undergoes a feminist awakening, deciding not only to enter the public sphere but also to attempt to change the male bias of the comedy industry. In this instance, her transformation is partially guided by a male figure (as it is in *Norma Rae*, *Absence of Malice*, *Places in the Heart*, and *Murphy's Romance*), this time in the form of a mentally unstable but highly talented comedian (Tom Hanks). Ultimately, she finds success within her chosen field of stand-up and strikes a balance between work and family (by achieving a satisfactory resolution with her husband). In *Punchline*, there is no mention of the second wave feminist movement (or of social move-

Sally Field passes the torch of stardom to Julia Roberts in the post-feminist *Steel Magnolias*.
Courtesy Jerry Ohlinger. Copyright Rastar Films, 1989.

ments in general), although it is implied that her escapes to New York transgress gender- and class-based rules that dictate remaining in the New Jersey suburbs.

As suggested by *Punchline* as well as numerous other Field films, her star persona had more room than Hawn's, somehow, to incorporate feminist politics. To a degree, this was attributable to class connotations. Hawn's cinematic associations with upper-class and upper-middle-class characters resulted in increased isolation as the decade wore on, especially as she aged. Field always appeared to reach out to causes and constituencies. In the 1980s, she played variations of the politicized mother (or one undergoing a social awakening) in *Places in the Heart*, *Murphy's Romance*, and *Punchline*. Hence, Field provided a feminist/post-feminist model for wives and mothers because she appeared to negotiate her multiple concerns with little conflict, off- and onscreen.

Field's last picture of the decade, *Steel Magnolias* (1989), contains many of these threads, yet this maternal melodrama-comedy is much more of a post-feminist film. Here, it is not Field that invokes the trope of the "daughter of Cinderella and Scarlett" but rather her own onscreen daughter, Julia

Roberts. Roberts plays Shelby, who chooses to have a baby even though she suffers from diabetes and could die from complications if she carries a child to term. Despite the fact that the film takes place in a contemporary small southern town with a cast of liberated female characters, the setting is whitewashed. The post-feminist *Steel Magnolias* sets aside racial and class politics in favor of a story about a middle-aged working mother and Shelby.

In part *Steel Magnolias* represents a symbolic passing of the torch of stardom from Field to Roberts, but as Deborah Barker argues it is also "in keeping with the backlash tendency to use metaphors of disease and death to characterize the end of feminism" (96). The film ostensibly celebrates Shelby's youthful world of "blush and bashful" (the pink colors of her wedding day), but at its true center are the friends who help her mother endure Shelby's loss. "The not so subtle postfeminist message of *Steel Magnolias* seems to be that the model of the superwoman is too much for the daughters of the next generation," Barker postulates (98). If representations of Field and Hawn had participated in questions of how to put feminism into practice at the beginning of the eighties, their cactus flower imagery—with its precarious negotiations and expressed vulnerabilities—was anything but flourishing by decade's end.

# 10 ★★★★★★★★★★★
# Meryl Streep
## Feminism and Femininity in the Era of Backlash

LINDA MIZEJEWSKI

In a December 1988 cover story in *Ms.*, film critic Molly Haskell remarked that Meryl Streep "made a fetish out of not giving the public what it wants and expects from a star" ("Meryl Streep: Hiding in the Spotlight," 68). This assessment suggests the specifically feminist stakes of her stardom in the 1980s that saw Streep's rapid ascent to fame and acclaim followed by gradual decline in popularity and reputation. In a period characterized by bitter backlash against feminism, the media bristled with contentions about femininity, changing gender roles, and the new figure of the superwoman who tantalizingly balanced family and career. Although Streep resisted and protested the roles of both superwoman and superstar, her career trajectory in the 1980s is haunted by these cultural figurations and by conflicting discourses about her femininity. Indeed, her perceived lack of glamour—the essence of femininity for Hollywood stardom—was a key element of the failed expectations referenced by Haskell. Femininity was a prickly topic in the aftermath of the women's movement, as suggested by the film with which Streep capped the 1980s, the feminist satire *She-Devil* (1989), in which she parodied an ultra-feminine celebrity whose luxurious lifestyle is ruined by marriage and children.

The expectations for Streep's stardom had been especially high at the beginning of the decade. Appearing on the covers of major magazines, Streep was named "America's best actress" (*Life*, April 1981, 80), "A Star for the 80s" (*Newsweek*, 7 January 1980), and "Magic" (*Time*, 7 September 1981, 38). Streep starred in a major motion picture every year, moving easily across nationalities and social strata in roles that revealed her exceptional range and virtuosity as an actress, and in particular her skill with voices and languages, enabling her to take on entirely different accents and personae: British, *The French Lieutenant's Woman* (1981); Polish, *Sophie's Choice* (1982); Danish, *Out of Africa* (1985); Australian, *A Cry in the Dark/Evil Angels* (1988); working-class activist, *Silkwood* (1983); disillusioned resistance fighter, *Plenty* (1985); and homeless alcoholic, *Ironweed* (1987). By the end of the 1980s, there had emerged what Karen Hollinger calls a "Meryl Streep film"—complex, literate, and focused on a challenging, multifaceted heroine (73–74).

In the first half of the decade, Streep appeared in high-profile films with mainstream appeal. Except for *Plenty*, all these films resulted in Academy Award nominations for Best Actress, with a win for *Sophie's Choice*. In less notable films, she portrayed an alluring murder suspect in the psychological thriller *Still of the Night* (1982), a married woman resisting adultery in *Falling in Love* (1984), and a betrayed wife and mother in *Heartburn* (1986). Throughout this time, she was honored with multiple awards and tributes, evidence that peers and reviewers indeed considered her one of America's best actresses.[1] Yet despite this standing, Streep's box office appeal and grosses greatly diminished by the end of the decade. Her reputation suffered regarding her acting style, her refusal of celebrity, and her choice of increasingly unpleasant character roles; her remarkable skill with accents and her ability to assume any nationality or ethnicity were admired but also criticized as impersonation rather than acting.

Indeed, as a star better known for her voice than for her body, Streep's stardom posed a significant disruption of the image-based Hollywood star system. Theater critic Hilton Als describes her estrangement from this system as "her disavowal of the American urge to cultivate personal glamour" ("Wagon Train: 'Mother Courage' at the Delacorte," *New Yorker*, 4 September 2006, 132). Although Streep took some traditionally glamorous roles at the beginning of the decade, she was entirely willing to portray unattractive women as well, and reviewers' hostility toward the roles or the social messages of these films are often manifested in comments on her appearance—that is, her refusal to *look* like a movie star or to act like one as well, and eschewing publicity, guarding her privacy, and, as Haskell put it, refusing to give the public "what it wants and expects from a star."

Even Streep's reputation as a hard-working actress sometimes ricocheted. Some critics reproached her for an acting style that foregrounded its own techniques. Paul Attanasio said her critics "charged that she always seemed to be watching herself in the mirror, that her performances are too 'worked out'" ("Meryl Streep and the Human Connection," *Washington Post*, 25 July 1986). A related objection was Streep's "predeliction for picking roles that efface all trace of her own identity" (Ron Rosenbaum, "Unnatural Actresses," *Mademoiselle*, January 1989, 46). *New Yorker* critic Pauline Kael, who had disliked Streep's mannerisms from the start, was the most prominent voice among her detractors, complaining that the lack of identity from role to role amounted to a lack of "presence" in Streep's performances: "An actress with a vivid presence might give the role something of her own substance," she wrote of Streep's acting in *Plenty*, "but Meryl Streep isn't that kind of actress. She's strictly an interpreter" (7 October 1985, 129).

These responses to Streep's self-conscious techniques and lack of a core persona or "presence" are crucial to the conflicted status of her stardom, a status she herself disdained. In one interview Streep said, "If you want to be a superstar, it seems to me you have to hire a press agent and do kinky things to get into the columns. If that's what it takes, I don't want to be a superstar" (*Ladies' Home Journal*, March 1980, 36.). Eight years later, she reiterated, "I'm not a star. I think you become a star only if you want it" (*Ladies' Home Journal*, October 1988, 62). In these and other dismissals of stardom, Streep seemed to equate stardom with the "superstardom" of celebrity—the focus on an actor's personality and personal life rather than the film texts. Indeed, Streep fiercely guarded the details of her personal life, refusing to "become 'celebrity junk food,'" as she told Brad Darrach (*Life*, December 1987, 78). She shunned public events, granted few interviews, and tightly controlled information about herself and her family.

Mapping Streep's stardom onto the issues of motherhood, feminism, and femininity in the 1980s, Karen Hollinger describes Streep as "the postfeminist woman in crisis, torn between her career aspirations and her desire to be a traditional housewife" (96). She suggests that Streep's stardom exposes rather than resolves the contradictory demands of post-feminism, a term that emerged in the early 1980s with multiple meanings. The term most often implies that the women's movement succeeded in securing equal rights for women so that feminism is no longer relevant and women can now enjoy endless choices concerning career, personal lifestyle, and the pleasures of both sexuality and commodities. As this suggests, post-feminism trumps politics with consumerism, positing that women now face choices rather than conflicts. Focusing on gains made by white, upper-class, heterosexual women—exactly the kind of privileged professional exemplified by Streep—post-feminism tends to overlook the economic and racial problems of the less privileged.

The problem is that while the civil rights movement opened doors and passed legislation, many things about gender did not change at all—the assumption that women still assume responsibility for emotional relationships, the household, and childcare, for example, or the double standard about attractiveness that makes a woman's looks a priority in how she is perceived. As a "star for the 80s," Streep was prime material for these cultural narratives about gender roles in transition. It was a decade in which *Glamour* magazine ran an editorial entitled, "When Someone Calls You 'Feminine,' Is That a Compliment or Not?" (July 1988, 44). The question goes to the heart of Streep's significance in cinema and culture.

## ★★★★★  The Crossroads of Gender

Streep's box office appeal slipped most for her 1987 and 1988 film roles as the homely bag woman in *Ironweed* and the pregnant, unsympathetic victim of media hysteria in *A Cry in the Dark*, films that generated Best Actress nominations but mixed reviews and poor ticket sales. "Even reviewers who dubbed her 'Magic Meryl' have begun to criticize her humorless selection of characters," the *Ladies' Home Journal* reported in 1988 in an essay reprinted in newspapers around the country (October 1988, 62).

The word "humorless" is a code for "feminist," a reference to the stereotype of the dour women's libber of the previous decade. The grammatical slip (humorless selection/humorless characters) suggests this quality is shared by the star and the characters she plays. Such an identification points to a broader issue, for Streep often defined herself as a feminist and advocate of women's rights at a moment when Hollywood films registered the impact of the feminist movement in contradictory ways (Claudia Dreifus, "Meryl Streep: Why I've Taken a Year Off for Motherhood," *Ladies' Home Journal*, April 1984, 154; see also *Redbook*, September 1982, 14; *Time*, 7 September 1981, 47).

The controversy about women's roles was galvanized in 1980, when President Jimmy Carter, proposing to reinstate the Selective Service, proclaimed that women should also register. In 1981 the Supreme Court ruled that only men could be registered for military service in case the draft had to be reintroduced, but the specter of women infusing "every profession"—and thus threatening traditional concepts of femininity—caught the public imagination. As Susan Faludi has documented, women did *not* in fact make significant gains in salary and professional status during the 1980s. The Bureau of Labor statistics instead show that women's wages stalled and the workforce became more sex-segregated. Nevertheless, the media played up individual success stories and then eulogized the loss of traditional femininity with features such as "What Has Happened to American Women?" (Faludi, *Backlash* [1991] 77–79, 365). In 1987, a Lifetime Women's Pulse Poll found American women divided about the issues of both feminism and femininity, with 50 percent feeling the women's movement had made no impact on their lives, but 41 percent believing femininity was a negative trait ("Feminist or Feminine?," *Executive Female*, July-August 1989, 6).[2]

★★★★★ **Who Will Rock the Cradle?**

This nervous question is the axis running through Streep's stardom and films at the peak of her career. Her breakthrough film character, after all, was the woman willing to leave her child in order to pursue her own needs in *Kramer vs. Kramer*, a film cited in *Newsweek*'s 1980 cover story on the growing divorce rate and its effect on children ("The Children of Divorce," 11 February 1980, 58). In several of Streep's major films of the 1980s, motherhood is a crisis or even a nightmare for the main character; at the same time, Streep's publicity focused on a narrative of the superstar as mom—in fact, as the 1980s superwoman, post-feminism's heroine and nemesis.

The criticism that Streep lacked a core persona in her films, with screen characters that changed radically from film to film, was reinforced by the contrast with her consistent persona as traditional wife and mother in "real" life. This dualism (private life versus screen life, "real" life versus fiction, "ordinary" life versus Hollywood) characterizes the construction of stardom itself as inevitably an unstable, contradictory entity (Geraghty 184–85). During this decade, in which she gave birth to three children in a stable, decidedly non-Hollywood marriage, Streep granted few interviews and most often selected journalists writing for women's and family magazines. This is significant because tabloid celebrity news had gone mainstream with the launching of "Entertainment Tonight" on CBS (1981) and the growing ubiquity of magazines like *People* (1974), *Star* (1974), and *US* (1977) through the 1980s. For the entire decade, *People* published only three stories on Streep, one involving her nervousness during the 1980 Academy Award ceremony ("Crossed Fingers but Then Meryl Left Her Oscar in the John," 28 April 1980), one on her campaign against pesticides in food ("Ms. Streep Goes to Washington to Stop a Bitter Harvest," 20 March 1989), and a third describing the wildlife dangers of filming *Out of Africa* on location ("Streep and Redford Battle Lions, Snakes, Storms, and Controversy," 20 January 1986). Gossip-hungry readers may have hoped for intimations of on-location romance between Streep and co-star Robert Redford in the latter article, which instead emphasized that both stars had brought along their families.

Streep married New York sculptor Don Gummer in 1978, and Henry, their first child, was born in 1979. In 1983 they had their first daughter, Mary Willa, and a second daughter, Grace Jane, in 1986.[3] The Gummer family, as they preferred to be called, lived first in a SoHo apartment and then, to protect their privacy, moved to a secluded country house two hours north of Manhattan. If there were conflicts between the famous wife and the more moderately successful artist husband, no interview or story ever hinted at it. Nor did either party describe the relationship in romantic terms. For the 1980 *Newsweek* cover story, Gummer spoke of trust and friendship in a quotation picked up in later feature articles: "There are many different levels of love," he said. "Ours is founded in a very deep-rooted feeling of trust. We're best friends" (7 January 1980, 56). Streep often spoke of their similar antisocial inclinations. "Don and I are a lot alike. . . . He's a hermit and so am I. We like to be alone—with each other and with our kids. We don't like the razzmatazz, the photographers and the glitz" (Dreifus, "Why I've Taken a Year Off," *Ladies' Home Journal*, April 1984, 153). The lack of romance in this and other accounts of Streep's marriage contributed, in the long run, to a public image devoid of glamour, as did the emphasis on family life.

Family life, in fact, was the element most romanticized about Streep, particularly before her decline in popularity after 1986. After the birth of Henry, Streep told *Redbook* that "Motherhood is a great thing, easier and more fun than anyone had told me" (September 1982, 14). A *McCall's* feature in 1983 described how she breast-fed her baby on breaks during the filming of *The French Lieutenant's Woman* and went home to cook dinner every night during the shooting of the New York sequences of *Sophie's Choice* (Natalie Gittelson, "Meryl Streep: Surprising Superstar," March 1983, 34). A 1986 cover story in the *Ladies' Home Journal* claimed that Streep could be found in local stores in the small town where the Gummers lived, "just another mother in an old sweatshirt" (August 1986, 150); the article explained that Streep is "a megastar who commands millions of dollars per picture, but it's her role as wife and mother that Meryl Streep says she could never live without" (100). In similar terms, a 1986 newspaper article praised Streep as the most respected actress of her times, and then qualified her status: "But most of all, Meryl Streep is a housewife. At home in Connecticut . . . there's no such thing as Meryl The Movie Star. There is only Meryl The Mom. Her all-time favorite role" (Rob Salem, "The Sunny Side of la Streep," *Toronto Star*, 13 July 1986). Feature stories occasionally added feminist language about shared domestic roles: "Meryl and Don have the kind of marriage in which old-fashioned ideas about love, marriage and commitment are blended with up-to-date notions about male-female equality," a 1984 article proclaimed, pointing out their efforts to share family time and household chores (Dreifus, "Why I've Taken a Year Off," *Ladies' Home Journal*, April 1984, 153).

Given the cultural climate of anxiety about motherhood, it is not surprising that feature stories focused on this aspect of Streep's life. As Richard Dyer points out, stars often "embody social values that are to some degree in crisis" (*Stars* 25–26). *Ladies' Home Journal* reported in 1980 that "despite the success of her career, it is obvious that Meryl's husband and child have now become the focus of her life and everything else is peripheral" (March 1980, 43). The comment that "everything else is peripheral" suggests a comforting cultural fantasy about the true place and heart of the superwoman, and Streep's interviews encouraged this slant. The same journalist asked if she would actually give up her career, and Streep's answer is telling: "I don't think that will be necessary. But yes, of course, I don't think that any enterprise is bigger than your life's needs or your humanity" (43). As Hollinger reminds us, Streep repeatedly claimed that she would always choose her family over her career, but no such melodramatic choice was ever required, making her "a safe role model for contemporary women" (95–96).

In actuality, Streep was on the screen nearly continuously throughout the years when she had her children in the 1980s. In April 1984, as noted, a *Ladies' Home Journal* cover ran the headline, accompanying Dreifus's article, "Meryl Streep: Why I've Taken a Year Off for Motherhood." However, Streep timed the break so that her career did not miss a beat. *Silkwood* had been released in December 1983, and *Falling in Love* was released in November 1984. Both *Plenty* and *Out of Africa* were released the following year. Hollinger points out that Streep's career was in fact inflected by her family life. Streep turned down roles that would have separated her from her family, while she chose to do *Falling in Love* and *Heartburn* mainly because she could shoot them close to home (83). Ironically, Streep's character in *Heartburn* is a food writer, a career that seems especially amenable to balancing family and work, but the marriage is a disaster. The scenes of heartbreak revolve around the household and kitchen, culminating in Streep's Rachel Samstat dumping a key lime pie into the face of her errant husband.

A successful high-end career in combination with insistence that the career was actually "peripheral" positioned Streep as the bifurcated superwoman, with the public narrative of the happy housewife running parallel to and on some level contradicting the public narrative of Streep's devotion to her craft. The feature stories about her were laced with details of her thorough preparations and professionalism: she read aloud from Jane Austen and George Eliot to perfect the cadences of a Victorian voice for *The French Lieutenant's Woman*; rehearsed tirelessly to get the posture right for *Silkwood*; ignored a giant bug inside her blouse so Sydney Pollock could get a long take in *Out of Africa*; and worked through take after take wearing a wig in the unbearable heat of Australia for *A Cry in the Dark* (*Rolling Stone*, 15 October 1981, 17; *Newsweek*, 10 October 1983, 89; *Films and Filming*, May 1989, 16). A journalist who observed her on the set of *Ironweed* commented, "Nothing, but nothing, gets in the way of her work. She arrives on the set in character and stays that way all day" (*Life*, December 1987, 78).

Directors and co-stars unanimously praised her cooperation, punctuality, good humor during shoots, and, most of all, her acting skills. Robert De Niro, her co-star in *Falling in Love*, commended her as a "pure actress," and interviews confirmed the deep respect De Niro and Streep had for each other despite their wholly different approaches to their art. Director Ulu Grosbard described De Niro as an actor gifted in performing scenes most actors find difficult, while Streep, he said, "is much more articulate; hers is an extraordinarily sharp intelligence. She is one of the brightest people I've ever met" (*Newsweek*, 3 December 1984; *Globe and Mail*, 21 November 1984). Alan J. Pakula, who directed Streep in *Sophie's Choice*, pointed out that the later backlash against Streep's painstaking acting techniques actually says more about the culture than about her: "We live in a society that cherishes spontaneity to such an extent that skill is thought of as second-rate" (*Washington Post*, 25 July 1986).

Streep's interviews about acting likewise emphasized it as craft and labor, especially because, as she said in an interview, it is "not popular" to analyze acting and much easier to think of it as "magic" (*Washington Post*, 25 July 1986). "The news is that most of the great practitioners of the art of acting know exactly what they're doing," she asserted in a 1988 interview with playwright Wendy Wasserstein. "There is a craft" ("Streeping Beauty," *Interview*, December 1988, 87). Streep never identified exactly which techniques or methods she used, and in the same interview she summarized her approach as an instinctual application of various techniques. In a strikingly superwoman moment, the "Star of the 80s" insisted on being recognized for her skills but also insisted on putting it in domestic terms—the housewife peering into the refrigerator, imagining a family dinner. Some people, she said, know how to pull things out of the refrigerator "and concoct a feast. But that is how I act: I just see what's there in me that I can apply to the task at hand" (87).

Streep occasionally bristled at the superwoman romanticization of her dual family-career life and spoke openly about the hard work of mothering, despite her breezy comment in 1982 that motherhood was fun and easy. "I resent that I'm held up as someone who's able to juggle two lives and make everything work. I'm just balancing like Blind Justice—I mean barely holding it all together," she said in a *Life* profile (December 1987, 81). She told *Esquire* that being a housewife and mother is much harder than making movies (December 1984, 444). However, her language in interviews sometimes mimicked the superwoman discourse, as in the quotation headline on the August 1986 *Ladies' Home Journal* cover: "Meryl Streep: 'What Do I Want? I Want it All.'" The accompanying story added the rest of the quotation from Streep, who said she "wanted it all, but in manageable proportions" (154). Nevertheless, the headline and story offered up Meryl Streep as a real-life configuration of a post-feminist success story, the 1980s superwoman.

In a similar fashion, Streep carefully framed her political activities as part of her family life. She won the Helen Caldicott Leadership Award in 1984 for her activism against nuclear warfare and in the later part of the decade immersed herself in environmental issues, eventually becoming the spokesperson for the Natural Resources Defense Council, an environmental action group. In interviews, Streep tied her activism in various political causes directly to her motherhood. She told *Redbook* in 1982 that "issues such as disarmament, equal rights, looking out for the disadvantaged" were all about her small son Henry (September 1982, 14). After her first daughter was born, she described her anti-nuclear activism as likewise personally motivated: "I watch the news and I think, 'goddamn these guys; they're going to blow up the world, just when I've got this beautiful little peach here'" (Dreifus, "Why I've Taken a Year Off," *Ladies' Home Journal*, April 1984, 154). In her 1988 interview with Wasserstein, Streep spoke at length about her involvement with environmental causes, adding, "Of course, none of this meant as much to me, either, before my children were born." In the same interview, she explicitly voiced the post-feminist dilemma of how traditional expectations of women continue even for women who are the wage earners: "I just think it's hard to be the person who provides food and takes out the garbage, because you also have to be the conscience of the family. And I think that's still largely left to women" (87).

Streep's film choices during this decade suggest her awareness of the cultural complexities of motherhood and its social inequities. During the period when Streep was most vocal about the importance of motherhood in her life, she played a series of guilt-wracked or traumatized mothers. *Silkwood* is even more significant because it strikingly combines themes that recurred in Streep's interviews, motherhood and social activism, in a true story. Karen Silkwood loves her children but cannot provide a good home for them, so they live in another state with her ex-husband. Yet the parental melodrama in this film is subsumed by its narrative about Silkwood's gradual political awakening as she realizes she and her colleagues in a plutonium plant are being contaminated while the corporation falsifies safety documents. Silkwood died in a car crash on her way to meet a reporter with incriminating documentation, and the cause of the crash was never determined.

*Silkwood* lends striking perspective to the question of career versus family, illustrating the privileges such a question takes for granted. In the gritty factory life of rural Oklahoma portrayed in this film, few women have choices. The film shows Silkwood gradually isolated even from her friends and colleagues as she battles the corporation for self-survival and as the contamination makes her progressively more ill. The camera often shifts to show Silkwood's photographs of her children, images that resonate with Streep's frequent comments that children are the whole point of political activism—and particularly activism about nuclear and pesticide contamination.

However, the two most horrific films about motherhood were the ones that bookended Streep's 1980s career: *Sophie's Choice* and *A Cry in the Dark*. *Sophie's Choice*, which won Streep her most acclaim, is structured around a ghastly moment in which an Auschwitz survivor is forced to choose which of her two young children will live. Critics had mixed responses to the screen adaptation of William Styron's novel, but Streep's performance won nearly unanimous accolades for its portrayal of a deeply conflicted character. In particular, she was singled out for her ability to carry out the series of confessional monologues that gradually reveal Sophie's agonizing secret. Nonetheless, Styron's story dramatizing this horrible "choice" has the unsettling effect of shifting the guilt of the Holocaust onto the wrong shoulders, as pointed out by film reviewer John Simon, who protested the dubious culpability of a young, anguished mother in this fiction ("Harrowed Heroine, Harassed Audience," *National Review*, 21 January 1983, 62). Most reviewers interpreted the film's pivotal moment as an insight into the nature of evil, but the insight costs the tormented mother her sanity and her life.

*A Cry in the Dark* ups the ante by relating a true story about a mother put into an impossible position. In a docudrama about an event that rocked Australia in the early 1980s, Streep plays Lindy Chamberlain, a minister's wife falsely accused of murdering her nine-week-old baby. Even though there was neither physical evidence nor even a recovered body, Chamberlain was imprisoned for more than three years until proof emerged that— as she had ascertained—the baby had been carried away from the family's campsite by a dingo.

Thus while Streep was deeply implicated in the superwoman narrative of "having it all," some of her most prominent choices of film roles reveal disturbing counter-narratives about guilt and motherhood circulating during this decade. A *Washington Post* review of *A Cry in the Dark* commented on the simultaneous release of this film and *The Good Mother* (1988), which is also about a woman on trial, facing the custody loss of her child: "These days, to Hollywood's way of thinking, the only perfect mothers are the daddies in 'Three Men and a Baby'" ("Streep's Forceful 'Cry,'" 11 November 1988, B1).

## ★★★★★ Glamour, Body, and Voice

Streep's women's-magazine image as superwoman in one sense positioned her squarely within the traditional feminine ideal of homemaker and mother. It also positioned her at odds with Hollywood's sexier and racier images of femininity. In the latter part of the decade, her refusal of glamour was criticized in terms of her film choices, though the criticisms often extended to her public profile. Her looks in *A Cry in the Dark* were especially targeted because her physical transformation was pointedly unflattering—oddly winged eyebrows, a severe haircut, and a body bloated by pregnancy in the second half of the film. The film takes pains to show that, stoic and unconcerned with her appearance, Chamberlain was under suspicion not only because of her cool demeanor but because of what she

Playing a mother wrongly accused of murdering her baby in *A Cry in the Dark*, Meryl Streep drew criticism for portraying an unpleasant character. Courtesy Jerry Ohlinger. Copyright Cannon Entertainment/Warner Bros., 1988.

looked like, eventually losing even the support of her husband. Speaking about the Chamberlain character, Streep emphasized how the expectations of gender role swayed public opinion: "How she held herself and behaved and looked and dressed had a lot to do with how people judged her as feminine or not feminine" (*Premiere*, December 1989, 77).

The statement eerily echoes discourses around Streep's own ambiguous femininity in the 1980s, for she was an A-list star whose attractiveness was frequently the object of contention in press coverage. In a 2008 retrospective of Streep's career, Molly Haskell summed up the controversy about her attractiveness as part of the difficulty of tracking Streep's star image : "Her off-center looks have always been part of the puzzle: is she beautiful or strikingly plain? . . . Does she obscure her 'beauty' in order to be taken seriously, or are her frequent disguises distractions from what she perceives as a lack of beauty?" ("Finding Herself" 34). The topic was complicated by Streep's refusal to look and act like a movie star, as is evident in a scathing 1989 feature article in *Mademoiselle* that took Streep to task for her attempt to resemble the real Lindy Chamberlain. The writer admits that Streep may have made herself "a little strange" in *A Cry in the Dark* to show how Chamberlain's appearance biased Australian public opinion (January 1989, 48). Because that was, in fact, the point of the film, the article's barely disguised subtext is frustration with Streep for her own strangeness. Pleading with Streep to drop her accents and play American roles, the writer sarcastically concludes, "She wouldn't have to play her *self*, compromise her privacy, be anything less than a serious actress (not, horror of horrors, a 'movie star')" (49).

As Jackie Stacey suggests, class and distance are important elements in determining the relationship between film spectators and stars. This insight helps explain why glamour was a slippery variable in Streep's film roles and a telling absence in her public image (see *Star Gazing*). Her preference for *Ladies' Home Journal* and *McCall's* as her publicity venues situated her in the domestic, middle-class world of recipes, hairstyling secrets, and diet tips. In addition, her insistence on prioritizing her family in her interviews further shortened the distance between the actress and the ordinary lives of readers and spectators. The privileges of a star making millions of dollars per picture were occasionally in view through references to the nanny or gardener in Streep's household. Nevertheless, the relative simplicity of her family's life was often referenced in feature articles: Streep "lives almost as far removed from Hollywood glamour as a person can get on this planet," a *McCall's* piece reported (March 1983, 34). The premise that the Gummers lived ordinary lives may have been ingenuous, but the repetition of this theme in feature articles suggests its appeal to middlebrow readers.

Streep's looks, like her persona, changed radically from film to film, from glamorous to ghastly, so her relationship to traditional femininity was an unstable one. In contrast to contemporary stars such as Michelle Pfeiffer, Kathleen Turner, or Faye Dunaway, who were always characterized as beautiful (and thus feminine), Streep was instead described in more uncertain terms. A 1988 *Photoplay* essay, "The Changing Faces of Streep," points out that for *Ironweed* she had become "almost unrecognizable," but the accompanying photos from that film and from *Out of Africa* and *A Cry in the Dark* are so vastly different that it is not clear which image is "recognizable" as the "real" one (July 1988, 40). The 1989 *Films and Filming* profile, "The Many Faces of Meryl Streep," offers the insight that for Streep, beauty or lack of it was not an innate quality but a part of her craft: "She may not actually be as perfectly beautiful as Garbo . . . but she can act herself to be as exquisite as she wants" (16).

This insight is crucial. If Streep could perform beauty, glamour, and femininity rather than actually embodying these traits, then her images suggest the unstable nature of femininity itself. The tension between this instability and the comforting durability of Streep as *Ladies' Home Journal* mom illustrates the inconsistencies of stardom, how "the 'text' of an actor's image is full of discrepancies and incoherencies," as Judith Mayne puts it (128).

Overall, Streep's popularity was greatest during the era when she was taking roles that were more glamorous than ghastly. Eschewing the distancing devices that could romanticize their protagonists, *Silkwood, Ironweed*, and *A Cry in the Dark* delivered unflattering close-ups of difficult, scrappy heroines in factories and dismal small towns. In contrast, Streep's most glamorous roles, including the ones that most powerfully launched her career in the early 1980s, gave her the distancing devices of passionate romances in other historical eras and the opportunity to wear period costumes: *The French Lieutenant's Woman, Sophie's Choice*, and *Out of Africa*. In *Sophie's Choice*, which takes place in the 1940s, her postwar dresses are filmy and sumptuous, and Streep and her co-star Kevin Kline dress up in plantation costumes as a lark. Many of the reviews of these early films describe her beauty as part of the characters' fascination. "Miss Streep has never looked more beautiful," Vincent Canby said of *The French Lieutenant's Woman*, in which Streep plays two parts in a movie within a movie: a tantalizing "ruined" Victorian woman and a present-day actress playing this part and having an affair with one of her co-stars (*New York Times*, 18 September 1981, C4). *Newsweek* praised her "severe, almost witchlike beauty" in that film ("The Woman on the Quay," 21 September 1981, 96). For *Sophie's Choice*, reviewers often commented on the lush sexuality Streep

Meryl Streep, here with Jeremy Irons, portrayed a mysterious Victorian seductress in *The French Lieutenant's Woman*, a part for which she wished she were "more beautiful." Courtesy Photofest. Copyright Junper Films, 1981.

brought to her role. *Time* magazine described her performance as "a seamless, seductive piece" (13 December 1982, 79); the *New York Times*'s Janet Maslin called her "tragic, voluptuous" (10 December 1982, C12); Stanley Kauffmann described Streep as "more translucently beautiful than ever" (*New Republic*, 10 January 1983, 40–42); and David Denby proclaimed her "the first actress since the young Ingrid Bergman to make desolation ravishingly sexy" (*New York*, 20 December 1982, 64).

Streep's glamour in *Out of Africa* was discussed in edgier terms because its class and racial meanings—always implicit in the concept of glamour—were underscored in her depiction of colonial writer Karen Blixen in Kenya. As Canby pointed out, Blixen in her writing positioned herself as "a great white goddess," and the film portrays her as "Scarlett O'Hara fighting to save Tara" (*New York Times*, 18 December 1985, C17). Andrew Kopkind of *The Nation* pinpointed the racial basis of the film's allure: Streep and Redford "make a pretty white pair in darkest Africa" (25 January 1986, 88). Especially romanticized in this film was the lushness of the scenery and what Denby called "the Great Adventure stuff" of a vanished era (*New York*, 6 January 1986, 58). The enchantment of distance in this film is ironic, since the early-twentieth-century Africa it rhapsodizes was lost to colonial exploits like those of the Redford character. Confirming Stacey's insight that glamour is linked to wealth and property, the attractive coupling of Streep and Redford was culturally registered as access to certain commodities and travel. The sexy-khaki colonial look inspired by the film had an immediate effect on fashion, most notably with the successful Banana Republic stores and clothing lines (Jennet Conant, "Out of Africa: The Movie Has Inspired a Ruggedly Romantic Look," *Newsweek*, 17 February 1986, 61) and on fashionable tourism in Africa. "Packaged safari tours are sure the movie's scenic splendor, which has helped it gross more than $50 million at the box office, will lure bigger crowds this year," *Money* magazine reported ("Into Africa: Affordable African Safaris," March 1986, 94).

But even during the period when Streep undertook these lush roles, her attractiveness was often treated with ambiguity. "She is not pretty, perhaps," the 1981 cover story for *Life* reported, "but many find in her a singular beauty—fragile, feminine, absolutely compelling. . . . There is the fine blonde hair, the long beaked nose that adds a lovely quirk to the classic features" (80). Streep herself, asked why she had escaped the blonde bimbo stereotype, replied, "I'm not good looking enough!" (Joan Juliet Buck, "More Than a Star," *Vogue*, June 1980, 226). Streep admitted that when she watched *The French Lieutenant's Woman*, she was disappointed by her looks: "I couldn't help wishing that I was more beautiful. . . . I'm good looking enough to play any of the women I usually play. . . . But for the character with her intense beauty, it wasn't enough" (*Time*, 7 September 1981, 40).

Some assessments of Streep's appearance were far more brusque. Critic John Simon complained that even though other characters remark about her incredible beauty in *Sophie's Choice*, she is "only a decently ordinary-

looking woman whose wide, angular face is imperfectly filled out by her features, even when they are as large and wavy as her nose" (*National Review*,
21 January 1983, 62). Truman Capote reportedly described her as having
the nose of an anteater and the eyes of a hen (Maychick 4). Even a laudatory *Life* magazine essay introduced its praise by cataloging her deficiencies:
"Her legs are thick and short, her hips pudgy, her bust indistinct. . . . Her
eyes are small and almost colorless, the nose that wanders down between
them is alarmingly long and strangely skewed" (December 1987, 76–77).[4]

In Hollywood—where the female body is, above all, to be looked at—the
star body of Meryl Streep was oddly elusive. Tellingly, Pauline Kael described
Streep as disembodied: "After I've seen her in a movie, I can't visualize her
from the neck down," she wrote of Streep in *Sophie's Choice*. In that film, said
Kael, all attention goes to Streep's accent, so that "she in effect decorporeal-
izes herself" (*New Yorker*, 27 December 1982, 74). Granted that Kael was no
fan of Streep, her remark resonates in the context of the fluctuating press
comments about Streep's physical appearance. In contrast to these conflicting discourses about Streep's body, the assessments of her voice were solid.
Some critics may have mocked the endless accents, but by all accounts
Streep's command of languages, dialects, and brogues is formidable, most
impressively displayed in her Polish-tinged English and Polish-accented German in *Sophie's Choice*. Director Alan J. Pakula had intended to cast an Eastern European actress but changed his mind after Streep's audition. "On the
first day of rehearsals, Meryl opened her mouth and she was Polish," Pakula
reported (*Newsweek*, 17 May 1982, 68). Director Mike Nichols, who later
worked with Streep in *Silkwood*, judged her speech in *Sophie's Choice* with
particular rigor because he is himself a native speaker of German. "Meryl
spoke perfect German, with only a trace of a Polish accent, very fast. Now
that's not supposed to be possible," he said. "She has the absolutely specific,
accurate sound of a person from that particular place of origin" (*Washington
Post*, 25 July 1986, D1). In *Plenty* she was British again, then Danish in *Out
of Africa*, and then New York Jewish in *Heartburn*. Streep claimed that the
Australian accent for *A Cry in the Dark* was "the hardest one" she'd ever tried,
but once she'd mastered it, an Australian who had known Chamberlain said,
"'If you close your eyes when Meryl talks, you hear Lindy speak'" (*Ladies'
Home Journal*, October 1988, 64).

Like glamour, the voice in cinema is a gender issue, given the voice's
cultural association with qualities such as power and authority. Scholars
have argued that the female voice in Hollywood cinema is often rendered
as a fascination or dilemma, so that it can pose "a stress point in the func-
tioning of the entire cinematic apparatus" (Silverman 63).[5] Tellingly, Streep's

voice and the status of her speech are "stress points" in five of her six major films of the 1980s. Most obvious is *Sophie's Choice*, the film in which her voice is foregrounded as it moves among three languages. The narrative slowly reveals that Sophie is a liar and that her position as Holocaust survivor is actually murky and full of compromises. Her linguistic skills, we learn, enabled her to transcribe her father's vicious anti-Semitic tirades and later put her in the position of working for the Nazis. Imprisoned at Auschwitz, as a Polish Catholic she was spared to become a secretary to one of the Nazi generals. The perfect Polish-accented German triggers Sophie's moral anguish: it attracts the Nazi general and leads Sophie to make a desperate offer of her body in return for the safety of her child. Streep's Sarah Woodruff character in *The French Lieutenant's Woman* is also a liar whose pose of being a fallen woman is a manipulation that entices the hero Charles (Jeremy Irons) away from his fiancée. Like Sophie's lies, Sarah's are knotted in cultural complexities. Sarah's pose as fallen is her escape from the narrowness of Victorian mores and thus is a liberation for Charles as well. But in both cases, the heroine's lies and their dramatic exposure are the stress points of the narrative, the places where the spectator must suddenly reevaluate everything previously seen and heard.

In *Silkwood* and *A Cry in the Dark*, the opposite trajectory occurs but with the same focus on speech and contention. The female voice is discredited for threatening the status quo but ultimately exonerated. Lindy Chamberlain in *A Cry in the Dark*, widely believed to be lying about the death of her baby, speaks uncomfortable truths that are considered inappropriate or unseemly for a woman and mother. At one point, she gives an interview calmly explaining how a dingo catches its victim and then "unpeels its skin, like an orange." Statements like this were considered callous, and public outrage against her was inflamed by *how* she spoke, her coolness and composure. Lindy Chamberlain's appearance was instrumental in how "people judged her as feminine or not feminine," as Streep pointed out, but her voice—and its lack of suitable emotion and woe—was equally critical in this judgment about femininity, which was also the judgment about her guilt.

In *Silkwood*, the heroine's voice is likewise discordant and disbelieved, its working-class Texas-Oklahoma twang especially out of place at the moments when it most needs authority—up against the plutonium plant's owners and with union officials in New York City. Canby's review describes the film's conflict in terms of "lip" and "noise": "At the [plutonium] plant, Karen takes no lip from the company bosses and sounds off noisily about love, sex and whatever else that comes to mind, to the shocked delight of

Meryl Streep was willing to take on roles that were wholly unglamorous, as seen here in *Silkwood*, in which she portrayed the title role of the working-class activist and factory worker. Courtesy Photofest. Copyright ABC Motion Pictures, 1983.

her more conservative co-workers" (*New York Times*, 14 December 1983, C27). But her co-workers are less delighted and eventually very angry with Karen when their jobs are threatened because of her activism. Karen, sounding off "noisily," threatens not only the local economy but the larger corporate world that demands plutonium products. In this, as in the films Amy Lawrence describes in her work on female voices in cinema, "woman's speech sparks a crisis within the texts that mirrors a corresponding break-down within the dominant ideology" (111).

The dominant ideology is likewise the target of the disgruntled heroine of *Plenty*. Streep plays Susan Traherne, a young British courier for the French resistance during World War II who is disillusioned and disappointed in post-war culture. Moving restlessly through bohemian and then middle-class social spheres, she eventually marries a British diplomat and makes his life miserable with her outspoken political criticisms. Because Susan is some-times mentally unhinged and at other times incisively perceptive, *Plenty* aims for a subtle cultural critique that many critics judged a failure. Again, the heroine's disruptive speech drew critical attention; Kael called it "showoffy verbiage—Susan Traherne is a walking harangue" (*New Yorker*, 7 October, 1985, 129). Even the *Washington Post*, whose critic praised both the character and Streep's ability to assume "not just the accent of the English but the cadences and timbre," described Susan's speech as "the harpyish shrieking of a Brit in a dither" (20 September 1985, B1). Some reviewers could not differentiate Streep's performance from the offensive nature of her character. Canby, for example, capped his negative review by claiming that "Miss Streep's performance doesn't help. She does all the right things technically, including her English accent, but the character remains as chilly and distant as the North Pole" (*New York Times*, 19 September 1985, C22).

Though not as central to the narrative as in these other films, the voice of the heroine is used for an emotional and disruptive effect in *Ironweed* in a virtuoso scene in which Streep sings a song, "He's My Pal," in a dingy Depression-era bar. A former singer and now homeless alcoholic, the glum character Helen Archer brightens up when she's given the opportunity to take the stage and belt out a sentimental ballad to the delight and acclaim of everyone in the bar—a moment noted by reviewers as the high point of the film, and a high point of the filming as well. "'When she finished singing, there wasn't a dry eye in the house,' says Fred Gwynne, who plays a bartender in the scene. 'Her voice was like an angel's'" (*Ladies' Home Journal*, January 1988, 92). Shockingly, we immediately discover that most of the scene is Helen's fantasy. She has actually sung a broken, off-key song that almost no one listens to, and she stumbles back to her seat humiliated. The voice of her fantasy was her past, happier self, wholly lost and unable to be recovered.

## ★★★★★ The Devil and Ms. Streep

Fittingly, Streep's final film of the decade was *She-Devil*, a comedy by feminist filmmaker Susan Seidelman that skewers femininity, celebrity, and glamour. *She-Devil* specifically targets post-feminist narratives by showing how much they depend on class privilege and female attractiveness. Streep's character Mary Fisher, a gorgeous, pampered romance writer, falls for a married man, Bob Patchett (Ed Begley Jr.), who dumps his wife and children for her. Mary's career and indulgent lifestyle both deflate when Bob's ex-wife—she-devil Ruth Patchett (Roseanne Barr)—sends the children to live with Bob and Mary. The servants quit in disgust, and suddenly Mary's life is full of cracker crumbs and laundry. Desperately trying to balance romance and domesticity, she writes a terrible novel called *Love in the Rinse Cycle*, a wry comment on the decade's superwoman and on the glamorous fantasies that don't hold up in the real-life world of work and family. In an interview in *Premiere*, Streep expressed her enthusiasm about

participating in a film that so thoroughly debunks the feminine mystique—
"the inappropriate value placed on being young and thin and pretty"
(December 1989, 78).

In the same interview, Streep also angrily vented about the double
standard of male and female salaries in Hollywood. Noting that Jack Nicholson had just been paid $11 million for *Batman* (1989), Streep said, "He was
in *Ironweed*, if you recall . . . *I* was in *Out of* fucking *Africa*, remember?
*Kramer vs.* fucking *Kramer*! *Deer Hunter* . . . I'm saying it's a guy's game. If I
asked for $11 million, they would laugh" (79). The outburst was not some-
thing that would show up in *Ladies' Home Journal*, but Streep's complaint
about gender and salaries in the 1980s, even among top-ranked Hollywood
stars, is the flip side of the happy working mother she portrayed in women's
magazines.

Two tensions characterized Streep's stardom at the pinnacle of her
career—on the one hand, the contradictory discourses about career versus
motherhood, and on the other hand the resistance to glamour that often
played out as a privileging of voice over body. Both tensions involve the
larger question of femininity, the characteristic wickedly lampooned in *She-
Devil*. Wrapping up the decade with a comedy, Streep demonstrated the
wide range of her talents and also allowed her final cinematic performance
of the 1980s to be funny and transgressive. After her character Mary Fisher
is forced into everyday domestic life, she shows up for a high-power lunch-
eon and pulls a gummy bear out of her hair. It's a gesture emblematic of
Streep's dismissals of glamour and her insistence that she is an actress, not
a star.

### NOTES

1. During the 1980s, Streep was nominated for five Golden Globe awards, winning for
*Sophie's Choice* and *The French Lieutenant's Woman*. She also won three Los Angeles Film Critics Association Awards for *The French Lieutenant's Woman, Sophie's Choice*, and *Out of Africa*;
two New York Film Critics Circle Awards for *Sophie's Choice* and *A Cry in the Dark*; and both
the Cannes Film Festival Award and the Australian Film Institute's Best Actress Award for *A
Cry in the Dark*.

2. For a sampling of the media attention given to the superwoman, see Harriet Breiker,
"Does Superwoman Have It the Worst?," *Working Woman*, August 1988, 65; Donna Carty,
"Yes, I Was Doing More and Enjoying It Less: Confessions of a Superwoman," *Working
Woman*, February 1986, 86–87; and Lois Duncan, "'He Wants Me to Be Superwoman': What
Happens When a Couple Expect Too Much," *Ladies' Home Journal*, December 1985, 14–16.

3. A fourth child, Louisa Jacobson Gummer, would follow in 1991.

4. In 2007, Streep narrated a Turner Classic Movies tribute to Bette Davis in which she
quoted from a letter Davis had written to her early in Streep's career. In the letter, Davis
expresses her admiration and says that Streep reminds her of herself. Davis, too, was frequently disparaged for her lack of traditional beauty and glamour. See Fischer.

5. See Doane on the psychoanalytic implications of the gendered voice in cinema. This argument is extended in Silverman's account that the maternal voice shapes the child's self-perception. In traditional mother-child relationships, she says, "the maternal voice introduces the child to its mirror reflection," its initial sense of an autonomous self but also its traumatic entry into sexual difference (80). Also see Lawrence, who argues that "the speaking woman disrupts the dominant order" (32) or threatens it by evoking the ambivalence of the maternal voice as experienced in the womb.

# 11
# Clint Eastwood and Bruce Willis
## Enforcers Left and Right

JAMES MORRISON

By the end of the 1980s, Clint Eastwood's career as a Holly-wood star appeared to be in sharp decline. After *Die Hard* (1988), Bruce Willis was widely regarded as his most viable replacement, an action-movie star for the new generation. A comparison of the two throws into relief some of the key trends of the 1980s. Eastwood resisted many of the most significant of those trends, trying to preserve his established star image in a time when its currency was passing. In an era when the culture of images expanded into new domains—with the rise of home video, corporate mergers promoting

Both photos courtesy Larry Edmunds Bookstore.

hyper-synergy across multiple media, and the emergence of computer-generated imagery in commercial cinema, especially with *The Abyss* (1989)—Eastwood appeared to dig in his heels, reverting to the same formulas and characters, always "playing himself" (as critics rarely failed to note), and making movies that ignored the new technologies. Willis, meanwhile, embraced the rising order—in many ways, he was a product of it. Like Eastwood, he began his career in television, in the series "Moonlighting" (1985), but in Willis's case this was part of a multimedia celebrity blitz. A large share of his early fame derived from his appearances in television commercials for Seagram's liquor (1986–88), in one of which he appears as Bruno, an alter-ego in whose guise he also recorded a musical album, "The Return of Bruno" (1988), appearing the same year in a mock-documentary to promote the record, modeled on *This Is Spinal Tap* (1984). Later, he moved into CGI with a television show in which the Bruno persona recurred, "Bruno the Kid" (1996), also lending his voice and likeness to the PlayStation video game "Apocalypse" (1998).

The two stars may seem to present a study in contrasts, generational and otherwise, yet both negotiate the decade's trends by recourse to notions of authenticity. Eastwood's fate might have been to fall into the grizzled self-parody common among aging stars (like John Wayne in the seventies), but he turned this to his advantage in maintaining his image. The result was that, despite his stands against it, he did not appear so out of place after all in the new culture of images that Willis and other emerging stars represented—a consequence that enabled Eastwood's rebirth in the nineties. Willis's persona, meanwhile, synthesizes the "fake" and the "real" in a fusion of irony and sincerity. Both stars engage cultural politics in parallel ways. While both publicly avow conservatism—Eastwood made no secret of being a Republican, while Willis appeared on television promoting the sequel *Live Free or Die Hard* in 2007 and proclaiming his support of George W. Bush—each makes films in the 1980s that explore the fissures in Reagan's America. Eastwood seeks a mythic reconciliation of right-wing and left-wing politics—mostly by claiming to be outside both—while Willis dives headfirst into contradiction, quite content to declare "I'm a Republican" and "I'm not a Republican" in the same interview (Gregory Ellwood, "Willis is Mad as Hell . . . ," movies.msn.com/movies/hitlist/2–24–06). A film like *Die Hard* would seem wholeheartedly of the right if most of its energies were not devoted, equally wholeheartedly, to vacating politics altogether. That the narrative of these two cultural figures turns out in the long run to move beyond the *All about Eve* (1950) pairing of a rising star with a falling star only makes it more evocative of a decade in which stardom itself underwent marked changes.

## ★★★★★ Eastwood: Decline and Canonization

Already a top box-office draw by the time the decade began, Eastwood saw his star power erode significantly by the end of the 1980s, after a series of outright flops. As he reached the age of sixty in 1990—and released another certified failure, *The Rookie*—he seemed to be a has-been, poised to collect a few perfunctory lifetime achievement awards as he faded from view. Looking back now, after his rebirth in the 1990s and beyond, we see Eastwood's work of the 1980s emerge as a watershed, a preparation for an unexpected renaissance disguised as an inevitable deterioration, a canny laying of groundwork for his subsequent career. With no parallel in American movies, this resurgence bears important implications for some of the main developments in Hollywood cinema of the 1980s.

The decade witnessed an explosion of action films with conventions derived from Eastwood's earlier movies, at least in the qualities of their violence and the wisecracking cool of the antiheroes who by turns opposed that violence and dished it out. This new generation, however, pushed the genre in directions Eastwood could not or would not follow, toward an apotheosis of the antihero as "hard body," and in the direction of increasingly high-concept, big-budget production (see Jeffords, *Hard Bodies*). Figures like Sylvester Stallone and Arnold Schwarzenegger (with Willis occupying an intermediary position) replaced Eastwood's lean, mean enforcers with iron-pumped, steroid-steeped characters in expensive spectacles driven by high-tech special effects. One of the few stars of the era to maintain a staunch commitment to the low budget, Eastwood continued to work frugally throughout the 1980s (Prince, *Pot of Gold* 266–68), so much so that as costs and production values inflated, Eastwood's films were often accused of looking cheap and cheesy. Yet with a slight shift of angle, it was easy to see his movies as devoutly modest in an age of rampant overindulgence, in keeping with the image of relative moderation that had always counterbalanced the elements of excess in his star persona, that penchant for ultra-violence and vigilante fervor.

Eastwood's reaction to prevailing changes in 1980s Hollywood was to distance himself from these developments by embracing his own seeming obsolescence with an attitude of wry self-consciousness. Nearly all his films of the decade broach this kind of guarded self-parody, with the ultimate effect of bolstering his star image against its apparent anachronism rather than undercutting or demystifying his persona. The Eastwood self-parodies of the 1980s, amid his seeming decline, edge into an elegiac wistfulness. In retrospect, they seem remarkably prescient, prefiguring the emergence of overt pop self-consciousness as a defining value in American film of the next decade. In fact, a strain of muffled self-parody was already evident in action movies such as the Indiana Jones or Terminator films. If Eastwood's masculinity seemed heightened or exaggerated in his earlier star-making roles, it seemed positively normative by comparison to the robotic hyper-masculinity of a Schwarzenegger or a Stallone; Eastwood's evolving star image commented implicitly—and disapprovingly—on the exorbitance and grotesquerie of the images that were taking his place and preserved a human dimension they lacked.

As Susan Jeffords argues, the "hard body" action films were a cultural manifestation of Reagan-era politics, evincing a turn to the right in Holly-wood movies of the time (24–28). One might have expected Eastwood to follow this turn avidly since he was one of the industry's most high-profile conservatives, even serving as the Republican mayor of the city of Carmel, California, from 1986 to 1988. But Eastwood's work of the eighties sets the stage for a more complex political engagement—one that would bring him in successive decades to make films that lend themselves readily to leftist readings—negotiating between the left and the right even as the polarizing "culture wars" raged in the society at large.

Although such negotiations could be said to define Hollywood cinema as such, in this case they enabled a rethinking of Eastwood's work as "com-plex," even "ironic." This reconception was a crucial step toward the can-onization of the star as an auteur, a process that ran its course throughout the period of his seeming decline. As Paul Smith notes, the earliest desig-nations of Eastwood as an auteur occurred in the late seventies (Smith 244–45). In 1980, New York's Museum of Modern Art mounted a day-long tribute to Eastwood, followed five years later—in the same year in which *Pale Rider* (1985), Eastwood's only western of the decade, premiered by invitation at Cannes—by a four-month retrospective at the Cinémathèque Française. Thereafter, Eastwood became a fixture in the pages of *Cahiers du cinéma*, where his work as director was discussed in tandem with auteurs of the past such as Raoul Walsh and Jacques Tourneur, while his star image was aligned with that of such figures from classical Hollywood as Gary Cooper and Errol Flynn. Valued precisely for their qualities of "irony" and "distance," Eastwood's 1980s films were said to pose a central question: "After . . . Vietnam and *Apocalypse Now*, is it still possible to believe in" America and cinema itself (Chevrie 10; translation mine)?

By the mid-1980s, the popular press in America was taking note of the shift in Eastwood's profile. An article by Gene Siskel in the *Los Angeles Daily News* noted the "revisionist thinking" by which Eastwood was increasingly seen as an artist, not merely a movie star, and concluded that "Eastwood's time for recognition in intellectual circles is now" ("Eastwood Doesn't Play Dirty—Just Tough," 17 June 1985, E1). The most striking feature of Eastwood's canonization was a familiar strategy in auteurist criticism, the retrospective recuperation of slighted work as bearing a previously overlooked complexity. Throughout the 1980s, Eastwood capitalized on this, promoting a view of his current work, however maligned, as continuous with his previous work while actively courting the attentions of highbrow critics whose adulation would not have been possible before, as when Eastwood ran a full-page advertisement in the *New York Review of Books* to promote *Tightrope* in 1984 (Kapsis 69).[1] Many such critics, including some in that tony journal, obliged these efforts, and when Eastwood directed *Bird* (1988)—only the second of his thirteen films as director to that date in which he did not appear as star—*Cahiers du cinéma* hailed this seemingly anomalous flight into the realm of art cinema as a masterpiece (with a "musical" structure and a "purity of the image" not seen since Edgar G. Ulmer) that was an extension of Eastwood's past work rather than a departure from it: "No, the last cowboy hasn't changed. He always recounts the same thing"—a representation of America itself (Katsahnias 54; translation mine).

## ★★★★★ Eastwood, Sincerity, and Self-Parody

In Eastwood's work before the 1980s, the question of whether he was to be viewed as a hero or a villain began by remaining open, if not moot. What defined his character was a relentless, monomaniacal pursuit of a goal, and the films—always poised on the brink of parody themselves—depended on this unswerving extremism to secure their ultimate sense of conviction. Then, these characteristics—an extremist masculinity, unyielding commitment, a certain vacillation between heroism and villainy—coalesced into a complex of "sincerity" that defines his image from the 1970s on.

In one sense, this bespeaks the hoariest of cinematic clichés, displayed most potently in the western and its variants, that of the man who remains true to himself against all odds. In a more interesting sense, though, it brings into focus the central question of Eastwood's work in the 1980s: how to maintain this quality, and retain stardom, in a market where its value has dropped. According to Richard Dyer, "The values of masculine physicality are harder to maintain straight-facedly and unproblematically in an age of microchips and a large scale growth (in the USA) of women in traditional male occupations" (Dyer, *Heavenly Bodies* 12). One line of the male-oriented action movie of the eighties, the films of Chuck Norris, Jean-Claude Van

Damme, and Steven Seagal, simply ignores such circumstances. Eastwood's movies try to adapt, to confront shifting conditions of postmodern culture, and he resorts to self-parody in a paradoxical bid to redeem sincerity.

In *Film Parody*, Dan Harries outlines an anatomy of the mode with six main attributes: reiteration, inversion, misdirection, literalization, extraneous inclusion, and exaggeration (Harries 43–92). Eastwood's films of the 1980s draw upon only two of these—reiteration and exaggeration—avoiding the elements Harries associates with parody's subversive potential. This selective use of the mode's characteristics enables a form of self-parody that produces new ways of understanding Eastwood's persona rather than deconstructing it. Crucial to Eastwood's self-parody is that it remain fully coextensive with Eastwood's longstanding star image, his core of "authenticity" left untouched. Eastwood himself has not changed, these films declaim; it is the world around him that has transformed—very much for the worse. Self-parody becomes the vehicle by which Eastwood brandishes his own archaism and increasing marginalization as a badge of honor. If his films acknowledge that he has begun to appear out of place in the current cultural climate, it is only because, they suggest, that climate itself, always suspect, has undergone such certain dissipation, while Eastwood has remained very much himself, as he always will.

*Bronco Billy* (1980) and *Honkytonk Man* (1982) are throwbacks in more ways than one. In spirit, they closely resemble semi-parodies like Sam Peckinpah's *Junior Bonner* (1972) or Stuart Rosenberg's *Pocket Money* (1972), gently comic elegies for the western as a cinematic genre. That Eastwood's contributions to the cycle appeared ten years late, after the death of the western had become a widespread article of faith, only enhances their sense of belatedness. Like Steve McQueen in *Junior Bonner* and Paul Newman or Lee Marvin in *Pocket Money*, Eastwood in *Bronco Billy* and *Honkytonk Man* plays the role of an aging westerner faced with his own obsolescence. In the first film, he owns an itinerant circus made up of a cross-racial assortment of rag-tag runaways and refugees, roving from Montana to Idaho to raise money for a ranch where "city kids can come and see what cowboys and Indians are really like." In the second, he is a down-at-heels, tubercular musician on the road to Nashville for one last shot at fame. In both performances, beneath a surface of stoical isolationism, his character is ultimately revealed as humanitarian and egalitarian in the realm of race, and doggedly populist in the realms of gender and class.

Both movies mix wry nostalgia with an awareness of the increasing archaism of their own values, and both roles provide unprecedented opportunities for Eastwood to display a certain range and to play against type,

A looser, ganglier Eastwood in *Honkytonk Man*. Courtesy Larry Edmunds Bookstore. Copyright The Malpaso Company, 1982.

mingling previously little-seen characteristics, such as benevolence, vulnerability, or physical decrepitude, with traditional aspects of the star's persona. Eastwood's performances in these movies are looser, rangier, more relaxed than any he had given before. The cool control of his body in previous films—the sense of holding the long limbs in check—gives way to a new gangliness, as when he slouches in the back seat of a convertible in *Honkytonk Man*, or lolls in a claw-footed tub too small for him, with his bony knees jutting upward and his arms and legs sloping in all directions.

Deftly avoiding self-criticism, Eastwood's self-parody shores up his "authentic" masculinity by contrast to the degraded masculinity that now surrounds him. *Any Which Way You Can* (1980) is the last of his films to present him as a figure of unquestioned virility—and the last to display his semi-nude body at length—and even there, his character is associated with retro-athletics and marginal milieus, bare-knuckle boxing and working-class roadside culture. Thereafter, he appears as a mainstay of old-fashioned manhood among men who variously represent a redefined masculinity—more "sensitive" or otherwise adjusted—that subjects his own masculinity to question but is ultimately exposed as artificial or debased.

Often, Eastwood's character engages in overt mimicry of these new postures. As early as *Dirty Harry* (1971), Eastwood's Harry Callahan repeats the sardonic line, "That'll be the day"—a citation of Ethan Edwards's refrain in

*The Searchers* (1956), with connotations of a John Wayne–like masculinity. In general, his characters cite a range of figures from the humiliated to the revered, from his invocation of a classic W. C. Fields line in a caustic drawl when he is stranded in a one-horse town in *Honkytonk Man*—"I'd rather be in Philadelphia!"—to his allusion in the same film to Ronald Reagan's famous admonition to Jimmy Carter in a 1980 presidential debate: "There you go again!" he mutters to a pesky cop.

Despite his characteristic stolidity, Eastwood's persona has always depended on mimicry of a sort, and in his films of the 1980s, he increasingly mimics the discourse of other men to reveal its falseness. In a film like *Pink Cadillac* (1989), he impersonates a range of garrulous types—a manic radio disc jockey, a Vegas huckster decked out in Liberace-like lamé—to show how far removed these disguises are from his own persona, the familiar stolidity to which he reverts on a dime. When a faux-hipster in *The Dead Pool* (1988) refers to his interlocutors with the polymorphously perverse moniker of "Love," Eastwood as Callahan takes up the address, parroting it with a baleful edge to emphasize its fey milksoppery. In *Heartbreak Ridge* (1986), Eastwood throws his ex-wife for a loop by mimicking New Age babble and the "new" masculinity: "Did we mutually nurture each other? Did we communicate meaningfully?" His own signature catchphrases become increasingly ritualized, often mocking feel-good pieties by re-packaging them as aggressive taunts: "Go ahead . . . make my day!"—a line later taken up by Reagan, closing the circle of allusion. This pattern of mimicry incorporates discourses of "sensitivity" only to deride them as jargon. Indeed, Eastwood's persona flirts with a new "sensitivity" throughout the 1980s, as remarked in a *Ladies' Home Journal* profile by the best-selling romance novelist Rosemary Rogers, in which she confesses that Eastwood's combination of hardness and softness made him the secret model for many of the romantic leads of her books ("Sweet Savage Clint," June 1982, n.p.). But Eastwood's mimicry never implies his internalization of what he imitates. It is a form of distancing that assures the triumph of his own "authentic" masculinity, however outmoded it may seem.

Even when the joke is ostensibly on Eastwood himself, it usually reverberates against external conditions the films castigate for their failure to accommodate Eastwood's character. One running gag of the 1980s films, for instance, involves gradually weakening gun power. In *Sudden Impact* (1984), Callahan still brandishes his giant Magnum as he jeeringly invites punks to make his day, but subsequent films show Eastwood looking quizzically at the smaller guns decreed by insular department bureaucrats, ending with his fingering a tiny revolver in *Pink Cadillac* that emits a little flag that says "Bang!" Clearly, these changing technologies of violence reflect the loss of power of a diminished masculinity, and Eastwood's most direct response comes at the end of *The Dead Pool*, when, stripped of his downsized weapon, he hoists a huge harpoon with which he impales the villain—an over-the-top joke that doubles as a forceful reassertion of phallic power and the ultimate proof of Eastwood's refusal to accede to the new masculinity even when it seems to have won out once and for all.

★★★★★ **Dirty Harry in the 1980s**

By the 1980s, the title character of the "Dirty Harry" series is no longer a renegade, he's a "dinosaur," advised by his colleagues in *Sudden Impact* to "get with it—it's a whole new ball game these days." Imperturbable as always, Callahan greets this news with a dispassionate squint, rife with the contempt he only rarely deigns to vent in full. Yet the whole film is infused by the issue of Callahan's obsolescence, by the problem of how to propagate paeans to vigilante justice when the bureaucrats out to protect the criminals have clearly won the day. Callahan's own vigilante impulses are notably curbed in *Sudden Impact*, though he sheds no tears for dispatched perpetrators, as when he murmurs over the corpse of a downed criminal, "Maybe we saved the taxpayers some money." Still, the film remains a vigilante story, a revenge tale in which a woman (played by Eastwood regular Sondra Locke) who has been the victim of a gang rape systematically stalks and kills her assailants. This narrative displacement has the advantage of projecting an effect of absolution, exonerating Callahan himself while underlining his own putative motivations to take on the role of avenger beyond the law—a professed identification with the victim.

A basic implication of Eastwood's 1980s films is that it is not his own image that needs rehabilitation, but the incomprehension of others that requires redress. *Sudden Impact* bids for such social correction by replacing Callahan's vigilantism with that of the rape victim herself, thereby making common cause between right-wing and left-wing variants of victims' rights advocacy, which emerged in its contemporary forms from 1960s counterculture via feminist activism to reform rape prosecutions—as documented in Susan Brownmiller's book *Against Our Will* (1975)—but was co-opted in the seventies by the political right, mobilized as a movement to consolidate individual property rights. Throughout that decade, private claims of individual injury jostled with public needs for social order, until a rapprochement of a sort was broached in the Reagan era, when the president declared

Victims' Rights Awareness Week in April 1982, subsequently assembling a "task force" to investigate the issue.

The source of identification between Callahan and the rape victim is an anger deemed irrational by the powers that be, and the film's main charge is to expose such designations as the smug prerogative of those whose dispassionate authority within the system renders them incapable of adopting the victim's position. At the same time, Callahan functions as a kind of surrogate, never vulnerable himself, capable of a quasi-feminist identification with the victim yet moved to retaliation less by anything so feminized as empathy than by a properly masculine rage against the system and the criminals it benefits. His conclusive refusal to arrest the woman for her revenge killings, instead framing her last victim for her own crimes, is quintessential 1980s Eastwood, a seeming gesture of sympathy that doubles as self-justification, and an implicit reassertion of his own power, condoning at one remove the same vigilante impulses that previously defined his own character.

The last "Dirty Harry" movie, *The Dead Pool*, reworks the character's image to present a mellower Callahan, a "kinder, gentler" Dirty Harry (in the slogan of George H. W. Bush's 1988 presidential campaign), while mounting a critique of the production of images in postmodern culture. Part of this reworking involves Callahan being, for the first time, a target of the crimes that propel the film's story—his name turns up on a hit list alongside those of the victims whose murders he is investigating—and at the same time a celebrity who holds fame in contempt. Stalked alternately by thugs who are out for his head and by admirers seeking his autograph, he fends off both with his usual unflappable cool and brutal efficiency. When a reporter asks to do a "profile" of him as a TV puff piece, he turns the request down with bluff disdain, and when his superiors demand that he contribute to the enhancement of the department's image in the media, he replies with undisguised scorn. In its farewell to the character, the movie cultivates Callahan's image by displaying his aversion to the whole idea of images.

To that end, the film leaves behind the earnestly visceral depictions of violence of the earlier entries in the series and transfers Callahan's longstanding iconoclasm from an avenging spirit against social corruption to a gruff repudiation of cultural decline—as it always really was all along. Set in the milieu of trash culture, the movie concerns a murder on the set of a low-budget horror film (of an Axl Rose–like rock star played by Jim Carrey) and the subsequent revelation of a plot to kill a series of figures who function as cultural symbols, from a Pauline Kael–like movie critic to Callahan himself. The director of the film-within-the-film, an effete Britisher lam-

pooned for his cultural pretensions, defends his work: "People are fasci-
nated with death and violence, that's why my films make money—they're
an escape." Yet the killer is spurred to his crimes because he is traumatized
by these images. Of the filmmaker, he says, "He stole my nightmares and
made them real!" Although he constructs a "substitute identity from books,
movies, and magazines," as one analyst in the film puts it, the villain seeks
revenge against the producers of the very representations that have shaped
him. At a time when Eastwood himself was starting to question the role of
his own films in the rise of trash culture (Tibbets 173), *The Dead Pool* flirts
with self-conscious acknowledgment.

Ultimately, the movie's aim is to insulate Callahan from the taint of its
own critique, to position him as upholder of truth and honesty against the
hypocrisy and artifice of the constructed image. In previous "Dirty Harry"
films, Callahan's pairing with ethnically different partners enabled displays
of the racial egalitarianism ostensibly underlying Callahan's apparent
racism. *The Dead Pool* takes this conceit a step further when high-ranking
lackeys assign Callahan a Chinese American partner because an appearance
of multiculturalism is "good for the department's image." Callahan's initial
derision of the partner seems at first like the usual display of white privilege, but it is finally meant to be understood as a rejection of sham social
engineering, so that the bond the two men achieve can be seen as more
"authentic" than any imposed protocols of politically correct diversity. Similarly, Callahan later preempts a reprobate's demand that his self-immolation
be broadcast, a refusal portrayed as a noble, if futile, gesture of resistance
on Callahan's part to the influence of exploitative media. The movie's stran-
gulated satire—it seems to be trying laboriously to ape the effortlessly postmodern style and tone of Brian De Palma's *Body Double* (1984)—reflects its
partial recognition of its own complicity in the culture of images even as it
strives to redeem Callahan as the defender of the real.

## ★★★★★ Eastwood versus the Hard Bodies

*Heartbreak Ridge* is Eastwood's most direct confrontation of
the decade with the "hard body" ethos, condensing his putatively redemp-
tive self-parody, avowed contempt for the culture of images, and mediation
of left- and right-wing politics into one long sneer at the new order. As a
lifetime marine reassigned to a reconnaissance mission, Eastwood plays
Sergeant Highway, charged with whipping young recruits into shape for the
invasion of Grenada. His superiors are all petty functionaries and college
boys who care about nothing but public relations. "This is the new marines,"

one of them advises him, "and you're an anachronism." Another calls him a "relic," but once again the point is to uphold the value of the old ways against the corroding forces of the new. The recruits are all young, muscular hard bodies, ripped and toned but ineffectual and undisciplined. By contrast to Highway's foursquare, effortless virility, the movie portrays the hard bodies as all image—a superficial appearance of strength concealing an underlying weakness.

In the contest between the buff and the bluff—in the dictionary sense of rough and unyielding but not unkind—the latter wins. Three quick fight scenes show Highway subduing a hard body gone to seed, a hard body in his prime, and, climactically, one of the bureaucratic officers. Except for the amorphous, extended brawls at the end of the *Every Which Way* films, fights in Eastwood movies of the 1980s are never prolonged affairs. Eastwood's fights are short and efficient, to demonstrate that his opponent never really has a chance. At the beginning of *Heartbreak Ridge*, Highway is jailed for disturbing the peace when a large, menacing type challenges him. Beefy enough to suggest the frame of a former bodybuilder, this foe is now an overweight redneck, and Highway has no trouble defeating him. Similarly, when Highway's men suffer under his disciplinary regimen, they await the return from the brig of one of their number, "the Swede," who will stand up to him. When the Swede appears, he proves to be a gargantuan Aryan, yet despite his hard body bearing he is gone in less than sixty seconds.

As if in reply to the rise of bodybuilder stars like Stallone and Schwarzenegger, Eastwood goes out of his way to mock the fad of pumping iron in the 1980s. In *Any Which Way You Can*, for example, he meets his future opponent, another bodybuilder he ultimately beats. Instead of hostility, the two men engage in a mutual admiration of each other's bodies. "You look like you lift," coos the bodybuilder, like a stock character from gay porn, to which Eastwood, playing a mechanic, replies, "Mostly motor blocks." We are to make no mistake that Eastwood's lanky musculature is the product of anything but real work, while the pumpers of iron engage in trumped-up labor producing artificial muscles that are little more than fat in disguise.

In the training scenes of *Heartbreak Ridge*, the film makes much of the contrast between Eastwood's clothed lankiness and his men's chiseled naked torsos. Typical as these young men are of the new masculinity, Highway rebukes them for effeminacy, viewing their hard bodies as signifiers not of fitness but of selfishness and laziness. At the center of the movie is a quasi-buddy pairing of Highway and Corporal Stitch (Mario Van Peebles), a young black man with aspirations to be a pop singer. This ambition reveals an addiction to pleasure, in the film's terms, that is also visible in the nar-

Eastwood versus the hard bodies. *Heartbreak Ridge.* Courtesy Larry Edmunds Bookstore.
Copyright Jay Weston Productions/The Malpaso Company, 1986.

cissistic display of the hard body, an addiction that must be overcome to
achieve real discipline. "No pleasure" is Highway's mantra—and even the
Swede, in the end, becomes a convert to his reign.

Defending themselves from Marxist guerillas, Highway's men conquer
a hill against hypocritical commands from the military brass as they try to
conceal the real crux of the mission. Called on to account for disobeying
orders his superiors knew he would ultimately be forced to abrogate, Highway declares, "We're paid to improvise, overcome, adapt!" As an allegory of
Eastwood's 1980s adaptations, *Heartbreak Ridge* demonstrates the star's eagerness to show himself at odds with both the left and the right in the service
of a greater honesty. On one hand, the film illustrates Highway's compli-
ance—however inadvertent—with covert military objectives, while on the
other it illustrates his exposure of the administration's recourse to sub-
terfuge. Clearly, any ideologue counting on Eastwood's allegiance would be
guilty of misjudging his faith in the higher cause of truth. Other, earlier
films allegorize this theme too, as such misjudgments litter the movies—
from the right-wing vigilantes in *Magnum Force* (1973) who expect him to
ally with them, only to be told they have "misjudged" him, to the renegade
biker gang in the *Every Which Way* films, combining countercultural accou-
trements with neo-Nazi regalia, who ultimately admit, to his gratification,
that they too have "misjudged" him. By the end of the decade, the message

was clear: misjudged as a racist, a sexist, a hawk, a fascist, a pawn of the left or the right, Eastwood would be redeemed as an auteur, above it all.

## ★★★★★ Willis and Postmodern Stardom

One of the key stars to emerge in the decade, Bruce Willis quickly became the type of the post-Eastwood action hero. Before this, he made two films with Blake Edwards, the romantic comedy *Blind Date* (1987) followed by the hybrid western/murder-mystery *Sunset* (1988). Considering his apotheosis as action star, both films seem like false starts, though both display Willis's deconstructions of traditional stardom. The latter is of special interest for its direct connection to *City Heat* (1984), Eastwood's most overt (and least successful) self-parody of the 1980s. Both *Sunset* and *City Heat* are buddy movies and both, like *Blind Date*, began as Blake Edwards projects (Edwards was replaced as director of *City Heat* by Richard Benjamin). *City Heat* pairs Eastwood and Burt Reynolds as hostile associates trying to find the killer of Eastwood's former partner in 1930s Kansas City, while *Sunset* brings Willis together with James Garner, the two playing Tom Mix and Wyatt Earp, respectively, to solve a murder in 1920s Hollywood. Both films follow two of Edwards's signature eighties projects, *S.O.B.* (1981), an aftershock of the New Hollywood bent on exposing the hypocrisy and perniciousness of the film industry, and *Victor/Victoria* (1982), a cross-dressing, gay-friendly, "gender-bending" farce. Like many of Edwards's films after these successes, *City Heat* and *Sunset* both trade in campy nostalgia and a penchant for questioning traditional masculinity, often by deconstructing the iconographies of aging stars. Among the stars that make up these buddy pairings, Willis is the only one from the generation of the eighties, suggesting his position as at once an atavistic and transitional figure, whose persona (like Reynolds's) entails a send-up of the idea of stardom. In his performance in *Sunset*, Willis becomes a virtual walking palimpsest of the older stars, mixing some of Reynolds's wry knowingness and Garner's sly folksiness with a bit of Eastwood's staunch taciturnity.

Retaining little of its edge, *Sunset* leavens the sourness of *S.O.B.* as well as its last-ditch mania to lay bare the rapacity of the Hollywood system. Like many of Edwards's subsequent films, *Sunset* has a gentle, punch-drunk blowsiness, expressing a druggy, vanquished perplexity over the paradox that the same old illusions persist long after they have been debunked. The plot pairs Mix, the old-time western movie star, and Earp, an actual, albeit mythic, western hero, to investigate a murder in a bordello featuring call girls who impersonate film stars of the day (Greta Garbo, Pola Negri, Mae

Between the Real and the Fake: Bruce Willis as Tom Mix with co-star Mariel Hemingway in *Sunset*. Courtesy Larry Edmunds Bookstore. Copyright The Blake Edwards Company/ TriStar Pictures, 1988.

West). Willis renders Mix as both a nostalgic cliché and a direct forerunner of the Eastwood iconography, a western antihero famous for playing himself: "I didn't become Numero Uno at the box-office by playing other people," he retorts when a sadistic studio head (Malcolm McDowell) orders him to play Earp in a biopic. Arriving in Hollywood to assist with the film about his own life, Earp rebuffs an autograph hound: "I'm a technical advisor, not a celebrity." Meanwhile, another fan snippily observes, "He looks more like a Texas oilman than a sheriff." The film treats the relation between self and image, strikingly, without proposing a binary link between the terms. Rather, it suggests mutual entanglements between identity and cultural representation. Even Mix's fans know he is a "fake," yet they lap up his movies all the same. The point is neither to engage in inveterate myth-making by showing how Mix rises to the occasion when forced to perform his movie roles in "real life," nor to demonstrate his failure by contrast to the triumphs of the "real life" hero, Earp. In the movie's terms both Earp and Mix *are* fake—and "real" at the same time. Casting Willis in the role suggests Edwards's early recognition of him as a star whose image would effortlessly traverse contradictory elements—the real and the fake, the mythic and the ironic.

A similar synthesis spurred Willis's move into action films. His John McClane in *Die Hard* begins as an Eastwood clone—a tight-lipped but sardonic reluctant antihero estranged from his wife and embroiled as a lone crusader in the robbery of a high-rise office building—and ends as a hard body. The movie marks a key moment in what Susan Jeffords calls "the big switch" (see Jeffords, *Hard Bodies*; Jeffords, "The Big Switch" 196–208), the transition from the post-Vietnam "remasculinization" films of the 1980s to the "kinder, gentler" model of American manhood that emerged in the nineties. To be sure, that model is still largely dedicated to the business of "kicking ass," in the recurrent phrase of *Die Hard*. The problem of these films is how to portray their heroes as "kinder" and "gentler" without portraying them as weak.

To that end, *Die Hard* explicitly disavows 1980s strategies of remasculinization. Where the Rambo movies hawked compensatory narratives of victory in Vietnam, *Die Hard* mocks such fantasies. As darting choppers circle the besieged building, one awe-stricken observer remarks, "It's like fuckin' Saigon!"—to which another sarcastically replies, speaking for the movie's target demographic, "I was in junior high [during the Vietnam War]." The movie's obsessive intertextual echoes of prior displays of cinematic heroism are mostly dedicated to removing McClane from the lineage of action heroes old and new, cited by name: John Wayne, Marshall Dillon, Rambo himself. McClane prefers a different precursor: "I was always partial to Roy Rogers," he says, adopting the alias "Roy" and shouting the tagline of the singing cowboy—"Happy Trails!"—as he dispatches villains. When McClane discovers the robbers' stash of ammunition, meanwhile, he notifies police that "they have enough plastic explosives to orbit Arnold Schwarzenegger!" Eastwood is just about the only action hero spared from the movie's jibes, as if to settle its debt to him.

The villains in *Die Hard* pose as international revolutionary terrorists taking revenge against the Japanese corporation that owns the building for the depredations and inequities—the "legacy of greed"—of their multinational power (this was the year before Sony bought Columbia Pictures), but they turn out to be ordinary thieves, motivated not by politics but by their own greed. It may be the beginning of globalization, this film would have us believe, but it's still the end of ideology. This assurance extends to the film's gender politics. By contrast to Eastwood's inveterate loners, most of Willis's heroes from *Die Hard* on are family men drawn into larger intrigues not by political or professional commitments but by a practical necessity to protect their domestic entitlements. McClane's wife (Bonnie Bedelia) is an executive for the Japanese corporation, taken hostage by the thieves, and her job has created rifts in the marriage that are ultimately mended by the spectacle of McClane's heroism. Yet, though she is a marginalized damsel in distress for much of the film, the couple's reconciliation depends on McClane's reconciliation to her independence and her right to work, a resolution that has caused some difficulty for critics seeking to parse the film's perspectives on domestic ideology between the right and the left (Overpeck 202).

Willis's performance in *Die Hard* is a veritable striptease, as he sheds clothing amid the mounting explosions to reveal himself ultimately as a full-on hard body. If in his films after the spaghetti westerns and before *Unforgiven* (1992) (and with the exception of *The Beguiled* [1971]) Eastwood rarely breaks a sweat and never gets his hair mussed, by the end of *Die Hard* Willis's naked body is covered in ash, gunpowder, blood, and sweat—a walking palimpsest, now, of all he's been through. Eastwood's imperviousness gives way to Willis's willingness to get down in the muck, not for a cause, but for personal stakes and—ultimately—for the fun of it. The effect is to suggest a sharp disconnect between this more "realistic" depiction of the body under duress and the lack of ordinary affect that accompanies it. Even as Willis's body becomes a visual signifier of physical pain, he expresses none, emitting aggressive wisecracks or primal screams of triumph in place of agony. As he digs a bullet out of his own foot, he talks by radio to police who are placing bets on him: "What kind of odds am I getting?" he asks with his usual snarky equanimity, and with nary a grimace.

As many commentators have noted, a crucial influence on the action films of the 1980s and 1990s was the popularization of the video game among the young males these films targeted (Gallagher 64). As in a video game, the movies' structures place their hero in a labyrinthine setting, in which new corridors open up successively, presenting ever greater hindrances in an escalating sequence of violent confrontations. The very embodiment of the gaming hero, Willis moves through the obstacle course with skill and aplomb, reacting with visceral instinct while also retaining a posture of distance predicated on (and producing) an understanding of the violence as pure display.

From 1985 to 1989, as his movie career began, Willis continued to appear on television in the series "Moonlighting," co-starring with Cybill Shepherd as the joint proprietors of a detective agency. Willis's wiseguy character defined his persona as he made the move into film stardom, and the show's sensibility, combining quirky parody with straightforward action scenes, provided a worthy springboard for his career while also demarcating the limitations of his early work. Even after his starring role in *Blind*

*Date*, Willis was still identified in the popular press in an oft-repeated coinage as "the smirkaleck star of *Moonlighting*" ("Gambling that Their Love Is Here to Stay, Bruce Willis and Demi Moore Hit Vegas to Get Seriously Married," *People*, 7 December 1987, 71). *Die Hard* did little to alter this profile, but Willis's subsequent film, *In Country* (1989), seemed like a calculated bid to extend his range, in something like the style of Eastwood's "sincere" roles. Press surrounding the production makes much of this transformation; in one interview, Willis enters as "the manic, doo-wappin' character that made him a star in TV's *Moonlighting*" (Daniel Cerone, "Bruce Willis Living Out a Dramedy," *Los Angeles Times*, 21 September 1989, E1–E3), but quickly morphs into "a far different Willis—calmer, more thoughtful and less performance-oriented," marking a turn from "the offscreen antics that for a while made him the poster boy of the tabloids." Willis himself weighs in on the metamorphosis in the course of the interview. To play the part, he remarks, "I had to let go of thinking about how I looked physically. I had to let go of that element of vanity that men in the late '80s have." The interviewer approvingly quotes from reviews of the film to the effect that, by contrast to "the problem most critics have had with him in the past . . . 'There is not a trace of his wisecracking celebrity persona.'"

As a traumatized veteran of the Vietnam War struggling to reintegrate into civilian life, Willis displays "his somber side" in *In Country* as part of a ritual obeisance to the "serious" that had already been heralded two months before the film was released in the title of a profile in *McCall's*, "Bruce Willis: From 'Wild Man' to Family Man" (Fred Robbins, June 1989, 82–84). Impressive though Willis's performance may be, it is difficult to view it apart from a consumer logic geared to produce an impression of depth in order to sustain the marketability of a commodified surface. Indeed, after *Die Hard*, interviews and profiles of Willis rarely fail to note the actor's astronomical paycheck: "And now you're getting five million for the movie *Die Hard*?" one interviewer asks forthrightly (Dennis Watlington, "Spruce Bruce," *Vanity Fair*, May 1988, 132). Typically, such inquiries move Willis to heroic acts of disavowal: asked what he aspires to, he says, "without hesitation," "Love of my wife and my friends . . . and—whether it's for a hundred dollars or a million dollars—the chance to act." Elsewhere, he notes that he would "accept just ten bucks" for the chance to work with Meryl Streep (Robbins, "From 'Wild Man,'" *McCall's*, June 1989, 84).

Willis's subsequent film seems so far removed from the reserved, quiet, middlebrow territory of *In Country* that it suggests a certain backlash. In *Look Who's Talking* (1989), only two years into his movie career, he mocks both his own celebrity and any pretensions to seriousness by lending his voice to the character of a baby in an unapologetically lowbrow comedy. Because Willis's persona in its most characteristic moments seems so fully dedicated to the pleasure principle, his association with infantilism comes as no surprise. Indeed, he had voiced a baby's thoughts in an episode of "Moonlighting" only the year before, granting a certain intertextual resonance to *Look Who's Talking* that belies its mixture of treacly cuteness and gross-out humor. The conceit of the television episode involves a fetus, offspring of Willis and Shepherd's characters, reluctant to emerge from the womb due to his parents' bickering and other unappealing features of "this thing called life." The question is rendered moot when the baby miscarries in a sudden turn to pathos. Similarly, in *Look Who's Talking*, Willis's antic monologue accompanies images of a child's development from birth through toddlerhood, the allegedly comic effects deriving from the notion that a pre-vocal infant naturally entertains the thoughts of an adult heterosexual male. The implication that identity is a set of stand-up jokes, fixed at birth, with a depthlessness sounded by the schismatic relation of voice and body, makes this film a fitting capstone to Willis's career of the eighties.

In *Die Hard*, Willis adapts the Eastwood persona for the high-tech age, proving that even in the era of the microchip—*pace* Dyer—the traditional hero needs only a few minor adjustments to kick ass effectively. Willis replaces Eastwood's slow-burning stare with an insouciant smirk, substituting postmodern ennui for repressed rage, and he hoists multi-round assault weapons in place of Eastwood's steady Magnum. Eastwood's increasing pop self-reflexivity in his 1980s action films signified an unflappable cool amid the relative earnestness of his surroundings, but in *Die Hard*, a similar self-reflexiveness bleeds into the general surround—everyone shares it, as part of the game. This free-floating spirit came to dominate the action genre so mightily that stars who did not follow it (Seagal, Norris, Van Damme) fell into shadow. Even Eastwood, after his bids for an alternative kind of relevance throughout the 1980s, tried his hand at it. When he finally entered the world of the high-tech po-mo action film with *The Rookie*, he was derided for this failed attempt to imitate *Die Hard* (Schickel 451).

If Eastwood is the quintessential *late* cold warrior, Willis is the quintessential *post*–cold warrior. Eastwood's persona remains that of the stoic isolato, defending individualism against conspiracies to condition it or bring it under the sway of organized society. Willis embodies the delirious roleplaying postmodern self, for whom politics is largely irrelevant and the world of multinational capitalism is not so much a threat as an opportunity for the intensification and dispersal of sensation—which is what, in Willis's movies, selfhood is largely about. His subsequent career alternates between action movies and "character" roles within ensembles. In most of these, modernist alienation appears as a joke, a holdover from when people still worried about having authentic selves. Still, Willis's "authenticity" is a constituent part of his image: "I'm the hero, I always mean what I say," he tells an admirer in *Sunset*, following up with a smirk and a wink. Yet this authenticity is not a "deeper" principle underlying the surface smart-aleck—it's just another part of the surface, coexisting with the cheekiness without generating any anxiety to speak of. He is nearly always both playing himself and parodying himself—as was true from his very first roles, when audiences had no reference points for the parody. While Clint Eastwood remained a one-track star, assuming the stability of his image could be assured by confining it to a single medium, Bruce Willis reveled in the euphoric proliferation of images and the dispersal of selves, identities, and stardom that came with it.

### NOTES

Thanks to Jean Walton for assistance with French translations.

1. *Tightrope* is the closest Eastwood comes to deconstructing his persona, paralleling the psychosexual proclivities of the Eastwood antihero with those of a homicidal maniac. Not surprisingly, this is also the Eastwood film of the eighties that has received, by far, the fullest treatment elsewhere. For that reason, I have chosen to focus on films that have garnered less attention. For a treatment of *Tightrope* as a deconstruction of the Eastwood persona and traditional cinematic representations of masculinity, see Holmlund "Sexuality and Power."

# 12 ★★★★★★★★★★

# Steve Martin and John Candy

## Penny Wise and Pound Foolish

JERRY MOSHER

There is a scene in *Planes, Trains and Automobiles* (1987) when Neal Page, the snobby, uptight businessman played by Steve Martin, attempts to contribute to a passenger sing-along during a long highway bus ride. Neal begins to sing the opening lines of the 1954 Jule Styne–Sammy Cahn song "Three Coins in the Fountain," but no passengers join in; instead, all heads silently turn to stare at the pompous fool who would know such an arcane tune. His traveling companion, Del Griffith, a loud, buffoonish salesman played by John Candy, saves Neal by quickly launching into the TV cartoon theme "Meet the Flintstones," and the busload of passengers joyfully unite in song. Eyes cast downward, Neal remains silent, embarrassed both for himself and for the ignorant proles around him.

This scene, in the only film in which Martin and Candy appeared together, nicely encapsulates the actors' star personas in the mid-1980s. Martin, the first stand-up comedian to play arenas and achieve rock-star status, had quickly alienated his younger fans with his forays into historical pastiche: lip-synching and dancing to Depression-era Tin Pan Alley tunes in *Pennies from Heaven* (1981) and interacting with clips from 1940s films noirs in *Dead Men Don't Wear Plaid* (1982). His well-publicized interest in studying philosophy and collecting modern art only magnified the public's suspicion that he was too intellectual and detached to play romantic comedy, despite the exquisite physicality he often invested in his roles. Candy, on the other hand, was commonly perceived as an eager-to-please everyman who tried too hard to be the life of the party, arousing both love and pity as he cheerfully plodded through a series of bad movies. Before entering feature films at the end of the 1970s, both actors had honed their comedic skills in front of live audiences (Martin in stand-up, Candy at Second City) and in television sketch comedy (Martin writing for variety shows and regularly hosting "Saturday Night Live," Candy on "SCTV"). Both actors appeared in box office smashes early in their film careers (Martin in *The Jerk* [1979], Candy in *Stripes* [1981]), and both had starred in a number of lackluster mid-1980s films that did not meet industry expectations. *Planes, Trains and Automobiles*, the first adult comedy written and directed by teen-film sensation John Hughes, was not a big box-office hit after it opened on Thanksgiving weekend of 1987, but the interplay between Martin and Candy generated enough critical acclaim and financial success to boost Martin's career and to reestablish Candy as a bankable headlining star—indeed, Candy considered it the pivotal film of his career. "The partnering between Martin and Candy here is the most inspired form of comic symbiosis," noted *Washington Post* film critic Hal Hinson. "There's real chemistry between these two, and you can feel their elation at being teamed together" (25 November 1987, C1).

In the 1980s, both Martin and Candy were at the peak of their film careers. Both comically portrayed models of American male whiteness that had become unfashionable after the social upheavals of the 1960s and 1970s: Martin as a caricature of uptight, status-conscious WASP culture, and Candy as a beleaguered common man who was often too tired or too loutish to care about fashion or feminism. In the 1980s the Hollywood comedy genre was moving away from counterculture humor toward situation comedy geared for wide release in multiplexes and ancillary sales to cable and video markets. Martin and Candy would struggle to make the transition from stand-up and sketch comedy to feature-length filmmaking, but they would be more successful than many of their "SNL" and "SCTV" brethren.

## ★★★★★ Steve Martin: Anti-Comedian

Steve Martin had already forged a well-known comic persona by the time he appeared in *The Jerk*, his first starring role in a feature-length film, in December 1979. Through incessant touring of clubs and arenas, hundreds of television appearances, the release of three Top Ten record albums, and cover stories in major periodicals, Martin had become a pop culture phenomenon: the prematurely gray, skinny white guy in a white three-piece suit who wore fake rabbit ears or plastic arrows and yelled catchphrases like "Excuse me!" and "I'm a wild and crazy guy," which quickly became household words. During the 1970s Martin had become the most successful among a group of young comedians—including Albert Brooks, Martin Mull, and Andy Kaufman—whose work would be dubbed "post-funny" or "anti-comedy": telling jokes without punch lines, or punch lines before the jokes; setting up tension and then refusing to break it with a joke, which forced the audience to choose when to laugh; using the audience as a prop (which sometimes entailed taking them outside); and satirizing the hoary tradition of "show business" by acting out shopworn Vaudeville-era gags, which got laughs precisely because the jokes themselves were no longer funny. Delivery was everything; the amount of audience laughter depended on its awareness of Martin's ironic distance from his material, an approach that would later inform (and sometimes plague) his screen acting. Martin was a comedian, he reasoned, because he said he was. He was also solipsistic and apolitical, which the prescient Martin recognized was exactly what audiences were looking for in the mid-1970s, after the previous decade's promise of personal freedom and social change had entered its dark aftermath in drug overdoses, Vietnam, and Watergate. In 1972, Martin later recalled, "I cut my hair, shaved my beard, and put on a suit" (Martin 144).

Martin often claimed that his choice of a white three-piece gabardine suit was pragmatic—it increased his visibility and the lightweight material gave him more physical freedom—but the suit's conservative connotations also gave the comedian another stage prop for his increasingly absurd act.[1] The incongruity of the performer's square appearance and wild behavior became crucial to his persona. Carl Reiner, who directed four of Martin's films, noted, "People look at Steve and think he's some WASP insurance salesman, and then he comes out with these ridiculous things. He comes on very poker-faced, like he doesn't expect what he's saying to be funny" (Kenneth Turan, *Rolling Stone*, 8 November 1984, 18). The dapper suit worked perfectly with Martin's deliberate caricature of show business success, suggesting that he was as suave as Cary Grant—until he shattered the illusion by talking in a smarmy faux-hipster voice or putting balloons on his head. By assuming the stereotypical image of a WASP, Martin also began to undermine assumptions about white entitlement and propriety: here was a character so committed to hard work and success that he always gave "110 percent" but lacked any real talent or skills, and whose pompous attempts to appear sincere and principled resulted in vulgarity and humiliation. That stand-up character, Martin noted, "assumed that everything he said was brilliant. He had total confidence, with *nothing* to back it up" (Adam Gopnik, *New Yorker*, 29 November 1993, 101). Martin, who was clearly aware of American stand-up comedy's history as a bully pulpit for minorities and outsiders looking in, satirized WASP privilege and reticence from within and turned them inside out. "My comedy is definitely linked to the white man," Martin told Lawrence Grobel during his *Playboy* interview in 1980. But he recoiled at being dubbed "the Great WASP Hope," noting that he didn't consider himself a WASP. "That term is derogatory. It implies simplicity and propriety, and I don't think of myself like that" (January 1980, 108).[2]

Martin funneled his stand-up act's absurd premises—and his reputation as "the Great WASP Hope"—into his screenplay for *The Jerk*, which he co-wrote with Carl Gottlieb. Navin Johnson, played by Martin, "once had wealth, power, and the love of a beautiful woman," but he is now living on skid row. The narrative goes into flashbacks as Navin tells his story: "It was never easy for me. I was born a poor black child. I remember the days, sitting on the porch with my family, singing and dancing down in Mississippi." Navin, it seems, is the only member of this black sharecropping family who prefers Lawrence Welk to rhythm and blues and whose favorite meal is tuna, Tab, and Twinkies, the familiar staples of white America. Navin's parents finally reveal the news that he is not their natural child, and Navin goes on the road in search of work and adventure. He gets rich but loses it all, is dumped by his girlfriend (Bernadette Peters), and winds up on skid row. In the end, his black family finds him and takes him back to Mississippi, where they have wisely invested the money Navin sent home.

Again, delivery was everything: *The Jerk*'s comedic momentum was achieved not by plotting but by the visual gags and wordplay that replicated the self-reflexive, anarchic energy of Martin's stand-up routines. "*The Jerk* wasn't really a parody of a particular kind of movie, like a Mel Brooks parody," Martin recalled in the *New Yorker*. "It was more abstract than that. It wasn't a parody of a particular kind of beginning, middle, and end. It was a parody of the whole idea that a movie should have a beginning and a middle and an end." Navin Johnson, a terribly untalented individual who assumes that unflagging optimism alone can guarantee his success, was a variation on Martin's stand-up character, steeped in show business lore, "who had once seen Fred Astaire and thought that he could tap-dance" (Gopnik, 29 November 1993, 101–02). Satirizing the egalitarian notions of stardom that appeared in so many Hollywood rags-to-riches stories, Navin gets his name published in the phone book and exclaims, "I'm somebody now! Millions of people look at this book everyday! This is the kind of spontaneous publicity—your name in print—that makes people." Released on 14 December 1979, *The Jerk* delivered on the promise of Martin's stand-up innovations and became a box office hit, grossing almost $74 million. The film's success allowed the comedian to retire from stand-up performing, but it would be a decade before another Martin film (*Parenthood*, 1989) achieved this level of box office earnings.

★★★★★ **Growing Distant**

*Daily Variety* gossip columnist Army Archerd visited Martin on the set of *Pennies from Heaven*, his follow-up to *The Jerk*, and filed a report: "Steve Martin no longer looks like the Martin of old with or without an arrow through his head," Archerd wrote. "His hair is dyed brown, cut short, parted severely and plastered down in 1934-style. Is he worried about losing his fanatic, faithful fans? 'Maybe I'll get some new ones,' he said seriously" (5 February 1981, 3). The fact that Archerd had to indicate that Martin wasn't joking suggests that the columnist already foresaw a box office disappointment in the making. MGM would spend $22 million on *Pennies from Heaven*, hoping to capitalize on Martin's popularity and reclaim the studio's past glory as the world's leading producer of musicals. The critical reputation of Dennis Potter's original six-hour BBC-TV production (1978) attracted gifted veterans such as director Herbert Ross, cinematographer Gordon Willis, production designer Ken Adam, and fashion designer Bob Mackie. Martin studied dramatic acting with Ross and spent more than six months learning how to tap dance for the film's musical numbers.

Advertising for *Pennies from Heaven* focused on the music and the re-teaming of Martin and Bernadette Peters, his co-star from *The Jerk* (and real-life girlfriend). The actual film was a self-consciously artistic portrayal of Depression-era America, by turns grim and ebullient, in which desperate, browbeaten characters escape into the fantasy world of an upbeat 1930s musical and lip-synch to popular tunes. It also operated as a metatextual commentary on the mythical status of the American musical, which could only resonate with viewers who possessed some degree of historical awareness and cultural sophistication. Critic Roger Ebert noted that "Hollywood is always pragmatic in these matters: If the filmmakers haven't made the film the studio had in mind, the studio simply advertises the film they wish had been made. That led to some thoroughly puzzled audiences, as Martin fans lined up for a wild and crazy musical and discovered they were in a musical that wanted to subvert musicals" (*Chicago Sun-Times*, 1 January 1982). Indeed, at a preview screening in Denver, producers had to beg masses of teen viewers to stay until the end. In *The Jerk*, Martin had given fans a glimpse of his interests when he and Peters sang the 1926 standard "Tonight You Belong to Me" while playing ukulele and cornet, but that scene could be tolerated as a charming interlude, akin to Martin's bluegrass banjo playing during his stand-up performances. *Pennies from Heaven*'s elaborate musical numbers and exquisite production values simply did not interest most younger viewers unfamiliar with Tin Pan Alley and the paintings of Edward Hopper and Reginald Marsh, which were the sources for several astonishing tableaux vivants. Critics generally admired the film, and Pauline Kael began her rave review for the *New Yorker* by calling *Pennies from Heaven* "the most emotional movie musical I have ever seen" (21 December 1981, 122). The film subsequently did good business in New York, but it bombed everywhere else, taking in $9 million and imposing heavy losses at MGM. *Pennies from Heaven* remains Martin's most impressive artistic achievement, but it also alienated the comedian's fan base and created a major setback in his film career.

"He shouldn't be doing a dramatic role at this point," Martin's manager Bill McEuen told *Rolling Stone* a few weeks before *Pennies from Heaven* opened. "I would've been happier if he'd done a couple of more comedies first, then tried something different" (Ben Fong-Torres, "Steve Martin Sings," *Rolling Stone*, 18 February 1982, 10). Why, then, did Martin do it? "There was no hesitation," Martin told the *Rolling Stone* reporter. "When I first started doing my act, it was not . . . normal. It was not what was expected. That's what the public caught onto. And I said, 'If I start getting trapped by my own sameness, I'm not doing what they secretly want, which is for me to do what I want to do'" (12). Years later, Martin remained unrepentant. "I had to do it," he told an interviewer in 1988. "I had just finished *The Jerk*, and I was sick of my act. . . . What was I going to do next? *The Jerk II?* I thought, is this it, am I 'The Wild and Crazy Guy' for the rest

Steve Martin and Bernadette Peters imitate Fred Astaire and Ginger Rogers in *Pennies from Heaven*. Copyright Metro-Goldwyn-Mayer, 1981.

of my life?" (Elvis Mitchell, "I'm Just a White Guy from Orange County," *American Film*, November 1988, 24).

Riding high on the enormous success of his stand-up act and *The Jerk*, Martin had not fully realized the ramifications of taking artistic risks in feature filmmaking. In stand-up, a comedian can bomb one night, revise his material, and kill the next night. In Hollywood, the cycle of producing and marketing a film, and carefully building audience expectations, requires years and millions of dollars. A decade after the *Pennies from Heaven* debacle, Martin expressed a more savvy view of the film industry, and his satisfaction making the low-risk, middlebrow *Father of the Bride* (1991): "You could argue that perfect, honest, well-made comic entertainment is the best thing that movies can do, or ought to do. If you miss with something ambitious, you can miss so badly . . . making a movie means five thousand people with opinions, two years of work, $25 million of somebody else's money, and then I have to go on 'Entertainment Tonight'" (Gopnik, *New Yorker*, 29 November 1993, 98). Martin's experience of acute success and failure with *The Jerk* and *Pennies from Heaven* established a schism of expectations that would shape the rest of his film career: the first remains his best screen adaptation of anarchic "anti-comedy," and the second remains his pinnacle of artistic achievement. Both films were slaps in the face: the first to cinematic conventions, the second to his fans. Martin would spend the rest of the 1980s atoning for his sins in middlebrow projects in which he only occasionally aimed for anti-comedy or high art.

His third film, the clever film noir parody *Dead Men Don't Wear Plaid*, reenlisted the services of director Carl Reiner to create a more audience-friendly pastiche of American film history, but many critics found Martin's interaction with old movie clips too gimmicky. In 1983 Martin and Reiner returned to more familiar, "wild and crazy" territory with *The Man with Two Brains*, but it fell flat with audiences, barely surpassing the box office of *Pennies from Heaven*. *The Lonely Guy* (1984), adapted by Neil Simon from a Bruce Jay Friedman book and directed by Arthur Hiller, appeared promising but was hampered by the lackluster pairing of Martin and Charles Grodin, and represents the financial nadir of Martin's early career. After *The Jerk* drew almost $74 million, Martin's next four films totaled only $43 million. "There was this time, between *Pennies from Heaven* and *The Lonely Guy*, where I felt lost," Martin recalled in 1990. "I didn't know if I was supposed to do some of the old stuff or was I not? Does it work? So in *The Man with Two Brains*, I tried some of the old things. But halfheartedly" (Elvis Mitchell, "The King of Anti-Comedy," *GQ*, July 1990, 170).

Martin would recover from this string of flops; a bigger problem was overcoming the alienation of his fan base and the growing perception that he was too cerebral and aloof. The ironic distance Martin had created in his stand-up act had affected the reception of his filmic and extra-filmic behavior, raising doubts about his sincerity and emotional investment across the board. This distance had been magnified on the big screen in the anti-comedy of *The Jerk* and the Brechtian trappings of *Pennies from Heaven*. Roger Ebert's review argued that *Pennies from Heaven* was "all flash and style and no heart. That's the problem with the Steve Martin performance, too: He provides a technically excellent performance that does not seem to be inhabited by a person." Even *All of Me* (1984) and *Roxanne* (1987), the two character-driven romantic comedies that revived Martin's career, showcased the actor's physical technique rather than his emotional range. In *All of Me*, Martin portrayed a lawyer whose body is invaded by the spirit of a feisty rich woman (Lily Tomlin); the actor's performance of the war between the sexes within his body was a tour de force of physical comedy. Initially, Martin displayed the exaggerated feminine gestures of a drag queen as the warring partners negotiated his bodily activities, but as Martin warmed to Tomlin and fell in love with her, his movements became more delicate and refined. In *Roxanne*, a modern retelling of the Cyrano de Bergerac story, critical attention focused on Martin's physical comportment as his character comically struggled to negotiate the world with an extremely long nose. The National Society of Film Critics awarded Best Actor awards to Martin for both films, and Pauline Kael, always a fan of Martin's performing talents, noted that in *Roxanne* "Martin seems to cross-breed the skills of [W. C.] Fields and Buster Keaton, with some Fred Astaire mingled in" (*New Yorker*, 15 June 1987, 77).

In spite of the critical accolades, Martin's obsessive pursuit of technical perfection often made him appear too precise, too controlled. The joke of Martin being "a wild and crazy guy," of course, was that he was really the opposite. Another manic comedian, Robin Williams, would successfully transition into dramatic roles in *The World According to Garp* (1982) and *Dead Poet's Society* (1989), but such roles remained out of Martin's reach. In a 1984 profile, critic Kenneth Turan noted Martin's ability to be "inexpressively expressive . . . as if behind all that discipline and control is something else, something unknowable, maybe otherworldly" (*Rolling Stone*, 8 November 1984, 18). Martin was handsome enough to play a romantic lead, but his studied, conceptual approach to everything he did lacked vulnerability, which diminished his sex appeal.

Martin has consistently refused to talk about his romantic relationships in any detail, and his fastidiously managed career has avoided any hint of scandal—other than a quiet 1994 divorce from actress Victoria Tennant—that could make him appear vulnerable. (Tennant, who co-starred with the comedian in *All of Me* and *L.A. Story* [1991], was a sophisticated, ethereal, London-born blonde who often seemed as detached as Martin.) Sounding like the WASP he had satirized in his stand-up act, Martin noted in a 1980 *Playboy* interview that "I'm against talking about sex, I don't think it's essential to my personality" (January 1980, 96). In an 18 February 1982 *Rolling Stone* interview, writer Ben Fong-Torres confronted Martin about his emotional distance: "*Offstage, you're a very serious kind of distant.* That's what my close friends say, too, you know. *Why is it that you come off so cold to people?* I can't answer that. That's for a shrink to answer. I'm a lot better at it now than when I was touring. When you're touring and if you go to a party, there's automatically a celebrity-audience distance. . . . Any time there is awe, it gets very difficult to be normal, to be yourself. But I'm not saying that that's what made me the way I am. I've probably always been distant" (13).

Publicity about Martin's intellectual pursuits only contributed to his reputation as cerebral and aloof. Interviews often noted Stephen Glenn Martin's average, middle-class childhood in suburban Southern California and his teenage jobs at Disneyland, but they increasingly focused on his eclectic interests in philosophy and modern art. In a 1984 *Rolling Stone* interview Martin explained how he had developed his "comedic premises" from his studies of philosopher Ludwig Wittgenstein (*Rolling Stone*, 8 November 1984, 85), and in a 1989 poster campaign for the American Library Association that featured celebrities appearing with a book of their choice, Martin posed with Douglas Hofstadter's esoteric *Metamagical Themas: Questing for the Essence of Mind and Pattern* (1985). Martin's acquisition of modern art masterpieces was deemed extraordinary even among Hollywood stars and especially among wealthy comedians (Jerry Seinfeld and Jay Leno collect automobiles, and David Letterman co-owns an auto racing team). In a January 1980 *Playboy* interview Martin revealed that he owned more than forty early American paintings (190); the 18 February 1982 cover of *Rolling Stone* featured a now-famous Annie Leibovitz photograph of Martin, in his trademark white suit smeared with black paint, leaping in front of Franz Kline's 1959 black and white painting *Rue*, which Martin owned at the time; and a 1983 *GQ* profile noted that Martin's living room contained paintings by modern abstractionists Kline, Helen Frankenthaler, Kenneth Noland, and Cy Twombly. "Unlike many people who suddenly find themselves in a position to acquire art and then have someone go buy it for them," the *GQ* reporter noted, "Martin goes to galleries himself, reads and studies art history books, and is very knowledgeable about the current art scene" (Sarah Paley, "Hanging Out with Steve Martin," November 1983, 210). Even at a time when TV viewers were ogling movie stars' conspicuous consumption of homes, cars, and clothes on "Lifestyles of the Rich and Famous" (1984), spending millions on abstract paintings seemed inscrutable. In 1984 Martin donated $250,000 to the Los Angeles County Museum of Art and was elected to its board of trustees; a gallery in the museum was named for him. The actor's contributions to the art world, however, did little to endear him to the majority of Americans living outside of Los Angeles and New York—"Jerry's Kids" this was not.

★★★★★ **The Hollywood Professional**

After several disappointments, *All of Me*, again directed by Carl Reiner, drew a healthy $36 million in 1984 and reestablished Martin's viability as a comedic star. It also boosted his confidence: "I see that whole stretch of time now as learning how to make movies," Martin said. "By *All of Me*, I started to get a footing" (*GQ*, July 1990, 170). The anti-comedian who had boasted that *The Jerk* deconstructed narrative convention was now a Hollywood professional singing the praises of structure and causality: "*All of Me* was probably the first *whole* comedy movie I ever starred in: it had a beginning, middle and end. There was a story, you could see it and think, 'I wonder what's going to happen next'" (*American Film*, November 1988, 24–25). Martin was settling into middlebrow situation comedy that was well suited for multiplexes and TV screens. Indeed, after noting *All of Me*'s occasional inventiveness, Pauline Kael complained that the film "often has the bland ugliness of sitcoms" and its situation "seems a little dated, a little too 'nice'" (*New Yorker*, 17 September 1984, 127–28). Martin finished out the decade with four starring vehicles that earned healthy box-office returns: *The Three Amigos* (1986), a critical disappointment directed by comedy veteran John Landis and co-starring Chevy Chase and Martin Short; the charming yet mawkish *Roxanne* (directed by Fred Schepisi), in which screenwriter and executive producer Martin felt compelled to give Edmond Rostand's *Cyrano de Bergerac* a happy ending; *Planes, Trains and Automobiles* with John Candy; and *Dirty Rotten Scoundrels* (Frank Oz, 1988), which paired Martin with Michael Caine as competing confidence men on the French Riviera. *Parenthood*, Martin's final film of the decade, was a Ron Howard–directed ensemble comedy in which Martin capably played a beleaguered family man; in an emotionally nuanced performance, the comedian shed the detached irony that had confounded some viewers of his early films. *Parenthood* grossed more than $100 million and paved the way for Martin's patriarchal roles in the hugely successful but retrograde *Father of the Bride* and *Cheaper by the Dozen* franchises.

   *L.A. Story* (1991), Martin's most personal, "auteurist" film, can be seen as the culminations of a decade of cinematic work that began with *The Jerk*. In a deleted scene, an enigmatic freeway sign registers the complaint, "You think I'm dumb because I live in L.A" (Murray Murry, "You Think I'm Dumb Because I'm L.A.," *Buzz*, December/January 1991, 58). The lament is a familiar one among artists and intellectuals in Los Angeles, where the glamour of the city's film and television industries often blinds outsiders to its rich history of literature, art, music, and architecture. For Martin, a creatively and intellectually gifted young man who grew up in the shadow of Disneyland and built a successful career in Hollywood, the American intelligentsia's routine lack of respect for the West Coast and its popular culture must have stung.[3] In his stand-up act and early film career, he thus tried to have it both ways: ironic distance allowed him to perform in show business and also stand outside of it, submitting it to philosophical scrutiny. Performing with such critical detachment, however, could not open a romantic comedy on 1,000 screens across the country. After *L.A. Story*, Martin fully accepted the Hollywood film industry on its own terms and sought intellectual sustenance elsewhere, focusing his creative energies on writing novels, essays, and plays.

## ★★★★★ John Candy: Living Large

"There's relief in acting," John Candy told an interviewer in 1992, two years before his death. "There's an escape within a character, the ability to get lost and take up another life. I think I may have become an actor to hide from myself" (Dotson Rader, "John Candy Remembers: 'The Day the Acting Bug Bit Me,'" *Parade*, 1992). Standing six-feet-three and weighing approximately 300 pounds, Candy was extremely sensitive about his size; like a magician, he could often conceal it by doing everything in a big way. Although Candy's film career contained more flops than hits, he was adored by fans who responded to his big-heartedness and joy in living for the moment. "John Candy is perfectly named," Pauline Kael noted. "He's a mountainous lollipop of a man, and preposterously lovable" (*New Yorker*, 19 March 1984, 124).

Candy was never interested in doing stand-up comedy; it was too solitary, too introspective.[4] He preferred to have funny, outgoing people around him, and during his late teens he began to participate in sketch comedy in Toronto, where he befriended future "Saturday Night Live" stars Dan Aykroyd and Gilda Radner. When Chicago's fabled Second City improvisational theater announced in 1973 that it would open a satellite stage in Toronto, Aykroyd and Candy went to Chicago to audition. The Second City managers were so impressed with Candy's stage presence that they hired him to apprentice in Chicago, and at the age of twenty-two Candy was performing and hanging out with another future "SNL" star, Bill Murray. Candy's charisma was apparent from the start. "There's a moment or two at the beginning of any sketch when the audience tries to figure out whether it likes you or not," recalled Toronto Second City cast member Dave Thomas. "Whenever I went out there with John, the audience was immediately with us because they instantly liked him. They gravitated to him. They looked at his big, warm, lovable, chubby face and thought, 'We like you and trust you. Whatever that other guy with you is doing is okay with us because you're here'" ("Star Bigger Than Life," *Toronto Sun*, 29 October 1996, 34). In 1974 and 1975 Candy worked the Second City stage in Toronto with Thomas, Eugene Levy, Catherine O'Hara, Andrea Martin, and Joe Flaherty, all of whom would form the nucleus of "SCTV," an independently produced Canadian television show developed in 1976 to stem the flow of Second City actors to "Saturday Night Live" and foster Canadian comedic talent.

In contrast to the occasionally cerebral and literary humor displayed at Chicago's Second City and "Saturday Night Live," "SCTV" focused on satirizing television itself, spoofing a variety of TV genres and advertisements to create a viewing experience akin to channel surfing. Candy did not like to write, but the sheer volume of material needed at Second City and "SCTV" forced him to contribute and develop characters. "SCTV" became a popular late-night show in North America, and soon Candy was known for playing memorable characters such as unscrupulous TV personality Johnny LaRue; 3-D horror film host Doctor Tongue; sycophantic talk-show sidekick William B. Williams; and pipe-smoking Melonville mayor Tommy Shanks. He continued to appear on "SCTV" through 1983, but Candy increasingly focused his creative ambitions on the movies after playing small roles in *1941* (1979) and *The Blues Brothers* (1980), both of which starred his Second City pals John Belushi and Dan Aykroyd.

*Stripes* (1981), a boot-camp comedy starring Second City alumni Bill Murray and Harold Ramis, provided the supporting role that became Candy's first breakthrough; it was also a role that forced Candy to contemplate the exploitation of his size and the kind of screen image he wanted to develop early in his career. The descriptively named Pvt. Dewey "Ox" Oxberger, a fat recruit who struggles through boot camp, feels compelled to discuss his weight when he introduces himself to his fellow recruits: "You might have noticed that I've got a slight weight problem . . . I went to this doctor, well, he told me I swallow a lot of aggression, along with a lot of pizzas . . . I'm a shy guy, and he suggested taking one of these aggression training courses . . . I thought to myself, join the army—it's free . . . while I'm here I'll lose a few pounds." Oxberger was a character familiar to Candy—too familiar, in fact—and the litany of fat jokes the overweight recruit cheerfully endured through the film took their emotional toll on the actor. Director Ivan Reitman allowed Candy to rewrite some of his lines, but Reitman insisted on filming a scene in which Oxberger mud-wrestles against six women, which proved to be an agonizing experience for Candy. "He wondered whether he was doing the right thing by participating in the mud-wrestling scene," recalled friend George Bloomfield. "He was afraid he might come across as a pig in mud. He felt degraded." Candy, in fact, lobbied to change the scene from the first time he read the script. "I was fighting right up to the end to get out of it," he told a reporter. "It was so painful, and we spent three days doing it" (Knelman 87).

Candy was particularly hurt by a review of *Stripes* that referred to him as "the elephant," and he decided to refuse any more roles that degraded his size. "Sure, I'm sensitive about my weight," Candy told *People* after *Stripes* was released. "I realize I stand out, especially on TV. But I'm the one who has to look in the mirror, and after a while it begins to eat at you" (13

John Candy agonized over the exploitation of his body size in this mud-wrestling scene in *Stripes*. Copyright Columbia Pictures, 1981.

July 1981, 58). Candy recognized that his size was integral to his everyman persona, but he resolved that his screen comedy would be firmly based in characterization. "John Candy won't do fat jokes," *Newsweek* reported. "He'll do impersonations of fat *people*, but victims aren't his shtik" (26 August 1985, 63). Candy noted that his "SCTV" impersonations of fat cultural figures like Orson Welles and Alfred Hitchcock did not specifically demean their size, but there was a tinge of remorse in his voice: "I can do them better than most people, who have no idea what it's like to be fat, anyway," he said in 1985. "But I hate it . . . I think when you're fat, you're treated like some kind of freak by the public" ("E! True Hollywood Story," 3 April 2001).

After the Depression and World War II, fat lost any vestiges of its privileged, leisure-class signification; it now indicated a failure to "measure up" in an increasingly corporate society. In the mid-1980s, when public health officials were estimating that a majority of Americans were overweight, a fat person would seem to be an ordinary figure, but within the moneyed, image-conscious culture of Hollywood, a fat movie star was at best a curiosity and at worst a pariah, pathologized as an unpleasant reminder of the Fatty Arbuckle scandal of the early 1920s. As his stardom grew, Candy was praised as an authentic embodiment of the common man; at the same time, his weight attracted increasing scrutiny and he often dieted to avoid being treated like "a freak." Still, he worried that "his fans might not like him if he were thinner" (Knelman 116).

After achieving film stardom, Candy would spend the rest of his life on a roller-coaster ride of excessive living and extreme dieting. In 1981 Candy told *People* he had hired an exercise coach in hopes of losing forty pounds (13 July 1981, 58); in fall 1982 he told the *Playboy* fashion supplement that "I swear I'm going on a diet . . . I'm trying to lose 100 pounds in about one year" (Fall/Winter 1982). In 1984, he checked into the Pritikin Longevity Center in Santa Monica and lost seventy-five pounds in several months; but by the end of the decade he had regained the weight and more, prompting concern among his friends (Knelman 116, 171). Candy's weight sensitivity intensified. On 11 May 1989, *Los Angeles Herald-Examiner* columnist Mitchell Fink reported that Candy weighed 400 pounds and was trying to lose 100 by joining the Nutri System program in Beverly Hills. Fink then asked, "Does he really think that after 100 pounds he'll be *light*?" Enraged, Candy insisted that Fink retract the story: "We heard from Candy's attorney who said his client 'has never had any contact, participated in or had any involvement whatsoever with Nutri System,'" Fink wrote. "Candy's attorney also said his client did not weigh 400 pounds" (15 June 1989, A2). In 1992, Candy refused to host the Genie Awards, Canada's equivalent of the Academy Awards, after a promotion announced his involvement by stating, "We'll get you a star so unbelievably, incredibly big you won't believe your eyes!" (Karen Murray, "Candy Too Big for Genies," *Daily Variety*, 18 November 1992, 18).

Candy's publicized struggles with his weight raised industry concern about his health and professional commitment, but they only made him appear more genuine and likeable to his fans. *Playgirl* even put Candy on its list of "Ten Sexiest Men" in September 1985, noting, "John Candy makes us smile. . . . The shaggy moptop, the dimpled cheeks, the physical grace— nobody is sexier than this giant of comedy who turns us on with good humor." Candy also continued to bolster his reputation for living large. "SCTV" cast member Paul Flaherty recalled, "My nickname for Johnny was 'Johnny Deluxe,' because everything had to be big with John—everything had to be first class." Comedian Martin Short concurred: "If we went out to dinner, he had to pick up the tab; he always had the biggest apartment; he always seemed to have more money than anyone" ("E! True Hollywood Story"). Even when working on set, Candy insisted on being the life of the party. Tom Hanks recalled, "Ask any grip, driver, operator, costumer, actor, director, whatever—they'll all say the best time they had while working was with John" (John Housely, "John Candy, 1950–1994," *Premiere*, May 1994, 120).

After the huge success of *Stripes*, which earned over $83 million, Candy's film work intensified and his popularity continued to grow. His substantial supporting role as Freddie, Tom Hanks's freewheeling playboy brother in *Splash* (1984), gained critical accolades as well. Pauline Kael praised Ron Howard as "the first director who has let John Candy loose" and noted that Freddie "fancies himself debonair and light on his feet, and he is. But he also makes you aware of his bulk by the tricks in his verbal timing. . . . The picture probably wouldn't work without him; he doesn't add weight, he adds bounce and imagination" (*New Yorker*, 19 March 1984, 124). In Candy's most memorable scene, he plays racquetball with Hanks while drinking a beer and smoking a cigarette. Breathless and heaving in exhaustion, Candy displayed no self-consciousness or hypocrisy; the actor seemed to genuinely enjoy himself during every second he appeared onscreen.

## ★★★★★ When Bad Movies Happen to Good People

Is there any better measure of stardom than an actor's ability to persistently attract fans to bad movies? Candy appeared in a string of flops in the 1980s, but, like populist stars Burt Reynolds and Whoopi Goldberg, he starred in many "critic proof" lowbrow comedies that drew audiences on the basis of the headliner's likeability, regardless of negative reviews. For his first headlining role in the vacation comedy *Summer Rental* (1985), Candy was eager to work with director Carl Reiner, who had nurtured the career of Steve Martin. The premise was promising—Candy as a stressed-out air-traffic controller forced to take a family vacation—but the results were dismal; the film had a weak screenplay and had been hastily shot in March to achieve a summer release. Co-starring roles in three more disappointing films—*Brewster's Millions* with Richard Pryor (1985), *Volunteers* with Tom Hanks (1985), and *Armed and Dangerous* with Eugene Levy (1986)—prompted critics to wonder about Candy's management and career choices. Candy, they noted, had become the kind of rich, overrated movie star he would have parodied just a few years earlier on "SCTV." "You just wish that someone had whacked him over the head with a good script," noted Patrick Goldstein, "because, without it, *Summer Rental* forces Candy to carry the movie all by himself, a task too Herculean even for a comic of his bulk and talent" (*Los Angeles Times*, 9 August 1985, D16). *Chicago Tribune* critic Gene Siskel argued that the actor's flops "have at least temporarily delayed Candy's move to the top of the movie-comedy heap" (30 March 1986, 13:4). Yet Candy's inability to say no to potentially bad film projects only brought him more sympathy from audiences and critics. "There's an undeniable fascination watching John Candy as he always tries to do the right thing, the decent thing, and always obtains catastrophic results," noted *Newsday* critic Mike McGrady. "Sincere, intense, well-intentioned, naive, he is constantly digging and redigging his own grave. [His] appeal is phenomenal. He has been in more turkeys than stuffing mix, yet everyone seems to love him" (15 August 1986, 2:4).

After the financial and critical success of *Planes, Trains and Automobiles* in fall 1987, Candy followed up with three more disappointments: *The Great Outdoors* (1988), co-starring Dan Aykroyd and based on a second-rate John Hughes screenplay; the embarrassing detective comedy *Who's Harry Crumb?* (1989); and the abysmal *Speed Zone!* (1989), the third film in the *Cannonball Run* franchise that was so bad even Burt Reynolds's and Candy's fans stayed away. By this point Candy had such a reputation for appearing in flops that a *Playboy* interviewer asked, "What is it like to be the funniest part of an unfunny movie?" Candy diplomatically replied, "There have been times that a movie hasn't done so well and I, personally have done well in the reviews. . . . I'm a very hard judge, so it's difficult to think of myself as funny at all" (Robert Crane, "20 Questions: John Candy," August 1989, 124).

★★★★★ **The John Hughes Industry**

After suffering through his mid-1980s string of flops, Candy found self-respect and box office redemption in several collaborations with writer/director John Hughes. A former advertising copywriter who had grown up in suburban Chicago, Hughes had a perceptive grasp of Midwestern suburban culture and particularly the language of white, middle-class teenagers. In his teen hits such as *The Breakfast Club* (1985) and *Ferris Bueller's Day Off* (1986), the settings were sanitized and the stories sentimental, but the characters were always distinctive and memorable. By 1987, Hughes was ready to move into adult comedies, and for *Planes, Trains and Automobiles* he had the confidence and intuition to write basic (and often humiliating) situations for actors Candy and Martin and then simply let them react. There was much ad-libbing on the set, and Martin graciously played it straight (as businessman Neal Page) to give Candy more freedom to portray the comically loutish salesman Del Griffith.

In the film's most famous scene, Neal and Del share a motel room bed and wake up in the morning wrapped around each other. After realizing

Odd couple Steve Martin and John Candy in *Planes, Trains and Automobiles*. Copyright Paramount Pictures, 1987.

their predicament ("Those aren't pillows!"), the embarrassed men jump out of bed and immediately discuss sports in an awkward attempt to assert their heterosexual masculinity. The comedy generated by the "odd couple" pairing of Martin and Candy depended upon each star's deviance from popular masculine norms: Martin was too cerebral and fastidious, and Candy was too fat and obsequious. Martin's thin, uptight, upper-middle-class executive and Candy's fat, sloppy, lower-middle-class salesman had little in common except the loneliness they concealed by focusing on their jobs—a truth too discomforting to reveal until the end of the film.

In *Planes, Trains and Automobiles*, Martin and Candy displayed not only pitch-perfect comic timing but dramatic chops as well. "It was a comedy, but it was a real heart-wrenching movie for me," Candy told a radio interviewer. "I never looked at it like he was a buffoon—Del was a real character to me" ("E! True Hollywood Story"). Indeed, after Neal finally cracks and angrily enumerates Del's annoying habits, Candy gives a heartfelt response that could very well represent his feelings about the barrage of criticism he had endured during his film career: "You want to hurt me? Go right ahead, if it makes you feel any better. I'm an easy target. Yeah, you're right, I talk too much. I also listen too much. I could be a cold-hearted cynic like you. But I don't like to hurt people's feelings. Well, you think what you want about me. I'm not changing. I like me. My wife likes me. My customers like me. Because I'm the real article. What you see is what you get." By film's end, audiences learn that Del's relentlessly cheerful persona is really just an artifice to hide his emotional pain. Similar revelations would surface after Candy's death. "John had a big hurt inside him," recalled Tom Mankiewicz, who directed Candy in *Delirious* (1991). "He was always trying so hard to be everything to friends and family and was constantly afraid he was letting people down" (Knelman 171).

*Planes, Trains and Automobiles* received mixed reviews, but most critics agreed that Hughes had created a multifaceted, breakthrough role for Candy. "Since leaving 'SCTV' he's never had the showcase that his talents deserve," noted Hal Hinson. "Not so anymore. Candy has never been more boisterously cracked than he is here. This is Candy's bust-out performance, the one where he puts it all together" (*Washington Post*, 25 November 1987, C1). Despite its occasional mawkishness, *Planes, Trains and Automobiles* has gained in reputation over the years; it is included in Roger Ebert's *The Great Movies II* collection (334, 338) and current comedy producers like Judd Apatow name it as an influential film.

*Uncle Buck* (1989), Candy's follow-up collaboration with writer-director Hughes, served as a showcase for the actor's freewheeling but vulnerable persona. Black sheep and sad-sack bachelor Buck Russell is forced to supervise his sister-in-law's three children in their tony suburban home while she visits her sick father, and Buck's permissiveness and good humor are stretched to the breaking point, forcing him and the rebellious children to rethink their values. The film's tagline summed up Candy's box office appeal: "He's crude. He's crass. He's family." The sitcom trappings did not impress critics, but *Uncle Buck*, released in August to attract family audiences, was number one at the box office for four weeks, taking in a total of nearly $67 million. Candy thus ended the 1980s with a film that proved he could still headline a well-regarded and financially successful project.

## ★★★★★ Coda

In March 1994, John Candy died of heart failure at the age of forty-three while shooting on location in Mexico for the western parody *Wagons East* (1994). His death, like those of Second City alumni John Belushi and Chris Farley, would become a cautionary tale about Hollywood excess, but as a family man with a wife and two children he was not so willfully self-destructive. Even after achieving wealth and fame, Candy treated his colleagues, crew, and fans with equanimity; he was a big man who always tried to be a regular guy. "He played all those little guys that no one gives a damn about," Hughes recalled. "It takes a certain amount of guts to go out in every role and play the fool and bring the kind of voice he did to those seemingly insignificant characters. I don't know who's going to speak for those kind of characters now" (*Premiere*, May 1994, 120).

### NOTES

1. Martin was not concerned that his white suit might be construed as conservative; rather, he worried that it might appear that he was copying John Lennon (Martin 169). Lennon wears a white suit on the cover of the Beatles' *Abbey Road* (1969).

2. Martin has remained interested in the issue of WASP culture; in 1996 he published *WASP*, a one-act play that satirized 1950s family dynamics, which has been produced around the world.

3. "As a comedian, you must do silly things and silly things are not critically respected," Martin told *Los Angeles Times* writer Jack Mathews. "But it is just as hard to do silly things as it is to do dramatic things" (30 June 1987). Ironically, Martin's only Academy Award nomination was for *The Absent-Minded Waiter* (1977), a short film he wrote and starred in before launching his feature-length film career.

4. "I have never done standup comedy," Candy said. "I loved 'SCTV' because it was all sketch work and I feel at home doing that" (Vernon Scott, "The Candy Man of Comedy Is One Shy Guy," *Chicago Tribune*, 23 August 1987).

# In the Wings

ROBERT EBERWEIN

Among the stars whose 1980s films served as a prelude to more significant appearances in subsequent decades, Johnny Depp's career began inauspiciously, as one of Freddy's short-lived victims in the first *Nightmare on Elm Street* (1984) and a horny teenager in *Private Resort* (1985). His first significant role was as a translator in Oliver Stone's *Platoon* (1986). (In the DVD commentary Stone says he knew Depp would be a star after taking one look at him.) Television work as a cop in "21 Jump Street" (1987) introduced Depp to a youthful audience that would eagerly seek out his films. He became a major favorite in John Water's *Cry-Baby* and Tim Burton's *Edward Scissorhands* (both 1990) and rose quickly in the ranks of young stars with luminous performances: as a quirky Buster Keaton–Charlie Chaplin wannabe in *Benny and Joon* and a pressured son trying to keep his family together in *What's Eating Gilbert Grape* (both 1993), as the cross-dressing film director *Ed Wood* (1994), and as an undercover cop in *Donnie Brasco* (1997). Starring as Captain Jack Sparrow in the three *Pirates of the Caribbean* films (2003, 2006, 2007), he is at the center of a franchise that has grossed over $1 billion domestically.

Robert Downey Jr. played mainly supporting roles in 1980s films, such as *Less Than Zero* (1987), *Johnny Be Good* (1988), and *Chances Are* (1989). He achieved success in his Oscar-nominated performance as *Chaplin* (1992) and as the star-obsessed broadcaster in *Natural Born Killers* (1994). But his substance-abuse problems led to incarcerations that sidetracked his career in the 1990s. Recently, though, he has become a huge star on the basis of his roles as the action hero *Iron Man* (2008) (over $318 million gross) and has confirmed his comic genius in *Tropic Thunder* (2008).

Nicole Kidman worked primarily in her native Australia in the 1980s before coming to the attention of American audiences for the first time in the thriller *Dead Calm* (1989), playing a young wife who with her husband is threatened by a homicidal maniac they have taken on board their boat. Her career took off in the 1990s as she starred with future husband Tom

Cruise in *Days of Thunder* (1990) and *Far and Away* (1992), and played a murderous television star in *To Die For* (1995), a doctor in *Batman Forever* (1995), and a romantic heroine in *The Portrait of a Lady* (1996). Her last appearance with Cruise (and the prelude to their marital break-up) was in Stanley Kubrick's final film, the erotic drama *Eyes Wide Shut* (1999). Her career reached its pinnacle thus far with *Moulin Rouge!* (2001) and her Oscar win for Best Actress playing the author Virginia Woolf in *The Hours* (2002).

Brad Pitt's early work included an uncredited appearance in *Less Than Zero* and small parts in two 1989 films, *Cutting Class* and *Happy Together*. His appearance in *Thelma and Louise* (1991) as J.D., a hitchhiker who seduces and robs Thelma, began the star-making process since audiences recognized that he brought a truly distinctive face and persona to the screen. His subsequent films confirmed his star status: as an irresponsible brother in *A River Runs Through It* (1992), a homicidal killer in *Kalifornia* (1993), one of the undead in *Interview with the Vampire* (1994), the tortured cop in *Se7en* (1995), the alter ego of Edward Norton's character in *Fight Club* (1999), and one of the men in the successful *Ocean's* franchise (2001, 2004, 2007).

River Phoenix's drug-related death in 1993 cut short what would have been a major career that began in the 1980s with appearances in *Stand By Me* and *The Mosquito Coast* (both 1986), *A Night in the Life of Jimmy Reardon* (1988), *Running on Empty* (1988, Oscar nomination as Best Supporting Actor), and *Indiana Jones and the Last Crusade* (1989). His greatest role was as a teenage hustler in love with Keanu Reeves in Gun Van Sant's heartbreaking *My Own Private Idaho* (1991).

Reeves started to experience visibility in *River's Edge* (1986), *Dangerous Liaisons* (1988), and *Parenthood* (1989), with Steve Martin, but it was in *Bill & Ted's Excellent Adventure* (1989), playing a somewhat dim-witted but amiable teenager in the time-travel-comedy, that he developed a large teenage audience. A successful sequel, *Bill & Ted's Bogus Journey*, followed in 1991, the same year as *My Own Private Idaho*. Reeves followed this with Francis Ford Coppola's vampire film *Dracula* (1992). The critical and box office success of his action film *Speed* (1994) enhanced Reeves's star credibility, which was solidified by the first version of *The Matrix* (1999) and the two sequels (2003). The total domestic grosses of these four action films exceed $700 million to date.

Tim Robbins appeared in a number of unremarkable films in the 1980s, but became someone to notice as a goofy baseball player in *Bull Durham* (1988), the filming of which introduced him to Susan Sarandon, his partner of many years. Notable films of the 1990s confirmed his stardom: as a dying soldier in *Jacob's Ladder* (1990), a murderous Hollywood executive in

*The Player* (1992), and, memorably, a convict trying to escape in *The Shaw-shank Redemption* (1994). He expanded into directing, with *Bob Roberts* (1992) and *Dead Man Walking* (1995). His varied choices of roles sometimes have included smaller parts, and he won the Oscar as Best Supporting Actor for *Mystic River* (2003). But a case could be made that he was in fact the co-star, along with Sean Penn.

Julia Roberts came to audiences' attention in memorable roles in *Mystic Pizza* (1988) as Daisy, a Connecticut waitress, and in *Steel Magnolias* (1989) as Shelby, a new wife who dies young. Roberts instantly became a megastar the next year in *Pretty Woman* (1990), as a prostitute who is remade into a fashionable and refined woman through the agency of her erstwhile client and then lover Richard Gere. She demonstrated an impressive ability to work in a variety of genres: serious dramas like *Flatliners* (1990), costume and historical dramas such as *Mary Reilly* and *Michael Collins* (both 1996), comedies such as Woody Allen's *Everyone Says I Love You* (1996) and *My Best Friend's Wedding* (1997), and tear-jerkers like *Stepmom* (1998). Her big moment came when she won a Best Actress Oscar playing the title role in *Erin Brockovich* (2000), a film based on the true story of a social crusader who exposes a utility's pollution of land.

Meg Ryan had a small part in *Top Gun* (1986), the year's biggest financial success, and leading roles in some other films in the late 1980s, but it was her breakout role in the romantic comedy *When Harry Met Sally* (1989) that helped to make her a star. Her teaming with Tom Hanks in *Joe versus the Volcano* (1990) was the first of three comedies with him, the most notable being *Sleepless in Seattle* (1993), followed by *You've Got Mail* (1998). She has consistently pushed herself as an actress, playing an alcoholic in *When a Man Loves a Woman* (1994), a Medivac pilot in the Persian Gulf War drama *Courage Under Fire* (1996), and an empowered writer in Jane Campion's erotic and sexually explicit thriller *In the Cut* (2003).

Sharon Stone did a great deal of television work in the 1980s, but except for the modest financial successes *King Solomon's Mines* (1985) and *Police Academy 4: Citizens on Patrol* (1987), her films didn't perform well. She made a brief appearance in Paul Verhoeven's *Total Recall* (1990) as the adulterous wife whom Arnold Schwarzenegger kills ("Consider this a divorce!"). Some unremembered films after that were eclipsed by her notorious success in *Basic Instinct* (1992). Playing the bisexual Catherine Trammel, romantically involved with the police inspector (Michael Douglas), Stone became an instant celebrity when in crossing her legs she was seen to be without underclothing. While roles in other 1990s films confirmed her star status— such as *Sliver* (1993), *Intersection* (1994), and Martin Scorsese's *Casino*

(1995), for which she received an Oscar nomination and won the Golden Globe—her power as a star did not last into the next decade.

Among those whose fledgling careers in the 1980s were later confirmed by box office success are Kim Basinger, who started out in the 1980s mainly in television and appeared in Sean Connery's last Bond film, *Never Say Never Again* (1983) and in two Blake Edwards comedies, *The Man Who Loved Women* (1983) and *Blind Date* (1987). Her most important roles in the decade were her courageous portrayal of female abjection in Adrian Lyne's disturbing erotic melodrama *9½ Weeks* (1986) as a woman who plays sex games with Mickey Rourke, and as Vicky Vale, the heroine of the mega hit *Batman* (1989). Her work in the 1990s included two films with her then-husband Alec Baldwin, *The Marrying Man* (1991) and a remake of *The Getaway* (1994). Her role as a prostitute in Curtis Hanson's neo-noir *L.A. Confidential* (1997) brought her acclaim and the Best Supporting Actress Oscar.

Nicolas Cage forged an impressive career as a star early in the 1980s, playing teenagers in *Fast Times at Ridgemont High* (1982), *Valley Girl* (1983), and *Racing with the Moon* (1984). He is seen as both teenager and young adult in *Birdy* (1984), in which he is a Vietnam veteran trying to save his friend's sanity. His flair for lighter films was shown in *Peggy Sue Got Married* (1986), *Raising Arizona* (1987), and *Moonstruck* (1987). He became a more formally recognized star for his body of work in the 1990s: as an Elvis-imitating singer in *Wild at Heart* (1990) and the tortured suicidal hero of *Leaving Las Vegas* (Best Actor Oscar, 1995). His remarkable star turn in John Woo's *Face/Off* (1997) had him playing both a tender husband and a murderous thug. He is one of those stars who, to use the language of the entertainment industry, can "open" a film because his presence guarantees a solid first weekend, a fact demonstrated most recently by both the original and sequel to *National Treasure* (2004, 2007), and the recent *Knowing* (2009).

Morgan Freeman is testimony to the fact that someone known mainly as a supporting actor can still be considered a major star. After years of film work (beginning in the 1960s), Freeman had a remarkable year in 1989, when he was one of the courageous Civil War soldiers in *Glory*, a tough principal who encourages students to succeed in the fact-based *Lean on Me*, and a Best Actor nominee as the chauffeur in *Driving Miss Daisy*. Key roles in the 1990s include his work as Clint Eastwood's partner in *Unforgiven* (1992), a fellow prisoner with Tim Robbins in *The Shawshank Redemption* (Oscar nomination for Best Actor), and Brad Pitt's stoic police partner in *Se7en*. He won an Oscar for Best Supporting Actor as an ex-boxer in Eastwood's *Million Dollar Baby* (2004).

Whoopi Goldberg's first major appearance in films came as the oppressed heroine of *The Color Purple* (1985), for which she received an Oscar nomination. She made mostly comedies in the rest of the decade, some reasonably successful, like *Jumpin' Jack Flash* (1986). She won a Best Supporting Actress Oscar as Oda May Brown, a medium who helps the dead hero protect his wife from his murderer, in *Ghost* (1990). The film was enormously successful ($217 million, the second highest box office for the year). Her star status was confirmed by her role as a singer who masquerades as a nun to avoid being murdered in *Sister Act* (1992) ($139 million). She re-created this role again in a financially successful sequel, *Sister Act 2: Back in the Habit* (1993). Other notable roles included playing a police inspector investigating Tim Robbins in *The Player* and a lesbian who is unable to declare her love for a young woman dying of AIDS in *Boys on the Side* (1995). Her recent work has been mostly in television and as one of the star voices in animated films.

Tom Hanks had already become a star to watch in the 1980s, beginning with his popular television series "Bosom Buddies" (1980–1982) and the popular films *Splash* (1984), *Nothing in Common* (1986), and the comedy-drama *Punchline* (1988), with Sally Field. *Big* (1988), in which he plays a kid who suddenly inhabits a man's body, was the fourth highest grossing film of the year. His 1990s performances made him a superstar. He is only the second actor to win consecutive Best Acting Oscars (after Spencer Tracy), playing a gay man dying of AIDS in *Philadelphia* (1993) and a gentle and mentally limited man in *Forrest Gump* (1994). Other notable work in the decade included his romantic comedy *Sleepless in Seattle*, and his roles as Astronaut Jim Lovell in *Apollo 13* (1995) and as Captain Miller in *Saving Private Ryan* (1998). He has been a major force in producing HBO's series about World War II: "Band of Brothers" (2001) and "The Pacific" (2010).

Holly Hunter first achieved significant success in 1987 playing the wife of Nicolas Cage in *Raising Arizona*, Joel and Ethan Coen's comedy about a childless couple who kidnap a baby from a group of quintuplets. The same year she starred in James L. Brooks's *Broadcast News* as a television reporter competing with William Hurt. She co-starred in Steven Spielberg's *Always* (1989). Working with director Jane Campion, she won an Oscar for her acclaimed performance as the mute heroine of *The Piano* (1993), the same year she co-starred with Tom Cruise in the legal thriller *The Firm*. She co-starred in Jodie Foster's comedy about the pressures faced by a family in *Home for the Holidays* (1995). Her boldest move as an actress came in 1996 when she co-starred in David Cronenberg's disturbing adaptation of *Crash*, about couples who use automobile accidents as a means for sexual arousal.

Demi Moore enjoyed considerably more success than any of the other Brat Packers in the 1990s. Beginning with *Ghost,* she made a number of popular films, including A *Few Good Men* (1992), with Tom Cruise, *Indecent Proposal* (1993) with Robert Redford, and *Disclosure* (1994) with Michael Douglas. By 1996 she could command a reputed salary of $12.5 million for *Striptease* (1996), thus making her at the time the highest paid actress in the world.

Sean Penn, who appeared with Cage playing a teenager in *Fast Times at Ridgemont High* and *Racing with the Moon,* has forged a distinguished career in wide-ranging parts and a variety of genres that testify to his talent: as a young adult, acting with his brother Chris in *At Close Range* and with Madonna, his wife at the time, in *Shanghai Surprise* (both 1986); as a cop in *Colors* (1988) and *State of Grace* (1990); as a heartless platoon leader who rapes and kills an innocent Vietnamese girl in *Casualties of War* (1989); as a murderer preparing for his execution in *Dead Man Walking;* and as a noble sergeant leading soldiers in *The Thin Red Line* (1998). He has two Best Actor Oscars: one as the vigilante murderer in Clint Eastwood's *Mystic River* and one as the eponymous hero of Gus Van Sant's biopic *Milk* (2008).

Susan Sarandon's film career began in 1970 and triumphed fully in the 1990s, after moves toward stardom in the 1980s. She began in a small but memorable part as a hippie in *Joe* (1970) and made an indelible appearance as "Janet Weiss—A Heroine" in the cult favorite *The Rocky Horror Picture Show* (1975). Her early 1980s films included her Oscar-nominated performance in *Atlantic City* (1980), in which she plays an aspiring card dealer, and *The Hunger* (1983), a vampire film widely noted for its lesbian sex scene. After a string of undistinguished works, she had two major hits in successive years, *The Witches of Eastwick* (1987) and *Bull Durham.* She became an even bigger star in the 1990s with two extraordinary films: *Thelma & Louise* and *Dead Man Walking.* The first of these was the most important film made thus far to speak to the concerns of feminists. As Louise, she embodied all the tensions and aspirations associated with women trying to exist in a man's world. In the fact-based second film, for which she won the Oscar as Best Actress, she played Sister Helen Prejean, who helps a convicted killer come to terms with his guilt and the nature of religious love.

Denzel Washington had already achieved stardom in the 1980s, winning the Oscar as Best Supporting Actor as a black soldier fighting for the North in *Glory.* Like Hanks, he became a megastar in the next decade, winning praise in two films by Spike Lee: as a musician in *Mo' Better Blues* (1990) and as the eponymous hero of *Malcolm X* (1992). In a stunning pairing, he co-starred with Hanks in *Philadelphia* playing his lawyer who is initially terrified of AIDS but who comes to accept and respect his client. He was a veteran turned sleuth in the neo-noir *Devil in a Blue Dress* (1995) and a troubled Iraq War veteran investigating whether Meg Ryan's character should receive the Medal of Honor in *Courage Under Fire*. He received a Best Actor Oscar as a vicious drug cop in *Training Day* (2001) and is one of the few megastars who can negotiate "pay-or-play" contracts, under the terms of which he gets paid full salary even if the film he has signed for doesn't get made.

Forest Whitaker's film work in the 1980s began with a small part in *Platoon* (1986), a more prominent role in *Good Morning, Vietnam* (1987), and the starring role in Clint Eastwood's *Bird* (1988), the biography of Charlie "Bird" Parker, for which he won the Best Actor award in Cannes. Some of the parts he has chosen are of problematic and troubling characters: the bisexual Jody in *The Crying Game* (1992), the hit man in *Ghost Dog: The Way of the Samurai* (1999), and the home invader in *Panic Room* (2002). The pinnacle of his career came when he played an utter monster, Idi Amin, in *The Last King of Scotland* (2006), for which he received the Best Actor Oscar.

# WORKS CITED

☆☆☆☆☆☆☆☆☆☆☆

Fan magazines and other primary or archival materials are cited in the text of individual essays.

Allen, Robert C., and Douglas Gomery. *Film History: Theory and Practice*. New York: McGraw-Hill, 1985.

Ames, Christopher. "Restoring the Black Man's Lethal Weapon." *Journal of Popular Film and Television* 20:3 (Fall 1992), 52–60.

Anderson, Benedict. *Imagined Communities: Reflections on the Origin and Spread of Nationalism*. London: Verso, 2006.

Austin, Thomas, and Martin Baker, eds. *Contemporary Hollywood Stardom*. London: Arnold, 2003.

Balio, Tino. "Adjusting to the New Global Economy." *Film Policy*. Ed. Albert Moran. London: Routledge, 1996.

Barker, Deborah. "The Southern Fried Chick Flick: Postfeminism Goes to the Movies." *Chick Flicks: Contemporary Women at the Movies*. Ed. Suzanne Ferriss and Mallory Young. London: Routledge, 2008. 94–118.

Baxter, John. *De Niro: A Biography*. London: HarperCollins, 2003.

Bazin, André. *What Is Cinema? Volume 2*. Trans. Hugh Gray. Berkeley: U of California P, 1971.

Beavers, Herman. "'The Cool Pose': Intersectionality, Masculinity, and Quiescence in the Comedy and Films of Richard Pryor and Eddie Murphy." *Race and the Subject of Masculinities*. Ed. Harry Stecopoulos and Michael Uebel. Durham, N.C.: Duke UP, 1997. 253–85.

Bingham, Dennis. *Acting Male: Masculinities in the Films of James Stewart, Jack Nicholson and Clint Eastwood*. New Brunswick, N.J.: Rutgers UP, 2004.

Bonnen, James. "Why Is There No Coherent US Rural Policy?" *Policy Studies Journal* 20:2 (1992), 193–94.

Brackett, David. "Banjos, Biopics, and Compilation Scores: The Movies Go Country." *American Music* 19:3 (Autumn 2001), 247–90.

Britton, Andrew. "Blissing Out: The Politics of Reaganite Entertainment." *Movie* 31/32 (Winter 1986), 1–42.

———. "Stars and Genres." *Stardom: Industry of Desire*. Ed Christine Gledhill. London: Routledge, 198–206.

Brost, Molly. "Negotiating Authenticity: *Coal Miner's Daughter*, the Biopic, and Country Music." *Americana: The Journal of American Popular Culture, 1900 to Present*, http://www.americanpopularculture.com/journal/articles/fall_2008/brost.htm.

Brunsdon, Charlotte. "Post-feminism and Shopping Films." *Screen Tastes*. London: Routledge, 1997. 81–102.

Brunette, Peter, ed. *Martin Scorsese Interviews*. Jackson: UP of Mississippi, 1999.

Case, Brian. "Hard and Fast." *David Mamet in Conversation*. Ed. Leslie Kane. Ann Arbor: U of Michigan P, 2001. 100–104.

Cavell, Stanley. *Pursuits of Happiness: The Hollywood Comedy of Remarriage*. Cambridge, Mass.: Harvard UP, 1981.

Chevrie, Marc. "Le Dernier des Cow-Boys." *Cahiers du cinéma* 393 (March 1987), 9–11.

Chow, Lesley. "The Actor's Voice." *Cineaste* 31:4 (Fall 2006), 33–35.

Clinch, Minty. *Harrison Ford: Film Stars and Society.* London: New English Library, 1987.

Clover, Carol. *Men, Women, and Chain Saws: Gender in the Modern Horror Film.* Princeton: Princeton UP, 1993.

Cohan, Steven, and Ina Rae Hark, eds. *Screening the Male: Exploring Masculinities in Hollywood Cinema.* London: Routledge, 1993.

Collins, Jim, Hilary Radner, and Ava Preacher Collins, eds. *Film Theory Goes to the Movies.* New York: Routledge, 1993.

DeAngelis, Michael. *Gay Fandom and Crossover Stardom: James Dean, Mel Gibson, and Keanu Reeves.* Durham, N.C.: Duke UP, 2001.

DeCordova, Richard. *Picture Personalities: The Emergence of the Star System in America.* Urbana: U of Illinois P, 2001.

DeCurtis, Anthony. "What the Streets Mean." *Martin Scorsese Interviews.* Ed. Peter Brunette. Jackson: UP of Mississippi, 1999. 158–85.

D'Emilio, John. *Sexual Politics, Sexual Communities: The Making of a Homosexual Minority in the United States, 1940–1970.* Chicago: U of Chicago P, 1983.

De Lauretis, Teresa. *Alice Doesn't: Feminism, Semiotics, Cinema.* Bloomington: Indiana UP, 1984.

Derry, Charles. *The Suspense Thriller: Films in the Shadow of Alfred Hitchcock.* Jefferson, N.C.: McFarland, 1988.

Desjardins, Mary. "Meeting Two Queens: Feminist Film-making, Identity Politics, and Melo-dramatic Fantasy." *Film Quarterly* 48:3 (Spring 1995), 26–33.

"Dialogue on Film: Martin Scorsese." *Martin Scorsese Interviews.* Ed. Peter Brunette. Jackson: UP of Mississippi, 1999. 13–47.

Diawara, Manthia. "Black Spectatorship: Problems of Identification and Resistance." *Screen* 29:4 (1988), 66–76.

Doane, Mary Ann. "The Voice in Cinema: The Articulation of Body and Space." *Yale French Studies* 60 (1980), 33–50.

Doherty, Thomas. *Teenagers and Teenpics.* Rev. ed. Philadelphia: Temple UP, 2002.

Dougan, Andy. *Untouchable: A Biography of Robert De Niro.* 2nd ed. New York: Thunder's Mouth, 2002.

Dyer, Joyce. "Rural America in Film and Literature." *English Journal* 76:1 (January 1987), 54–57.

Dyer, Richard. *Heavenly Bodies: Film Stars and Society.* London: Routledge, 2003.

———. *Stars.* New ed. London: BFI, 1998.

———. *White.* London: Routledge, 1997.

Ebert, Roger. *The Great Movies II.* New York: Broadway, 2006.

Eco, Umberto. *Travels in Hyperreality: Essays.* Trans. William Weaver. London: Pan Books, 1987.

Edelman, Rob. "*Top Gun.*" *Cineaste* 15:1 (1987), 41–42.

Emerson, Mark, and Eugene E. Pfaff Jr. *Country Girl: The Life of Sissy Spacek.* New York: St. Martin's, 1988.

Evans, Sara M. *Tidal Wave: How Women Changed at Century's End.* New York: Free Press, 2003.

Faludi, Susan. *Backlash: The Undeclared War against Women.* New York: Crown, 1991.

———. *Backlash: The Undeclared War against American Women.* 2nd ed. New York: Three Rivers, 2006.

Fiedler, Leslie. *Love and Death in the American Novel*. New York: Stein and Day, 1960.

Fischer, Lucy. "Bette Davis: Worker and Queen." *Glamour in a Golden Age: Movie Stars of the 1930s*. Ed. Adrienne L. McLean. New Brunswick, N.J.: Rutgers UP, 2010.

Fish, Robert. *Cinematic Countrysides*. Manchester: Manchester UP, 2007.

Fowler, Catherine, and Gillian Helfield, eds. *Representing the Rural: Space, Place, and Identity in Films about the Land*. Detroit: Wayne State UP, 2006.

Fox, Michael J. *Lucky Man: A Memoir*. New York: Hyperion, 2003.

Frank, Barbara, and Bill Krohn. "Entretien avec Jessica Lange." Trans. Philippe Guilhon. *Cahiers du Cinéma* 337 (June 1982), 60–64.

Frayling, Christopher. *Sergio Leone*. London: Faber and Faber, 2000.

Fuchs, Cynthia. "Working Girl." *Cineaste* 17:2 (1989), 50–52.

Fussell, Paul. "Bodybuilder Americanus." *The Male Body*. Ed. Laurence Goldstein. Ann Arbor: U of Michigan P, 1994.

Gabbard, Krin. *Black Magic: White Hollywood and African American Culture*. New Brunswick, N.J.: Rutgers UP, 2004.

———, and Glen O. Gabbard. "Phallic Women in Contemporary Cinema." *American Imago* 50:4 (Winter 1993), 421–40.

Gallagher, Mark. *Action Figures: Men, Action Films, and Contemporary Adventure Narratives*. New York: Palgrave, 2006.

Gallardo C., Ximena, and C. Jason Smith. *Alien Woman: The Making of Lt. Ellen Ripley*. New York: Continuum, 2004.

Gehring, Wes. *Romantic vs. Screwball Comedy*. Lanham, Md.: Scarecrow, 2002.

Geraghty, Christine. "Re-examining Stardom: Questions of Texts, Bodies, and Performance." *Reinventing Film Studies*. Ed. Christine Gledhill and Linda Williams. London: Arnold, 2000. 183–201.

Glass, Fred. "Totally Recalling Arnold: Sex and Violence in the New Bad Future." *Film Quarterly* 44:1 (Autumn 1990), 2–13.

Gledhill, Christine, ed. *Industry of Desire*. London: Routledge, 1991.

Gledhill, Christine, and Linda Williams, eds. *Reinventing Film Studies*. London: Arnold, 2000.

Godden, Richard. "Maximizing the Noodles: Class, Memory and Capital in Sergio Leone's *Once Upon a Time in America*." *Journal of American Studies* 31:3 (1997), 361–84.

Greenberg, Harvey Roy. "Fembo: *Aliens'* Intention." *Journal of Popular Film and Television* 15:4 (Winter 1988), 164–71.

Harper, Sue. *Women in British Cinema: Mad, Bad, and Dangerous to Know*. London: Continuum, 2000.

Harries, Dan. *Film Parody*. London: BFI, 2000.

Harwood, Sarah. *Family Fictions: Representations of the Family in 1980s Hollywood Cinema*. Basingstoke: Macmillan, 1997.

Haskell, Molly. "Finding Herself: The Everlasting Prime of an Acting Powerhouse." *Film Comment* 44:2 (2008), 32–41.

———. *From Reverence to Rape: The Treatment of Women in the Movies*. 2nd ed. Chicago: U of Chicago P, 1987.

Hawn, Goldie. *Goldie: A Lotus in the Mud*. New York: Penguin, 2005.

Hayes, Kevin J., ed. *Martin Scorsese's Raging Bull*. Cambridge: Cambridge UP, 2005.

Hentzi, Gary. "Peter Weir and the Cinema of New Age Humanism." *Film Quarterly* 44:2 (Winter 1990–91), 2–12.

Hodenfield, Chris. "You've Got to Love Something Enough to Kill It." *Martin Scorsese Interviews*. Ed. Peter Brunette. Jackson: UP of Mississippi, 1999. 128–37.

Hollinger, Karen. *The Actress: Hollywood Acting and the Female Star*. London: Routledge, 2006.

Holmlund, Chris. "Masculinity as a Multiple Masquerade: The 'Mature' Stallone and the Stallone Clone." *Screening the Male: Exploring Masculinities in Hollywood Cinema*. Ed. Steven Cohan and Ina Rae Hark. London: Routledge, 1993. 9–20.

———. "New Cold War Sequels and Remakes." *Jump Cut* 35 (April 1990), 85–96.

———. "Sexuality and Power in Male Doppleganger Cinema: The Case of Clint Eastwood's *Tightrope*." *Cinema Journal* 26:1 (Fall 1986), 31–42.

Holt, Jennifer. "In Deregulation We Trust: The Synergy of Politics and Industry in Reagan-Era Hollywood." *Film Quarterly* 55:2 (2001), 22–29.

Hrabi, Dale. "Hail Mary." *The Advocate* (February 2009), 82.

Jeffords, Susan. "The Big Switch: Hollywood Masculinity in the 90s." *Film Theory Goes to the Movies*. Ed. Jim Collins, Hilary Radner, and Ava Preacher Collins. New York: Routledge, 1993. 196–208.

———. *Hard Bodies: Hollywood Masculinity in the Reagan Era*. New Brunswick, N.J.: Rutgers UP, 1994.

Jeffries, J. T. *Jessica Lange: A Biography*. New York: St. Martin's, 1986.

Johnson, E. Patrick. "The Specter of the Black Fag: Parody, Blackness, and Hetero/Homosexual B(r)others." *Journal of Homosexuality* 45:2/3/4 (2003), 217–34.

Jones, Kent. "Uncommon Valor: Kent Jones Salutes the Fearless Screen Presence of Jessica Lange." *Film Comment* 42:2 (March 2006), 34–36, 38–40.

Kane, Leslie. *David Mamet in Conversation*. Ann Arbor: U of Michigan P, 2001.

Kapsis, E. Robert. "Clint Eastwood's Politics of Reputation." *Society* 30:6 (September/October 1993), 68–72.

Katsahnias, Iannis. "Vent d'Est, Vent d'Ouest." *Cahiers du cinéma* 409 (June 1988), 54–59.

Katzenstein, Mary Fainsod. *Faithful and Fearless: Moving Feminist Protest inside the Church and Military*. Princeton, N.J.: Princeton UP, 1998.

Kearney, Richard. *Modern Movements in European Philosophy*. Manchester: Manchester UP, 1986.

Kimmel, Michael. *Manhood in America: A Cultural History*. 2nd ed. New York: Oxford UP, 2006.

King, Barry. "Articulating Stardom." *Stardom: Industry of Desire*. Ed. Christine Gledhill and Linda Williams. London: Arnold, 2000. 167–82.

Klevan, Andrew. *Film Performance: From Achievement to Appreciation*. London: Wallflower, 2005.

Knelman, Martin. *Laughing on the Outside: The Life of John Candy*. New York: St. Martin's, 1997.

Knepper, Marty S., and John S. Lawrence. "World War II and Iowa: Hollywood's Pastoral Myth for the Nation." *Representing the Rural: Space, Place, and Identity in Films about the Land*. Eds. Catherine Fowler and Gillian Helfield. Detroit: Wayne State UP, 2006. 323–339.

Kozloff, Sarah. *Overhearing Film Dialogue*. Berkeley: U of California P, 2000.

Krämer, Peter. "'A Woman in a Male-Dominated World': Jodie Foster, Stardom and 90s Hollywood." *Contemporary Hollywood Stardom*. Ed. Thomas Austin and Martin Baker. London: Arnold, 2003. 201–14.

Lawrence, Amy. *Echo and Narcissus: Women's Voices in Classical Hollywood Cinema*. Berkeley: U of California P, 1991.

Leamer, Laurence. *Fantastic: The Life of Arnold Schwarzenegger*. New York: St. Martin's, 2005.

Lehman, Peter. *Running Scared: Masculinity and the Representation of the Male Body*. 2nd ed. Detroit: Wayne State UP, 2007.

Lott, Eric. *Love and Theft: Blackface Minstrelsy and the American Working Class*. New York: Oxford UP, 1993.

Lovell, Alan. "I Went in Search of Deborah Kerr, Jodie Foster and Julianne Moore but Got Waylaid . . ." *Contemporary Hollywood Stardom*. Ed. Thomas Austin and Martin Baker. London: Arnold, 2003. 259–70.

Maguffee, T. D. *Sigourney Weaver*. New York: St. Martin's, 1989.

Maltby, Richard. *Hollywood Cinema*. 2nd ed. Malden, Mass.: Blackwell, 2003.

Martin, Steve. *Born Standing Up*. New York: Scribner, 2007.

Maychick, Diana. *Meryl Streep: The Reluctant Superstar*. New York: St. Martin's, 1984.

Mayne, Judith. *Cinema and Spectatorship*. London: Routledge, 1993.

McDonald, Paul. "Reconceptualizing Stardom." *Stars*. Richard Dyer. London: BFI, 1998. 175–200.

———. "Stars." *Schirmer Encyclopedia of Film*. Volume 4. Ed. Barry Keith Grant. Detroit: Thompson Gale, 2007. 155–64.

McKenzie, Alan. *The Harrison Ford Story*. New York: Arbor House, 1984.

Mulvey, Laura. *Death 24X a Second: Stillness and the Moving Image*. London: Reaktion Books, 2006.

———. *Visual and Other Pleasures*. 2nd ed. Hampshire: Palgrave Macmillan, 2004.

———. "Visual Pleasure and Narrative Cinema." *Screen* 16:3 (Autumn 1975), 6–18.

Naremore, James. *Acting in the Cinema*. Berkeley: U of California P, 1988.

Neale, Steve. *Genre and Hollywood*. London: Routledge, 2000.

———. "Masculinity as Spectacle: Reflections on Men in Mainstream Cinema." *Screening the Male: Exploring Masculinities in Hollywood Cinema*. Ed. Steven Cohan and Ina Rae Hark. London: Routledge, 1993. 9–20.

———, and Frank Krutnik. *Popular Film and Television Comedy*. London: Routledge, 1990.

Oram, James. *Reluctant Star: The Mel Gibson Story*. London: Fontana, 1991

Overpeck, Deron. "1988: Movies and Images of Reality." *American Cinema of the 1980s: Themes and Variations*. Ed. Stephen Prince. New Brunswick, N.J.: Rutgers UP, 2007. 188–209.

Pally, Marcia. "Sigourney Takes Control." *Film Comment* 22:6 (1986), 18–22.

Palmer, William J. *The Films of the Eighties: A Social History*. Carbondale: Southern Illinois UP, 1993.

Penley, Constance. *NASA/Trek: Popular Science and Sex in America*. New York: Verso, 1997.

Pfaff, Eugene E. Jr., and Mark Emerson. *Meryl Streep: A Critical Biography*. Jefferson, N.C.: McFarland, 1987.

Pfeil, Fred. "Rock Incorporated: Plugging in to Axl and Bruce." *White Guys: Studies in Postmodern Domination and Difference*. New York: Verso, 1995. 71–104.

Prince, Stephen, ed. *American Cinema of the 1980s: Themes and Variations*. New Brunswick, N.J.: Rutgers UP, 2007.

———. *A New Pot of Gold: Hollywood under the Electronic Rainbow, 1980–1989*. Berkeley: U of California P, 2000.

Pulver, Andrew, and Steven Paul Davies. *Brat Pack Confidential*. London: BT Basford, 2000.

Ray, Robert. *A Certain Tendency of the Hollywood Cinema, 1930–1980*. Princeton, N.J.: Princeton UP, 1985.

Rogin, Michael. *Ronald Reagan, The Movie: and Other Episodes in Political Demonology*. Berkeley: U of California P, 1987.

Rose, Cynthia. "The Riddle of the Rock Biopic." *Sight & Sound* 3:10 (October 1993), 14–16.

Rosen, Marjorie. *Popcorn Venus*. New York: Avon, 1974.

Rubin, Martin. *Thrillers*. Cambridge: Cambridge UP, 1999.

Russo, Vito. *The Celluloid Closet: Homosexuality in the Movies*. Rev. ed. New York: Harper & Row, 1987.

Ryan, Michael, and Douglas Kellner. *Camera Politica: The Politics and Ideology of Contemporary Hollywood Film*. Bloomington: Indiana UP, 1988.

Sanello, Frank. *Eddie Murphy: The Life and Times of a Comic on the Edge*. Secaucus, N.J.: Birch Lane, 1997.

Schickel, Richard. *Clint Eastwood: A Biography*. New York: Knopf, 1996.

Schlotterbeck, Jesse. "'Trying to Find a Heartbeat': Narrative Music in the Pop Performer Biopic." *Journal of Popular Film and Television* 36:2 (Summer 2008), 82–90.

Shales, Tom, and James Andrew Miller. *Live from New York: An Uncensored History of "Saturday Night Live."* Boston: Little, Brown, 2002.

Shary, Timothy. *Generation Multiplex: The Image of American Youth on Screen*. Austin: U of Texas P, 2002.

Silverman, Kaja. *The Acoustic Mirror: The Female Voice in Psychoanalysis and Cinema*. Bloomington: Indiana UP, 1988.

Sinyard, Neil. *Mel Gibson*. New York: Crescent Books, 1992.

Smith, Paul. *Clint Eastwood: A Cultural Production*. Minneapolis: U of Minnesota P, 1993.

Stacey, Jackie. *Star Gazing: Hollywood Cinema and Female Spectatorship*. London: Routledge, 1994.

Studlar, Gaylyn, and David Desser. "Never Having to Say You're Sorry: Rambo's Rewriting of the Vietnam War" *Film Quarterly* 42:1 (Autumn 1988), 9–16.

Tasker, Yvonne. *Spectacular Bodies: Gender, Genre, and the Action Cinema*. London: Routledge, 1993.

———. *Working Girls: Gender and Sexuality in Popular Cinema*. London: Routledge, 1998.

Tasker, Yvonne, and Diane Negra, eds. "In Focus: Postfeminism and Contemporary Media Studies." *Cinema Journal* 44:2 (2005), 107–10.

———. *Interrogating Postfeminism: Gender and the Politics of Popular Culture*. Durham, N.C.: Duke UP, 2007.

Taves, Brian. *The Romance of Adventure: The Genre of Historical Adventure Movies*. Jackson: UP of Mississippi, 1993.

Tibbets, John C. "The Machinery of Violence: Clint Eastwood Talks about *Unforgiven*." *Clint Eastwood, Actor and Director: New Perspectives*. Ed. Leonard Engel. Salt Lake City: U of Utah P, 2007. 171–80.

Tomasulo, Frank. "Mr. Jones Goes to Washington: Myth and Religion in *Raiders of the Lost Ark*." *Quarterly Review of Film Studies* 7:4 (Fall 1982), 331–38.

Vare, Ethlie Ann, and Mary Toledo. *Harrison Ford*. New York: St. Martin's, 1987.

Vineberg, Steve. "Acting without Fear." *Threepenny Review* 44 (Winter 1991), 26.

———. "Swing Shift: A Tale of Hollywood. (Jonathan Demme's *Swing Shift*)." *Sight & Sound* 60:1 (Winter 1990/1991), 8–14.

Watney, Simon. "Hollywood's Homosexual World." *Screen* 23:3–4 (November-December 1982), 107–22.

Whillock, David E. "The American Farmer as Hero: An Archetypal Study of Women on the Farm as Portrayed in *Country, Places in the Heart,* and *The River.*" *Journal of American Culture* 10:3 (June 2004), 27–31.

White, Mimi. "Rehearsing Feminism: Women/History in *The Life and Times of Rosie the Riveter* and *Swing Shift.*" *Multiple Voices in Feminist Film Criticism.* Ed. Diane Carson, Linda Dittmar, and Janice Welsch. Minneapolis: U of Minnesota P, 1994. 318–29.

Wiegman, Robyn. *American Anatomies: Theorizing Race and Gender.* Durham, N.C.: Duke UP, 1995.

Willis, Sharon. *High Contrast: Race and Gender in Contemporary Hollywood Film.* Durham, N.C.: Duke UP, 1997.

Wood, Robin. "80s Hollywood: Dominant Tendencies." *Cineaction* 1 (1986), 2–5.

———. *Hitchcock's Films Revisited.* New York: Columbia UP, 1989.

———. *Hollywood from Vietnam to Reagan.* New York: Columbia UP, 1986.

———. *Hollywood from Vietnam to Reagan . . . and Beyond.* Rev. ed. New York: Columbia UP, 2003.

———. "Ideology, Auteur, Genre." *Hitchcock's Films Revisited.* New York: Columbia UP, 1989. 288–302.

———. "Martin Scorsese." *The St. James Film Directors Encyclopedia.* Ed. Andrew Sarris. Detroit: Visible Ink, 1998. 453–57.

———. "Robert De Niro." http://www.filmreference.com. Accessed 1 January 2009.

Wyatt, Justin. *High Concept: Movies and Marketing in Hollywood.* Austin: U of Texas P, 1994.

# CONTRIBUTORS
★★★★★★★★★★★

AARON BAKER is an associate professor of Film and Media Studies at Arizona State University. He is the author of *Contesting Identities: Sports in American Film* (2006) and *The Films of Steven Soderbergh* (forthcoming).

REBECCA BELL-METEREAU directs the Media Studies Minor at Texas State University and has authored *Hollywood Androgyny* (1986), *Simone Weil* (1998), and numerous chapters and articles in anthologies, *Cinema Journal*, and *Journal of Popular Film and Television*.

WILLIAM BROWN is a lecturer in Film Studies at the University of St. Andrews, Scotland. His research interests include digital technology, cinema, and the stars. He has published a range of book chapters and articles, including a chapter on Audrey Hepburn in *Larger Than Life: Movie Stars of the 1950s* (forthcoming).

MICHAEL DeANGELIS is an associate professor at DePaul University's School for New Learning, where he teaches in the areas of media and cultural studies. He is currently writing a history of art cinema and exhibition practices in Chicago during the 1960s and 1970s.

ROBERT EBERWEIN is Distinguished Professor of English Emeritus at Oakland University. Recent books include *The Hollywood War Film* (2009) and *Armed Forces: Masculinity and Sexuality in the American War Film* (2007).

KRIN GABBARD is a professor in the Department of Comparative Literary and Cultural Studies at Stony Brook University. He is the author most recently of *Hotter Than That: The Trumpet, Jazz and American Culture* (2008) and the co-editor of *Screening Genders* (2008).

CHRIS HOLMLUND is a professor of cinema studies, women's studies, and French at the University of Tennessee–Knoxville. She is also chair of the Cinema Studies Program and author and editor of several books on film, including *American Cinema of the 1990s* (2008).

ADAM KNEE is an associate professor at the Wim Kee Wim School of Communication and Information at Singapore's Nanyang Technological University. He has previously published essays on the intersection of stardom, masculinity, and race in such anthologies as *Screening the Male* (1993) and *Soundtrack Available* (2002).

CHRISTINA LANE is an associate professor in film studies at the University of Miami. She is the author of *Feminist Hollywood: From Born in Flames to Point Break* (2000) and essays in the anthologies *Culture, Trauma, and Conflict: Cultural Studies Perspectives on War* (2007), *Contemporary American Independent Film* (2004), and *The West Wing* (2003).

LINDA MIZEJEWSKI is a professor of women's studies at Ohio State University. Her most recent books are *It Happened One Night* (2010), part of the Wiley-Blackwell Studies in Film and Television, and *Hardboiled and High Heeled: The Woman Detective in Popular Culture* (2004).

JAMES MORRISON is a professor of literature and film studies at Claremont McKenna College. He is the author, co-author, or editor of several books on film, most recently *Roman Polanski* (2007) and *The Cinema of Todd Haynes: All That Heaven Allows* (2006).

JERRY MOSHER is an assistant professor in the Department of Film and Electronic Arts at California State University, Long Beach. His research focuses on American cinema and its representations of the body. He has published essays on film and culture in numerous anthologies.

# I N D E X
★★★★★★★★★★★

Note: Featured stars in boldface; page numbers for illustrations in italic.

*About Last Night* (Edward Zwick, 1986), 112, 117–18, *118*
*Absence of Malice* (Sydney Pollack, 1981), 14, 185, 198
*Absent-Minded Waiter, The* (Steve Martin, 1977), 262n3
*Abyss, The* (James Cameron, 1989), 224
*Accidental Tourist, The* (Lawrence Kasdan, 1988), 17
*Accused, The* (Jonathan Kaplan, 1988), 13
Actors Studio, 21–22, 69, 184
Adler, Stella, 21–22
*Against Our Will* (Susan Brownmiller), 231
*Alien* (Ridley Scott, 1979), 61, 144, 157
*Aliens* (James Cameron, 1986), 11, 61, 139–42, *141*, 147, 152–54, 158
*Alien* series, 140, 150, 152
*All About Eve* (Joseph Mankiewicz, 1950), 224
Allen, Karen, 163
Allen, Robert, 144
Allen, Woody, 144
*All of Me* (Carl Reiner, 1984), 250, 252–53
*All That Jazz* (Bob Fosse, 1979), 60
Alonso, Maria Conchito, *51*
Als, Hilton, 203
*Altered States* (Ken Russell, 1980), 16
*Always* (Steven Spielberg, 1989), 267
*Amadeus* (Milos Forman, 1984), 9
*American Buffalo* (David Mamet, February 16, 1977), 31
American Movie Classics (AMC), 5
Ames, Christopher, 171–72
*Analyze This* (Harold Ramis, 1999), 21, 31
Anderson, Eddie "Rochester," 129
*And the Band Played On* (Randy Shilts), 6
*Animal House* (John Landis, 1978), 123
*Annie Hall* (Woody Allen, 1977), 113, 144
Ansen, David, 79, 90, 91, 185
Antonioni, Michelangelo, 137
*Any Which Way You Can* (Buddy Van Horn, 1980), 229, 234

Apatow, Judd, 261
*Apocalypse Now* (Francis Ford Coppola, 1979), 53, 226
*Apollo 13* (Ron Howard, 1995), 267
Arbuckle, Roscoe "Fatty," 256
*Armed and Dangerous* (Mark L. Lester, 1986), 258
Astaire, Fred, 247, 249, 251
*At Close Range* (James Foley, 1986), 269
*Atlantic City* (Louis Malle, 1980), 268
Austen, Jane, 208
*Author! Author!* (Arthur Hiller, 1980), 14
*Awakenings* (Penny Marshall, 1980), 18
Aykroyd, Dan, 123, 130–31, *131*, 149, 159n4, 254–55, 259

Bacall, Lauren, 110
*Backlash* (Susan Faludi), 181
*Back Roads* (Martin Ritt, 1981), 185
*Back to School* (Alan Metter, 1986), 9
*Back to the Future* (Robert Zemeckis, 1985), 8, 42, 74, 100, 101–103, *102*, 106, 108
*Back to the Future* series, 119
Bacon, Kevin, 9
Baldwin, Alec, 266
Balio, Tino, 46
Bancroft, Anne, 75
"Band of Brothers" (2001), 267
*Barfly* (Barbette Schroeder, 1987), 13
Barker, Deborah, 200
Barr, Roseanne, 221
*Basic Instinct* (Paul Verhoeven, 1992), 265
Basinger, Kim, 266
*Batman* (Tim Burton, 1989), 14, 17, 221, 266
*Batman Forever* (Joel Schumacher, 1995), 264
*Battleship Potemkin* (Sergei Eisenstein, 1925), 33
Baxter, John, 21, 22, 25, 27
Bazin, André, 62
*Beaches* (Garry Marshall, 1988), 14, 63
Beatles, 262n1

Beatty, Warren, 13
Beavers, Herman, 130
Bedelia, Bonnie, 238
*Beetle Juice* (Tim Burton, 1988), 9, 17
Begley, Ed Jr., 220
*Beguiled, The* (Don Siegel, 1971), 239
Belushi, Jim, 54
Belushi, John, 123, 255, 262
Benjamin, Richard, 236
Benny, Jack, 129
*Benny and Joon* (Jeremiah S. Chechik, 1993), 263
Benton, Robert, 189
Bergman, Ingrid, 147
Berrigan, Daniel, 29
Berry, Chuck, 101
*Best Little Whorehouse in Texas, The* (Colin Higgins, 1982), 17
*Beverly Hills Cop* (Martin Brest, 1984), 11, 120, 123, 130–31, 134, 136, 149
*Beverly Hills Cop II* (Tony Scott, 1987), 11, 136
*Beyond the Poseidon Adventure* (Irwin Allen, 1979), 185
*Beyond the Sea* (Kevin Spacey, 2004), 63
*Big* (Penny Marshall, 1988), 267
*Big Chill, The* (Lawrence Kasdan, 1983), 15, 16, 17
*Bill & Ted's Bogus Journey* (Peter Hewitt, 1991), 264
*Bill & Ted's Excellent Adventure* (Stephen Herek, 1989), 264
*Biloxi Blues* (Mike Nichols, 1988), 15
Bingham, Dennis, 50
*Bird* (Clint Eastwood, 1988), 227, 269
*Bird on a Wire* (John Badham, 1990), 182
*Birdy* (Alan Parker, 1984), 266
Bishop, Joey, 110
*Blade Runner* (Ridley Scott, 1982), 164–66, 168
*Blind Date* (Blake Edwards, 1987), 236, 239–40, 266
*Blow-Up* (Michelangelo Antonioni, 1966), 137
*Blue City* (Michelle Manning, 1986), 111, 112, 118
*Blues Brothers, The* (John Landis, 1980), 123, 255
*Blue Sky* (Tony Richardson, 1994), 59, 57, 76n5
Blum, David, 108–112, 114–16
*Bob Roberts* (Tim Robbins, 1992), 265
*Body Double* (Brian De Palma, 1984), 233

*Body Heat* (Lawrence Kasdan, 1981), 16, 17
Bogart, Humphrey, 110, 174
Bolt, Robert, 29
*Bonfire of the Vanities, The* (Tom Wolfe), 2
*Bonnie and Clyde* (Arthur Penn, 1967), 13
Bono, Sonny, 15
Borden, Lizzie, 11
*Born in Flames* (Lizzie Borden, 1983), 11
*Born on the Fourth of July* (Oliver Stone, 1989), 10, 89, 96–97
"Bosom Buddies" (1980–1982), 267
*Bounty, The* (Roger Donaldson, 984), 86
*Boys on the Side* (Herbert Ross, 1995), 267
Brackett, David, 64–65
Brando, Marlon, 25–26, 109, 119n1
**Brat Pack**, 1, 78, 99, 99–100, 103, 108–19, 268
*Breakfast Club, The* (John Hughes, 1985), 99, 100, 111, 114, 115, 259
*Breaking Away* (Peter Yates, 1979), 145
Brennan, Eileen, 187
Brest, Martin, 21
*Brewster's Millions* (Walter Hill, 1985), 258
*Bright Lights, Big City* (James Bridges, 1988), 106–107, 107, 110
Britton, Andrew, 60, 140, 142
*Broadcast News* (James L. Brooks, 1987), 17, 267
Broderick, Matthew, 15
*Bronco Billy* (Clint Eastwood, 1980), 228
Brooks, Albert, 245
Brooks, James L., 267
Brooks, Mel, 246
Brost, Molly, 65–66
Brown, Bryan, 155
Brownmiller, Susan, 231
*Brubaker* (Stuart Rosenberg, 1980), 14
Bruckheimer, Jerry, 8
Brunette, Peter, 22
Brunsdon, Charlotte, 151
Buchwald, Art, 135
*Bull Durham* (Ron Shelton, 1988), 15, 264, 268
Burrows, James, 85
Burton, Tim, 17, 263
Busey, Gary, 89
Bush, George H. W., 5, 84, 132, 151, 232
Bush, George W., 224

Cable News Network (CNN), 4
Cage, Nicolas, 119n1, 266, 267, 268

Cagney, James, 104
"Cagney and Lacey" (1982–1988), 7
Cain, Christopher, 112
Caine, Michael, 40, 139, 145, 253
Cameron, James, 42, 53, 152–53
Campion, Jane, 265, 267
Canby, Vincent, 214, 216, 218–19, 220
Candy, John, 1, 243, 243–45, 253–62, 256, 260, 262n4
Cannonball Run series, 259
Cape Fear (Martin Scorsese, 1991), 21
Capone, Al, 26, 30–34
Capote, Truman, 217
Capshaw, Kate, 166
Carpenter, John, 9
Carrey, Jim, 232
Carrie (Brian De Palma, 1976), 69
Carter, Jimmy, 2, 92, 205, 230
Case, Brian, 102
Casino (Martin Scorsese, 1995), 265–66
Casualties of War (Brian De Palma, 1989), 10, 107–108, 268
Cavell, Stanley, 187
Chances Are (Emile Ardolino, 1989), 263
Chapelle, Dave, 133
Chaplin (Richard Attenborough, 1992), 263
Chaplin, Charlie, 263
Chariots of Fire (Hugh Hudson, 1981), 9
Chase, Chevy, 123, 159, 253
Cheaper by the Dozen series, 253
"Cheers" (1982–1993), 7
Cher, 15, 17
Chinatown (Roman Polanski, 1974), 13, 14
Chow, Leslie, 67
"Christopher Columbus" (Alberto Lattuada, 1985), 13
Cinemax, 4
City Heat (Richard Benjamin, 1984), 236
Clay, Andrew "Dice," 133–34
Clean and Sober (Glenn Gordon Caron, 1988), 17
Clinch, Minty, 173–74
Cline, Patsy, 58, 64–66, 68
Close, Glenn, 15, 16
Clover, Carol, 9
Coal Miner's Daughter (Michael Apted, 1980), 11, 57, 59, 63–67, 70
Cocktail (Roger Donaldson, 1988), 90
Coen, Ethan, 267
Coen, Joel, 267

Color of Money, The (Martin Scorsese, 1987), 14, 90, 95–96, 96
Color Purple, The (Alice Walker), 11
Color Purple, The (Steven Spielberg, 1985), 11, 267
Colors (Dennis Hopper, 1988), 268
Come Back to the Five and Dime, Jimmy Dean, Jimmy Dean (Robert Altman, 1982), 15
Coming Home (Hal Ashby, 1978), 13
Coming to America (John Landis, 1988), 135–36
Commando (Mark L. Lester, 1985), 84
Conan the Barbarian (John Milius, 1982), 36, 48, 49, 84
Conan series, 48
Connery, Sean, 12, 13, 15, 32–33, 34, 176, 266
Cooper, Gary, 226
Coppola, Francis Ford, 9, 264
Corliss, Richard, 23, 103, 116, 143
Cosby, Bill, 104, 125, 132, 133, 136
"Cosby Show, The" (1984–1992), 6–7, 101
Costner, Kevin, 15, 32, 34
Country (Richard Pearce, 1984), 58, 59, 71, 72, 73, 74
Courage Under Fire (Edward Zwick, 1996), 265, 269
Crash (David Cronenberg, 1996), 267
Craven, Wes, 9
Crawford, Joan, 13
Creative Artists Agency (CAA), 21
Crenna, Richard, 41
Crimes of Passion (Ken Russell, 1984), 18
Crimes of the Heart (Bruce Beresford, 1986), 58, 59, 63, 66, 67, 70
Cronenberg, David, 267
Cruise, Tom, 1, 8, 13, 77, 77–78, 89–98, 93, 96, 100, 119n1, 263–64, 267, 268
Cruising (William Friedkin, 1980), 11, 14
Cry-Baby (John Waters, 1990), 263
Cry Freedom (Richard Attenborough, 1987), 17
Crying Game, The (Neil Jordan, 1992), 269
Cry in the Dark, A/Evil Angels (Fred Schepisi, 1988), 202, 204, 208, 210, 211–14, 212, 218, 221n1
Cunningham, Sean, 9
Curtis, Jamie Lee, 131
Cusack, Joan, 148, 151

*Cutting Class* (Rospo Pallenberg, 1989), 264
*Cyrano de Bergerac* (Edmond Rostand), 253

"Dallas" (1978–1991), 7
*Dangerous Liaisons* (Stephen Frears, 1988), 15, 17, 264
Dargis, Manohla, 132
Davies, Steven Paul, 119n1
Davis, Bette, 221n4
Davis, Miles, 137
Davis, Sammy Jr., 110
*Days of Thunder* (Tony Scott, 1994), 264
*Dead Calm* (Philip Noyce, 1989), 263
*Dead Man Walking* (Tim Robbins, 1995), 265, 268
*Dead Men Don't Wear Plaid* (Carl Reiner, 1982), 244, 250
*Dead Poets' Society, The* (Peter Weir, 1989), 18, 251
*Dead Pool, The* (Buddy Van Horn, 1988), 230–33
*Deal of the Century* (William Friedkin, 1983), 159n2
DeAngelis, Michael, 78
D'Angelo, Beverly, 66
DeCordova, Richard, 181
DeCurtis, Anthony, 22
*Deer Hunter, The* (Michael Cimino, 1978), 19, 27, 30, 221
*Defiant Ones, The* (Stanley Kramer, 1958), 128
De Laurentiis, Dino, 49, 60
De Lauretis, Teresa, 6
*Delirious* (Tom Mankiewicz, 1991), 261
D'Emilio, John, 6
Demme, Jonathan, 193–94
DeMornay, Rebecca, 90, 92
Denby, David, 106, 111–12, 215–16
**De Niro, Robert**, 1, *19*, 19–35, *23*, *28*, *32*, 109, 208
De Palma, Brian, 10, 26, 31–33, 107–108, 233
Depardieu, Gérard, 159n2
Depp, Johnny, 7, 263
Derry, Charles, 272
*Desert Hearts* (Donna Deitch, 1985), 11
Desjardins, Mary, 78
*Desperately Seeking Susan* (Susan Seidelman, 1985), 5
Desser, David, 41
*Devil in a Blue Dress* (Carl Franklin, 1995), 269

De Vito, Danny, 7, 55
Diawara, Manthia, 127
*Die Hard* (John McTiernan, 1988), 128, 223–34, 238–41
Dillon, Matt, 119n1
*Dirty Dancing* (Emile Ardolino, 1987), 9
*Dirty Harry* (Don Siegel, 1971), 229
*Dirty Rotten Scoundrels* (Frank Oz, 1988), 253
*Disclosure* (Barry Levinson, 1994), 268
Dixon, Ivan, 137
Doane, Mary Ann, 222n5
Doherty, Thomas, 8
*Dollmaker, The* (Daniel Petrie, 1984), 58
Donaldson, Roger, 62
*Donnie Brasco* (Mike Newell, 1997), 263
*Do the Right Thing* (Spike Lee, 1989), 11
Douglas, Michael, 13, 15, *16*, 17, 176, 265, 268
*Down and Out in Beverly Hills* (Paul Mazursky, 1986), 14
Downey, Robert Jr., 263
*Dracula* (Francis Ford Coppola, 1994), 264
*Driving Miss Daisy* (Bruce Beresford, 1989), 9, 11, 266
Dunaway, Faye, 13, 214
Durang, Christopher, 143, 157–58
Dutton, Charles, 30
Dyer, Richard, 20, 34, 38, 47, 62, 161, 207, 227, 241
"Dynasty" (1981–1989), 7

**Eastwood, Clint**, 1, 10, *223*, 223–42, *229*, *235*, 266, 268
Ebert, Roger, 56, 248, 250, 261
Eco, Umberto, 71
Edelman, Rob, 94–95
*Eddie Murphy Delirious* (Bruce Gowers, 1983), 132–34
*Eddie Murphy Raw* (Robert Townsend, 1987), 133, 136
Edwards, Anthony, 94
Edwards, Blake, 11, 85, 236–37, 266
*Edward Scissorhands* (Tim Burton, 1990), 263
*Ed Wood* (Tim Burton, 1994), 263
Ehrenreich, Barbara, 79
Eisenstein, Sergei, 33
Eisner, Michael, 27
Eliot, George, 208
Ellington, Edward Kennedy "Duke," 137

Emerson, Mark, 58, 65, 69, 76n1
*Empire Strikes Back, The* (George Lucas, 1980), 160–62, 166, 168
"Entertainment Tonight" (1981– ), 206, 249
*Erin Brockovich* (Stephen Soderbergh, 2000), 265
**Estevez, Emilio**, *99*, 100, 108–109, 111, 114, 115, 117, 119
*E.T.* (Steven Spielberg, 1982), 9, 43
Evans, Sara, 150
*Everybody's All American* (Taylor Hackford, 1988), 61, 67, 70, 75
*Everyone Says I Love You* (Woody Allen, 1996), 265
*Exorcist, The* (William Friedkin, 1973), 148
*Eyes Wide Shut* (Stanley Kubrick, 1999), 264
*Eyewitness* (Peter Yates, 1981), 145–46, 157

*Fabulous Baker Boys, The* (Steve Kloves, 1989), 17
*Face/Off* (John Woo, 1997), 266
*Falling in Love* (Ulu Grosbard, 1984), 20, 22, 27–29, *28*, 34, 202, 208
Faludi, Susan, 181, 205
*Fame* (Alan Parker, 1980), 9
*Family Business* (Sidney Lumet, 1989), 13, 15
"Family Ties" (1982–1987), 7, 101, 103, 105, 106, 109
*Far and Away* (Ron Howard, 1992), 264
Farley, Chris, 262
Farmer, Frances, 60, 66, 67, 75
*Far North* (Sam Shepard, 1988), 70, 71, 72, 73
*Fast Times at Ridgemont High* (Amy Heckerling, 1982), 8, 266, 268
*Fatal Attraction* (Adrian Lyne, 1987), 13, 15, *16*
*Father of the Bride* (Charles Shyer, 1991), 249
*Father of the Bride* series, 253
Ferraro, Geraldine, 5
*Ferris Bueller's Day Off* (John Hughes, 1986), 8, 15, 259
*Few Good Men, A* (Rob Reiner, 1992), 268
Feydeau, Georges, 157
Fiedler, Leslie, 128, 171

**Field, Sally**, 1, 57, 58, 68, *180*, 180–85, 188–92, *190*, 198–200, *199*, 267
*Field of Dreams* (Phil Alden Robinson, 1989), 15–16
Fields, W. C., 230, 251
Fierstein, Harvey, 11
*Fight Club* (David Fincher, 1999), 264
Fincher, David, 5
*Firm, The* (Sydney Pollack, 1993), 267
*First Blood* (Ted Kotcheff, 1982), 10, 38, 40–41, 47, 53, 84
Fischer, Lucy, 221n4
Fish, Robert, 71
*Fish Called Wanda, A* (Charles Crichton, 1988), 17
Fisher, Carrie, 163–64
Fisk, Jack, 58
*Five Corners* (Tony Bill, 1987), 13
*Flashdance* (Adrian Lyne, 1983), 9
*Flatliners* (Joel Schumacher, 1990), 265
Flynn, Errol, 226
Fonda, Jane, *12*, 13, 17, 57, 68, 189
Fonda, Henry, 13
*Footloose* (Herbert Ross, 1984), 9
**Ford, Harrison**, 1, 13, 139, 142, 148, 152, *160*, 160–79, *165*, *170*, 177
*Forrest Gump* (Robert Zemeckis, 1994), 267
*48 Hrs.* (Walter Hill, 1982), 120–23, *122*, 127–30, 136
Fosse, Bob, 60
Fosse, Dian, 142, 152, 154–57
Foster, Jodie, 13, 157, 267
Fowler, Catherine, 71–72
**Fox, Michael J.**, 1, 7, *99*, 99–109, *102*, *107*, 109, 113, 119
*Frances* (Graeme Clifford, 1982), 11, *57*, 59, 60, 63, 66, 67, 70, 74, 75
*Frantic* (Roman Polanski, 1988), 174–75
Frayling, Christopher, 26
Freeman, Morgan, *10*, 11, 12, 132, 266
*French Lieutenant's Woman, The* (Karel Reisz, 1981), 202, 207, 208, 214–16, *215*, 218, 221n1
*Fresh Horses* (David Anspaugh, 1988), 116
Freud, Sigmund, 41, 91
*Friday the 13th* (Sean Cunningham, 1980), 9
*Friday the 13th* series, 150
Friedman, Bruce J., 250
*From the Hip* (Bob Clark, 1987)
Fuchs, Cynthia, 151

*Full Metal Jacket* (Stanley Kubrick, 1987), 10, 116
Fussell, Paul, 47

Gabbard, Glen, 159n5
Gabbard, Krin, 128, 159n5
Gable, Clark, 174
Gallagher, Mark, 239
Gallardo C., Ximena, 153
*Gallipoli* (Peter Weir, 1981), 80–84, *82*, 88
*Gandhi* (Richard Attenborough, 1982), 9
Garbo, Greta, 214, 236
Garcia, Andy, 33
Garland, Judy, 110
Garner, James, 198, 236
Gehring, Wes, 159n3
Geraghty, Christine, 59, 140, 144, 170, 205
Gere, Richard, 265
*Getaway, The* (Roger Donaldson, 1994), 266
*Ghost* (Jerry Zucker, 1990), 267, 268
*Ghost Busters* (Ivan Reitman, 1984), 9, 136, 139–41, 147–50, *149*, 157
*Ghostbusters II* (Ivan Reitman, 1989), 9, 140, 142, 147–48, 150
*Ghost Dog: The Way of the Samurai* (Jim Jarmusch, 1999), 269
**Gibson, Mel**, 1, 11, 17, 77, 77–89, *82*, 91, 95, 97–98, 134, 139, 141, 145–47, 150
Glass, Fred, 56
Gledhill, Christine, 78
Glenn, Scott, 74
*Glory* (Edward Zwick, 1989), *10*, 11, 15, 266, 268
Glover, Danny, 11, 88, 172, 191
Godden, Richard, 26
*Godfather, The* (Francis Ford Coppola, 1972), 14
*Godfather: Part II, The* (Francis Ford Coppola, 1974), 14, 19
Goldberg, Whoopi, 11, 258, 267
*Golden Child, The* (Michael Ritchie, 1986), 134–36
"Golden Girls" (1985–1992), 7
Goldstein, Jeanette, *141*, 154
Gomery, Doug, 144
*Goodfellas* (Martin Scorsese, 1990), 21
Goodman, John, 198
"Good Morning America" (1975– ), 154
*Good Morning Vietnam* (Barry Levinson, 1987), 18, 269

*Good Mother, The* (Leonard Nimoy, 1988), 211
"Good Times" (1974–1979), 126
*Good Will Hunting* (Gus Van Sant, 1997), 18
Gopnik, Adam, 246–49
Gorbachev, Mikhail, 2, 44–45
*Gorillas in the Mist* (Michael Apted, 1988), 139–40, 142, 147, 154–57, *156*
Grammer, Kelsey, 7
Grant, Cary, 147, 246
*Great Outdoors, The* (Howard Deutch, 1988), 259
Greenberg, Harvey, 153
*Greetings* (Brian De Palma, 1968), 31
Gregory, Dick, 133
Griffith, Melanie, 142, 148, 176–77, *177*
Grodin, Charles, 21, 250
Grosbard, Ulu, 208
*Groundhog Day* (Harold Ramis, 1993), 123
Gwynne, Fred, 220

Haas, Lucas, 168
*Half Moon Street* (Bob Swaim, 1986), 145–46
**Hall, Anthony Michael**, *99*, 100, 111, 115, 116, 117, 119
*Halloween* (John Carpenter, 1978), 9
*Hamburger Hill* (John Irvin, 1987), 10
Hamill, Mark, 163
Hamilton, Linda, 52
*Hamlet* (Franco Zeffirelli, 1990), 88
Hancock, Herbie, 137
Hanks, Tom, 198, 257–58, 265, 267, 268–69
*Happy Together* (Mel Damski, 1989), 264
*Harlem Nights* (Eddie Murphy, 1989), 121, 136–38, *137*
Harmetz, Aljean, 90, 107, 189
Harper, Sue, 67
Harries, Dan, 228
Harris, Ed, 30, 64
*Harry Potter* series, 62
Harwood, Sarah, 62
Haskell, Molly, 57, 59, 61–62, 201–203, 213
Haufrect, Ian T., 42
**Hawn, Goldie**, 1, 58, *180*, 180–83, 185–89, 192–98, *197*
Hayes, Kevin, 24–25
Haysbert, Dennis, 132
HBO (Home Box Office), 4

*Heartbreak Ridge* (Clint Eastwood, 1986), 10, 230, 233–35, *235*
*Heartburn* (Mike Nichols, 1986), 208, 217
*Heat* (Michael Mann, 1995), 21
Helfield, Gillian, 71–72
Hemingway, Mariel, *237*
Henn, Carrie, 154
Hentzi, Gary, 173
*Heroes* (Jeremy Kagan, 1977), 162
*High School U.S.A.* (Rodney Amateau, 1983), 101, 103
Hill, Walter, 120–21, 128
Hiller, Arthur, 85
"Hill Street Blues" (1981–1987), 7
*Hi, Mom!* (Brian De Palma, 1970), 31
Hitchcock, Alfred, 146, 256
Hoberman, J., 103
Hoffman, Dustin, 13, 15
Hofstadter, Douglas, 252
Hollinger, Karen, 69, 202, 203–204, 207
Holmlund, Chris, 46, 153, 242n1
Holt, Jennifer, 72
*Home for the Holidays* (Jodie Foster, 1995), 267
*Honkytonk Man* (Clint Eastwood, 1982), 228–30, *229*
Hope, Bob, 125
Hopper, Edward, 249
*Hotel New Hampshire, The* (Tony Richardson, 1984), 13
*Hours, The* (Stephen Daldry, 2002), 263
Howard, Ron, 126, 253, 258
*How to Beat the High Co$t of Loving* (Robert Scheerer, 1980), 60, 61, 70
Hrabi, Dale, 143
*Huckleberry Finn* (Mark Twain), 128
Hudson, Ernie, 159n4
Hudson, Rock, 6
Hughes, John, 8, 15, 109, 113, 115, 244, 259–61
*Hunger, The* (Tony Scott, 1983), 268
Hunt, Linda, 85, 141
Hunter, Holly, 267
*Hurleyburly* (David Rabe, 1984), 157
Hurt, William, 16, 139, 145–46, 267
*Hustler, The* (Robert Rossen, 1962), 14
Huston, John, 40
Hutton, Timothy, 100, 119n1

*In Country* (Norman Jewison, 1989), 240
*Indecent Proposal* (Adrian Lyne, 1993), 268

*Indiana Jones and the Last Crusade* (Steven Spielberg, 1989), 13, 173, 176–78, 264
*Indiana Jones and the Temple of Doom* (Steven Spielberg, 1984), *160*, 166–68, 176, 178
*Indiana Jones* series, 9, 161, 166, 226
Innaurato, Albert, 143
*Intersection* (Mark Rydell, 1994), 265
*Interview with the Vampire* (Neil Jordan, 1994), 264
*In the Bedroom* (Todd Field, 2001), 59
*In the Cut* (Jane Campion, 2003), 265
*In the Heat of the Night* (Norman Jewison, 1967), 128
*Iron Man* (Jon Favreau, 2008), 263
Irons, Jeremy, 2, 29, *215*, 218
*Ironweed* (Hector Babenco, 1987), 202, 204, 208, 214, 220, 221
Irvin, John, 10
*Ishtar* (Elaine May, 1987), 13
*It Happened One Night* (Frank Capra, 1934), 186

*Jacknife* (David Hugh Jones, 1989), 20, 29, 30, 34
Jackson, Michael, 6
Jackson, Samuel L., 132
*Jacob's Ladder* (Adrian Lyne, 1990), 264
James, Rick, 135
*Jayne Mansfield Story, The* (Dick Lowry, 1980), 48
"Jeffersons, The" (1975–1985), 126
Jeffords, Susan, 10, 40–41, 50, 60, 91–92, 161, 178–79, 192, 225–26, 238
Jeffries, J. T., 68, 76n5
*Jerk, The* (Carl Reiner, 1979), 244–50
Jett, Joan, 105
*Jewel of the Nile, The* (Lewis Teague, 1985), 13
*Joe* (John G. Avildsen, 1970), 268
*Joe versus the Volcano* (John Patrick Shanley, 1990), 265
*Johnny Be Good* (Bud S. Smith, 1988), 263
Johnson, E. Patrick, 134
Jones, James Earl, 49, 132
Jones, Kent, 66, 68–69
Jones, Tommy Lee, 65, 67
Joplin, Janis, 14
Jordan, Richard, 105
*Jumpin' Jack Flash* (Penny Marshall, 1986), 267

*Junior* (Ivan Reitman, 1994), 55
*Junior Bonner* (Sam Peckinpah, 1972), 228

Kael, Pauline, 116, 147, 148, 155, 203, 217, 219, 232, 248, 251, 253, 254, 258
*Kalifornia* (Dominic Sena, 1993), 264
Kane, Leslie, 33
Kapsis, E. Robert, 227
*Karate Kid* series, 150
Katzenstein, Mary Fainsod, 153
Kauffmann, Stanley, 215
Kaufman, Andy, 245
Keaton, Buster, 251, 263
Keaton, Diane, 58, 113
Keitel, Harvey, 22, 28
Kellner, Douglas, 161
Kelly, David Patrick, 127
Kempley, Rita, 41, 46
Kennedy, Jihmi, *10*
Kidman, Nicole, 263–64
Kimmel, Michael, 27–28
King, Barry, 21, 22, 23, 25, 59, 69, 142, 157
*King Kong* (John Guillermin, 1976), 60, 61
*King of Comedy, The* (Martin Scorsese, 1982), 20, 25, 34
*King Solomon's Mines* (J. Lee Thompson, 1985), 265
*Kiss of the Spider Woman* (Hector Babenco, 1985), 17
Klavan, Andrew, 68
Kline, Franz, 252
Kline, Kevin, 17, 214
*Klute* (Alan J. Pakula, 1971), 13
Knelman, Martin, 257, 261
Knepper, Marty, 72–73
*Knowing* (Alex Proyas, 2009), 266
Konchalovsky, Andre, 47
Kotcheff, Ted, 119
Kovic, Ron, 97–98
Kozloff, Sarah, 26
Krämer, Peter, 63
*Kramer vs. Kramer* (Robert Benton, 1979), 205, 221
Kroll, Jack, 30, 31, 103, 112
Krutnik, Frank, 148
Kubrick, Stanley, 10, 116, 264

*L.A. Confidential* (Curtis Hanson, 1997), 266
"L.A. Law" (1986–1994), 7

LaMotta, Jake, 19, 22–25
Landis, John, 253
Lang, Fritz, 5
**Lange, Jessica**, 1, 57, 57–76, *64*, *71*, 157, 189
*Last Emperor, The* (Bernardo Bertolucci, 1987), 9
*Last King of Scotland, The* (Kevin Macdonald, 2006), 269
*Last of the Mohicans, The* (James Fenimore Cooper), 128
*L.A. Story* (Mick Jackson, 1991), 253
Lawford, Peter, 110
Lawrence, Amy, 219, 222n5
Lawrence, John, 72–73
Leamer, Laurence, 37
*Lean on Me* (John G. Avildsen, 1989), 266
*Leaving Las Vegas* (Mike Figgis, 1995), 266
Lee, Mark, *82*, 82–83
Lee, Spike, 11, 137, 268
Lehman, Peter, 48
Leibovitz, Annie, 252
Lennon, John, 262n1
Leno, Jay, 252
Leone, Sergei, 26
*Less Than Zero* (Marek Kanievska, 1987), 263, 264
*Lethal Weapon* (Richard Donner, 1987), 11, 46, 77, 78, 88, 128, 148
*Lethal Weapon 2* (Richard Donner, 1989), 11, 46
*Lethal Weapon* series, 77, 88
Letterman, David, 252
Levy, Eugene, 254, 258
Lewis, Jerry, 25, 34
Liberace, 230
*Life and Times of Rosie the Riveter, The* (Connie Field, 1980), 194
*Light of Day* (Paul Schrader, 1987), 105
*Live Free or Die Hard* (Len Wiseman, 2007), 224
Locke, Sondra, 231
*Lock Up* (John Flynn, 1989), 46
*Lonely Guy, The* (Arthur Hiller, 1984), 250
*Look Who's Talking* (Amy Heckerling, 1989), 240–41
*Lost Boys, The* (Joel Schumacher, 1987), 112
Lott, Eric, 133
Lovell, Alan, 69, 75
**Lowe, Rob**, 99, 100, 108–109, 111, 112, 114, 115, 117–18, *118*, 119

Lucas, George, 8, 9
*Lucas* (David Seltzer, 1986), 8
*Lucky Man: A Memoir* (Michael J. Fox),
    101
Lumet, Sidney, 185
Lundgrun, Dolph, 43
Lyne, Adrian, 266
Lynn, Loretta, 58, 63–66, 76n4

MacDonald, Paul, 158
MacLaine, Shirley, 14, 110, 157
*Mad Max* (George Miller, 1979), 80, 88
*Mad Max Beyond Thunderdome* (George
    Miller, George Ogilvie, 1985), 86
*Mad Max 2: The Road Warrior* (George
    Miller, 1982), 79–81, 83–84
Madonna, 5, 6, 45, 117, 268
*Magnum Force* (Ted Post, 1973), 235
"Magnum P.I." (1980–1988), 7
Maguffee, T. D., 148
*Making Love* (Arthur Hiller, 1982), 11, 85
*Malcolm X* (Spike Lee, 1992), 268
Malkovich, John, 191
Maltby, Richard, 21, 69
Mamet, David, 31–32
Mankiewicz, Tom, 261
*Mannequin* (Michael Gottlieb, 1987), 113
*Man Who Loved Women, The* (Blake
    Edwards, 1983), 267
*Man with Two Brains, The* (Carl Reiner,
    1983), 250
Mapplethorpe, Robert, 6
*Marie* (Roger Donaldson, 1985), 61–63,
    66, 67, 75
*Marrying Man, The* (Jerry Rees, 1991), 266
Marsh, Reginald, 248
Marshall, Garry, 196
Martin, Dean, 110
**Martin, Steve**, 1, *243*, 243–53, *249*,
    258–61, *260*, 262nn1–3, 264
Marvin, Lee, 228
*Mary Reilly* (Stephen Frears, 1996), 265
*Mask* (Peter Bogdanovich, 1985), 15
Maslin, Janet, 215
*Matrix, The* (Andy and Lana Wachowski,
    1999), 264
*Matrix, The*, series, 62, 264
*Maurice* (James Ivory, 1987), 11
Maychick, Diana, 51, 86–87, 116, 217
Mayne, Judith, 214
McBride, Joseph, 23
**McCarthy, Andrew**, *99*, 100, 111, 113,
    116, 119

McDonald, Paul, 20
McDowell, Malcolm, 237
McGillis, Kelly, 94, 169–70, *170*
McGovern, Elizabeth, 26
McInerny, Jay, 106
McKenzie, Alan, 167
McKeon, Nancy, 103
McQueen, Steve, 228
*Mean Streets* (Martin Scorsese, 1973), 19,
    22
*Meet the Fockers* (Jay Roach, 2004), 21
*Meet the Parents* (Jay Roach, 2000), 21
Method acting, 21–22, 25, 69, 145, 184
*Metropolis* (Fritz Lang, 1927), 5
"Miami Vice" (1984–1989), 7
*Michael Collins* (Neil Jordan, 1996), 265
Midler, Bette, 13
*Midnight Run* (Martin Brest, 1988), 21
Milius, John, 49
*Milk* (Gus Van Sant, 2008), 268
Miller, George, 80
Miller, James Andrew, 123
*Million Dollar Baby* (Clint Eastwood,
    2004), 266
*Missing* (Costa-Gavras, 1982), 59, 66, 67,
    70, 75
*Mission, The* (Roland Joffé, 1986), 20, 25,
    27, 34
Mix, Tom, 236–37
*Mo' Better Blues* (Spike Lee, 1990), 268
*Moby Dick* (Herman Melville), 128
*Mommie Dearest* (Frank Perry, 1981), 13
Mondale, Walter, 5
Monroe, Marilyn, 67
*Monster* (Patty Jenkins, 2003), 25
"Moonlighting" (1985–1989), 7, 224,
    239–41
*Moonstruck* (Norman Hudson, 1987), 15,
    266
**Moore, Demi**, *99*, 100, 111, 112,
    117–18, *118*, 119, 240, 268
Moranis, Rick, 148–49, *149*
Moriarty, Kathy, 23
"Mork and Mindy" (1978–1982), 18
*Morning After, The* (Sidney Lumet, 1986),
    13
*Moscow on the Hudson* (Paul Mazursky,
    1984), 18
*Mosquito Coast, The* (Peter Weir, 1986),
    172–73, 178, 264
*Moulin Rouge* (Baz Luhrmann, 2001), 264
The Movie Channel (TMC), 4
*Mr. Mom* (Stan Dragoti, 1983), 17

"Mr. Rogers' Neighborhood"
(1968–2001), 125
*Mr. Smith Goes to Washington* (Frank
Capra, 1939), 196
*Mrs. Soffel* (Gillian Armstrong, 1984), 86
MTV, 5
Mueller-Stahl, Armin, 66
Mull, Martin, 245
Mulvey, Laura, 6, 63, 76
**Murphy, Eddie,** 1, 11, *120,* 120–38,
*122, 131, 137*
*Murphy's Romance* (Martin Ritt, 1985),
189, 198–99
Murray, Bill, 123, 136, 141, 149, 150,
159n4, 254–55
*Music Box* (Costa-Gavras, 1989), 59, 67
*My Beautiful Laundrette* (Stephen Frears,
1985), 11, 46
*My Best Friend's Wedding* (P. J. Hogan,
1997), 265
*My Man Godfrey* (Gregory LaCava, 1936),
187
*My Own Private Idaho* (Gus Van Sant,
1991), 264
*Mystic Pizza* (Donald Petrie, 1988), 265
*Mystic River* (Clint Eastwood, 2003), 265,
268

*Name of the Rose, The* (Jean-Jacques
Annaud, 1986), 12
Naremore, James, 24, 34, 68
*National Treasure* (Jon Turteltaub, 2004),
266
*National Treasure: Book of Secrets* (Jon
Turteltaub, 2007), 266
*Natural, The* (Barry Levinson, 1984), 14,
15
*Natural Born Killers* (Oliver Stone, 1994),
263
Neale, Steve, 89, 148
Negra, Diane, 182
Negri, Pola, 236
**Nelson, Judd,** *99,* 100, 108–109, 111,
112, 113, 114, 115, 118, 119
*Network* (Sidney Lumet, 1976), 13
*Never Say Never Again* (Irwin Kershner,
1983), 12, 266
Newman, Paul, 14, 185, 228
*New York, New York* (Martin Scorsese,
1977), 19
Nichols, Mike, 139, 217
Nicholson, Jack, 14, 15, 221
Nickson-Soul, Julia, 42

Nielsen, Brigitte, 37, 43, 48
*Nighthawks* (Bruce Malmouth, 1981), 38,
39
*Night in the Life of Jimmy Reardon, A*
(William Richert, 1988), 264
*Nightmare on Elm Street, A* (Wes Craven,
1984), 9, 263
*Nightmare on Elm Street, A,* series, 150
*'night Mother* (Tom Moore, 1986), 70, 75
*Night Shift* (Ron Howard, 1982), 126
*9½ Weeks* (Adrian Lyne, 1986), 266
*1984* (George Orwell), 4
*1941* (Steven Spielberg, 1979), 255
*Nine to Five* (Colin Higgins, 1980), 11, *12,*
13, 17, 151
Nolte, Nick, 120, *122,* 127
*Norma Rae* (Martin Ritt, 1979), *180,*
182–85, 198
Norris, Chuck, 227, 241
Norton, Edward, 264
*Nothing in Common* (Garry Marshall,
1986), 267
*Notorious* (Alfred Hitchcock, 1946), 147
*No Way Out* (Roger Donaldson, 1987), 15
*Nutty Professor, The* (Tom Shadyac, 1996),
138

Obama, Barack, 132
*Ocean's Eleven* series, 264
O'Connor, Sandra Day, 5
O'Hara, Catherine, 254
*Omen, The* (Richard Donner, 1976), 148
*Once Upon a Time in America* (Sergio
Leone, 1984), 20, 26–27, 34
*One Flew Over the Cuckoo's Nest* (Milos
Forman, 1975), 14
*On Golden Pond* (Mark Rydell, 1981), 13
*On the Waterfront* (Elia Kazan, 1954),
25–26
Oram, James, 87
*Ordinary People* (Robert Redford, 1980),
9, 14
Orwell, George, 4
*Our Gang* comedies, 125–26
*Out of Africa* (Sydney Pollack, 1985), 9,
14, 158, 202, 206, 208, 214–16, 221,
221n1
*Outrageous Fortune* (Arthur Hiller, 1987),
14
*Outsiders, The* (Francis Ford Coppola,
1983), 90
*Overboard* (Garry Marshall, 1987), 182,
196–98, *197*

Overpeck, Deron, 239
Ovitz, Michael, 21, 60
Oz, Frank, 253

"Pacific, The" (2010), 267
Pacino, Al, 14, 17, 109
Pakula, Alan J., 208, 217
Pale Rider (Clint Eastwood, 1985), 226
Pally, Marcia, 154
Palmer, William J., 8, 57, 58
Palminteri, Chazz, 25
Panic Room, The (David Fincher, 2002), 269
Parenthood (Ron Howard, 1989), 247, 253, 264
Parker, Charlie "Bird," 269
Parting Glances (Bill Sherwood, 1986), 11
Partners (James Burrows, 1982), 85
Parton, Dolly, 12, 17, 42
Peckinpah, Sam, 228
Peggy Sue Got Married (Francis Ford Coppola, 1986), 17, 74, 266
Pelé, 40
Penley, Constance, 128
Penn, Chris, 268
Penn, Sean, 100, 119n1, 265, 268
Pennies from Heaven (Herbert Ross, 1981), 244, 247–50, 249
Perry, Roland, 86
Personal Best (Robert Towne, 1982), 11
Pesci, Joe, 23–24
Peters, Bernadette, 246–47, 249
Pinter, Harold, 157
Pfaff, Eugene E. Jr., 58, 67, 69, 76n1
Pfeiffer, Michelle, 17, 214
Pfeil, Fred, 128
Philadelphia (Jonathan Demme, 1993), 267, 268–69
Phoenix, River, 173, 264
Piano, The (Jane Campion, 1993), 267
Pinchot, Bronson, 134
Pink Cadillac (Buddy Van Horn, 1989), 230
Pinter, Harold, 157
Pirates of the Caribbean series, 263
Pitt, Brad, 264, 266
Places in the Heart (Robert Benton, 1984), 58, 180, 182, 188–92, 190, 198–99
Planes, Trains, and Automobiles (John Hughes, 1987), 243–44, 253, 259–61, 260
Platoon (Oliver Stone, 1986), 9, 263, 268

Player, The (Robert Altman, 1992), 264–65, 267
Plenty (Fred Schepisi, 1985), 202, 203, 208, 219–20
Pocket Money (Stuart Rosenberg, 1972), 228
Poison Ivy (Larry Elikann, 1985), 103
Poitier, Sidney, 132
Polanski, Roman, 174, 178
Police Academy (Hugh Wilson, 1984), 9
Police Academy 4: Citizens on Patrol (Jim Drake, 1987), 265
Pollack, Sydney, 208
Pollan, Tracy, 100, 106–107, 107
Popeye (Robert Altman, 1980), 18
Porky's (Bob Clark, 1981), 8
Portrait of a Lady, The (Jane Campion, 1996), 264
Postman Always Rings Twice, The (Bob Rafelson, 1981), 60, 67
Potter, Dennis, 247
Predator (John McTiernan, 1987), 43, 53
Presley, Elvis, 125, 266
Presumed Innocent (Alan J. Pakula, 1990), 178
Pretty in Pink (John Hughes, 1986), 8, 109, 113, 116
Pretty Woman (Garry Marshall, 1990), 265
Prince, Stephen, 8, 57, 58, 60, 63, 71, 73, 225
Private Benjamin (Howard Zieff, 1980), 180, 182, 185–88, 192
Private Resort (George Bowers, 1985), 263
Protocol (Herbert Ross, 1984), 196
Pryor, Richard, 121, 125, 133, 136–37, 137, 258
Pulver, Andrew, 119n1
Punchline (David Seltzer, 1988), 182, 198–99, 267

Quaid, Dennis, 61
Quinn, Aiden, 29

Rabe, David, 157
Racing with the Moon (Richard Benjamin, 1984), 266, 269
Radner, Gilda, 123, 254
Ragan, David, 81
Raggedy Man (Jack Fisk, 1981), 59, 70
Ragghianti, Marie, 61–62, 66
Raging Bull (Martin Scorsese, 1980), 19, 22–26, 23, 28, 31, 34

*Raiders of the Lost Ark* (Steven Spielberg, 1981), 160, 162–64, 174

*Rain Man* (Barry Levinson, 1988), 9, 13, 95

*Raising Arizona* (Joel Coen, 1987), 9, 266, 267

*Rambo: First Blood Part II* (George Cosmatos, 1985), 10, *36*, 42, 53, 84, 101, 140

*Rambo* series, 46,192, 238

*Rambo III* (Peter MacDonald, 1988), 38, 45, 55

Ramis, Harold, 159n4, 255

Ray, Robert, 20

*Ray* (Taylor Hackford, 2004), 63

Reagan, Ronald, 1, 2, 5, 8, 25, 45, 60, 70, 71, 72–73, 75, 76, 84, 87, 88, 91–92, 94, 100, 101, 106, 132, 151, 153, 154, 160, 161, 175, 178, 181, 192, 196, 224, 226, 230, 231–32

Redford, Robert, 14, 15, 206, 216

*Red Heat* (Walter Hill, 1988), 52, 53–54, *54*, 55

*Red Sonja* (Richard Fleischer, 1985), 48–49, 52

Reed, Rex, 112

Reese, Della, 137

Reeves, Keanu, 264

*Regarding Henry* (Mike Nichols, 1991), 178–79

Reiner, Carl, 245–46, 250, 252, 258

Reiser, Paul, 153

Reitman, Ivan, 139, 255

Remar, James, 120

*Return of the Jedi, The* (George Lucas, 1982), 13, 16

Reynolds, Burt, 17, 185, 236, 258, 259

*Rhinestone* (Bob Clark, 1984), 17, 38, 41

Rhys-Davies, John, 163

**Ringwald, Molly**, *99*, 100, 111, 113, 114, 116, 117, 119

*Risky Business* (Paul Brickman, 1983), 90, 92–94, *93*, 95

Ritt, Martin, 184–85

*River, The* (Mark Rydell, 1984), 58, 59, 70, 71, 72, *73*, 74, 86

*River Runs Through It, A* (Robert Redford, 1992), 264

*River's Edge* (Tim Hunter, 1986), 9, 264

Robbins, Tim, 264–65, 266, 267

Roberts, Julia, *199*, 199–200, 265

*Robin Hood: Prince of Thieves* (Kevin Reynolds, 1991), 128

Rock, Chris, 132, 133

*Rocky* (John G. Avildsen, 1976), 38

*Rocky IV* (Sylvester Stallone, 1985), 38, 42, 43, *44*, 55

*Rocky Horror Picture Show, The* (Jim Sharman, 1975), 268

*Rocky III* (Sylvester Stallone, 1982), 38

*Rocky* series, 39

Rogers, Ginger, 249

Rogers, Roy, 238

Rogin, Michael, 192

*Romancing the Stone* (Robert Zemeckis, 1984), 13

*Rookie, The* (Clint Eastwood, 1990), 225, 241

Rooney, Mickey, 103

Rose, Axl, 232

Rose, Cynthia, 65

*Rose, The* (Mark Rydell, 1979), 14

"Roseanne" (1988–1997), 7

*Rosemary's Baby* (Roman Polanski, 1968), 148

Rosen, Marjorie, 67

Ross, Herbert, 247

Rourke, Mickey, 266

Rowlands, Gena, 105

*Roxanne* (Fred Schepisi, 1987), 250–51, 253

Rubin, Martin, 145

*Rumble Fish* (Francis Ford Coppola, 1983), 9

*Running Man, The* (Paul Michael Glaser, 1987), *51*

*Running on Empty* (Sidney Lumet, 1988), 264

Russell, Kurt, 46, 47, 193–94, 196–97, *197*

Russo, Rene, 88

Russo, Vito, 6

*Ruthless People* (Jim Abraham, David Zucker, Jerry Zucker, 1986), 14

Ryan, Meg, 265, 269

Ryan, Michael, 161

Rydell, Mark, 86, 87

Sanello, Frank, 124

Sarandon, Susan, 15, 17, 264, 268

Sarris, Andrew, 147

"Saturday Night Live" (SNL) (1975– ), 115, 123–27, 133, 134, 244–45, 254

*Saving Private Ryan* (Steven Spielberg, 1998), 267

*Scarface* (Brian De Palma, 1983), 14, 17

Schepisi, Fred, 253

Schickel, Richard, 152, 241
Schlotterbeck, Jesse, 63
Schoonmaker, Thelma, 22–23
Schroeder, Patricia, 106
Schumacher, Joel, 100, 113
**Schwarzenegger, Arnold**, 1, *36*, 36–38, 43, 45, 46, 48–56, *51*, *54*, 84, 153, 160, 225–26, 238, 265
Scorsese, Martin, 19, 22, 90
Scott, A. O., 132
Scott, Ridley, 4, 139, 144, 164
Seagal, Steven, 228, 241
*Sea of Love* (Harold Becker, 1989), 14
*Searchers, The* (John Ford, 1956), 229–30
"Second City TV" (SCTV) (1976–1984), 244–45, 254–55, 256, 257, 258, 261, 262n4
*Secret of My Succe$s, The* (Herbert Ross, 1987), 105
Seidelman, Susan, 220
Seinfeld, Jerry, 252
Selleck, Tom, 7
*Se7en* (David Fincher, 1995), 264, 266
*sex, lies, and videotape* (Steven Soderbergh, 1989), 119
Shales, Tom, 92, 123
*Shanghai Surprise* (Jim Goddard, 1986), 268
Shary, Timothy, 8
*Shawshank Redemption, The* (Frank Darabont, 1994), 265, 266
*She-Devil* (Susan Seidelman, 1989), 202, 220–21
**Sheedy, Ally**, 99, 100, 111, 112, 113, 114, 118, 119
Sheen, Charlie, 118
Shepard, Sam, 58, 73, 74
Shepherd, Cybill, 239, 241
Shields, Brooke, 155
Shilts, Randy, 6
Shire, Talia, 44
Short, Martin, 253, 257
Showtime, 4
*Siesta* (Mary Lambert, 1987), 13
*Silkwood* (Mike Nichols, 1983), 15, 202, 208, 210, 211, 217–19, *219*
*Silverado* (Lawrence Kasdan, 1985), 17
Silverman, Kaja, 5, 217, 222n5
*Silver Streak* (Arthur Hiller, 1976), 128
Simmons, Richard, 123, 132
Simon, John, 211, 216–17
Simon, Neil, 249
Simpson, Don, 8

Sinyard, Neil, 88
Siskel, Gene, 68, 69, 76n5, 226–27, 258
*Sister Act* (Emile Ardolino, 1992), 267
*Sister Act 2: Back in the Habit* (Bill Duke, 1993), 267
*Sixteen Candles* (John Hughes, 1984), 113, 115, 116, 117
"60 Minutes" (1968– ), 124
Slater, Helen, 106
*Sleepless in Seattle* (Nora Ephron, 1993), 265, 267
*Sliver* (Philip Noyce, 1993), 265
Smith, C. Jason, 153
Smith, Paul, 226
Smith, Will, 132
*Smokey and the Bandit* (Hal Needham, 1977), 185
*S.O.B.* (Blake Edwards, 1981), 236
Soderbergh, Steven, 119
*Sophie's Choice* (Alan J. Pakula, 1982), 17, 202, 207, 208, 210–11, 214, 216–18, 221n1
*Sophie's Choice* (William Styron), 207, 210–11
**Spacek, Sissy**, 1, *57*, 57–76, *73*
*Speed* (Jan de Bont, 1994), 264
*Speed Zone* (Jim Drake, 1989), 259
Spielberg, Steven, 8, 9, 11, 13, 101, 267
*Splash* (Ron Howard, 1984), 258, 267
*Spook Who Sat by the Door, The* (Ivan Dixon, 1973), 137
Stanislavski, Konstantin, 22
Stacey, Jackie, 213
**Stallone, Sylvester**, 1, 10, 17, *36*, 36–48, *44*, 49, 55–56, *57*, 61, 84, 131, 140, 153, 161, 225–26
*Stand by Me* (Rob Reiner, 1986), 9, 264
Stanley, Kim, 60
*Stardust* (Matthew Vaughn, 1997), 21
*Star Trek* series, 150
*Star Wars* (George Lucas, 1977), 160–63, *165*
*Star Wars* series, 9, 62, 161, 164
*State of Grace* (Phil Joanou, 1990), 268
*Steel Magnolias* (Herbert Ross, 1989), 11, 17, 63, 182, *199*, 199–200, 265
*St. Elmo's Fire* (Joel Schumacher, 1985), 99, 100, 108, 109, 111 112, 113
"St. Elsewhere" (1982–1988), 7
*Stepmom* (Chris Columbus, 1998), 265
*Still of the Night* (Robert Benton, 1982), 202
Sting, 121

Stoltz, Eric, 101
Stone, Oliver, 2, 9, 73, 97
Strasberg, Lee, 21, 69, 184
**Streep, Meryl**, 1, 14, 15, 22, 27–28, 143, 158, 198, *201*, 201–22, *212*, *215*, *219*, 240
*Streetcar Named Desire, A* (Tennessee Williams, December 3, 1947), 25
Streisand, Barbra, 58, 189
*Stripes* (Ivan Reitman, 1981), 9, 244, 255–56, *256*
*Striptease* (Andrew Bergman, 1996), 268
Studlar, Gaylyn, 41
Styron, William, 210–11
*Sudden Impact* (Clint Eastwood, 1983), 230–31
*Summer of '42* (Robert Mulligan, 1971), 111
*Summer Rental* (Carl Reiner, 1985), 258
*Sunset* (Blake Edwards, 1988), 236–37, *237*, 242
Sutherland, Kiefer, 112
Swayze, Patrick, 9
*Sweet Dreams* (Karel Reisz, 1985), 58, 63–67, *64*, 67
*Swing Shift* (Jonathan Demme, 1984), 182, 192–95
"Sybil" (Daniel Petrie, 1976), 184
Sykes, Wanda, 132

*Tango & Cash* (Andrei Konchalovsky, 1989), 38, 45, 46, 47
*Taps* (Harold Becker, 1981), 89, 90, 100
Tasker, Yvonne, 153, 163, 176, 182
Taves, Brian, 145
Taylor, Elizabeth, 155
"Taxi" (1978–1982), 7
*Taxi Driver* (Martin Scorsese, 1976), 13, 19, 20, 30, 34
*Teen Wolf* (Rod Daniel, 1985), 100, 103
Tennant, Victoria, 251
*Tequila Sunrise* (Robert Towne, 1988), 17
*Terminator, The* (James Cameron, 1984), 48, 50, 51–54
*Terminator* series, 226
*Terminator 2: Judgment Day* (James Cameron, 1991), 50
*Terms of Endearment* (James L. Brooks, 1983), 9, 11, 14, 63
Tesich, Steve, 145
*Thelma and Louise* (Ridley Scott, 1991), 264, 268
Theron, Charlize, 25

Theroux, Paul, 78–79
*Thin Red Line, The* (Terrence Malick, 1998), 268
"thirtysomething" (1987–1991), 7
*This Is Spinal Tap* (Rob Reiner, 1984), 224
*Three Amigos, The* (John Landis, 1986), 253
*3 Men and a Baby* (Leonard Nimoy, 1987), 9, 211
*3 Women* (Robert Altman, 1977), 69
"Thriller" (John Landis, 1982), 6
Tibbets, John C., 233
*Tightrope* (Richard Tuggle, 1984), 227, 242
"Today Show, The" (1952– ), 154
*To Die For* (Gus Van Sant, 1995), 264
Tomasulo, Frank, 161
Tomlin, Lily, *12*, 17, 250
*Tootsie* (Sydney Pollack, 1982), 13, 60–61, 66, 76
*Top Gun* (Tony Scott, 1986), 8, 77, 90, 94–95, 265
*Torch Song Trilogy* (Paul Bogart, 1988), 11, 15
*Total Recall* (Paul Verhoeven, 1990), 265
Tourneur, Jacques, 226
Tracy, Spencer, 267
*Trading Places* (John Landis, 1983), 123, 130–132, *131*
*Training Day* (Antoine Fuqua, 2001), 269
*Tropic Thunder* (Ben Stiller, 2008), 263
*True Confessions* (Ulu Grosbard, 1981), 20
Turner, Kathleen, 13, 16, 17, 214
Turner Classic Movies (TCM), 221
Turner Network Television (TNT), 4
"21 Jump Street" (1987–1990), 263
*Twins* (Ivan Reitman, 1988), 54–55

Ulmer, Edgar G., 227
*Uncle Buck* (John Hughes, 1989), 261–62
*Une femme ou deux* (Daniel Vigne, 1985), 159n2
*Unforgiven* (Clint Eastwood, 1992), 239, 266
*Untouchables, The* (Brian De Palma, 1987), 12, 15, 20, 30–34, *32*

Valentino, Rudolph, 158
*Valley Girl* (Martha Coolidge, 1983), 266
Van Damme, Jean-Claude, 227–28, 241
Van Peebles, Mario, 234
Van Sant, Gus, 264, 268

Vare, Ethlie Ann, 173
*Verdict, The* (Sidney Lumet, 1982), 14
Verhoeven, Paul, 265
*Victor/Victoria* (Blake Edwards, 1982), 11, 85, 236
*Victory* (John Huston, 1981), 38, 39
Vineberg, Steve, 69, 194
*Violets Are Blue* (Jack Fisk, 1986), 70
*Volunteers* (Nicholas Meyer, 1985), 258
Von Sydow, Max, 39–40

*Wagons East* (Peter Markle, 1994), 262
Walker, Alice, 11
*Wall Street* (Oliver Stone, 1987), 2, 13, 73, 176
Walsh, Raoul, 226
Walters, Barbara, 87
*War Games* (John Badham, 1983), 15
*War of the Roses, The* (Danny De Vito, 1989)
Washington, Denzel, 7, *10*, 17, 268–69
Wasserstein, Wendy, 143, 209, 210
Waters, John, 263
Watney, Simon, 83
Wayne, John, 37, 174, 224, 230, 238
"Way We Live Now, The" (Susan Sontag), 6
**Weaver, Sigourney,** 1, 61, 85, *139*, 139–59, *141*, *149*, *156*, 176–77, *177*
"Webster" (1983–1989), 126
*Wedding Party, The* (Brian De Palma, 1969), 31
*Weekend at Bernie's* (Ted Kotcheff, 1989), 100, 119
*We Get to Win This Time* (Ian T. Haufrect, 2002), 42
Weir, Peter, 81, 85, 146–47, 168, 172
*Weird Science* (John Hughes, 1985), 115
Welles, Orson, 256
West, Mae, 236–37
*What's Eating Gilbert Grape* (Lasse Halström, 1993), 263
*When a Man Loves a Woman* (Luis Mandoki, 1994), 265

*When Harry Met Sally* (Rob Reiner, 1989), 265
Whitaker, Forest, 269
White, Mimi, 195
Whitton, Margaret, 106
*Who's Harry Crumb?* (Paul Flaherty, 1989), 259
Wiegman, Robyn, 128
*Wild at Heart* (David Lynch, 1990), 266
Williams, Robin, 17, 251
Williams, Tennessee, 157
**Willis, Bruce,** 1, 7, 117, *223*, 223–25, 236–42, *237*
Willis, Gordon, 247
Willis, Sharon, 128
Winfrey, Oprah, 11
Winningham, Mare, *99*
*Wisdom* (Emilio Estevez, 1986), 114, 117
*Witches of Eastwick, The* (George Miller, 1987), 15, 17, 268
*Witness* (Peter Weir, 1985), 168–72, *170*
Wittgenstein, Ludwig, 252
Wonder, Stevie, 136
Woo, John, 266
Wood, Robin, 20, 60, 63, 83, 88
Woolf, Virginia, 264
*Working Girl* (Mike Nichols, 1988), 11, 61, 140, 142, 147, 151–52, 175–78, *177*
*Working Girls* (Lizzie Borden, 1986), 11
*World According to Garp, The* (George Roy Hill, 1982), 15, 18, 251
Wyatt, Justin, 8, 148

Yates, Peter, 145
*Year of Living Dangerously, The* (Peter Weir, 1982), 85, 145–47, 157, 158
Young, Sean, 165
*Young Guns* (Christopher Cain, 1988), 100, 112–13, 114, 119
*You've Got Mail* (Nora Ephron, 1998), 265

Zavattini, Cesare, 62
Zemeckis, Robert, 8, 100
Zwick, Edward, 7